CW00503515

CHILDREN OF ABRAHAM AT WAR
The Clash of Messianic Militarisms

CHILDREN OF ABRAHAM AT WAR
The Clash of Messianic Militarisms

TALMIZ AHMAD

AAKAR

Children of Abraham at War: The Clash of Messianic Militarisms
Talmiz Ahmad

© Author

First Published, 2010

ISBN 978-93-5002-080-7

All rights reserved. No part of this book may
be reproduced or transmitted, in any form or
by any means, without prior permission
of the Publisher.

Published by
AAKAR BOOKS
28 E Pocket IV, Mayur Vihar Phase I, Delhi-110 091
Phone : 011-2279 5505 Telefax : 011-2279 5641
aakarbooks@gmail.com; www.aakarbooks.com

Printed at
Mudrak, Delhi-110 091

Contents

Preface

A year ago, two important developments took place: first, the three-week Israeli assault upon Gaza and second, the swearing in of the 44th US President, Barack Hussain Obama.

The Israeli assault on Gaza was the latest in a series of vicious and bloody exchanges between the Israeli and Palestinian people over the last sixty years. The pattern in Gaza was similar to what had taken place earlier: fierce Israeli criticism of Palestinian terrorism, in response to which a devastating military assault is undertaken. In Gaza, the instigation for the assault was the rockets that Hamas had been unleashing upon Israel: from January 2007 up to the eve of the Israeli assault on Gaza at the end of December 2008, twenty-three Israeli citizens had been killed and about 600 injured as a result of these rocket attacks. The Israeli retaliation, consisting of large-scale aerial bombardment over one week followed by ground action, left about 1,300 Palestinians dead (forty per cent of them women and children), the territory devastated and normal life in ruins.

The assault on Gaza, in terms of the disproportionate use of force and disproportionate Palestinian casualties, echoed the assault two years earlier on Lebanon when Israel had attempted to cripple Hezbollah militarily and politically, through a massive aerial assault that had left more than 3,000 Lebanese dead. Since after the attack the Hezbollah remained an effective political force in Lebanon, many observers, including several Israelis, saw the Lebanese operation as a 'defeat', leading to the resignations of the then Israeli Defence Minister and the Chief of Staff. The Prime Ministership of Ehud Olmert was also adversely affected, though he finally resigned due to unrelated 'corruption' charges and remained head of a 'caretaker' administration.

Throughout the Gaza operation, as earlier during the Lebanese attacks, and, indeed, in all previous such attacks, the Israeli government enjoyed the total support of the US. Both during the Lebanese and Gaza operations, the Bush administration refused to call for a ceasefire and thwarted every other attempt to do so, in spite of horrendous casualties being suffered, primarily by civilians, in order to enable Israel to complete the operations to its satisfaction.

There is, at present, an uneasy truce in Gaza and a general air of uncertainty and insecurity across West Asia and the Gulf. Though there are suggestions from the American side that the situation in Iraq is improving, the continuing suicide bombings, insurgency and sectarian violence would suggest otherwise. Afghanistan, after nine years of NATO-led military operations, is seeing a resurgent Taliban in control of over one-third of Afghan territory and a flourishing poppy cultivation feeding the global drugs trade. In terms of the so-called Global War on Terror (GWOT), the situation at the Afghanistan-Pakistan border and within Pakistan itself has deteriorated considerably. While the Al-Qaeda is not the same cohesive entity it was earlier, it remains a robust inspirational force and continues to instigate violence and terror not only in the Arab world and other parts of Asia but also in Europe. Pakistan, which readily provided sanctuary to Al-Qaeda and Taliban elements in the face of US assaults on Afghanistan in November-December 2001, is today awash with militant jihadis who are not only perpetrating sectarian and other violence in Pakistan itself but are the fountainhead of terror in the region in general, a matter of considerable concern to India, particularly after the Mumbai attacks in November 2008.

The situation relating to Iran remains uncertain, albeit with widespread hope that the Obama administration will do away with the hostile policies of previous US administrations since the Islamic revolution in 1979, and initiate a process of engagement and dialogue. Indeed, no other region in the world has such high expectations from President Barack Obama as West Asia, since no other region has felt the adverse impact of the outgoing Bush administration more than this region. Since Obama's electoral victory, the mood in West Asia has been swinging from overwhelming optimism to cold despair, from fervent hope that the advent of the new presidency will somehow magically change everything for the better, to acute despair and pessimism based on the memory of previous high expectations followed by deep disappointments.

I have been working on this book for over five years. Its origins lie in the concern that, after 9/11, Western, particularly US, discourse was increasingly demonizing Islam the religion, and Muslims the people. Bernard Lewis' two books, *What Went Wrong* and *The Crisis of Islam*, though a regurgitation of some of his earlier rather shallow and polemical writings, were readily seized upon by the American public and had considerable impact in solidifying the prejudices and animosities of Western readers with regard to Islam and Muslims. In Bernard Lewis' writings, as also those of Samuel Huntington and other contributions from the neo-conservative think tanks, an essentialized stereotype of Muslims was being painted in the worst tradition of nineteenth and twentieth century Orientalist writing, so that, before our very eyes, the clash of civilizations was being given concrete shape, with the Muslim as the Satanic 'other'.

Such a broad-brush approach denied all political context or legitimacy to Muslim grievances, and did not attempt to take into account the complexity of Islamic history and contemporary politics and culture. Above all, such an approach entirely failed to address Western culpability, through specific betrayals and interventions, for the anger and despair in the Muslim world over the last century, when the West was the hegemonic power, and, after the end of imperialism, continued as the dominant political and economic influence in West Asia. Instead, it was asserted by several Right-wing commentators that, given the essentialized character of Islam and the Muslims, conflict between Islam and the West was both inherent and inevitable, and contemporary animosities merely reflected age-old mutual hatred and mutual intolerance. To buttress this view, it was added that Muslim anger was due to their inability to cope with the modernity and secularism of the West and, indeed, was based on a rejection of the values of the West. The fact that such views had little historical validity and, at best, represented a selective and grossly inadequate assessment of the complex reality, was deliberately glossed over by neocon and orientalist intellectuals who dominated the discourse and the debate.

This book is an attempt to correct these false premises and to present a narrative of the conflict amongst the peoples of the three Abrahamic traditions in a more balanced historical context. It focuses on their common messianic tradition which, in the view of the author, when refreshed and given a contemporary resonance due to contemporary political developments, constitutes the basis of much present-day animosity. I have attempted to be as fair as possible in analyzing the three traditions and their interaction with one another over the last several centuries, presenting facts rather than passing judgement on crimes and misdemeanours of the past. I have also attempted to be balanced in analyzing the contemporary conflicts in West Asia, setting out in as much detail as possible the contemporary political contexts in which these struggles are taking place.

As I have indicated above, the discourse relating to conflict between the children of Abraham is, today, largely dominated by Jewish and Christian Right-wing commentators whose writings are intensely polemical; they feed the current animosities and justify disproportionate violence against the Palestinians and Muslims in general. Thankfully, as my studies have shown, while prejudiced and polemical writers dominate the intellectual landscape, they do not have exclusive control over it. Indeed, it is a matter of satisfaction that some of the best minds from the three traditions are actually extremely fair and balanced: they reject the argument of inherent and inevitable animosity, are vigorously self-critical in regard to their own community's heritage, and call for the pursuit of mutual understanding and accommodative policies. I have been particularly impressed with the writings of Israeli commentators such as Ehud Sprinzak and Israel Shahak of the earlier generation, and contemporary writers such as Zeev Sternhell, Ilan Pappe, Akiva Eldar, Idith Zertal and, recently, Avraham Burg.

Similarly, Western scholars, such as Richard Bulliet, Hugh Goddard, Richard Fletcher and Karen Armstrong, have rejected the narrative of sustained West-Islam hostility, while others, such as Edward Said earlier and now Tomaz Mastnak, have placed Christian animosity to Islam and Muslims in the imperialist period firmly in the Orientalist tradition. Many Arab and Muslim writers too, such as Albert Hourani, Shibley Telhami and Rashid Khalidi, have rejected the essentialized history of Muslim-Christian or Muslim-Jewish conflict, and have placed contemporary differences within the context of contemporary political events.

The eight years of the Bush presidency loom large as an influence and role-player in the current events discussed in this book pertaining to West Asia and the GWOT. Hence, the thinking of American neocons and the Christian Right-wing and the religious orientation of the former President himself have been provided considerable attention and space in this work. I am aware that every book is, itself, a child of its times and the context in which it was developed. Now, at the commencement of the Obama era, it is quite possible that many aspects of US policy will be subjected to review and could be significantly modified if not given up altogether. While the Bush era is writ large in these pages, I still believe that the study of the interactions of the Jewish, Christian and Muslim peoples with one another over the last several centuries will yield a broader context and promote an understanding which would go beyond the timeframe of a particular presidency.

A word about the subtitle: the term 'messianic militarism' was first used by the American activist Ralph Nader in describing the Bush presidency, which emphasized the role of the messianic impulse in motivating the president in his response to the conflict in Afghanistan and Iraq and against Al-Qaeda in the GWOT. However, I think this term can be used to describe the motivating spirit of all the three principal actors presently engaged in perpetrating violence in West Asia and beyond in a dance of death where contemporary political and military actions are justified on the basis of time-honoured divine sanctions.

Readers will observe that this work is replete with quotations from primary sources as also from some important writers who have commented on the issues under consideration. I have deliberately adopted this approach in order to enable readers who might not be familiar with the relevant literature or have access to it to read first-hand the thinking and views of earlier commentators. Given the vast scope of their work, I cannot but acknowledge my debt to the extensive commentaries on the subject by a number of authors whose works I have taken advantage of. I have made every effort to ensure that every source, be it book, paper or article, including those drawn from the Internet, has been carefully cited in the endnotes that accompany each chapter.

This book is a result of extensive readings on the subject, a bibliographical voyage that has taken me into fascinating areas of ancient belief and faith, particularly messianism, both in its religious and secular manifestations. The people of the three Semitic traditions, in their own faith and in interactions with each other, are heavily influenced by *current* perspectives with regard to the past. Hence, it is important to go beyond the written word and to obtain a first-hand experience of the region and its people. I have travelled through and lived in many of the countries that are, today, at the heart of contemporary conflict between the children of Abraham, and have been consistently influenced by the intellectually vigorous people—Arab, Christian and Jewish—I have met in my diplomatic career of 35 years, most of which has spent in or in dealing with West Asia.

Above all, I have benefited from my engagement with the best minds of the Indian Foreign Service, with whom I have been privileged to serve India's interests at home and in different parts of the world. However, having set out the debt of gratitude I owe to my colleagues in Government, I would like to stress that the views expressed in this book are entirely my own and do not necessarily reflect the views of the Government of India.

January 2010   **Talmiz Ahmad**

Acknowledgements

This book has obviously been influenced not only by extensive readings on the subject but also by my personal encounters with outstanding personalities in India and abroad. I have been deeply influenced in my intellectual evolution by certain people I have had the privilege of working with very closely, namely, Mr. Mohammad Hamid Ansari, my former colleague in the Foreign Service and now the respected Vice President of India, and Mr. Ishrat Aziz, my Ambassador in Saudi Arabia for four years when I was Consul General in Jeddah. My colleagues in the 1974 batch of the Foreign Service, who have been my friends and companions for 35 years, include in their ranks some of the best minds our nation has produced for the pursuit of our national interests. Close association with these outstanding colleagues has broadened my outlook and sharpened my understanding of the complex environment within which we have to pursue our national goals. Outside the service, I have benefited from interaction with some of India's best writers and commentators, among whom I must name: M.J. Akbar, Atul Aneja, Sidharth Bhatia, Professor Mushirul Hasan, Saeed Naqvi, Dileep Padgaonkar, Siddharth Varadarajan, C. Raja Mohan, Maroof Raza and Pranay Sharma.

Some friends, Michael Dwyer, Professor Abdul Nafey, Meena and N. Janardhan, carefully went through an earlier draft of this book and made substantial comments which have served to improve this work significantly. I also benefited from some diligent research work done by Prakash Jha, a doctoral student at JNU, who took time off from his own studies to dig up some useful material for me.

The writing of a book is a self-centred and lonely endeavour: intellectual pursuit isolates one from familial responsibilities and can only be attempted successfully if one is blessed with an understanding and supportive family. I am privileged in this regard: my wife, Sunita Mainee, has consistently supported my desire to read and write, even when it has meant long periods of self-imposed isolation as also amnesia relating to day-to-day responsibilities. This work, as it continued to expand in scope and content, would not have been completed but for her insisting that I go back to my study and peruse the new texts I had indulgently ordered from different parts of the world. My children Ashwin, Rahul, Tara and Anchal, my daughter-in-law, Anoothi and my brother, Tanvir Ahmad, have been a sustained source of support, and have helped to make this book a labour of joy.

This book could not have taken shape without the assistance I have received from colleagues in my offices in different countries: Swaminathan in Riyadh; Harish Kharbanda in Muscat; Narendra Kumar in Delhi; and above all, Ashok Yadav in Abu Dhabi, who has made the bulk of the contribution. Ashok cheerfully revised the text several times, ensuring that errors were painstakingly corrected, and the manuscript was attractive and accurate. Finally, I am most grateful to my two colleagues in Riyadh, Ashok Dhawan and Sanjay Banga, who, with dedication and commitment, worked on the text in its final stages and made it ready for publication.

I am most grateful to Mr. K.K. Saxena of Aakar Books for taking up the publication of this work so enthusiastically. I am also grateful to him for assigning the editing of this book to Ms. Ritu Singh. I share with him his shock and grief at her tragic demise at the end of January 2010. Though I did not meet Ritu Singh, I had a robust exchange of emails with her and was deeply impressed with her diligence and commitment. She worked on my manuscript with great care, meticulously correcting numerous blemishes in content and style. The rough manuscript that came into her hands emerged much improved as a result of her extraordinary attention to detail. Though she was battling a grave illness, she ensured that almost all the editing work was completed before she breathed her last. I am confident this book will remain a lasting tribute to an excellent editor. I am grateful to Ms. Padmamalini G. Rao for taking up the editing of the manuscript and finalizing the manuscript for publication.

Throughout my career in the Indian Foreign Service, I have enjoyed the friendship of a person I have admired and attempted to emulate, though without success. He has been an inspirational figure since we first worked together in Baghdad over 30 years ago. He has instilled in me, by precept and personal example, the qualities of intellectual integrity, commitment to excellence, and an understanding of our national interest which eschews xenophobia and is, instead, founded on the understanding of the perceptions of the other side and an accommodativeness that serves mutual interests. This book, which discusses age-old animosities and calls for a better understanding and accommodation in place of historic feuds, is an appropriate tribute to him and, hence, it is to Mr. Mani Shankar Aiyar, mentor and friend, that I dedicate this work, hoping (against hope) that it will meet his exacting standards.

This narrative of hatred, conflict and war, of mistakes made and opportunities lost, of old ties callously abandoned or coloured with modern-day prejudices, is likely to fill one with anguish and pessimism. In this despair, I take great joy in the happy face and bright smile of my granddaughter, Aalia, who has brought enchantment in the late afternoon of my mortal sojourn, and whose generation, I hope, will achieve the peace denied the Children of Abraham in my life.

Talmiz Ahmad

Introduction

Mine eyes have seen the glory of the coming of the Lord;
He is trampling out the vintage where the grapes of wrath are stored;
He hath loosed the fateful lightning of His terrible swift sword;
His truth is marching on.

...

In the beauty of the lilies Christ was born across the sea,
With a glory in His bosom that transfigures you and me;
As He died to make men holy, let us die to make them free,
While God is marching on.

Julia Ward Howe, 'The Battle Hymn of the Republic' (1861)

In recent years, violence based on religious zeal has replaced violence emerging from secular sources and interests.In the period 1970–95, there were 64,319 acts of violence, with religious terrorism accounting for half of them.[1] Bruce Hoffman has noted that:[2]

> ... the religious imperative for terrorism is the most important defining characteristic of terrorist activity today. The revolution that transformed Iran into an Islamic republic in 1979 played a crucial role in the modern advent of religious terrorism, but it has not been confined to Iran, to the Middle East, or to Islam. Since t he 1980s, this resurgence has involved elements of the entire world's major religious as well as some smaller sets of cults.

Religion is increasingly providing the ideology, motivation and organizational strength for groups in different parts of the world to perpetrate violence. By 1992, the number of religious terrorist groups had increased from two to eleven and embraced major world religions as well as obscure sects and cults.[3] Again, during the 1990s, the proportion of religious terrorist groups among all active international terrorist organizations grew significantly: in 1994, sixteen, nearly a third of the forty-nine (49) identifiable organizations, could be classified as religious; in 1995, their number grew to twenty-six (26)—nearly half of the fifty-six (56) organizations identified.[4]

Again, as Hoffman has pointed out, terrorism, motivated in whole or in part by religious imperatives, often leads to more intense acts of violence, producing considerably more fatalities than the relatively discriminating acts of violence perpetrated by secular terrorist organizations. Thus, although religious terrorists committed only 25 per cent of the recorded international terrorist incidents in 1995, their acts were responsible for 58 per cent of the terrorist-related fatalities recorded that year. The attacks that caused the greatest numbers of death in 1995, that is, those that killed eight or more people, were *all* perpetrated by religious terrorists.[5]

Every organized religion today is imbued with a 'strain of violence' and includes aspects that would suggest a 'divine mandate for destruction'.[6] As a scholar has noted, 'Religiously justified violence first and foremost is a problem of "sacred" texts and not a problem of misinterpretation of the texts'.[7] The role of religion as the basis for conflict primarily emerges from what are referred to as 'fundamentalist movements' within a particular religion. Every principal religion today has its 'fundamentalist' groups but all fundamentalists tend to share certain common features. Karen Armstrong points out:[8]

> [Fundamentalisms] are embattled forms of spirituality, which have emerged as a response to a perceived crisis. They are engaged in a conflict with enemies whose secular policies and beliefs seem inimical to religion itself.Fundamentalists do not regard this battle as a conventional political struggle, *but experience it as a cosmic war between the forces of good and evil.* [Emphasis added.]

Bruce Lawrence sees fundamentalism as a kind of religious ideology which consists of 'an affirmation of religious authority as holistic and absolute, admitting of neither criticism nor reduction'.[9] It also demands that 'specific creedal and ethical dictates derived from scripture be publicly recognized and legally enforced'[10]

At the end of their 'Fundamentalism' project, which went into several thousand pages, Appleby, Sivan and Almond had identified five 'ideological' characteristics of fundamentalists:[11]

(*i*) they are concerned above all with the erosion of religion and its proper role in society;

(*ii*) they are selective in regard to what part of their tradition they would wish to retain, and what part of modernity they choose to react against: from tradition they select those aspects that support their fundamentalist ideology and reject other aspects associated with mainstream religion; again, they accept the technological and organisational aspects of modernity while rejecting its ideological values, e.g. secularism, pluralism, etc.; indeed, some modern values are identified for 'focused opposition';

(*iii*) they embrace some form of dualism, usually centred around the moral absolutes of good vs. evil, with all good being on one side and all evil on the other; one side is pure and redeemed while the other is 'contaminated, sinful, doomed';

(*iv*) they stress absolutism and inerrancy in *their* sources of revelation; and,

(*v*) they are often imbued with some form of Millennialism or Messianism: history will end miraculously when 'good will triumph over evil'; the end-days will be preceded by severe trials, though the righteous will be saved by a Messiah.

Religious fundamentalism obtains its credibility from the perceived 'failure' of secular models of progress to address the problems of transition from an agrarian to an urban, industrial society. This, coupled with the perceived domination of the moral and political doctrines of the West, has encouraged native populations in the developing world (as also in some sections of the West) to assert 'nativist religions as an alternative ideological vehicle for resistance against both foreign powers and indigenous secular rulers ... cultural survival, national independence and social transformation are the dominant themes of such fundamentalist movements and discourses'.[12] As Francis Fukuyama has noted succinctly: 'One is inclined to say that the revival of religion in some way attests to a broad unhappiness with the impersonality and spiritual vacuity of liberal consumerist societies'.[13]

Religious militancy and fundamentalist ideologies and movements present a common challenge to the dominant secular ideologies of progress: religious militants hold before believers the promise of a return to the certitudes of religious traditions, indigenous cultural roots, sacred languages, and primordial identities.[14] Still, however strong their belief and however fervent their advocacy, 'not all fundamentalists are terrorists or even potential terrorists'.[15] It is the alliance of fundamentalism with messianism that creates a political force, and it is 'messianic fundamentalism' that constitutes a significant challenge to the political order.[16]

Messianism

First, three related concepts, often used interchangeably, Apocalypticism, Millennialism and Messianism, need to be defined. Apocalypticism refers to the belief in the imminent total transformation of this world (the earthly kingdom) through divine intervention. Millennialism refers to the expectation of a radical break in the present at the end of a thousand-year age; in general, it refers to a period of chaos and destruction, culminating in a period of redemption through divine intervention. Messianism refers to the expectation of the appearance of a divinely ordained saviour, the Messiah, who will lead the war of believers against evil and herald the millennial era.[17] Though found in all major cultures, these three concepts are central to Jewish and Christian traditions, and have a strong resonance in Islam as well, particularly in Shia Islam.

In the Semitic traditions, the three concepts centre around 'the struggle between good and evil which has endured since the dawn of creation, [which] will culminate in a destructive final battle in which the victory of the forces of good over evil will be followed by divine judgment and reward of a time-less bliss'.[18] These concepts are 'intrinsically tied to humanity's striving to imagine, articulate and help bring about a tormenting End, and, through that agony, a fresh Beginning'.[19]

The narrative of messianism begins with Zoroaster (fl. 1500–1200 BC) who saw human history in terms of a struggle between light and darkness, with final victory going to the former.[20] The Iranian prophet Mani (c. AD 210–76) built on this binary view, though, unlike Zoroaster, he thought of good and evil as permanent features of the world.[21] Biblical messianism may have borrowed some ideas from foreign, particularly Persian sources, but scholars now tend to believe that many features of the apocalyptic tradition were already a part of Jewish world view, such as the ideas of judgment and salvation, though the dualistic world view did not fit into orthodox Jewish messianic thinking.[22]

Jesus Christ spoke of ushering in a new kingdom – a land of abundance, free of corruption and illnesses. His crucifixion and death did not mark the end of his message: since he had risen to heaven, there would be a 'second coming', when a messiah sent by God would descend to earth, heralding an end-time marked by a cosmic struggle between good and evil, culminating in the permanent destruction of the latter and the setting up of the promised kingdom of happiness and bliss.[23] St. Augustine (AD 354–430) later suggested that the message of end-time should not be read literally; it was an allegory and pertained to inner transformation (the victory of good over evil) which was not linked to any specific time frame.[24]

This early evolution of Christian faith gave shape to certain fundamental beliefs that reverberate in Christianity (and secular schools inspired by it) to this day: first, that evil can be conquered, and second, that heavenly perfection, Utopia, can be attained on earth as a result of human effort.[25] In due course, a third idea also began to emerge, though it took final shape only when the age of religious faith had commenced its retreat: the idea of immutable progress at the heart of human history.[26] At the same time, in spite of St. Augustine's teachings, belief in end-times and the coming of the messiah never died away. From time to time, between the eleventh and sixteenth centuries, a number of movements based on millennial expectations emerged in Europe, particularly when people were going through periods of serious hardship, such as war, plague or economic difficulties, or when major changes had occurred in societies that alienated certain sections of their members, primarily due to unbearable feudal extraction or corruption of the religious establishment. Mark Lilla has described the power of messianic belief in Christianity thus:[27]

> As a religion of redemption, Christianity nurses hopes of a transformation of earthy existence through divine action, and these hopes are articulated in terms of Christ's Second Coming and the enduring presence of the Holy Spirit. While Christ's death, resurrection, and ascension leave some Christians with a sense of void, causing them to withdraw from the world, the redemptive promise of his return can also inspire quite different thoughts and emotions – about the struggle against Satan in the present, about the apocalyptic destruction of the world, about lands of milk and honey, about a New Jerusalem.

In her brilliant 'reflections' on the aftermath of September 11, Pnina Werbner has noted the following characteristics shared by messianism in the three Semitic traditions:[28]

(*i*) messianic movements in the Semitic traditions usually occur during periods when societies are going through major and painful transitions, involving large-scale dislocations and deep uncertainties;

(*ii*) a world of 'absolute perfection', Utopia, is achieved through the defeat of an evil satanic force, the forces of good usually represented by a uniquely empowered 'chosen people'; and,

(*iii*) this Utopia is in sharp contrast to the present world of chaos and anarchy.

The persistent wars of religion over a few hundred years, ending with the Thirty Years' War (1618–48), led to the insistent questioning of the religious Christian state and the need to separate Church and State. The British intellectual Thomas Hobbes (1588–1679) mounted the first robust assault in this regard. He contended that the years of religious wars had led to anarchy in which men's basic instincts of fear, ignorance and desire had been given free rein; this had led to conditions of civic and political breakdown, which was described by him in this well-known passage:[29]

> In such condition there is no place for industry, because the fruit thereof is uncertain, and consequently, no culture of the earth, no navigation, nor use of the commodities that may be imported by sea, no commodious building, no instruments of moving and removing such things as require much force, no knowledge of the face of the earth, no account of time, no arts, no letters, no society, and, which is worst of all, *continual fear and danger of violent death, and the life of man, solitary, poor, nasty, brutish, and short.* [Emphasis added.]

Besides his powerful criticism of the 'Kingdom of darkness' and the untrammelled power of the papacy, Hobbes also expressed deep concerns about the power of messianism on the minds and actions of believers. Mark Lilla describes his worries:[30]

> It was the intellectual horsemen of the apocalypse who worried him [Hobbes] most. It was the mystic who believed he heard voices, the dissenter who claimed an absolute right to follow his conscience, the mountebank prophet who raised an army of fanatics to defend the New Jerusalem. Hobbes and his early followers knew from experience how weak the hold of orthodox theology was on the minds and actions of believers, once rumours began to circulate of an imminent redeeming God.

Hobbes' fervent hope was that the 'Great Separation' (between Church and State) that he was advocating would delink politics from theological and cosmological speculation.[31] His concerns were valid but his expectations were doomed: powerful messianic movements centred around charismatic personalities continued to emerge in the West at regular intervals. More importantly, the messianic impulse began to manifest itself in movements professing *secular* visions and ideologies, what John Gray refers to as 'secular millennialism'.[32] These movements borrowed from Christianity the idea of human redemption based on human effort and the idea of the inevitability of human progress. These were still 'faith-based' upheavals, with faith not in the divine presence but in their own vision and ideology. Like religious messianic movements, these secular messianic movements too emerged and held sway during periods of severe social dislocations, promising, in good Biblical tradition, the emergence of a 'new man' and a heaven on earth.[33]

Secular messianism contributed one new idea to the messianism discourse that 'humanly initiated terror could create a new world'.[34] Such an idea was absent in Christianity: though Europe had been wracked with bloody wars over several hundred years, particularly religious wars, no one had contended that violence would perfect humanity and speed up end-times. It was the leaders of the French Revolution, the Jacobins, who believed that 'society had become corrupt as a result of repression but could be transformed by the methodical use of force'.[35] This idea took thousands of people to the guillotine.

After a detailed study of European messianic movements in the Middle Ages, the American author, Norman Cohn (1915–2007), wrote his pathbreaking study, *The Pursuit of the Millennium*, in 1957, in which he pointed out that the twentieth century movements, Nazism and Communism, were indeed 'rooted in an earlier forgotten Age' and in their basic attitudes followed 'an ancient tradition' of the Middle Ages in which:[36]

> A boundless, millennial promise [was] made with boundless, prophet-like conviction to a number of rootless and desperate men in the midst of a society where traditional norms and relationships are disintegrating – here, it would seem, lay the source of that subterranean medieval fanaticism which has been studied in this book. It may be suggested that here, too, lies the source of the giant fanaticisms which in our day have convulsed the world.

Twentieth century secular messianism was exemplified by Communism, Fascism and Nazism as implemented in the Soviet Union, Italy and

Germany, where the harmony of Utopia was pursued: Marxism accommodated millennial aspiration by promising an egalitarian paradise of plenty and freedom of choice; in Germany a proud nation sought to recover its lost self-respect by exalting its unique racial superiority. Both visions of Utopia ended in violence on an unprecedented scale, leaving their polities shattered and their peoples ruined. Later, the anti-communist rhetoric of the Cold War also drew from apocalyptic imagery such millennial references as 'Doomsday' and 'Armageddon' and the concept of the 'Evil Empire'.In the 1960s, the radical Left Movement in Europe picked up the baton of secular messianism, ending up by perpetrating sporadic acts of mindless violence and murder. In the post-Cold War era, scenarios of environmental catastrophe have also evoked the imagery of the Apocalypse.[37]

It is important to note that secular messianism has frequently shown a deep affiliation with its religious manifestation. Thus, in 1920, during a visit to the Soviet Union, the philosopher Bertrand Russell saw the close connection between them:[38]

> *The hopes which inspire Communism are, in the main, as admirable as those instilled by the Sermon on the Mount, but they are held as fanatically, and are likely to do as much harm ...* The war has left throughout Europe a mood of disillusionment and despair which calls aloud for a new religion, as the only force capable of giving men the energy to live vigorously. Bolshevism has supplied the new religion. It promises glorious things ... [Emphasis added.]

Again, even before the Soviet Revolution, the Russian religious philosopher Semyon Frank had already sensed the similarity in character and consequences between the messianic enthusiasm generated by Semitic tradition and that which emerged from Socialist idealism: [39]

> Among his contemporaries he[the Socialist] sees either merely the victims of the world's evil he dreams of eradicating or the perpetrators of that evil ... This feeling of hatred for the enemies of the people forms the concrete and active psychological foundation of his life. *Thus the great love of mankind of the future gives birth to a great hatred for people; the passion for organizing an earthly paradise becomes a passion for destruction..* [Emphasis added.]

Similarly, both Italian Fascism and German Nazism reflected in their secular idealism the powerful impact of Semitic messianic tradition. Mussolini said in 1926:[40]

Fascism is not only a party, it is a regime, it is not only a regime, but a faith, it is not only a faith, but a religion that is conquering the labouring masses of the Italian people.

In this spirit, fascist cadres were exalted as missionaries and martyrs in the Christian tradition, with Mussolini as the central messiah figure.[41] In public articulations in Nazi Germany, the distinction between the National Socialist belief system and Christian faith was so blurred as to be nearly obliterated. Thus, before Christmas of 1925, referring to Jesus Christ clearing the temple of Jewish moneylenders, Hitler said:[42]

Then too, victory did not come by virtue of the power of the State, but through a redemptive doctrine, whose herald was born under the most wretched circumstances. Despite this, people of Aryan blood, still celebrate this birth. Christ had Aryan blood. Today, we have also given birth to a poisonous period with the State being totally incapable of mastering the situation ... *We National Socialists see in the work of Christ the possibility of achieving the unimaginable through fanatical belief.* [Emphasis added.]

Hitler was convinced of his special relationship with God and saw himself as the instrument of God's will. Thus, he said in June 1937:[43]

... when I look back on the five years behind us, I cannot help but say: this has not been the work of man alone. Had Providence not guided us, I surely would often have been unable to follow these dizzying paths. That is something our critics should above all know. At the bottom of our hearts, we National Socialists are devout! We have no choice: no one can make national or world history if his deeds and abilities are not blessed by Providence.

In his public speeches, Hitler drew numerous references from the Lutheran Bible which were familiar to his listeners: the march of the German people from dejection and failure to success and glory on the basis of true belief in Nazi ideology was a recurring theme in Hitler's proclamations, described by Michael Burleigh as a 'redemptive story of suffering and deliverance, a sentimental journey from misery to glory, from division to mystic unity based on the blood bond that linked souls'.[44] This redemption, in Hitler's view, was the unique destiny *not* of the German people but of the 'Aryan-Germanic race' which was the true instrument for the realization of God's purposes on earth.[45] From this, the demonization of the Jews was the logical next step. In 1921 itself, Hitler had set out his thoughts clearly thus:[46]

> I can imagine Christ as nothing other than blond and with blue eyes, the
> devil however only with a Jewish grimace.
>
> ...
>
> Of course, [Christ] made no secret of his attitude towards the Jewish people,
> and when necessary he even took to the whip to drive from the temple of
> the lord *this adversary of all humanity*, who then as always saw in religion
> nothing but an instrument for his business existence. [Emphasis in the
> original.]

Arjomand has made the important point that 'an apocalyptic world view
is compatible with both quietistic and revolutionary attitudes, with
militancy as well as pacifism'. However, as he has noted, it is political
messianism that motivates militant activism.[47] Barbara Stowasser echoes
this by pointing out that apocalyptic movements emerge in different ages
in response to prevailing circumstances and seek salvation through a
variety of means, including 'a combination of quietism and a withdrawal
from the world, or on reform, or radical segregation of the righteous from
the sinful majority'. They could also express themselves through 'militant
activism', in order to restructure society to hasten the final event.[48]
However, the promise of collective deliverance, both in its religious and
secular manifestations, often becomes a 'collective nightmare'.[49] Since the
process of redemption is itself based on a struggle between good and evil,
it follows that secular messianism would borrow from Christianity the
idea of demonology, the belief in hostile conspiracies that are out to
thwart the realization of Utopia (and human advance), and can only be
confronted through violence, particularly pre-emptive violence. This
takes a heavy toll in human life, but, as Robespierre had said, in the larger
interest of the Revolution, 'Pity is treason'.[50]

Contemporary Messianic Conflicts

It is the conviction of the protagonists in present-day messianic conflicts
that their war with the 'other' is a 'millennial religious duty',[51] a holy
war urged upon the faithful by divine injunction. While the earliest
Christian tradition had rejected the concept of 'holy war', a thousand
years after Christ, the Crusades broke with earlier tradition and, at Papal
insistence, pursued war in support of the Christian faith and church.
Though again, five hundred years later, Christian tradition generally
did away with the concept of holy war, the vocabulary and legal
terminology of the Crusades, as Peter Partner has noted, deeply affected

the mindset of the Western colonial leadership and influenced its interaction with the subject Muslim peoples.[52] One of the most pernicious aspects of this colonial interaction was for travellers, popular writers and artists, statesmen at home and even genuine scholars to develop and propagate an essentialized view of 'Islam' by seeing it as a single cultural identity, with common attributes and characteristics that had remained largely unchanged from the inception of Islam. The end of imperialism and the later changes in global power equations have not effected any significant change in these perceptions.

The mainstream Western view of 'Islam', encompassing the faith and its followers, is generally founded on the following principal premises:

(i) 'Islam' is a permanent bundle of similar beliefs and practices across the Muslim realm, which have remained unchanged over the last several centuries.

(ii) 'Islam' encompasses all aspects of the life of the believer, public and private, and has done so through all stages of its history. Thus, the political, social and moral aspects of an individual or the polity to which he belongs constitute an integral whole that is incapable of fundamental change. It does not have the Western separation between Church and State. Consequently, 'Islam' rejects Western values of modernity and secularism.

(iii) It follows that 'Islam' is inevitably at war with the 'West' and this state of conflict has continued through the entire history of Islam's encounter with the West. Thus, it is not surprising that 'Islam' should pursue a fanatical jihad, a 'holy war' against the West: the core identity of the modern-day Muslim is that of the 'mujahid' (holy warrior).

These premises have so long and hoary a tradition as to be an integral part of the Western belief system vis-à-vis Islam. Most recently, it was set out in categorical terms by Samuel Huntington:[53]

> The underlying problem for the West is not Islamic fundamentalism. It is Islam, a different civilization whose people are convinced of the superiority of their culture and are obsessed with the inferiority of their power. The problem for Islam is not the CIA or the U.S. Department of Defense. It is the West, a different civilization whose people are convinced of the universality of their culture.

Every one of the above propositions is inaccurate and a-historical. 'Islam' over the last 1,400 years has gone through remarkable mutations in its doctrinal, political, social and moral aspects, and in reality exhibits an extraordinary diversity, both in terms of its attributes and practices as also in terms of its geographical spread. As Richard Jackson has pointed out:[54]

> There is simply too much variation within 'Islam' and Islamic movements for meaningful or illuminating generalizations, not least because 'Islam' consists of over a billion people from dozens of different countries, languages and cultures, five major doctrinal groupings and hundreds of smaller sects, theological traditions and cultural-religious variants.

Again, Islam, as an all-encompassing way of life, has been more a pious canonical hope and aspiration than realized experience. All too frequently through Islamic history, as in the history of the West, the secular interests of the state and its rulers have triumphed over the precepts of the faith and the assertions of the clergy, so that Muslim empires through the ages have manifested and celebrated the colourful tapestry of multicultural diversity rather than the monochrome homogeneity of a dominant unchanging faith.

The assertion that one of the principal reasons for Muslim 'backwardness' is the lack of separation between Church and State, as in the Christian tradition, is of doubtful validity. Such a distinction was neither inherent in Christian tradition nor was it pervasive in its history. In fact, the Christian Church has consistently and directly exercised power in matters pertaining to the community – religious, economic, social, and has also enjoyed remarkable political authority and influence in state matters.[55] Once Christianity became the state religion of the Roman Empire, it, over the centuries: eliminated or marginalized all other religious beliefs and practices; acquired ownership over extensive properties; exercised near-exclusive control over education; and set the framework for the moral values of the state. Above all, as Shahid Alam has pointed out, the Church, through much of its history, sanctioned intolerance of all other faiths, which included discrimination and even violence against Jews.[56] Even today, the influence of the Church in state matters continues, particularly in the United States, an issue that is examined in some detail in Chapters V and VI.

At the same time, the assertion that the Islamic state had a monolithic religious character is a gross exaggeration. In actual practice, as brought out in Chapter VII, there was a regular struggle for influence between the political ruler and the *ulema*, with long periods of mutual accommodation for mutual benefit. Though the balance of power often tilted in favour of the political leader, the ulema retained considerable autonomy with regard to the 'legislative' aspect of the Islamic state: they developed and fine-tuned, over the centuries, various aspects of law to cover personal, social and commercial matters, thus setting up an effective, albeit informal, separation between the executive and legislative branches of government, well before this had been achieved in the West.[57]

That 'Islam' has consistently rejected modernity remains an erroneous assertion in spite of the frequency with which it is averred. Without entering into a theoretical discussion of what constitutes modernity, suffice it to say that, in their interaction with the West, Muslim statesmen and intellectuals from the earliest times evinced a deep interest in the instruments, institutions and achievements of the West, and attempted emulation, at times half-hearted, at other times enthusiastic.[58] While Islamic intellectuals in the nineteenth and early twentieth centuries were generally hostile to the West on account of its hegemonic and intrusive policies, and saw the West as a threat to their religion and way of life, they willingly sought to study and imbibe those aspects of Western civilization that were constructive, particularly science and technology. Prominent Islamist scholars such as Hassan-Al Banna, Abul Ala Maududi and Sayyid Qutb were deeply familiar with contemporary Western works and, in fact, all three of them in their writings frequently quoted from Western popular scientific literature. More important, while Islamist writers often used traditional religious language and celebrated life in pristine Islam, their mindset, concepts and institutions were thoroughly modern and were deeply influenced by contemporary European developments. Thus, Maududi innovatively projected 'Islam' as an ideology and a system, and set it up in opposition to (imperialist) Western ideology and system.[59]

However, whatever the later significance of these Islamist intellectuals, for over 50 years, from the end of the First World War up to the 1960s, 'Islam' hardly made any political impact in the Muslim world. The two principal ideas which resonated in 'Islam' at that time were nationalism and socialism, which constituted the ideological base of the 'Third World' in its confrontation with Western imperialism. In the Arab world, nationalism effectively ousted pan-Islamism and, instead, opted (with moderate success) for the ideal of pan-Arabism, which was pursued not on the basis of Islam but through such secular ideologies as Nasserism or Baathism. Even the conflict with Israel had no religious character or orientation, being led by the staunchly secular Palestine Liberation Organization (PLO). Through the Cold War, the Arab world was divided into traditional monarchies and revolutionary regimes that had emerged as a result of military or party political coups d'états. The former were Islam-oriented, but they were consistently and actively pro-West, and 'Islam' was seen by the West as a 'natural ally' against godless Communism. The revolutionary regimes were Left-oriented, but neither side, at this time, espoused a robust Islamic ideology or belief system. Outside the Arab world, in Turkey, Pakistan and Iran, religious groups were generally at the margins of nationalist politics.

With the Arab defeat in the 1967 war, the bases and structures of the West-oriented secular system received a powerful blow. This defeat, followed rapidly by the compromise of Camp David-I and the Israeli attack on Lebanon in 1982, which ousted the PLO as a political and military force in the region, for the first time in contemporary history gave 'Islam' some space in the consciousness and, later, in the politics of the region. However, Islam's progress was slow since the state powers ruthlessly crushed their domestic Islamic movements, while the Iran-Iraq war confined the fervour of the Islamic revolution in Iran to its national boundaries.

What gave special impetus to 'Islam' from the 1980s was the successful jihad in Afghanistan, initiated for short-term, tactical advantage by Saudi Arabia, Pakistan and, ironically, the United States. Later, in the 1990s, the neglect (the USA) or indifference (Saudi Arabia) or active support (Pakistan) of the principal role-players ensured the emergence of Al-Qaeda as the principal face of modern-day Islamic militancy. The ideological and political narrative of militant Islam is set out in Chapters VII and VIII. Suffice it to say here that contemporary resurgent Islam is the product of specific contemporary political circumstances and opportunities provided by global and regional role-players that were quickly taken advantage of by the nascent radical movement that had defeated one superpower in Afghanistan and now turned its attention to the other superpower and its allies – Israel and pro-West regimes in different parts of the Islamic realm.

Today, the political scenario of West Asia lies at the root of contemporary assertions of a 'millennial religious duty' or 'holy war'. However, regardless of the insistence of the principal protagonists, the duty of waging holy war remains rooted not in history but in 'the passions of contemporary politics', even if it is expressed in the 'archaic language of religion'.[60]

The Israeli-Palestinian conflict in West Asia and the Al-Qaeda-led jihad in Afghanistan, that had parallel trajectories through the 1980s and 1990s, have merged with the insurgency in Iraq and the confrontation with Iran, to define the so-called contemporary conflict between 'Islam' and the 'West', thus providing an opportunity to scholars, committed on one side or the other, to project this modern-day confrontation, emerging from specific contemporary political contexts, as an age-old civilizational war. Such a projection, however false in historical terms, has acquired a certain validity since the three Semitic faiths engaged in this conflict have long traditions of holy war, even if, in practice, holy war may not have been pursued for a long period or, when invoked, was in reality a case of archaic terminology being utilized for contemporary political advantage. The reason why holy war has retained a contemporary resonance is because, while Christian leaders over the last few centuries have hardly ever been involved in holy war, the language utilized by them in their political encounters with adversaries, both in the colonial period and later in the 'secular' conflicts of the twentieth century, has frequently evoked the crusading spirit, as a result of which:[61]

> Crusading has had a much longer afterlife than is generally thought, and ... Christian attitudes of mind that we think of as long-dead may exercise a greater influence upon our present point of view than we imagine.

In the Jewish tradition, holy war has been more muted, the last such conflicts having taken place in the first two centuries of our era (AD 70 and AD 132-5), which resulted in the destruction of the Jewish Temple in Jerusalem and the expulsion of Jews into the diaspora. However, for the last 1800 years, though holy war was not part of Jewish experience, messianic expectation, with its promise of redemption for the Jewish people through their return to the 'promised land', remained a vibrant tradition and sustained the community with hope amidst its severe tribulations in exile. Twentieth-century experiences such as the

Holocaust, the Zionist project and the setting up of the State of Israel, and Israel's victories against the Arabs on the battlefield, taken together appear to have affirmed the central prophecies of the Jewish messianism in modern-day Israel and among its allies in the West.

At the same time, the present era, marked by horrendous conflict, economic upheaval and uncertainty, the assertions of a secular order that have undermined traditional norms and values, and, above all, the uncertainties and fears emerging from a nascent globalization, all of these have taken the confidence and the passion out of the rationalism of the Enlightenment,[62] and given way to a 'time of troubles', thus engendering grave apocalyptic fears.[63] These uncertain times have given a new strength and credibility to Christian fundamentalist revival, particularly in the USA, so that most American evangelical groups now espouse literalist end-time beliefs, and see their destiny firmly intertwined with the fate of the Jewish people and, hence, the politics of West Asia. This constitutes the basis of the novel concept of a 'Judeo-Christian' civilization, which has tied American Jewry, in alliance with Right-wing US Christianity, to the interests of Israel, that is total and unquestioning support for all of Israel's policies, including large-scale expansion of settlements in occupied Palestinian territories and massive violence against the Palestinian populace.

The present scenario reverses the much older tradition of 2,000 years of Christian-Jewish animosity, which continued into the Enlightenment, and, in its secular manifestations, was as fierce and wanton in its assault upon the Jew as it had been earlier when religious identities were in conflict. This contemporary Christian-Jewish alliance has now gone well beyond the specificities of the Palestinian issue and has ranged itself against 'Islam', thus carrying forward into the twenty-first century the Orientalist discourse relating to Islam and Muslims from the colonial era. The Jew, on his part, rejecting nearly 1,400 years of reasonably comfortable and mutually advantageous cohabitation with 'Islam', now sees the Muslim as his traditional Biblical enemy (variously, the Amalek, the Philistine or Canaanite) who, with Biblical sanction, deserves annihilation.

In contrast to this, there is the pervasive sense of defeat and demoralization in the Islamic world as a result of political and economic failure at home and sustained defeat and humiliation abroad. In their despair, many Muslims have sought solace in religious belief and some have become active supporters of Islamic fundamentalist groups and movements, the most radical of which believe they, too, have divine sanction to perpetrate wanton violence upon the demonized 'Other'.

While fundamentalism mobilizes a native religious tradition to confront the alien, modern and secular order, its alliance with messianism strengthens the motivation and enthusiasm of the believer by providing him with the promise of a world of perfect harmony, and imbues him with zeal since he knows he is in the right and that God is on his side. This conviction enables him to justify and perpetrate the most heinous violence upon the enemy. Thus, the stage is now set for a renewed conflict among the children of Abraham who are united in drawing from their shared traditions new justifications and doctrines in support of animosity, conflict and war.

NOTES

1. Dr. Magnus Ranstorp, 'Terrorism in the Name of Religion', *Journal of International Affairs,* Summer 1996, 50, no. 1; downloaded from http://www.ciaonet.org/wps/ram01/;

2. Bruce Hoffman, 'Old Madness, New Methods – Revival of Religious Terrorism Begs for Broader US Policy', *Rand Review,* Winter 1998-9; downloaded from: http://rand.org/publications/randreview/issues/rr.winter98.9/methods.html.

3. Hoffman.

4. ibid.

5. ibid.

6. Mark Juergensmeyer, *Terror in the Mind of God – The Global Rise of Religious Violence* (New Delhi: Oxford University Press, 2000) p. 6.

7. Jack Nelson Pallmeyer, *Is Religion Killing Us? Violence in the Bible and the Quran* (Harrisburg, PA: Trinity Press International, 2003) p. xiv.

8. Karen Armstrong, *The Battle for God-Fundamentalism in Judaism, Christianity and Islam* (London: Harper Collins Publishers, 2001) p. xi.

9. Quoted in: Dr. Fazlur Rehman, 'Religious Fundamentalism – Causes and Remedies', *HSSRD Science-Religion Dialogue*, Manshera, Pakistan, Spring 2004; downloaded from: http://www.hssrd.org/journals/2004/english/fundamentalism.htm

10. ibid.

11. Luca Ozzana, 'Religious Terrorist Groups and Political Power: An Ambiguous Relationship' SGIR Turin Conference, September 2007,

Online Paper Archive; downloaded from: www.sgir.org/archive/turin/uploads/Ozzano-paper_sgir_to_2007_def.pdf.

12. Majid Tehranian, 'Religious Resurgence in a Global Perspective', *Economic and Political Weekly*, 32:50, New Delhi, 13-19 December 1997; downloaded from: http://www2.hawaii.edu/ majid/journal_articles/rr.html.

13. Mark Burgess, 'Explaining Religious Terrorism – Part I: The Axis of Good and Evil', Centre for Defense Information, 20 May 2004; downloaded from: http://cdi.org/friendlyversion/printversion.cfm?documentID=2381.

14. Tehranian.

15. Ozzano.

16. William Maley, 'Messianism and Political Action – Some Contextual Characteristics', in K.P.S. Gill and Ajai Sahni (Ed), *The Global Threat of Terror*, The Institute for Conflict Management, New Delhi, 2002; downloaded from: http://www.satp.org/satporgtp/publication/books/global/maley.htm.

17. Said Amir Arjomand, 'Messianism, Millennialism and Revolution in Early Islamic History', in Abbas Amanat and Magnus Bernhardsson (Eds.), *Imagining the End: Visions of Apocalypse from the Ancient Middle East to Modern America* (London: I.B. Tauris Publishers, 2002) p. 106.

18. Abbas Amanat, 'Introduction: Apocalyptic Anxieties and Millennial Hopes in the Salvation Religions of the Middle East', in Abbas Amanat and Magnus Bernhardsson (Eds.), *Imaging the End: Visions of Apocalypse from the Ancient Middle East to Modern America* (London: I.B. Tauris Publishers, 2002) p. 2.

19. Amanat, p. 1.

20. John Gray, *Black Mass – Apocalyptic Religion and the Death of Utopia* (London: Penguin Books, 2008) pp. 13–14.

21. Gray, p. 14.

22. Robert R. Wilson, 'The Biblical Roots of Apocalyptic', in Abbas Amanat and Magnus Bernhardsson (Eds.), *Imaging the End: Visions of Apocalyptic from the Ancient Middle East to Modern America* (London: I.B. Tauris, , 2002) pp. 63–6.

23. Mark Lilla, *The Stillborn God – Religion, Politics, and the Modern West* (New York: Alfred A. Knopf,, 2007) pp. 33–4; Gray, p. 9.

24. Gray, pp. 10–11.

25. ibid., pp. 29–30.

26. ibid., p. 30.

27. Lilla, pp. 48–9.

28. Pnina Werbner 'The Predicament of Diaspora and Millennial Islam:

Reflections in the Aftermath of September 11', Public lecture, February 2002; downloaded from http://www.ssrc.org/sept11/essays/ werbner_text_only.htm.
29. Lilla, pp. 82–3.
30. ibid., pp. 253–4.
31. ibid., p. 254.
32. Gray, p. 61.
33. Michael Burleigh, *Sacred Causes – Religion and Politics from the European Dictators to Al Qaeda* (London: Harper Press,, 2006), p. xii.
34. Gray, p. 36.
35. ibid.
36. Norman Cohn, *The Pursuit of the Millennium* (London: Pimlico, First Published 1957, Pimlico edition 2004) p. 288.
37. Amanat, p. 17.
38. Burleigh, p. 39.
39. ibid.
40. ibid., p. 57.
41. ibid., pp. 60–1.
42. ibid., p. 101.
43. ibid., pp. 102–3.
44. ibid., p. 105.
45. ibid.
46. Burleigh, p. 108.
47. Said Amir Arjomand, p. 108.
48. Barbara Freyer Stowasser, 'The End is Near: Minor and Major Signs of the Hour in Islamic Texts and Contexts', Council on Middle East Studies, The MacMillanCentre for International and Area Studies, Yale University, New Haven, Working Paper, 24 April, 2006; downloaded from: http://128.36.236.77/workpaper/pdfs/MESV6-3.pdf
49. Gray, p. 24.
50. ibid., p. 37.
51. Peter Partner, *God of Battles – Holy Wars of Christianity and Islam*, (Princeton, NJ: Princeton University press, 1997), p. xvii.
52. Partner, p. xviii.
53. Quoted in Stanley Kurtz, 'The Future of History', *Policy Review*, No. 113, June 2002; downloaded from: http://www.policyreview.org/JUN02/ kurtz_print.html
54. Richard Jackson, 'Religion, Politics and Terrorism: A Critical Analysis of Narratives of "Islamic Terrorism,"' Centre for International Politics, Working Paper Series, No. 21, October 2006, University of Manchester, p. 14; downloaded from: http://www.socialsciences.manchester.ac.uk/

disciplines/politics/researchgroups/cip/publications/documents/
Jackson_000.pdf

55. M. Shahid Alam, 'Scholarship or Sophistry? Bernard Lewis and the New
Orientalism', *Counterpunch*, June 28, 2003, pp. 17-18; downloaded from:
http://www.counterpunch.org/alam06282003.html.

56. Alam, p. 18.

57. ibid., p. 17.

58. ibid., pp. 5–10.

59. Partner, p. 236.

60. ibid., p. xvii.

61. ibid., p. xxvii.

62. Amanat, p. 18.

63. Arthur P. Mendel, *Vision and Violence* (Ann Arbor, Michigan: The
University of Michigan Press, 2002) p. 268.

1

Messianism in Semitic Traditions

In the salvation religions of the Middle East, the binary of the Beginning and the End paradigms is particularly powerful ... The struggle between good and evil, which has endured since the dawn of creation, will culminate in a destructive final battle in which the victory of the forces of good over evil will be followed by divine judgment and the reward of a timeless bliss.

... believers have found in the allegorical reading of the biblical and Qur'anic prophecies, keys to the understanding of the troubling questions of their own times ... Beyond the religious domain, though not necessarily detached from its memory, the paradigm of the End and the rhetoric of renewal seem likely to endure for as long as there are anxieties about the moral and material troubles ahead.

> [Abbas Amanat, *Imaging the End: Visions of Apocalypse from the Ancient Middle East to Modern America*][1]

Almost all ancient civilizations—Mesopotamian, Egyptian, Indian, Greek and Roman—nurtured 'combat myths', that is, narratives which envisaged heroic gods engaged in battles to maintain cosmic order against forces of evil, disruption and chaos which threatened universal peace and prosperity.[2] This dichotomy of good versus evil was central to the thinking of the prophet Zoroaster (fl. 1600–1200 BC), who visualized a struggle between the great god Ahura Mazda ('Lord Wisdom') and the force of chaos and destruction, Angra Mainya or Ahriman (the origin of the biblical Satan). In this struggle, Ahura Mazda created time; at the end of time, that is, in a specific finite period, Ahriman would be defeated and destroyed, after which, the world would continue in peace till eternity.[3] This bliss would be enjoyed by all faithful followers, including the dead who would be resurrected. Men would be active participants in this struggle: they would strengthen the good side through 'virtuous actions, sacrifices and obedience to the rules of purity'.[4] This would be followed by the last judgment when 'the good would be lavishly rewarded and the wicked agonizingly annihilated'.[5]

The extent of Zoroaster's impact on Jewish thinking continues to be debated. Norman Cohn believes that Jews in exile in Babylon (586-39 BC) obtained their ideas of the struggle between good and evil, and of judgment, reward and punishment, from Zoroaster.[6] Robert Wilson, on the other hand, points out that, even before the Zoroastrian impact on the Jews in exile, the Hebrew Bible had already developed the ideas of the unique identity of Jews as the 'chosen people of God', of divine intervention in human affairs, and of the divine role in regard to judgment and salvation. Thus, according to him, even if certain ideas were borrowed from Zoroaster by the exile Jews, those ideas 'received a distinctive Jewish development' in the Hebrew Bible.[7]

Jewish Messianism

Arthur Mendel has provided a lucid account of the evolution of apocalyptic thinking in the Hebrew Bible. He points out that the Bible was based on the notion of progress towards peace and social justice based entirely on human will; God's role was benign, being limited to giving direction, promising protection, blessing the righteous and punishing the evil-doers.[8] As Mendel has noted:[9]

> Such, in essence, is the Hebrew Bible's gradualist project and its assumptions. Made in the image of God, man has freedom, reason and conscience to undertake the repair and completion of the world ... To complete the work of creation meant to heal the world's wounds and repair its flaws, bringing peace where there is war, justice where there is injustice, freedom where there is repression, welfare where there is material deprivation, joy where there is pain. Given man's inherently dual nature and manifold limitations, it was assumed the realization of those ideas necessarily lay far in the future and could only be achieved slowly. Yet, given as well the fact that the world was created by a loving parent who cared boundlessly for the well-being of his children, it was also taken for granted that the ideals could and would be fulfilled, that God's world smiled on the dreams of his children.

From this benign scenario, the Hebrew Bible evolved in five steps to the

Apocalypse: the first step was the Bible's divine blessing for violence against alien nations and their gods. As Mendel has said:[10]

> It was at God's command that Joshua brought down the walls of Jericho and destroyed 'utterly all that was in the city, both man and woman, young and old, and ox, and sheep, and ass, with the edge of the sword' (Joshua 6.21). 'So Joshua smote the whole country of the hills, and of the south, and of the vale, and of the springs, and all their kinds: he left none remaining, but utterly destroyed all that breathed, as the Lord God of Israel commanded' (Joshua 10.40) ... priests and prophets not only blessed the campaigns but inspired and even initiated them in the name of Yahweh, as Samuel did when he told Saul of God's orders to 'smite Amalek, and utterly destroy all they have, and spare them not, but slay both man and woman, infant and suckling, ox and sheep, camel and ass' (1 Samuel 15.3).

The second step emerged from a cruel predicament: as the Jewish people faced military defeats, disasters and exiles, they were unable to understand why the hitherto benign divine father had turned against them; it was then explained to them that they had only themselves to blame and that their severe setbacks were divine chastisement for their sins:[11]

> As the tongue of fire devours the stubble,
> As the dry grass sinks down in the flame,
> So their root will be rottenness,
> And their blossom go up like dust ...
> For all this His anger is not turned away
> And His hand is stretched out still
> So the Lord cut off from Israel head and tail,
> Palm branch and reed in one day ...
> The Lord ... has no compassion on the fatherless and widows;
> For everyone is godless and an evildoer,
> And every mouth speaks folly ...
> Through the wrath of the Lord of hosts
> The land is burned
> And the people are like fuel for the fire;
> No man spares his brother.
>
> (Isaiah 5.24, 10–14, 17, 19)

The third step provided that the sinful would have to be redeemed only through divine intervention:[12]

> But this is the covenant that I will make with the house of Israel after those days, saith the Lord, I will put My law in their inward parts, and in their heart will I write it; and I will be their God, and they shall be My

people; and they shall teach no more every man his neighbour, and every man his brother, saying: 'Know the Lord' for they shall all know Me, from the least of them unto the greatest of them, saith the Lord; for I will forgive their iniquity, and their sin will I remember no more. (Jeremiah 31.31-34)

With divine support, the fortunes of the Jews would be reversed: their enemies would be totally annihilated, they would return to Israel from exile, and the Temple would be rebuilt. Yahweh would then emerge as the universal God, and all the other nations would be subordinate to the reunited Israel:[13]

Strangers shall build up thy walls, and their kings shall minister unto thee
...
The nation and kingdom that will not serve thee shall perish; yea, those nations shall be utterly wasted.

The sons also of them that afflicted thee shall come bending unto thee; and all they that despised thee shall bow themselves down at the soles of thy feet ... (Isaiah 60.10, 12, 14)

And, all the nature shall celebrate this great victory:[14]

The mountains and hills shall break forth before you into singing, and all the trees of the field shall clap their hands.
Instead of the thorn shall come up the fir tree, and instead of the brier shall come up the myrtle tree. (Isaiah 55.12–13)

Human and animal nature would change and all life would be blissful:[15]

The wolf and the lamb shall feed together; and the lion shall eat straw like the ox; and dust shall be the serpent's meat. They shall not hurt nor destroy in all my holy mountain, saith the Lord. (Isaiah 65.25)

At the fourth stage, there was a refinement in regard to reward and punishment: while there would be divine chastisement for the sinners, a pure 'remnant' would be saved:[16]

A remnant will return, the remnant of Jacob, to the mighty God, for though your people Israel be as the sand of the sea, only a remnant of them will return. (Isaiah 10.21–22)

Their prophet in the 'Second Isaiah' revealed to the Jews in exile in Babylon a new god imbued with 'loving kindness' and tender mercy, who gave them hope amidst their misery:[17]

The spirit of the Lord God is upon me; because the Lord hath anointed me to preach good tidings unto the meek; he hath sent me to bind up the broken-hearted, to proclaim liberty to the captives, and the opening of the prison to them that are bound.

This new god would rescue his people from bondage:[18]

The voice of him that crieth in the wilderness, Prepare ye the way of the Lord, make straight in the desert a highway for our God. Every valley shall be exalted, and every mountain and hill shall be made low; and the crooked shall be made straight, and the rough places plain ... Behold, the Lord God will come with strong hand, and his arm shall rule for him ... He shall feed his flock like a shepherd; he shall gather the lambs with his arm, and carry them in his bosom and shall gently lead those that are with young.

This prophet also foretold the coming of a 'Servant' who with his sacrifice would redeem the Jewish people:[19]

He is despised and rejected of men; a man of sorrows, and acquainted with grief; ... he was despised, and we esteemed him not. Surely he hath borne our griefs, and carried our sorrows; yet we did esteem him striken, smitten of God, and afflicted. But he was wounded for our transgressions, he was bruised for our iniquities; the chastisement of our peace was upon him; and with his stripes we are healed ... The Lord hath laid on him the iniquity of us all.

At the fifth and final stage, all the details of the Apocalypse came to be incorporated in the Hebrew Bible, and marked the apogee of God's intervention in human affairs in the most dramatic form possible: the world will come to be dominated by an 'evil, tyrannous power of boundless destructiveness';[20] when the tyranny becomes more and more outrageous and the sufferings of the people increasingly onerous, the divine power will unleash the catastrophic destruction of the earth and all mankind at one stroke and its replacement by a new world of 'peace, justice and material abundance'.[21] The Book of Daniel, the final work of the Jewish Bible composed in the third or early second century BC, provided the crucial link between the previous sinful world and the coming apocalypse in the person of the Messiah (though this word is not used in the text). After describing in graphic detail the person and power of the 'Ancient One', Daniel went on to say:[22]

As I watched in the night visions, I saw one like a human being [literally, 'one like a son of man'] coming with the clouds of heaven. And he came to the Ancient One and was presented before him. To him was given dominion and glory and kingship, that all peoples, nations, and languages should serve him. His dominion is an everlasting dominion that shall not pass away and his kingship is one that shall never be destroyed. (Daniel 7. 13–14)

The advent of 'the great prince, the protector of your people' amidst the extraordinary suffering of the Jewish people will bring about a great transformation:[23]

There shall be a time of anguish, such as has never occurred since nations first came into existence. But at that time your people shall be delivered, everyone who is found written in the book. Many of those who sleep in the dust of the earth shall awake, some to everlasting life, and some to shame and everlasting contempt. Those who are wise shall shine like the brightness of the sky, and those who lead many to righteousness, like the stars for ever and ever. (Daniel 12.1–3)

After the Book of Daniel, references to the Apocalypse and the Messiah became more frequent in later Jewish writings composed contemporaneously with the rise of Christianity; these included the First Book of Enoch, the Book of Jubilees, and the Testaments of the Twelve Patriarchs. These books, which were written in the context of the tribulations of the Jewish people in the Roman empire, taken together set out 'the essentials of the apocalyptic pattern' thus: total rejection of the present world; absolute faith in the imminence of the ideal, divine kingdom of the saved; certainty that a divinely sent Messiah will bring about this salvation; and emphasis on the terrible violence that will accomplish the miraculous transformation.[24]

The concept of a 'fresh Beginning' has as its central figure a divinely ordained saviour (referred to as the *messiah* in the three Semitic religions) who, at the end of the world, engages in combat with his arch-enemy whom he will vanquish and then usher in an era of eternal bliss, the Utopia in Western religious and literary traditions, in which the faithful will be rewarded for their goodness and piety. The later Jewish apocalyptic writings specifically reflected the acute predicament of the Jews under Rome's tyranny; hence, in their apocalyptic prophecies, they envisaged the advent of a divinely sent Messiah who would destroy the Romans and take the Roman leader in chains to Mount Zion where he would be executed; the Messiah would then establish his kingdom and, after defeating all the enemies of the Jews, inaugurate an 'age of bliss' in which 'pain, disease, untimely death, violence and strife, want and hunger will be unknown ...'[25] Great violence would accompany these catastrophic events; the Apocalypse was described thus:[26]

> In these days downcast in countenance shall the kings of the earth have become,
> And the strong who possess the land because of the works of their hands,
> For on the day of their anguish and affliction they shall not (be able to) save themselves.
> And I will give them over into the hands of Mine elect:
> As straw in the fire so shall they burn before the face of the holy:
> As lead in the water shall they sink before the face of the righteous
> And no trace of them shall any more be found ...
> And then shall all the righteous escape,
> And shall live till they beget thousands of children,
> And all the days of their youth and their old age
> Shall they complete in peace.

In this messianic kingdom on earth, the saved remnant would live in 'light and joy and peace ... and their lives shall be increased in peace and the years of their joy shall be multi-plied in eternal gladness and peace, all the days of their life':[27]

> And cleanse thou the earth from all oppression, and from all unrighteousness and from all sin, and from all godlessness: and all the uncleanness that is wrought upon the earth destroy from off the earth. And all the children of men shall become righteous and all nations shall offer adoration and shall praise Me, and all shall worship Me. And the earth shall be cleansed from all defilement, and from all sin, and from all punishment, and from all torment, and I will never again send [them] upon it from generation to generation and forever.

In the Roman Empire, even as the condition of the Jews became more desperate, the intensity of their messianic expectations increased, and they warmly welcomed new leaders as messiahs who would restore to the Jews their national home.

The Romans took control of Jerusalem in 37 BC. Herod (37–4 BC), the first Rome-nominated king of Judea, thoroughly expanded and renovated the Jewish Temple during his reign. For over the next one hundred years, the Jews' lives were generally peaceful, with the Roman leaders viewing their idiosyncratic beliefs and practices with amused tolerance, while, with some exceptions, letting them practise their religion. There were occasional disturbances and conflicts, particularly when Roman governors and over-zealous local officials attempted to restrict Jewish religious practices, though the Jews did not exhibit any structured or sustained anti-Roman ideology and organized dissent.[28] The Romans, on their part, ruled with a 'light hand',[29] permitting Jews to congregate in Jerusalem in large numbers for their festivals, respecting the Sabbath by exempting Jews from appearing before magistrates on those days, avoiding depiction of human figures on coins used in Judea and generally respecting their customs.[30]

This environment of mutual goodwill was brought to an abrupt end by the war of AD 66–70. Martin Goodman has argued that at the commencement of the conflict, originating in the long period of misrule by local governors and sparked by the initiative of a young Jewish priest not to continue the tradition of offering sacrifices to the Jewish god on behalf of the Roman emperor, there was no intention on the part of the Romans to go beyond local police action.[31] It escalated into total war due to the incompetence of the local Roman military commanders and the robust response of the Jewish religious and military leaders, who, in inflicting initial defeats upon the Roman force, obtained for their community four years of freedom.[32]

This conflict culminated in the fierce assault on the Jewish forces besieged in the Temple in Jerusalem in AD 70 by the Roman forces led by Titus (AD 39–81, son of emperor Vespasian (AD 9–79), and his successor as emperor). Goodman believes Titus had no interest in destroying the Jewish sanctuary and, indeed, even in the midst of battle tried to protect the sacred structure. However, he could not control his troops, who were by then 'overpowered by their rage, their hatred of the Jews, and a lust for battle', as also by the hope of plunder.[33] In this battle, between half to a million Jews were killed, while another 100,000 were caught and sold as slaves. With their Temple destroyed and their province despoiled, the Jews dispersed across the Mediterranean, thus dating their diaspora from the destruction of their Temple in AD 70.[34]

After the defeat of the Jewish forces, not only was the Temple completely destroyed, the Romans also did not again approve the reconstruction of the shrine. Successive emperors regularly glorified the destruction of the Temple as a great Roman victory, which, in time, led to two further Jewish uprisings, in 115 and 132.[35] After the uprising of

AD 115–117, which saw the extensive participation of Diaspora Jews, emperor Hadrian (AD 76–138) issued an order (in AD 130) forbidding circumcision and public instruction of Jewish law and also announced that a temple devoted to Jupiter would be constructed on the site of the Jewish temple.[36]

This led to the last major Jewish revolt which took place in AD 132–5 and was headed by the military leader Shimon bar Kosiba. He was initially seen as the expected messianic leader who would lead the Jews to salvation, his name being modified to mean 'Son of the Star'. With the failure of the military effort, his name was re-modified to 'son of the lie' by the same Rabbis who had earlier exalted him as 'king Messiah' and 'Prince of Israel'.[37] In this uprising, over half a million Jews were killed and a larger number were enslaved or died of starvation.[38]

The consequences of this defeat were more devastating than that of AD 70. The name of the province was changed to 'Syria Palaestina' and Jews were forbidden to observe their religious customs or to observe the Sabbath. They were expelled from Jerusalem which they could enter only one day in the year to mourn before their razed Temple.[39] In due course, the Jews 'ceased to exist as a nation in their own land'.[40] From this date also commenced a deep mutual antipathy between Roman and Jew, which Goodman describes as 'the Clash of Ancient Civilizations'; he goes on to say:[41]

> To what extent the hostility of the state was reflected in the attitude of ordinary Romans towards the Jews can be surmised only from occasional hints in the extant literature, and from plausibility. Violent terminology occasionally surfaces. Under Domitian, the great authority on rhetoric Quintilian wrote of Jews as a baleful nation (*perniciosa gens*). For Tacitus in the reign of Trajan, most Jewish customs are base, abominable and depraved, so that 'the Jews regard as profane all that we hold sacred, while they permit all that we abhor. To Florus, a younger contemporary, Jews were an 'impious nation'. In the distant city of Oenoanda in what is now Turkey, the Epicurean philosopher Diogenes had inscribed, probably during the reign of Hadrian, in large letters for the benefit of his fellow citizens advice to seek contentment by not behaving credulously like the Jews: 'A clear indication of the complete inability of the gods to prevent wrong-doings is provided by the nations of the Jews and Egyptians, who, while being the most superstitious of all peoples, are the vilest of all peoples.'

The Jews on their part equated Rome with their hereditary biblical enemy, Edom, and prayed for the final destruction of the evil empire of Rome.[42] Will Durant has described their situation most eloquently:[43]

> No other people has ever known so long an exile, or so hard a fate. Shut out from their Holy City, the Jews were compelled to surrender it first to paganism, then to Christianity. Scattered into every province and beyond, condemned to poverty and humiliation, unbefriended even by philosophers and saints, they retired from public affairs into private study and worship, passionately preserving the words of their scholars, and preparing to write them down at last in the Talmuds of Babylonia and Palestine. Judaism hid in fear and obscurity while its offspring, Christianity, went out to conquer the world.

Following this catastrophic experience, all through the medieval period the Jewish community in the diaspora was severely enjoined by its priests to reject all expectation of the Messiah: they were aware of the destruction wreaked upon the Jewish people as a result of their messianic beliefs when their Temple had been destroyed, their communities annihilated and the entire people driven into exile. The greater scholar, Maimonides (1135–1204), gave this assurance to his people:[44]

> The Messiah will arise and restore the kingdom of David to its former might. He will rebuild the sanctuary and gather the dispersed of Israel. Do not think that the Messiah needs to perform signs and miracles, bring about a new state of things in the world, revive the dead, and the like. It is not so ... Let no one think that in the days of the Messiah anything of the natural course of the world will cease or that any innovation will be introduced into creation. Rather, the world will continue in its accustomed course.

In spite of this assurance, apocalyptic messianism was not to be eradicated: the deep despair of the Jewish people *required* the expectation that their fortunes would turn at some future date with divine support; Max Weber has explained this fervent belief thus:[45]

> For the Jew the religious promise was the very opposite [of that of Hinduism]. The social order of the world was conceived to have been turned into the opposite of that promised for the future, but in the future it was to be over-turned so that Jewry would be once again dominant ... *The whole attitude toward life of ancient Jewry was determined by this conception of a future God-guided political and social revolution.* [Emphasis added.]

However, the Jewish messianic prophecy that emerged referred not to a kingdom of God emerging at some unknown future but, instead, had a more immediate and terrestrial resonance: 'The goal of repossessing this specific geographic territory promised by God to Abraham and his heirs further strengthened the attachment to the world already reflected in the Biblical idea of achieving a future good society on earth through human moral progress'.[46] The role of the Messiah was central to the realization of these expectations. The great Rabbi of the mid-thirteenth century, Nachmanides (1194–1270) claimed that the Messiah had not yet come though he was born on the day of the destruction of the Temple:[47]

> He was born on the day of the destruction [of the Temple]: for was it not on the day that Moses was born that he immediately went to redeem Israel? He arrived only a number of days later, under the command of the Holy One, Blessed be He, and [then] said to Pharaoh: 'Let my people go that they may serve Me!' So, too, when the end of time will have arrived, the Messiah will go to the Pope under the command of God and say, 'Let my people go that they may serve Me,' and until that time we will not say regarding him that he arrived, for he is not [yet] the Messiah.

Later, Jewish messianic writings were influenced by developments in Europe. Europe in the thirteenth century was convulsed in considerable chaos and uncertainty, with war and fear of anarchy causing large-scale insecurity and dislocation in the lives of the people. The most serious sources of anxiety were: the failure of the Crusades to retake the holy places; the attack upon the Islamic Caliphate by the Mongols; and the emergence of the Mamelukes from Egypt who fought both the Christians and the Mongols and asserted Islamic authority over the Holy Land. The Jews, now suffering under Christian hegemony, in their desperation, saw, in the Mongols, the Biblical Ten Lost Tribes who would avenge the sufferings of the Jews at the hands of the Christians. One Jewish seer prophesied:[48]

> The sons of Israel will be liberated from captivity. A certain people called 'without a head' or reputed to be wanderers, will come. Woe to the clergy! A new order thrives: if it should fall, woe to the church! There will be many battles in the world. There will be mutations of faith, of laws, and of kingdoms. The land of the Saracens will be destroyed.

In medieval Europe there also emerged a school of Jewish mysticism called *Kaballah* (inherited tradition), which in time became a mass movement.[49] In the context of the Mongol invasions, one of its protagonists prophesied:[50]

> The sons of Ishmael [Muslims] will cause fierce wars in the world and the sons of Edom [i.e. the Roman Empire] will gather and wage battles against them, one on the dry earth, another on the sea, and one near Jerusalem. And each of them will rule over the other. And the land of Israel will not be given to the sons of Edom. At that same time, a nation [coming] from the end of the world will awake against the wicked Rome and will fight there for three months. And [other] nations will gather there and fall into its hands, until all the sons of Rome will gather together from all the corners of the world ... and it will expel the sons of Ishmael from there.

The third nation mentioned here refers to the Mongols who would defeat the oppressive Christians, a belief that strengthened messianic expectations among the beleaguered people.[51] Kaballah sages confidently foretold the imminent end-times thus:[52]

> The coming day is the Day of Judgment,
> And it is called the day of remembrance.
> And the time of the trial has arrived,
> And the time of the end has been accomplished.
> The heaven will become earth,
> And earth will become celestial,
> Because the Lord of the trial is called by the name YHWH
> And his judgment is one of truth
> And his trial is upright.

Christian Messianism

Norman Cohn describes Jesus as 'Jewish through and through' in that his message, as conveyed in his lifetime, was in the tradition of Daniel and the later Jewish apocalyptic literature.[53] As Dale Allison has noted, his eschatological views 'were well known in the Judaism that nurtured Jesus; and his apocalyptic views were held by many Jews of the time.'[54] Thus his references to the 'Kingdom of God' were contained in several Jewish texts. Again, he drew from Jewish traditions the idea of a struggle between good and evil and the final defeat of Satan. Several of Jesus's eschatological predictions had their origin in the Hebrew Bible.[55]

Allison has pointed out that some of Jesus's contemporaries thought him a prophet, and that there is 'every reason to suppose that Jesus himself shared this evaluation'.[56] She argues that he saw his Ministry in terms of Isaiah 61, which said:[57]

> The spirit of the Lord God is upon me,
> because the Lord has anointed me;
> he has sent me to bring good news to the poor,
> to bind up the broken-hearted,
> to proclaim liberty to the captives,
> and release to the prisoners
> to proclaim the year of the Lord's favour,
> and the day of vengeance of our God;
> to comfort all who mourn

Allison goes on to point out that Jesus 'may well have believed himself to be Israel's messianic king': he placed himself outside the symbolic groups of twelve (apostles), presented himself as their leader and so, 'implicitly, made himself out to be the leader of re-gathered Israel'.[58]

The crucifixion and resurrection of Jesus fundamentally transformed his status from that of the leader of a Jewish cult to the progenitor (over time) of a separate global faith. This was a slow process, influenced by doctrinal evolution as also external political developments, all of which taken together served to gradually distance the faith from Judaism and imparted to it its own distinct character and identity. The most important factor in regard to the former was the consolidation of Jesus's status as a messiah and, flowing from this, the belief in his 'second coming' to defeat the forces of evil and commence his thousand-year reign on earth. Thus, departing from Jewish tradition, St. Paul (AD 5–67) asserted that, while the Jews continued to await their messiah, for the Christians the Messiah had already arrived in the person of Jesus, so that, with Christ's death and resurrection, 'God ended the old course of the world and introduced a new aeon'.[59] Adela Yarbro Collins has noted that, at this time, while the movement started by Jesus 'could still be defined as a type of Judaism', certain differences and even tensions between the two communities had already become apparent.[60] Goodman has explained the situation thus:[61]

> Among the most important reasons for the growth and spread of Christianity during these years, one must be that after 70, and even more after 135 [the years of Jewish insurrection against the Romans], Christians presented themselves to the gentile world as unconnected to the Jews, whose alienation from mainstream Roman society had been sealed by the destruction of the Temple in Jerusalem. The very earliest Christians, like Jesus himself, were all Jews, but by the early fourth century, when Constantine became the first Roman emperor to portray himself as a

devotee of Christ, the links between Christianity and Judaism had been deliberately obscured by Christians themselves. Most Christians in the second and third centuries avoided calling themselves Jews, and, far from hoping for the rebuilding of the Temple, they reveled in its demise, which they portrayed as confirmation of the prophecies which Jesus had spoken in his lifetime.

Goodman also points out that the 'sense of mission' of the early Christians and their strong sense of exclusive identity fostered unity amongst them even as it separated them from people of other faiths.[62] He says:[63]

> Christians had a strong feeling of belonging to a single community of belief and practice, and the most striking innovation of all in terms of ancient religious history was the gradual defining of Christianity in the last years of the second century by the systematic exclusion of ideas not deemed acceptable to the mainstream ... In contrast to the uncertainty, agnosticism or denial of many Roman pagans and some Jews, all Christians asserted with total confidence their belief in a life after death and the restriction of that life to those saved through Christ.

Jewish persecution of Christians took place mainly in the first century AD, after which the Jews became more accommodative in the religious area, with differences mainly emerging on social and political issues.[64] On the other hand, the Roman persecution of Christians was theological: not due to the gods that the Christians worshipped, but on account of their failure to worship the gods of the Romans; this resulted in the martyrdom of numerous Christian heroes.[65]

Goodman suggests cautiously that 'at some time in the first four centuries AD the ways of the two religious [Judaism and Christianity] parted'.[66] Concurrent with the sharpening distinction between the two communities was the evolution of a more pernicious mindset, the portrayal of the Jews as the arch-enemies of Christians. This had its roots in early Christianity itself. In ca. AD 50, St. Paul had referred to Jews as those who 'killed the Lord Jesus and their own prophets, and have persecuted us'.[67] The Gospel of Mathews, written in the last quarter of the first century, distinguished between the synagogue of the Jews and the church. In succeeding decades there were more frequent references to 'lawless Israel' and their role in Christ's crucifixion.[68]

The early Christians could not reject the Hebrew Bible since they based Jesus' messianic status on its passages, but they, in time, usurped the name 'Israel' for themselves and maintained a consistent denigration of the name 'Jew'.[69] Goodman has argued that the Christians did this primarily to avoid the hostility with which the Romans had come to view the Jews, particularly after the uprisings of the early second century AD.[70] Generally, as Goodman notes, large-scale persecution of Christians by the Roman state was rare, with attacks on the former being generally caused by local reasons; however, such episodes did cause considerable trauma to the community, and imbued in it a sense of being beleaguered and in danger.[71] In fact, accounts of persecution and martyrdom served to strengthen the faith of the believers: 'the blood of the martyrs is seed', said a prominent Christian leader of the day.[72] Will Durant describes this scenario thus:[73]

> There is no greater drama in human record than the sight of a few Christians, scorned or oppressed by a succession of emperors, bearing all trials with a fierce tenacity, multiplying quietly, building order while their enemies generated chaos, fighting the sword with the word, brutality with hope, and at last defeating the strongest state that history has known. Caesar and Christ had met in the arena, and Christ had won.

With the conversion of the Roman emperor Constantine (272–337) to Christianity in AD 312, and the issue of the edict of Milan (313) committing the Roman state to religious tolerance, the Christian faith became pervasive across the Roman empire, from Rome to Constantinople. Will Durant notes that Constantine strengthened the unity of the Church even as he put in place the 'unanimity of basic belief which gave the medieval Church its Catholic name'.[74] Durant concludes:[75]

> A new civilization, based on a new religion, would now rise over the ruins of an exhausted culture and a dying creed. The Middle Ages had begun.

Unfortunately, there was no respite for the Jews: Constantine made anti-Jewish pronouncements that were more vituperative than the pagan rulers before him, even as privileges and wealth were granted to the Christian clergy.[76]

Constantine played a lead role in developing Jerusalem as the religious centre for Christians, but not, as Goodman has noted, 'for the wicked Jews, whose Temple had been destroyed because of "the bloody murder of the Lord" '.[77] The Christian clergy of this period had no difficulty in identifying the Jews as the enemies of the Church who would be suitably chastised at the 'second coming' of Jesus Christ. Thus, Cyril, Bishop of Jerusalem, explained to Constantine's son, Constantius, the meaning of the signs of the imminent coming of the Lord Jesus which would be mourned by Jews:[78]

> A sign of a luminous cross precedes the King, showing Him who was formerly crucified; in order that the Jews, who before had pierced Him and plotted [against Him], on seeing it, will mourn tribe-by-tribe, saying, 'This is He who was struck with blows, this is He whose face they spat upon, this is He whom they fastened with bonds; this is He whom of old they crucified and held in derision. Where shall we *flee* from the face of your wrath?' They will ask, but, surrounded by the angelic hosts, they will not be able to escape anywhere. The sign of the Cross brings fear to the enemy.

The Christian scholar and ascetic St. Jerome (AD 347–420) asserted that the Jews should come to Jerusalem only to mourn the destruction of their Temple due to their sins:[79]

> Right up to the present day the treacherous inhabitants, having killed the servants and finally the Son of God, are prohibited to enter Jerusalem except to lament, and they pay a price to be allowed to weep over the ruin of their state. Thus those who once bought the blood of Christ buy now their own fears, and not even their grief is free. On the day when Jerusalem was captured and destroyed by the Romans you may see a mournful populace arrive, a confluence of decrepit females and old men 'covered with rags and years', demonstrating in their bodies and their condition the wrath of the Lord. The congregation is a crowd of wretches, but as the yoke of the Lord glitters, and His surrection shines, and from the Mount of Olives the standard of His cross gleams, the populace keening over the ruins of their Temple is pitiable, yet not suitably to be pitied.

Christian Biblical Messianism

Christian apocalyptic tradition reached its apogee with the *Book of Revelation*, written in the second half of the first century AD. *Revelation* provided the most vivid imagery of end-times; chapter 19 describes the defeat of the 'Beast' and the 'false prophet' thus:[80]

> Then I saw an angel standing in the sun, and with a loud voice he called to all the birds that fly in midheaven, 'Come, gather for the great supper of God, to eat the flesh of kings, and flesh of captains, the flesh of mighty men, the flesh of horses and their riders, and the flesh of all men, both free

and slave, both small and great'. And I saw the beast and the kings of the earth with their armies gathered to make war against him who sits upon the horse and against his army. And the beast was captured, and with it the false prophet who in its presence had worked the signs by which he deceived those who had received the mark of the beast and those who worshipped its image. These two were thrown alive into the lake of fire that burns with brimstone. And the rest were slain by the sword of him who sits upon the horse, the sword that issues from his mouth; and all the birds were gorged with their flesh. (Revelation 19.13–21)

Then follows chapter 20, which describes the millennial kingdom to be ruled by Jesus Christ:[81]

And I saw an angel come down from heaven, having the key of the bottomless pit and a great chain in his hand. And he laid hold on the dragon, that old serpent, which is the Devil, and Satan, and bound him a thousand year, and cast him into the bottomless pit, and shut him up, and set a seal upon him, that he should deceive the nations no more, till the thousand years should be fulfilled: and after that he must be loosed a little season. And I saw thrones, and they sat upon them, and judgment was given unto them: and I saw the souls of them that were beheaded for the witness of Jesus, and for the word of God, and which had not worshiped the beast, neither his image, neither had they received his mark upon their foreheads, or in their hands; and they lived and reigned with Christ a thousand years. But the rest of the dead lived not again until the thousand years were finished. This is the first resurrection. Blessed and holy is he that hath part in the first resurrection: on such the second death hath no power, but they shall be priests of God and of Christ, and shall reign with him a thousand years.

Mendel says of Revelation:[82]

Virtually the whole of that text is an account of the violence, devastation, suffering, and death necessary to purge the world and clear the way for the pure and perfect Kingdom. Wave after wave of horrendous suffering cascade down on the sinful world as the seals of secret scrolls are broken, trumpets sounded, bowls of divine wrath overturned, and the forces of the Apocalypse given 'power over a fourth of the earth, to kill with sword and famine, by pestilence and wild beasts', then 'to kill a third of mankind', as 'men gnawed their tongues in agony' (Revelation 6.8, 9.15, 16.10).

This vision of apocalyptic war set out in Revelations led Carl Jung to comment:[83]

[it] is a terrifying picture that blatantly contradicts all ideas of Christian humility, tolerance, love of your neighbor and your enemies, and makes nonsense of a loving father in heaven and rescuer of mankind. A veritable orgy of hatred, wrath, vindictiveness and blind destructive fury that revels in fantastic images of terror and fire overwhelms a world which Christ had just endeavoured to restore to the original state of innocence and loving communion with God.

This cataclysmic violence is echoed in other parts of the Bible:[84]

Do not think that I have come to bring peace on earth; I have not come to bring peace, but a sword. For I have come to set a man against his father, and a daughter against her mother, and a daughter-in-law against her mother-in-law; and man's foes will be those of his own household ... (Mathew 10.34–36).

And when you hear of wars and rumors of wars, do not be alarmed; this must take place, but the end is not yet. For nation will rise against nation, and kingdom against kingdom; there will be earthquakes in various places, there will be famines; this is but the beginning of the sufferings. (Mark 13.7–8)

The various aspects of the apocalyptic vision in the Judeo-Christian tradition had now been given final shape, and it was this vision that would reverberate over the centuries; Mendel has explained this vividly thus: [85]

The Apocalypse was now complete and ready to begin its long and violent career in our history. All apocalyptic movements thereafter mirrored the original model. For all of them, the existing society is beyond repair, too corrupt for reforms and doomed to complete annihilation; for all of them, the coming Kingdom, the 'new heaven and new earth,' is beyond compare or criticism, purged of the sins of the old aeon; and for all of them, the transition between the two realms is beyond compassion, cataclysmically violent and unforgiving toward those condemned to 'mourn and weep ...'

Similarly, they all agree that those hoping to be saved and to enter the Kingdom must heed the message of the Savior Leader and his small band of disciples since only the Leader and his disciples know the Truth and the Way, as revealed to them by the supreme power.

Several early Christian writers saw Revelations as a prophecy of an imminent 'second coming' of Christ and the setting up of his kingdom on earth for one thousand years. Such a literalist view was challenged from time to time by other scholars who read in Revelations a message to seek spiritual salvation on the basis of the triumph of good over evil rather than an imminent blissful *earthly* kingdom. This view was most powerfully (and influentially) advocated by St. Augustine (AD 354–430), who synthesized the two positions by suggesting that the thousand-year reign should be seen as the reign of the Christian Church when evil (Satan) would be under control (bound); though the Church would be the divine instrument of salvation, it would remain imperfect and the struggle between good and evil would continue up to Judgment Day. He rejected interpretations that literally linked events/personalities of the Revelation with contemporary figures and events, and envisaged the 'end-time' in the distant future. The Augustinian view remained dominant till 1100 AD.[86]

However, the apocalyptic view did not die away and, from time to time, amidst periods of political persecution, social malaise and anxiety, it emerged robustly. These apocalyptic expectations, generally based on Revelations, were articulated by religious scholars during periods of severe hardship, and drew specific details from contemporary events or personalities to set out the scenario of an imminent apocalypse. Often, the Antichrist depicted in these descriptions was a Jewish figure who would assume the attributes of the Messiah, but would work towards consolidating Jewish interests at the expense of the Christian Church.[87]

Later, in spite of the edict of universal religious tolerance issued by Constantine in 313, which ended Christian persecution at the hands of political rulers, Christian apocalyptic visions continued to be articulated in the face of depredations by the Northern tribes of the Goths, Huns and Vandals, with scenarios of widespread disaster and the emergence of the powerful Antichrist who would attempt to re-establish Jewish law, and thus prepare the ground for Christ's second coming.[88]

Apocalyptic scenarios were developed in the Byzantine empire in response to periodic external attacks on it, and prophesied the latter's ultimate triumph. The Byzantine apocalypses generally saw the empire as the 'Roman' empire, its Christian people as God's 'chosen people' and its capital, Constantinople, as the 'New Jerusalem', with apocalyptic writers also referring to their empire as the 'New Israel'. This was aimed at ensuring that 'the prophecies that pertained to the kingdom of Israel now properly belonged to the Christian empire of the Romans'. Thus, the earlier struggle of imperial Rome with barbarians now became a struggle of Christians against heathens.[89]

The seventh century witnessed some of the major defeats of this Christian empire, particularly at the hands of the Arabs professing the new faith of Islam. These defeats gave rise to some powerful apocalyptic writings, which, in line with Hebrew and early Christian traditions, projected the same scenario of punishment for Christian sinfulness, divine intervention, and the ultimate defeat of the heathens. The Arabs were thus seen as mere instruments of God's chastisement of Christians, not as his favoured children, and it was confidently asserted that Christian repentance would restore the Lord's grace.[90] These apocalyptic visions culminated in the vision of the 'Last (Christian) Emperor' who would defeat all opponents of Christianity and re-conquer Jerusalem. At Jerusalem, he would 'take his crown, and set it upon the cross and stretch his hands to heaven, and hand over his empire to God the Father'. After his reign of peace and plenty, the last emperor would go to heaven. He would be replaced by the Antichrist enthroned in the Temple in Jerusalem, who would be finally destroyed by Christ, when the Apocalypse and the world would come to an end.[91]

Bernard McGinn has pointed out that apocalypticism remained pervasive all through to AD 1500; he notes that medieval folk, consumed with 'fear and hope', 'lived in a more or less constant state of apocalyptic expectation'.[92] The various apocalyptic movements across Europe reflected the anxieties of deprived groups, seeking to give vent to their fears and aspirations through apocalyptic visions.[93] Norman Cohn has noted how, 'again and again', in periods of severe dislocation and anxiety, the poor in medieval Empire would be seized by fantasies (propagated by 'would-be prophets or would-be messiahs') of a future golden age or messianic kingdom which would come into being after a final apocalyptic massacre of the evil ones (Jews, clergy or the wealthy) and their replacement by the faithful believers, the poor themselves.[94] This 'messianism of the poor' flourished most successfully in the times of the early Crusades (1096–1146).[95]

The decade 1085–1095 was particularly harsh for the people in West Europe on account of floods, droughts and famines, as well as plague from 1089.[96] The call to the Crusade to liberate the Holy Land by Pope Urban II in 1095 gave the opportunity to these people to set up 'salvation groups' around holy men as also to escape from their intolerable conditions.[97] The unorganized and impoverished hordes saw the Crusade as 'an armed and militant pilgrimage', with the strong messianic ideal of liberating Jerusalem, which had occupied a central position in Jewish and Christian apocalyptic literature from Isaiah to Revelation.[98] As Cohn has pointed out:[99]

> No wonder that – as contemporaries noted – in the minds of simple folk the idea of the earthly Jerusalem became so confused with and transfused by that of the Heavenly Jerusalem that the Palestinian city seemed itself a miraculous realm, abounding both in spiritual and in material blessings. And no wonder that when the masses of the poor set off on their long pilgrimage the children cried out at every town and castle: 'Is that Jerusalem?' – while high in the heavens there was seen a mysterious city with vast multitudes hurrying towards it.

The messianic zeal of the Crusaders, the knight and the pauper, was given a further inspirational impetus by the conviction that the liberation of Jerusalem would be achieved through the massacre of the infidel, the extermination of 'the sons of whores, the race of Cain'.[100] The biblical injunction of extermination of evil as a divine duty was translated into a sanction to freely perpetrate violence on Jews and Muslims, and even Christians who were seen to deviate from the true path. The following, as elucidated in John Capek and Peter Chelcicky's *Book of a Hundred Chapters*, is illustrative of contemporary thinking:[101]

> Accursed be the man who withholds his sword from shedding the blood of the enemies of Christ. Every believer must wash his hands in that blood ... every priest may lawfully pursue, wound and kill sinners ... The just ... will now rejoice seeing vengeance, and washing their hands in the blood of the sinner ... Whoever strikes a wicked man for his evil doing, for instance for blasphemy—if he beats him to death, he shall be called a servant of God; for everyone is duty bound to punish wickedness.

Thomas Muntzer, in the same vein, states:

> The sword is necessary to exterminate them. And so that it shall be done honestly and properly, our dear fathers, the princes must do it, who confess Christ with us. But if they don't do it, the sword shall be taken from them ... If they resist, let them be slaughtered without mercy ... At the harvest time one must pluck the weeds out of God's vineyard ... But the angels who are sharpening their sickles for that work are no other than the earnest servants of God ... For the ungodly have no right to live, save what the Elect choose to allow them.

This commitment to violence was translated in practical terms during the Crusades, as in the the 'Prophet' Rudolph's *People's Crusade*:[102]

> We have set out to march a long way to fight the enemies of God in the East; and, behold, before our very eyes are His worst foes, the Jews. They must be dealt with first ... You are the descendents of those who killed and hanged our God. Moreover, [God] himself said: 'The day will yet dawn when my children will come and avenge my blood.' We are His children and it is our task to carry out His vengeance upon you ... Those who will not accept baptism are no Christians or people of Holy Scripture, so they are to be killed, then they will be baptized in their own blood.

The *Chanson de Roland* further describes:

> The emperor has taken Saragossa. A thousand Franks are sent to search thoroughly the town, the mosques, and synagogues. With iron hammers and axes they smash the images and all the idols; henceforth there will be no place there for spells or sorceries. The King believes in God, he desires to serve Him. His bishops bless the water and the heathen are brought to the baptistery. If any one of them resists Charlemagne, the King has him hanged or burnt to death or slain with the sword.

The first great massacre of European Jews took place during the First Crusade, when, between May and June 1096, about four to eight thousand Jews were killed by Crusaders on their way to the Holy Land, thus, in Cohn's words, marking 'the beginning of a tradition'.[103] After this, the massacre of Jews was 'to remain a normal feature of popular, as distinct from knightly, crusaders'.[104] The Crusaders were not just seeking booty from the Jews; they saw them as the 'worst foes' of God; they had 'killed and hanged our God'; the Crusaders also sought vengeance for 'your obstinate and blasphemous' attitude to him.[105] The messianic excitement generated by the Crusades, imbued with the vision of the recapture of the Holy Land, also served to define the evil enemy, 'The Other', in the shape of Jews and Muslims who then assumed the identity of the biblical Antichrist. The annihilation of Jews and Muslims was seen by the Crusaders as the first step in the ushering in of end-times which would culminate in the destruction of Evil and the setting up of the Kingdom to be ruled by Jesus.[106]

Both Jews and Muslims became an integral part of popular demonology in Europe. This led in due course, to 'the peculiarly intense and unremitting hatred in Christendom (that) has been directed against Jewry above all "outgroups" ... what accounts for that is the wholly phantasmic image of the Jew which suddenly gripped the imagination of the new masses at the time of the first Crusades'.[107]

The Jews came to be portrayed increasingly as 'uncanny and sinister' and as incarnations of evil, capable of ever more harm to Christians.[108] This identity became integral to Christian end-times expectations: the Jews would help the Antichrist to conquer the world; later, after Christ's second coming, the Jews and the Antichrist (meaning Satan) would be annihilated.[109] As a result, as Cohn has asserted, 'hatred of Jews (became) endemic in the European masses', while the Jews themselves became 'a terrorized society locked in perpetual warfare with the greater society around it'.[110]

The Crusaders also put in place the West European demonization of Muslims, commencing with the massacre of Muslim inhabitants of Jerusalem after the First Crusade in 1099. As Karen Armstrong has pointed out, 'Western Christians would never again regard Jews and Muslims as normal human beings. They saw them as inhuman monsters and developed fantasies about them which bore no relation to the truth...'[111] Norman Daniel has noted that Christian attitude to Islam and Muslims became, during the medieval period 'established canon',[112] which continues to dominate Western understanding and attitude to this day.

Messianism in the Islamic Tradition

Apocalypticism and Messianism came to Islam from Jewish and Christian traditions. Said Amir Arjomand has emphasized the importance of the impact of the Book of Daniel on early Islam, identifying numerous points where, according to him, the Koran indicates the influence of this biblical text, particularly the status of Prophet Mohammed as the 'Seal of the Prophets' (Daniel 9.24).[113] He notes that, Daniel had spoken of the time for setting the seal on prophecy but was told by Gabriel to 'keep the book sealed until the end time' (Daniel 12.1).[114] Again, in verse 61:6 of the Koran, Jesus son of Mary presents himself to the children of Israel as the messenger of God who confirms the Torah and is the 'bearer of good tidings of a messenger, who shall come after me and whose name shall be Ahmad (Ismuhu Ahmadu)'. This echoes the promise in John 16.13-14, where it was said: 'when the Spirit of truth comes ... he will not be speaking of his own accord but will only say what he has been told; and he will reveal to you the things to come. He will glorify me.'[115] This also affirms the Koranic concept of the divine revelation as the unaltered recitation by the Prophet of the divine words brought down by Gabriel who is the holy/trustworthy spirit *[ruh]* mentioned in the Koran. Again, the Koran also adopts the Biblical belief in the second coming of Jesus Christ: Jesus 'is the sign of the Hour' (Q. 43.61).[116]

Abdulaziz Abdulhussein Sachedina has acknowledged that the concept of the *Mahdi,* or Islamic Messianism, is drawn from Judeo-Christian roots, but points out that it evolved over time in a vibrant Islamic context; he describes Islamic Messianism thus:[117]

> The term 'messianism' in the Islamic context is frequently used to translate the important concept of an eschatological figure, the Mahdi, who, as the foreordained leader, 'will rise' to launch a great social transformation in order to restore and adjust all things under divine guidance. The Islamic Messiah, thus, embodies the aspirations of his followers in the restoration of the purity of the Faith which will bring true and uncorrupted guidance to all mankind, creating a just social order and a world free from oppression in which the Islamic revelation will be the norm for all nations.

The messianic persona of the Mahdi acquired a sharper image in the turbulent years of the early civil wars involving Hazrat Ali and his son Imam Husain against the Umayyads centred at Damascus. The first declared Mahdi was Hazrat Ali's third son, Muhammad Al Hanafiyya (d. 700). When he died, his supporters said he was in concealment or occultation, and would return as the Mahdi and the *Qa'im* (the Standing One, the Riser). In due course, the concept of the Mahdi and Al-Qa'im became part of the Shia messianic tradition.

Early Shi'ite traditions represent the Qa'im as the expected redresser of the cause of God (*al-qa'im bi amr Allah*) and the redresser by the sword (*al-qa'im bi'l-sayf*), wearing the armour of the Prophet and wielding his sword, the *dhu'l-fiqar*. This picture can be supplemented by the early Shi'ite traditions which present the Qa'im the redresser of the House of Mohammed (*qa'im al Mohammed*), modeled on the Messiah as the restorer of the house of David. He is at the same time the 'Lord of the Sword' (*sahib al-sayf*), and the avenger of the wrong done to the House of Muhammad by the usurpers: 'The weapon [of the Prophet] with us is like the ark with the children of Israel.' The Qa'im will establish the empire of truth (*dawlat al-haqq*).[118]

In Shia tradition, the Mahdi is the Imam (from the House of Hazrat Ali) who has gone into a state of '*ghayba*' (occultation). This hidden

Imam will emerge as the Mahdi, the deliverer of the Islamic community. Shia sects differ as regards from which lineage a descendant of Hazrat Ali the Mahdi will appear. The Zaidis believe he will come from the line of the 5th Imam, Zayd; the Ismailis believe he will come from the line of Ismail, the 7th Imam, while the largest Shia group, the Twelvers, believes he will emerge from the line of the 12th Imam, Mohammed Al Mahdi.[119]

In Shia hagiographic literature, the Mahdi is described thus:[120]

> A figure more legendary than that of the Mahdi, the Awaited Saviour, has not been seen in the history of mankind. The threads of the world events have woven many a fine design in human life but the pattern of the Mahdi stands high above every other pattern. He has been the vision of the visionaries in history. He has been the dream of all the dreamers of the world. For the ultimate salvation of mankind, he is the Pole Star of hope on which the gaze of humanity if fixed ... He stands resplendent high above the narrow walls in which humanity is cut up and divided. He belongs to everybody.

While Shia Islam has a broadly consensual position about the Mahdi, Sunni traditions are less unanimous. After the *Hadith* collections of *Al Bukhari* and *Muslim*, which make no reference to the Mahdi, there were four more Sunni Hadith collections, of which three make references to the Mahdi. On the basis of these references, Muslim commentators over the centuries have laboured to identify the 'signs of the hour' which will herald the arrival of the Mahdi. Though there are a variety of traditions, the general scenario preceding the advent of the Mahdi will consist of: deep divisions in the Muslim community; decline in faith, morality, honesty and human decency; collapse of political accountability, justice and public civility—in short the near-total destruction of the fabric of Muslim society. Amidst this situation of despair, the Mahdi will make his appearance. The Mahdi's arrival is certain; he will come from the family of Prophet Mohammed; and, he will have an appearance that is similar to that of the Prophet. The Mahdi will rule the earth with justice for seven to nine years, providing peace and harmony to the people. The earth will bear vegetation due to plentiful rain; wealth will be abundant but will be divided equitably.[121] In short, the reign of the Mahdi will mean 'a brief return to the State of spiritual lucidity and primordial integrity that obtained at the dawn of time'.[122]

After this peaceful reign, the *Maseeh Al-Dajjal* [Antichrist] will appear from the East, who will tempt people from their true faith through false 'miracles'. These traditions contain long passages depicting the dramatic developments surrounding 'end-time', with important roles being played by the Mahdi and Jesus Christ. Jesus will proclaim Islam as the universal religion and will call upon 'the people of the book' to join Islam. He, in association with the Mahdi, will lead the righteous Muslim armies against *Dajjal* and will slay him. Jesus' reign will last for an undetermined period, after which the end-times will unfold with signs that include the arrival of the evil forces Gog and Magog (to be finally destroyed by God Himself), three solar eclipses, sunrise from the West, appearance of the beast from the earth and a great fire.[123]

The principal attributes and achievements of the Mahdi, as drawn from various Islamic traditions and commentaries, may be summarized as follows:[124]

- (*i*) The Mahdi will be a descendant of Prophet Mohammed and will bear his name (Mohammed bin Abdullah).
- (*ii*) He will emerge upon the earth after a period of great turmoil and suffering.
- (*iii*) He will establish justice and righteousness throughout the world, eradicate tyranny and oppression and establish a new world order.
- (*iv*) He will be the Caliph and Imam (vice-regent and leader) of Muslims worldwide.
- (*v*) He will make a seven-year peace treaty with a Jew of priestly lineage.
- (*vi*) He will conquer Israel for Islam and lead the 'faithful Muslims' in a final battle against Jews.
- (*vii*) He will establish the new Islamic world headquarters from Jerusalem.
- (*viii*) He will rule for seven years (though possibly as much as eight or nine).
- (*ix*) He will cause Islam to be the only religion practised on the earth.
- (*x*) He will discover some previously undiscovered biblical manuscripts that he will use to argue with the Jews and cause some Jews to convert to Islam.

(*xi*) He will also re-discover the Ark of the Covenant from the Sea of Galilee, which he will bring to Jerusalem.

In Islamic history, the Sunni political and religious establishments strongly discouraged apocalyptic and messianic beliefs in favour of mainstream practices flowing from the Koran and Hadith. In spite of this, a number of personalities emerged throughout Muslim history claiming to be the awaited Mahdi. Timothy Furnish has analyzed several significant Mahdist movements in the Sunni tradition in different parts of the Islamic world in which their protagonists claimed Mahdi status, even as every one of them was destroyed by the superior force of the Muslim or non-Muslim ruler they had rebelled against.[125]

In recent years, the most significant Mahdist movements have been those of Mohammed Ahmad ibn Abdullah [1843–85], the Mahdi of Sudan and that of Juhayman Al Utaybi and Mohammed Al Qahtani in Saudi Arabia in 1979. The movement in Sudan has been the most successful in Islamic history in that the Mahdi actually set up a state in Sudan that was independent of the British and which survived for about twenty years. After initial victories against Egyptian and Ottoman forces, the Mahdi army besieged Khartoum in August 1884, and finally succeeded in taking the city and killing the British General defending the city.[126]

The reign of Mohammed bin Abdullah Al Qahtani as Mahdi of Saudi Arabia, though extremely short, was also very dramatic in that it involved the capture of the Holy Mosque in Makkah by the Mahdi forces led by Juhayman Al Utaybi, the brother-in-law of the proclaimed Mahdi. The forces occupying the Haram Sharief called for the overthrow of the Saudi royal family, the expulsion of all foreigners, severing of ties with Western countries and redistribution of Saudi wealth. The occupation of the Haram Sharief lasted just 15 days, when the Saudi forces succeeded in retaking the mosque and capturing or killing the Mahdi and his supporters. While the failed Mahdi, Al Qahtani, was killed in the fighting, Juhyaman Al Utaybi was captured alive and then beheaded in public with his supporters in January 1980. The writings of Al Utaybi were published only after his death. In one of these writings, Al Utaybi described the Islamic world as in a state of acute crisis and predicted that the coming of the Mahdi was imminent.[127]

It is interesting to note that the Muslim state powers, Ottoman and

Saudi, that crushed the two Mahdi movements, criticized the movements on the same bases:[128]

  (*i*) that the self-proclaimed Mahdis were actually rebels in that they had killed fellow Muslims;

  (*ii*) that the purported Mahdis did not have the characteristics set out in Islamic traditions; and,

  (*iii*) that the governments they had rebelled against were already Islamic.

However, it is noteworthy that though the specific Mahdi movements were attacked, Mahdism itself was accepted as a legitimate part of Islamic tradition. Thus, in 1976, the Jeddah-based Muslim World League which is sponsored by the Saudi Government and broadly reflects the Saudi world view and politico-religious interests, issued a *fatwa* saying:[129]

> The memorizers and scholars of Hadith have verified that there are reliable and acceptable reports among the Hadiths on the Mahdi; the majority of them are narrated through numerous authorities. There is no doubt about their status as unbroken and sound reports. And the belief in the appearance of the Mahdi is obligatory ... none denies it except those who are ignorant of the Sunnah and innovators in doctrine.

Conclusion

All early West Asian civilizations developed 'combat myths' in which Gods battled the forces of evil in order to maintain cosmic order. The Iranian prophet Zoroaster developed this concept by envisaging a struggle between the Lord Wisdom, Ahura Mazda, and the force of evil, Ahriman. The Hebrew Bible also contained in it the concepts of good versus evil and of divine judgment, reward and punishment.

As the Bible developed over several centuries before Christ, it evolved over five stages to give shape to the idea of the Apocalypse: divine sanction for violence against alien nations; divine chastisement of the believers who sin; redemption for the sinful through divine intervention; a further refinement that a 'remnant' among the sinful would be saved by a kind and loving god; and, finally, the total destruction of the sinful world in a catastrophic apocalypse, and its replacement by a new world of peace, justice and material abundance. The later texts of the Hebrew Bible, perhaps drawing from Zoroastrianism, spoke of the Messiah, a divine saviour who would personally bring about the salvation of God's people, specifically by ensuring the return of the Jews in exile in Babylon to their holy land and the restoration of their destroyed Temple.

Later, such messianic expectations provided great solace to the Jews living under Roman oppression and even encouraged them in their various uprisings. The failure of the uprising of AD 66–70 ended in the final destruction of the Jewish Temple in Jerusalem and the dispersal of the entire Jewish community across West Asia, the Roman Empire and North Africa. This and the later uprising of AD 132–135 in fact laid the basis for a deep-seated Roman antipathy for the Jewish people as a race, constituting, in the words of a modern author, 'the clash of ancient civilizations'.

In the diaspora, the Jews were discouraged by their religious leaders from pursuing messianic beliefs since these had brought only catastrophe to the Jewish people in the past. However, messianic traditions did not die away and, from time to time, Jewish sages did give vent to their fervent hope that their enemies (the Christians from the fourth century AD) would be annihilated and they would be restored to their promised homeland.

The religious tenets of Christianity and, hence, of Christian messianism drew heavily from Jewish traditions, though, unlike the Jews, the Christians saw in Jesus Christ the Messiah foretold in the Hebrew Bible. From this belief emerged the Christian messianic notion that the end-times would see Jesus' 'second coming' to defeat evil and commence his thousand-year rule on the earth, a millennium of perfect peace and harmony. After the millennium, the forces of evil headed by the Antichrist would re-emerge; however, they would be vanquished in a final cosmic battle, in which evil would be finally destroyed and believers would find their eternal home in paradise.

Most Christian messianic scenarios in the early Christian and medieval periods saw the Jews as agents of the Antichrist. Later, with the rise of Islam and the enthusiasm generated by the Popes to liberate the Christian holy lands from the Muslims, the latter joined the Jews in Christian demonology. Given the biblical sanction to exterminate evil as a divine duty, Christians were encouraged to perpetrate violence on Jews and Muslims, which was undertaken most robustly in the Crusades, thus, consolidating the depiction of Jews and Muslims as the personification of the evil 'Other' in Christian messianic tradition.

Islamic messianism drew heavily from Jewish and Christian traditions, envisaging a central role for Jesus Christ at the end-times. However, the evolution of Islamic messianism took place in a vibrant Islamic context and provided for a Mahdi (the Directed One; the Guide, Leader) who would restore the purity of the Islamic faith and set up a just social order under divine guidance. Shia Islam readily embraced the notion of the Mahdi who, according to the Hadith would emerge from the Prophet's family, by expecting him in the person of the last Imam who has gone into occultation and will re-emerge at the end of the world. Sunni Islam's approach to messianism has been a little less assured since, of the six Hadith collections, only three refer to the Mahdi. While mainstream Sunni Islam accepts the notion of the Mahdi, the claims to Mahdi status of leaders of various Islamic movements, such as Mohammed Ahmad in Sudan in the late nineteenth century and Mohammed bin Abdullah Al Qahtani in the late twentieth century in Saudi Arabia, have been vehemently denied by the Muslim state powers concerned.

While the expectation of the Messiah and the attendant promise of redemption have provided hope and comfort to believers in times of political anarchy, societal breakdown and personal despair, they have also consistently served to define the satanic 'other' and sanctioned violence. This link between messianic belief and violence, a recurring feature throughout Semitic history, is examined in the next chapter.

NOTES

1. Abbas Amanat and Magnus T. Bernhardsson, *Imaging the End: Visions of Apocalypse from the Ancient Middle East to Modern America* (London & New York: I.B. Tauris Publishers, 2002) pp. 2 and 19.
2. John J. Collins, 'Eschatological Dynamics and Utopian Ideals in Early Judaism', in *Amanat*, p. 72; and Jasper Griffin, 'New Heaven, New Earth', *The New York Review of Books*, Vol. 41, Number 21, 22 December 1994; downloaded from: http://www.nybooks.com/articles/2043.
3. Griffin.
4. ibid.
5. ibid.
6. ibid.
7. Robert R. Wilson, 'The Biblical Roots of Apocalyptic', in Amanat, pp. 63–5.

8. Arthur P. Mendel, *Vision and Violence* (Ann Arbor, Michigan: The University of Michigan Press, 2002) pp. 8–9; henceforth Mendel.
9. Mendel, pp. 17–18.
10. ibid., p. 19.
11. ibid., p. 21.
12. ibid., p. 22.
13. Griffin.
14. ibid.
15. ibid.
16. Mendel, p. 23
17. Will Durant, *Our Oriental Heritage* (New York: Simon and Schuster, 1954, Copyright renewed 1963) p. 325.
18. ibid.
19. ibid., p. 326.
20. Norman Cohn, *The Pursuit of the Millennium – Revolutionary Millenarians and Mystical Anarchists of the Middle Ages,* (London: Pimlico, 2004) p. 21; henceforth Cohn.
21. Mendel, p. 31.
22. Harald W. Attridge, 'The Messiah and the Millennium: The Roots of Two Jewish-Christian Symbols', Amanat, p. 92.
23. Attridge, p. 93.
24. Mendel, p. 31.
25. Cohn, p. 22.
26. Mendel, pp. 31–32.
27. ibid., pp. 32–3.
28. Martin Goodman, *Rome and Jerusalem – The Clash of Ancient Civilisations,* (London: Allen Lane/Penguin Books, 2007) p. 414.
29. Goodman, p. 416.
30. ibid., p. 417.
31. ibid., p. 422.
32. ibid., pp. 425–30.
33. ibid., p. 442.
34. Will Durant, *Caesar and Christ* (New York: Simon and Schuster, Copyright 1944, copyright renewed 1972) p. 545.
35. Goodman, p. 464.
36. ibid., p. 485.
37. ibid., p. 491.
38. *Caesar and Christ*, p. 548.
39. Goodman, p. 494; *Caesar and Christ*, pp. 548–9.
40. ibid., p. 494.
41. ibid.

42. Goodman, p. 502.
43. *Caesar and Christ*, p. 549.
44. Mendel, p. 54.
45. Quoted in Said Amir Arjomand, 'Origins and Development of Apocalyptic and Messianism in Early Islam: 610–750 CE', Congress of the International Committee of the Historical Sciences, Oslo, August 2000; downloaded from: Oslo2000.uio.no/program/papers/m2b/m2b-arjomand.pdf
46. Mendel, p. 55.
47. Moshe Idel, 'Jewish Apocalypticism—670–1670', in Bernard J. McGinn et al (Eds), *The Continuum History of Apocalypticism*, (New York: Continuum, 2003) p. 362.
48. Idel., p. 367.
49. Karen Armstrong, *The Bible—The Biography* (London: Atlantic Books, 2007), p. 153.
50. Idel, p. 368.
51. ibid.
52. ibid., p. 373.
53. Griffin.
54. Dale C. Allison Jr, 'The Eschatology of Jesus', in McGinn, p. 145.
55. Allison, pp. 147–50.
56. ibid., p. 156.
57. ibid.
58. ibid., p. 158.
59. M.C. de Boer, 'Paul and Apocalyptic Literature', in McGinn, p. 179.
60. Adela Yarbro Collins, 'The Books of Revelation', in McGinn p. 201.
61. Goodman, p. 512.
62. ibid., p. 517.
63. ibid., p. 519.
64. ibid., p. 521.
65. ibid.
66. ibid., p. 525.
67. ibid., p. 527.
68. ibid.
69. ibid., p. 530.
70. ibid., p. 531.
71. ibid., p. 534.
72. *Caesar and Christ*, p. 652.
73. ibid.
74. *Caesar and Christ*, p. 661.
75. ibid.

76. Goodman, p. 544.
77. ibid., p. 560.
78. ibid., p. 575.
79. ibid., pp. 575–6.
80. Mendel, p. 40.
81. Downloaded from: www.christiananswers.net/bible/rev20.html
82. Mendel, p. 39.
83. Quoted in: David C. Rapoport, 'Messianic Sanctions for Terror', *Comparative Politics*, Vol. 20, No. 2, (Jan. 1988), pp. 209–10; downloaded from:http://links.jstor.org/sici?sici=0010-4159%28198801% 2920%3A2%3C195% 3AMSFT%3E2.0.CO%3B2-C
84. Mendel, pp. 40–1.
85. ibid., pp. 43–4.
86. Adela Collins, p. 214; Cohn, p. 29.
87. Brian Daley, S.J., 'Apocalypticism in Early Christian Theology', in McGinn, pp. 223, 228–9.
88. Daley, pp. 232–7.
89. David Olster, 'Byzantine Apocalypses', in McGinn, pp. 258–59.
90. Olster, p. 265.
91. ibid., pp. 265–6.
92. Bernard McGinn, 'Apocalypticism and Church Reform: 1100-1500', in McGinn, p. 273.
93. ibid.
94. Cohn, pp. 14–15.
95. ibid., p. 61.
96. ibid., p. 63.
97. ibid.
98. ibid.
99. ibid., pp. 64–5.
100. ibid., p. 67.
101. Mendel, pp. 64–5.
102. ibid., p. 67.
103. ibid., pp. 68–9.
104. ibid., p. 70.
105. ibid.
106. ibid., pp. 71, 76.
107. ibid., p. 77.
108. ibid., p. 78.
109. ibid., p. 79.
110. ibid., p. 80.

111. Karen Armstrong, *Holy War – The Crusades and Their Impact on Today's World* (New York: Anchor Books, 2001) p. 374.
112. Norman Daniel, *Islam and the West – The Making of an Image*, (Oxford, England: One World Publications, 1993) p. 302.
113. Said Amir Arjomand, p. 110.
114. ibid.
115. ibid., p. 112.
116. ibid.
117. Quoted by Joel Richardson, 'The Mahdi: Islam's Awaited Messiah'; downloaded from: http:answering-islam.org.uk?Authors/JR/Future/ch04_the_mahdi.htm.
118. Said Amir Arjomand, 'Islamic Apocalypticism in the Classic Period', in: Bernard J. McGinn et al. (Eds.), *The Continuum History of Apocalypticism*, Continuum, New York, 2003, p. 390.
119. Said Amir Arjomand, pp. 116–19.
120. Joel Richardson.
121. Joel Richardson; -Arjomand, pp. 381–7; David Cook, *Contemporary Muslim Apocalyptic Literature* (Syracuse, New York: Syracuse University Press, 2005) pp. 7–10.
122. Cyril Glasse, *The Concise Encyclopaedia of Islam* (London: Stacey International, 1989) p. 107.
123. Joel Richardson; Said Amir Arjomand, pp. 112–15; Cook, pp. 9–10.
124. Joel Richardson.
125. Timothy R. Furnish, *Holiest Wars-Islamic Mahdis, Their Jihads, and Osama bin Laden* (Westport, CT: Praeger, 2005).
126. Furnish, pp. 45–58.
127. ibid., p. 61.
128. ibid., pp. 83–4.
129. ibid., p. 87.

2

Messianism and Violence

Wherever it is happening, the revival of religion is mixed up with political conflicts, including an intensifying struggle over Earth's shrinking reserves of natural resources; but there can be no doubt that religion is once again a power in its own right. *With the death of Utopia, apocalyptic religion has re-emerged, naked and unadorned, as a force in world politics.* [Emphasis added.]

John Gray, *Black Mass – Apocalyptic Religion and the Death of Utopia*

I have come to see that *apocalyptic violence intended to 'cleanse' the world of 'impurities' can create a transcendent state.* All the terrorist groups examined in this book believe – or at least started out believing – that they are creating a more perfect world. From their perspective, they are purifying the world of injustice, cruelty, and all that is antihuman. When I began this project, I could not understand why the killers I met seemed spiritually intoxicated. Now, I think I understand. They seem that way because they are. Only a few of the terrorists discussed in these pages have had visions or felt themselves to be in direct communication with God. But all of them describe themselves as responding to a spiritual calling, and many report a kind of spiritual high or addiction related to its fulfillment.

As odd as it sounds, *a sense of transcendence is one of many attractions of religious violence for terrorists, beyond the appeal of achieving their goals.* [Emphasis added.]

Jessica Stern, *Terror in the Name of God – Why Religious Militants Kill*

David Rapoport played a pioneering role in drawing attention to the 'holy' and the 'sacred' in acts of terror. Writing in 1984, he disagreed with the then mainstream thinking that had focused only on the role of

modern technology in regard to the various acts of violence of the 1960s
and 1970s.[1] Analyzing in detail the wellsprings of violence of three diverse
groups in history—the Zealots, the Assassins and the Thugs-Rapoport
had argued that 'sacred terror' had never disappeared altogether, and
that 'there are signs that it is reviving in unusual forms'.[2] He had described
the 'holy terrorist' thus:[3]

> The holy terrorist believes that only a transcendent purpose which fulfills
> the meaning of the universe can justify terror, and that the deity reveals at
> some early moment in time both the end and means and may even
> participate in the process as well.

Rapoport pointed out that, while the Thugs were impelled by religious
conviction in carrying out their murders, their violence had served no
political purpose nor did it seek an audience to witness their deeds. On
the other hand, in respect of the Assassins and the Zealots, Rapoport
noted the central role of messianism in their violence as also the
importance of the public spectacle.[4] Thus, the Zealots drew from Jewish
messianic doctrines 'the object of their terror and the permitted method
necessary to achieve it'.[5] Rapoport recalled, in this context, the Jewish
apocalyptic prophecies that were widely prevalent at the time of the
insurrection of the Zealots against the Romans (AD 66–73), which saw
the imminent arrival of the Messiah in a series of massive catastrophies.
As a scholar quoted by Rapoport pointed out:[6]

> Almost every event was seized upon ... to discover how and in what way it
> represented a Sign of the Times and threw light on the approach of the
> End of the Days. The whole condition of the Jewish people was
> psychologically abnormal. The strongest tales and imaginings could find
> ready credence ... New messianic pretenders flourished everywhere, because
> so many people believed that the signs indicating a messianic intervention
> were quite conspicuous: Judea was occupied by an alien military power,
> and prominent Jews were acquiescing in "the desecration of God's name"
> or accepting the culture of the conqueror.

The Zealots utilized tactics that, in terms of their impact, would
anticipate the motivations of later sacred terrorists; as Rapoport has
said:[7]

> Participants [in the Zealots' violence] (despite their contrary intentions)
> were pulled into an ever-escalating struggle by shock tactics which
> manipulated their fear, outrage, sympathy, and guilt. Sometimes these

emotional effects were provoked by terrorist atrocities which went beyond the consensual norms governing violence; at other times they were produced by provoking the enemy into committing atrocities against his will.

The Assassins (1090–1275) were a manifestation of an Islamic (Shia) messianic movement whose central belief pertained to the emergence of a Mahdi (Messiah) as a result of holy war (jihad) against the Orthodox establishment to cleanse Islam. The victims of the Assassins were Orthodox Muslim religious and political leaders who were deemed to be complicit in the corruption of their religion, so that their assassination was necessary to 'renew the communities' faith'.[8]

At the end of his study, Rapoport firmly asserted the 'uniqueness of sacred terror', pointing out that technological changes only changed the weapons of terror, but it was 'doctrine rather than technology (that) is the ultimate source of terror'.[9] He identified four characteristics that made 'sacred terror' different from other forms of terror:[10]

(*i*) The transcendent source of holy terror, i.e. God, is directly involved in the means and the ends.

(*ii*) Flowing from (i), holy terror draws its rationale from the past, 'either in divine instructions transmitted long ago or in interpretations of precedents from founding periods of the parent religions'.

(*iii*) Holy terror is a 'war without limits', i.e. the holy war in the Semitic tradition requires the total elimination of the deemed enemy; as Rapoport noted: 'The belief that assimilation [of the enemy] impeded messianic deliverance and that all members of the community (of the enemy) were – culpable gave Jewish terror a character that seemed indiscriminate ...'In fact, the early Zealots obtained biblical sanction for their pursuit of war without limits since the protection of *herem* (sacred space; *haram* in Arabic) imposed an obligation to destroy all persons [i.e. enemies] with their property who remain in the land, lest they become sources of corruption.

(*iv*) Rapoport's study of the Zealots and the Assassins confirmed that 'martyrdom is a central, perhaps, critical method of message-giving religions used both to dispel the doubts of believers and to aid proselytizing effort'.[11]

Four years later, Rapoport revisited the issue of 'holy terror' and noted the increasing tendency to use 'theological concepts to justify terrorist activity'.[12] For purposes of his analysis, Rapoport provided a broad definition of terrorism as 'extra-normal or extra-moral violence, a type that goes beyond the conventions of boundaries particular societies establish to coercion'.[13] Holy terror, he noted, 'is usually linked to messianism'[14] and described the Messianic believer as 'one who has faith that there will be a day in which history or life on *this* earth will be transformed totally and irreversibly from the condition of perpetual strife which we have all experienced to one of perfect harmony that many dream about.'[15] Based on a study of messianic movements in different cultures over several centuries, Rapoport concluded that 'messianism would be conducive to terrorism in a given set of circumstances that is when believers think that the day of deliverance is near or imminent and that their actions can or must consummate the process'.[16]

Rapoport also examined in some detail the 'necessary conditions' that impel the messianic believer into perpetrating terrorist acts. He identified six such conditions:

First is the belief in the imminence of the messianic era, together with the conviction of the believer that *he* can influence messianic events, particularly its character and timing, through his own actions.[17]

Second, once the messianic believer comes to accept that his actions can influence and even precipitate the advent of the messianic era, it is very likely that the believer would first consider some non-violent action such as self-purification, migration and creation of a (secluded) sacred community. He could reject these options in favour of violent action (that is, terror) if he felt these non-violent actions would not lead to the desired end, that is, the ushering in of the messianic era.[18]

The *third* element pertains to the 'proof' to be provided by the believer in regard to his faith and his 'moral worthiness': he does this primarily through an eagerness to seek martyrdom which is common to all three Semitic traditions.[19]

The *fourth* element pertains to 'signs' or portents that herald the messianic era. These generally are a series of cataclysmic events such as natural disasters, wars, famines, gruesome massacres, which are read as portents of a messianic era; such events can provoke believers into a 'commission or provocation' of atrocities they believe would precipitate the end of the current era and herald a new messianic era.[20]

The *fifth* element pertains to the demonization of the enemy, seeing him as the Son of Darkness, Satan or Antichrist: 'The enemy is wholly evil, always dangerous, in short, something other than human. Binding agreements with him are impossible because the restraints which the enemy accepts or proposes are designed for the sole purpose of lulling us into complacency. Against such an antagonist the temptation becomes so overwhelming to argue that everything is permissible and that he must be mercilessly destroyed.'[21]

The *sixth* element is the believers' understanding of God's role in the imminent struggle heralding the messianic era. Both Judaism and Christianity see an active divine role in these struggles:[22]

> God fights by means of famine, pestilence, and other natural disasters which spread devastation indiscriminately. At its worst, a violent conflict between humans gives the victor a choice concerning the lives and fortunes of the defeated, and normally conquerors preserve in order to possess. At their best, such wars may be subject to conventions concerning the disposition of populations and properties never engaged or no longer involved in the conflict. But in sharp contrast to this practice, the enemy and its properties had to be exterminated completely in Israel's early holy wars, lest its continued existence corrupt Israel. *In the later messianic wars, terror seems to be violence without restraint or violence that transcends those limits which ordinary concerns for utility and morality dictate.* [Emphasis added.]

David Rapoport ended his study with this sobering reflection:[23]

> Once a messianic advent appears imminent, in every case powerful impulses towards terror are inherent in the beliefs of a world about to be destroyed, the gains imagined, the character of the participants, and God's methods. Beyond all this, and I cannot emphasize the point enough, *terror is attractive in itself to messianists just because it is outside the normal range of violence and for this reason represents a break with the past ....* [Emphasis added.]

In a rigorously argued paper written in 1996, Sonia Alianak applied Rapoport's 'messianic model' of holy terror to the assassinations of Egyptian President Anwar Sadat in 1981 and Israeli Prime Minister Yitzhak Rabin in 1995, and concluded that Rapoport's model was fully applicable to the two events; she said:[24]

> 'Holy assassinations' tend to occur in the Middle East under two necessary conditions: religious delegitimization of the ruler or rulers and the existence of a 'devout' human agent or agents from a militant religious minority,

who are ready to participate violently at any stage of the messianic process, rejecting democracy.

The sub-factors are the following: This human agent considers himself to be morally worthy because he has an unshakable faith, his 'sins' are potentially holy, and he believes in martyrdom. However, he feels powerless in the ruler's political system. Therefore, he must resort to violence to prevent the ruler's threat to the messianic process. This threat is seen through physical signs, Western innovations, and/or major reversals of policy by the ruler causing psychological shocks. The assassin might perceive the ruler as slowing down or stopping the messianic process. He is often under the influence of competing messianic views about violence, whether verbal or involving civil disobedience, which targets the ruler or rulers.

Other critics have also seen similarities between otherwise antagonistic religious groups. Thus, Ranstorp has pointed out:[25]

> There is a great degree of similarity between the stands of the Jewish Kach and Islamic Hamas organization: Both share a vision of a religious state between Jordan River and the Mediterranean Sea; a xenophobia against everything alien or secular which must be removed from the entire land and a vehement rejection of western culture. This distinction between the faithful and those standing outside the group is reinforced in the daily discourse of the clerics of these terrorist groups. The clerics' language and phraseology shapes the followers' reality, reinforcing the loyalty and social obligation of the members to the group and reminding them of the sacrifices already made, as well as the direction of the struggle.

The great scholar of religious fundamentalism, R. Scott Appleby, has linked fundamentalism with messianism by speaking of the *'fundamentalist apocalyptic imagination'*,[26] which, according to him, is shaped by a 'torture vision of the past, construction of history tht attempts to cast the long and otherwise dispiriting record of the humiliation, persecution and exile of the true believers (punctuated by an occasional, atypical 'golden age' of faith) as a necessary prelude to and prerequisite for the decisive intervention of God and the final vanishing of the apostates'.[27] He goes on to point out:[28]

> Religious fundamentalists are dualists at heart; they imagine the world divided into unambiguous realms of light and darkness peopled by the elect and reprobate, the pure and impure, the orthodox and the infidel. Many if not all fundamentalists further dramatize this Manichaean

worldview by setting it within an apocalyptic framework: the world is in spiritual crisis, perhaps near its end, when God will bring terrible judgment upon the children of darkness. When the children of light are depicted in such millenarian imaginings as the agents of this divine wrath, violent intolerance toward outsiders appears justified on theological grounds.

The messianic world view, according to Appleby, has the following attributes:[29]

(*i*)   It is based on the conviction that these are not normal times: there is a threat to one's way of life from encroaching foreign norms and secular threats, in short what Jessica Stern describes as 'the engine of modernity that is stealing the identity of the oppressed'.[30]

(*ii*)   This absence of normal times has evolved into a crisis which consists of a mortal threat or apocalypse so that one's own existence as a people is threatened.

(*iii*)   Since these are exceptional times and we are in a state of crisis and our very existence as a people is under threat, the exceptional times require exceptional measures, such as self-sacrifices, which will in time help to prepare devout cadres for physical warfare.

On similar lines, James Rinehart too has seen messianism (referred to as 'millenarianism' by him) as a factor in political violence. Rinehart has described the 'messianic paradigm' as:[31]

a community composed of deeply ethnocentric people, disrupted by a perceptibly wicked, evil, and alienating power of seemingly demonic dimension that upsets and menaces their traditional way of life. In the presence of such danger, the community becomes convinced that its role and purpose must be defended to the death, largely because they are God's chosen Elect, destined to ensure that righteousness overcomes evil; triumph is inexorable and according to God's plan, represents the true end of history which will reveals itself as heaven on earth.

He noted that, historically, movements in Christian tradition suggesting the imminent return of the Messiah made their deepest impact in places which were going through social and economic change which had brought in its wake cultural shock and disorientation, diversified the existing socio-economic order and had a powerful impact on traditional life.[32]

Messianism and Terror

As Juergensmeyer has pointed out, acts of terror are executed in a deliberately intense and vivid manner as to inspire anger and hatred. Terrorist killings are generally 'vivid and horrifying',[33] and are aimed not only to obtain a political purpose or strategic advantage but also to make a powerful 'symbolic statement' from a stage that provides 'mind-numbing mesmerizing theatre'.[34] The most powerful acts of violence are those that embody 'a grander conquest, a struggle more awesome than what meets the eye'.[35] The invocation of powerful religious belief imbues the dramatic act of killing with an intensity that far transcends the value of any secular cause, however significant it might be for human welfare; for it is religion alone that can imbue violence with a sense of 'great momentum in history' and elevate earthly conflict to a 'cosmic' dimension.[36]

The radical religious movements that have emerged from the cultures of violence in different parts of the world have three common attributes:[37]

(*i*) they reject all compromise with liberal values and secular institutions;

(*ii*) they refuse to accept the central attribute of a secular society that religion is a private matter; they believe instead that religion is a significant role player in the public domain;

(*iii*) they seek to replace mainstream religious belief and practice (which they see as weak and accommodative), with an alternative that they believe is more vibrant and demanding and, above all, more in conformity with the origins of the tradition of their religion: religious radicals not only see themselves as defenders of their ancient true faith, they are also engaged in a quest 'for a deeper level of spirituality' that they are unable to find in mainstream religious practice.

Protagonists of religious violence invoke images of divine warfare:[38] recalling the great battles of the past, they separate them from their original political or strategic significance and project them as conflicts between good and evil on a cosmic scale. This sense of a 'cosmic war'[39] emerges from certain powerful beliefs and impulses:

(*i*) the certainty about the correctness on one's own position or belief, with the attendant willingness to defend it or to impose it on others to the very end;[40]

(*ii*) the conviction that no compromise with the other belief or institution is possible;[41]

(*iii*) the belief that the present-day struggle far transcends the immediate identities and interests of the parties involved, e.g. the protagonists involved in the Arab-Israeli-Palestine conflict do not see their struggle merely as competing claims over control of land; it is elevated to a cosmic struggle that goes back to biblical times;[42]

(*iv*) the fact that the cosmic struggle inevitably acquires a Manichaean character: it becomes a combat between good and evil; the conviction that good is on one's own side provides a ready justification for the most extreme acts of violence;[43] and,

(*v*) the apocalyptic violence that is aimed at cleaning the world of 'impurities' can induce in its protagonists a sense of spiritual intoxication brought out by their sense of 'responding to a spiritual calling';[44] as Stern has pointed out, 'a sense of transcendence is one of the many attractions of religious violence for terrorists, beyond the appeal of achieving their goals'.[45]

A detailed study of violence emanating from religious groups in different parts of the world has led Mark Juergensmeyer to identify the attributes of a 'cosmic war'. First, the struggle is in defence of basic identity and dignity; defeat in this struggle is not an option.

The second attribute emerges from the sense that the struggle is facing obstacles on the secular plane and, hence, needs to be 'reconceived' on a sacred plane, with God being mobilized on one side; that is, the struggle may begin on a worldly plane but in time may acquire the character of the cosmic war as a solution or settlement of the dispute at the secular level becomes increasingly unlikely; this leads to:

(a) the antagonism evolving from the worldly plane and assuming transcendental proportions;

(b) acts of violence becoming legitimate instruments in the cosmic war; and,

(c) the opposing sides getting sharply divided on a Manichaean basis, with all good being on one side and all evil on the other.[46]

Third, the 'invention of the enemy' is a central characteristic of the religious war;[47] this demonizing of 'the other' involves:[48]

(*a*) his expulsion or annihilation;

(*b*) imbuing a satanic character to even relatively innocent enemies;

(*c*) caricaturing the enemy, thus, denying him human character and personality; and,

(*d*) stereotyping and categorizing people as collective enemies, thus ensuring that the label of Satan includes the entire collective of 'the Other'; this leads to the further conviction that, in a cosmic struggle, among the enemy 'no one is innocent'.

Juergensmeyer has described satanization as a 'creation of a mythic monster in the cosmic war whom ultimately only divine power could subdue'.[49] The process of satanization and stereotyping the collective enemy permits a group on one side of the cosmic war to commit the most heinous atrocities without any doubt or hesitation.[50]

Finally, since the struggle is part of the pursuit of God's interests and purposes, 'sacrifice' is central to the struggle. ('Sacrifice' is derived from the Latin world 'sacrificium' which means 'to make holy'.) Personal sacrifice or martyrdom elevates the protagonist and ennobles him. Such a supreme sacrifice makes sense only in the context of a cosmic war. As Juergensmeyer has noted, in spiritualizing violence, religion has imbued terrorism with extraordinary power, since a terrorist will do anything if he thinks it has been sanctioned by divine mandate or conceived 'in the mind of God'.[51]

Suicide Attacks

Robert Pape has described suicide attacks as operations that are designed in such a way that the terrorist does not expect to survive them, even if he or she is actually killed by police or other defenders.[52] Though suicide attacks go back to the Jewish Zealots and the Islamic Assassins, they have acquired an extraordinary resonance in recent years, particularly after the dramatic events of 9/11.

Pape has noted that while terrorist incidents declined from a high of 666 in 1987 to 348 in 2001, suicide attacks have increased from three per year in the 1980s, to 10 per year in the 1990s, to over 40 per year in 2001 and 2002, and nearly 50 in 2003.[53] He has counted a total of 315 suicide attacks between 1980 and 2003.[54] These attacks were just three per cent of all terrorist incidents in this period, but accounted for 48 per cent of the fatalities, making the average suicide terrorist attacks twelve times more deadly than other forms of terrorism.[55] Islamic extremism has been associated with about half of the suicide attacks between 1980 and 2003.[56]

New figures cited by Ahmed Rashid confirm that suicide attacks are increasingly becoming the weapon of choice in arenas involving confrontations with radical Islam.[57] Thus, in Afghanistan, where suicide bombings were a mere twenty-one in 2005, they rose to 136 in 2006 and 137 in 2007. They also became more lethal: while the number of attacks was nearly the same, in 2006, there were 1,100 casualties as against 1730 casualties in 2007; these included 900 Afghan policemen and foreign aid workers.

There has been a similar pattern in Pakistan: while there had been only six attacks in Pakistan in 2006, there were fifty-six in 2007, in which 419 security personnel and 217 civilians were killed. In the period January-April 2008, there were nineteen attacks, killing 274 security personnel and injuring several hundred persons. However, the most horrendous arena is Iraq: in 2008, there has been an average of nineteen suicide attacks per month, as against eight to ten attacks per month in 2007.

Ehud Sprinzak has described suicide attacks as 'almost supernatural, extremely lethal, and impossible to stop'.[58] The principal reason for the proliferation of suicide attacks has been their effectiveness from the perspective of the organizations that support them. This is borne out by the following:

(*i*)   they enable the organization to choose the time and location of the assault, so that the maximum and/or the most damaging wound can be inflicted on the enemy;

(*ii*) they yield a large number of casualties: thus between 2000 and 2002, suicide attacks by Palestinians constituted only one per cent of the total attacks but caused 44 per cent of Israeli casualties;[59]

(*iii*) they provide great publicity on account of the number of casualities, the deep sense of tragedy universally inherent in wanton death, and the dramatic value that universally informs martyrdom, particularly when women 'martyrs' are involved;

(*iv*) in a cost-benefit analysis, they yield extraordinary net gain both in financial and political terms, besides boosting the morale of supporters and obtaining new adherents; and, (*v*) they powerfully intimidate large sections of the target population: they erode confidence in the authorities (security and political); over time, they encourage pressure on governments to compromise established positions and even avowed national values by inciting xenophobic responses and demanding immediate, quick-fix solutions; such responses, by their very nature, could harm the long-term interests of the target country/people, even as they dramatically focus attention on the 'cause' espoused by the attacking entity.

Before 9/11, government officials in West Asia, on the basis of their experiences till then, had worked out a fairly detailed 'profile' of a Palestinian suicide terrorist, which had, inter alia, included the following characteristics:[60]

(*i*) He is young and mentally immature.

(*ii*) He is under personal pressure due to unemployment.

(*iii*) He has very low self-esteem and is without a social safety net.

(*iv*) He is generally without female company due to inadequate resources.

(*v*) He seeks solace in religion and becomes a regular visitor to the local mosque, where he might get recruited by an extremist organization.

An Israeli expert had added to this list by noting that most of the suicide attackers came from refugee camps, they were of average economic status and most of them had spent time in Israeli prisons.[61]

However, the 'profiles' of the perpetrators of the 9/11 events were so much at variance with what had been experienced earlier that scholars have had to review their understanding of the typical suicide terrorist. This has led Jessica Stern to note that, after 9/11, 'it has become clear that developing a single profile of suicide bombers is nearly impossible;'[62] she goes on to say:[63]

Candidates are not necessarily poor; they may in fact be wealthy. Nor are they necessarily uneducated. Women are now getting involved. Women have been responsible for over a third of the suicide bombings carried out by the Liberation Tigers of Tamil Eelam in Sri Lanka, and over two-thirds of those perpetrated by the Kurdish Workers' Party, PKK. But until recently, female suicide bombers were considered rare among Muslims. Hamas no longer needs to recruit suicide bombers; they are swamped with volunteers requiring little indoctrination.

Robert Pape echoed this view when he pointed out that 'suicide attacks are likely to come from a broad cross-section of society', and that many of them are 'secular, employed, reasonably well educated and otherwise contributing members of society'.[64] He has pointed out that Hamas in Palestine and Hizbullah in Lebanon, both of whom advocate martyrdom operations', explain their position on the ground that such operations are 'a justifiable response to the specific circumstances of a foreign occupation'.[65] Their detailed justification is as follows:[66]

(*i*) martyrdom operations are aimed at ending foreign occupation of the homeland;

(*ii*) the imbalance of conventional military power between the occupier and the occupied justifies their use; and,

(*iii*) they are likely to be effective as the occupier is susceptible to coercive force; thus, Hizbullah stated:[67]

With the blood of its martyrs and the struggle of its heroes, the Islamic resistance has been able to force the enemy for the first time in the history of the conflict against it to make a decision to retreat and withdraw from Lebanon without any American influence.

Fadlallah, Hezbollah's spiritual leader, said:[68]

The self-martyring operation is not permitted unless it can convulse the enemy. The believer cannot blow himself up unless the results will equal or exceed the loss of the believer's soul. Self-martyring operations are not fatal accidents but legal obligations governed by rules.

A Hamas statement went as follows:[69]

The Zionist enemy does not understand the language of begging and submission, which only increases its aggressiveness and arrogance. It only understands the language of Jihad, resistance and martyrdom, that was the language that led to its blatant defeat in South Lebanon and it will be the language that will defeat it on the land of Palestine.

Louise Richardson plays down the religious factor in motivating suicide attacks, stressing that suicide terror should be seen as a strategic weapon rather than as a *religious* response to a deeply felt grievance. She believes that suicide terrorism is 'simply the tactic of choice among many terrorist groups', with the terrorist being motivated by long-term political objectives as also short-term immediate objectives inherent in all terrorist acts – revenge, renown and reaction.[70] She notes that suicide operations require a disaffected individual, a supportive community and a legitimizing ideology.[71] Since many suicide operations are group operations, the comradeship of the group inculcates in each individual an 'intense small-group loyalty'.[72] She quotes two scholars who have studied Hamas as saying:[73]

> What the rank and file [of Hamas] seemed to live and die for, in the end, was neither hospitals nor politics nor ideology nor religion nor the Apocalypse, but rather *an ecstatic camaraderie in the face of death on the path to Allah*. [Emphasis added.]

While it is true that, in the West Asian context, suicide attacks have been carried out by members of secular as well as religious groups, the religious factor has come to play an increasingly important role in motivating the attackers. The early attacks in Lebanon in 1981 against French and American soldiers were carried out by Islamic militants.[74] Later, they were undertaken by other Palestinian groups, both religious and secular, and then expanded rapidly to Islamic groups in Pakistan (from where suicide attacks were launched both within the country and in Kashmir), Afghanistan and, above all, Iraq. While the principal motivation in Iraq and Palestine is to rid the homeland of foreign occupation, in Pakistan and Afghanistan the targets are foreign troops, foreign (Western) citizens and domestic leaders and officials seen as allied to the West. A 'martyr-in-waiting' in Iraq informed a foreign correspondent that he was fighting first for Islam, second to become a martyr and go to heaven, and third for his country.[75]

Robert Pape has forcefully argued that the 'strategic logic of suicide terrorism' emerges from foreign occupation,[76] fanning an anger that expresses itself in suicide missions in faraway countries, with Islamic organizations, including Al-Qaeda being impelled by political rather than religious goals.[77] Pape has also emphasized the importance of the group in suicide operations, noting that the militants have a close band of loyalty to comrades and loyalty to leaders.[78] However, Pape does recognize the overwhelming significance of the religious factor in suicide attacks: after a detailed analysis of suicide terrorism between 1980 and 2003, he concluded:

> Nationalist rebellion and religious difference between the rebels and a dominant democratic state are the main considerations under which the foreign occupation of a community's homeland is likely to lead to a campaign of suicide terrorism as part of a national liberation strategy ...

Since 1980, religious difference has accounted for much of the variance
in the pattern of when nationalist rebellions against occupation by a
democratic state evolve into terrorist campaigns.[79]

Under circumstances of a foreign occupation ... Religious difference
can influence nationalist sentiments in ways that encourage mass support
for martyrdom and suicide terrorism.[80]

Conclusion

Violence based on messianic religious belief, referred to by Rapoport as
'sacred terror', is different from other forms of violence in that it directly
involves God as an active role-player and pursues a 'war without limits'
in which the total destruction of the 'Other' is the cherished aim and
martyrdom of the protagonist is the eagerly anticipated prize. The
messianic believer is convinced that the day of redemption is near and
his intervention can actually precipitate the advent of the messianic era.
Hence, he confronts a demonized enemy with unlimited violence, with
the conviction that the divine entity is on his side.

Messianic religious movements share certain common attributes:
they reject all compromise with secular values and institutions; they
believe that religion has a major role in the public domain; and they
replace their mainstream religious traditions with what they believe is
the essence of their true faith, which is at once rigid and
uncompromising.

This confrontation is truly a 'cosmic war' since it is fought in defence
of core values; thus, compromise cannot be considered and defeat is not
an option. Messianic belief also sanctions the most extreme violence to
cleanse the world of an 'impure' Other. This conflict calls for personal
sacrifice, which elevates the struggle and is in accord with its divine,
cosmic character. Suicide bombings have now emerged as the most
pervasive form of personal sacrifice in the 'cosmic' struggle. The strongest
motivation for suicide terror is to rid the homeland of alien occupation.
Though the principal role-players in specific episodes may have their
religious impulse buttressed by other sources that strengthen grievance
and victimhood, religious differences between the occupier and the
occupied encourage suicide terrorism as part of a national liberation
strategy.

In the following chapters we will look at contemporary manifestations of messianism in the three Semitic traditions.

NOTES

1. David C. Rapoport, 'Fear and Trembling: Terrorism in Three Religious Traditions', *The American Political Science Review*, Vol. 78, No. 3 September 1984, p. 658; downloaded from:http://www.international. ucla.edu/media/files/fear-trembling.pdf.

2. Rapoport 1984, p. 659; the *Zealots* are described in the *Jewish Encyclopedia* thus:

   Zealots: Zealous defenders of the Law and of the national life of the Jewish people; name of a party opposing with relentless rigor any attempt to bring Judea under the dominion of idolatrous Rome, and especially of the aggressive and fanatical war party from the time of Herod until the fall of Jerusalem and Masada. The members of this party bore also the name Sicarii, from their custom of going about with daggers ("sicae") hidden beneath their cloaks, with which they would stab any one found committing a sacrilegious act or anything provoking anti-Jewish feeling. [Kaufmann Kohler: 'Zealots', downloaded from: http://www.jewishencyclopedia.com/view_friendly.jsp?artid= 49&letter=Z.]

   The Zealots flourished between 5 and AD 70. They emerged early in the reign of Herod and were active in opposing Roman oppression. They attacked Romans as also Jews who cooperated with their rule. They carried out their murders in public, choosing holidays when they could mingle with crowds and stab their victims. They also participated in military action, killing hostages and also terrorizing wealthy Jewish landowners to compel land re-distribution according to religious tradition. They played a lead role in the capture of Masada fortress in AD 66. Most of them were killed when the Roman legions re-took Jerusalem (AD 70) and Masada (AD 73).

   The **Assassins** were active over nearly two centuries (1090-1275). They carried out assassinations in order to purify Islam. They killed prominent Muslim personalities, often at shrines and even at royal courts. After carrying out the murders, they made little effort to escape and appeared to welcome martyrdom.

   The **Thugs** flourished in India over several centuries till they were systematically annihilated by British-Indian armed forces in the nineteenth century. They may have flourished for over 600 years, though there are suggestions that they might even have existed for about 2,500 years. Again, they are believed to have killed at least half a million people. The Thugs were motivated by deep religious belief which caused them to attack travellers, though they were forbidden to kill certain specific categories of people such as women, lepers, the handicapped, certain categories of artisans and Europeans. In their actions, they were governed by strict rules pertaining to choice of victims, methods of attack, division of labour amongst themselves, disposal of bodies, distribution of booty and training of new members.

3. ibid.
4. ibid., p. 668.
5. ibid., p. 669.
6. ibid.
7. ibid., p. 670.
8. ibid., p. 665.
9. ibid., p. 672.
10. ibid., p. 674
11. ibid., p. 665.
12. David. C. Rapoport, 'Messianic Sanctions for Terror,' *Comparative Politics*, Vol. 20, No. 2 (Jan. 1988), p. 195; downloaded from: http:// links.jstor.org/sici=0010-4159%28198801%2920%3A2%3C195% 3AMSFT%3E2.CO%3B2-C; henceforth Rapoport 1988.
13. Rapoport 1988, p. 196.
14. ibid., p. 195.
15. ibid., p. 197.
16. ibid.
17. ibid., p. 201.
18. ibid., p. 204.
19. ibid., p. 206.
20. ibid., p. 208.
21. ibid.
22. ibid., p. 209.
23. ibid., p. 210.
24. Sonia L. Alianak, 'Religion, Politics and Assassination in the Middle East', *World Affairs*, 1 Jan 1998; downloaded from: www.encyclopedia. com/printable.espx? id = 1G1:20380795.
25. Dr. Magnus Ranstorp, 'Terrorism in the Name of Religion', *Journal of International Affairs*, Summer 1996, 50, No.I; downloaded from: www.ciaonet.org/wps/ram01.
26. R. Scott Appleby, 'The Unholy Uses of the Apocalyptic Imagination: Twentieth Century Patterns', revised text of a conference presentation based on earlier published material of 2002; downloaded from: 128.36.236.77/workpaper/pdfs/MESV6-4.pdf.
27. Appleby.
28. ibid.
29. ibid.

30. Jessica Stern, *Terror in the Name of God – Why Religious Militants Kill* (New York: Harper Collins, 2003) p. 283.
31. James F. Rinehart, *Apocalyptic Faith and Political Violence – Prophets of Terror* (Hampshire, England: Palgrave MacMillam, 2006) p. 23.
32. Rinehart, pp. 22–3.
33. Mark Juergensmeyer, *Terror in the Mind of God—The Global Rise of Religious Violence* (New Delhi: Oxford University Press, 2000) p. 120.
34. Juergensmeyer, p. 122.
35. ibid., p. 123.
36. ibid., p. 137.
37. ibid., pp. 221–2.
39. ibid., p. 146.
39. ibid.
40. ibid., p. 149.
41. Ibid.
42. ibid., p. 153.
43. ibid.
44. Stern, p. 281.
45. ibid., p. 282.
46. Juergensmeyer, pp. 161–3.
47. ibid., p. 171.
48. ibid., pp. 171–5.
49. ibid., p. 182.
50. ibid., p. 183.
51. ibid., p. 216.
52. Robert A. Pape, *Dying to Win – Why Suicide Terrorists Do It*, (London: Gibson Square, 2006) p. 10.
53. ibid., p. 6.
54. ibid., p. 3.
55. ibid., p. 6.
56. ibid., p. 17.
57. Ahmed Rashid, 'Jihad: Suicide Bombers: The New Wave', *New York Review of Books*, Vol. LV, No. 10, 12 June 2008, p.20.
58. Ehud Sprinzak 'Outsmarting Suicide Terrorists', *Christian Science Monitor*, 24 October 2000; downloaded from: http// www.csmonitor.com/cgi-bin/durableRedirect.pl?/durable/2000/10/24/ fp9s1-csm.shtml
59. Audrey Kurth Cronin, 'Terrorists and Suicide Attacks', *CRS Report for Congress*, 28 August 2003; p. CRS-9; downloaded from:www.fas.org/ irp/crs/Rl32058.pdf
60. Stern, p. 50.

61. ibid., p. 51.
62. ibid.
63. ibid., pp. 51–2.
64. Pape, p. 198.
65. ibid., p. 189.
66. ibid., pp. 189-90.
67. ibid., p.190.
68. ibid.
69. ibid., p. 193.
70. Louise Richardson, *What Terrorists Want—Understanding the Terrorist Threat* (London: John Murray, 2006) p. 135.
71. ibid.
72. ibid., p. 159.
73. ibid.
74. ibid., p. 143.
75. ibid., p. 151.
76. Pape, p. v.
77. ibid., p. vi.
78. ibid., p. 8.
79. ibid., p. 101.
80. ibid., p. 88.

3

Jewish Messianism

Ode to the Nation

What shall they do here today,
Your sons and daughters,
In the fullness of their vigor,
With the storm of their dammed-up fury,
The force of revolt within them?
What shall they do
With the pulse of battle pounding in their blood?
Bid them conquer the land,
Scale the peaks with standards flying;
Storm the walls of Titus, raze Bastilles;
As rebels they will go forth,
And you shall hear them, singing their song
Of freedom and conquest and redemption,
Full redemption!

Uri Zvi Greenberg
(downloaded from: www.saveisrael.com/greenberg/greenbergnation.htm)

Zionism was a Jewish nationalist movement aimed at setting up a Jewish state that emerged in nineteenth century Europe in response to exclusionary and repressive anti-Semitism, with periodic pogroms against local Jewish populations. Israel's first Prime Minister, David Ben Gurion, described it as 'the desire for a Jewish State, a country and authority in that country'.[1] It arose from the conviction that the Jews were 'abnormal' in that they had no state of their own and hence were constantly threatened with being suppressed or massacred.[2] In late nineteenth century West Europe, many Jews had attempted to get 'assimilated' and become 'normal' Europeans. However, repeated experiences of anti-Semitism indicated how futile such an approach was. The Jewish journalist and playwright, Theodor Herzl, was shocked by the Dreyfus Affair in Paris, in 1894, which confirmed to him the failure of assimilation. He then committed himself to setting up a Jewish state; he wrote: 'Let sovereignty be granted us over a portion of the globe adequate to meet our rightful national requirement. We will attend to the rest.'[3]

Zionism had many strands—Socialist, Religious and 'Revisionist'— as different groups, united in the cause of a Jewish State, drew their ideas from Judaism as also from the numerous European political ideas that flourished through the nineteenth and early twentieth centuries. All of these influences and movements taken together crystallized 'the modern Jewish political identity'.[4]

Early debates among the votaries of Zionism centred around the link of this avowedly secular movement with its religious moorings. These debates led finally to the broad consensual position that religion defined the identity of the Jewish people; it would therefore continue to define the *national* identity of the Jewish people in their state.

Alain Dieckhoff has emphasized that religion was not just a tool defining the Jewish state: the pioneers who laboured to create their Jewish state 'were driven on by the Messianic idea of the renewal the nation on its own land';[5] their present tribulations were endurable because they were spurred by a messianic impulse that promised them 'a radiant and magnificent future'. Indeed, as Dieckhoff suggests, this promise of a bright future blinded the Jewish pioneers to the present-day reality of the Arabs residing in Palestine, who were seen as 'part of the provisional reality that was to fade steadily away before the new reality forged by the Jews'.[6]

While the most important role players in the Zionist movement and in the first twenty years of the Israeli state were secular socialists, it is important to recall that the Zionist movement from its advent had a parallel religious movement, referred to by scholars as 'Religious Zionism', that frequently interacted with and influenced the secular side, and, after 1967, came to dominate Israeli society, culture and politics.

Religious Zionism

The evolution of Jewish messianic thinking over the previous several centuries crystallized, in the late nineteenth and early twentiethth centuries, into two diametrically opposite views pertaining to the nature

and purposes of the Zionist movement and generally the destiny of the
Jewish people in the diaspora.

In Jewish tradition, the Messiah was the person, human or divine,
who was destined to appear as the divinely ordained deliverer of his
people. The Jewish community waited for the Messiah who would bring
salvation for them, judge them righteously and ensure peace and
prosperity: thus, in Isaiah it was proclaimed:[7]

> And there shall come forth a shoot out of the stock of Jesse [father of the
> Biblical David], and a twig shall grow forth out of his roots. And the spirit
> of the Lord shall rest upon him, the spirit of wisdom and understanding,
> the spirit of counsel and might, the spirit of knowledge and of the fear of
> the Lord. And his delight shall be in the fear of the Lord; and he shall not
> judge after the sight of his eyes, neither decide after the hearing of his ears;
> but with righteousness shall he judge the poor, and decide with equity for
> the meek of the land ...they shall not hurt nor destroy in all My holy
> mountain; for the earth shall be full of the knowledge of the Lord, as the
> waters cover the sea. And it shall come to pass in that day, that the root of
> Jesse, that standeth for an ensign of the peoples, unto him shall the nations
> seek; and his resting-place shall be glorious. (Isaiah 11.1–4, 9–10).

The traditional Orthodox view that prevailed over several centuries was
that the coming of the expected Messiah would occur amidst an 'abrupt
apocalypse' that would bring 'instant glory to Israel's faithful (that is,
the Jewish people) and destruction upon her enemies'. However, from
medieval times there were also votaries of an opposite view that the
coming of the Messiah would be 'a compelling human drama in which
the national energies of the people are harnessed, *on their own initiative*,
to a resourceful redemptive process, pursuing the restoration of Jewish
sovereignty and collective restrain to Jewish spirituality'.[8] In the early
twentiethth century, Rav Avraham Kook (1865-1935) upheld this
tradition. He robustly moved away from the Orthodox view and, instead,
saw in the secular, human effort of the Zionist movement the hand of
divine providence. As Martin Gordon has noted, manifest messianism
was implicit in the development of the land 'both culturally and
materially' which would take shape in a national entity, which would in
turn benefit from 'inspired direction'.[9] This was the path then taken by
'Religious Zionism'.

Religious Zionism differed from Orthodox Jewry in that the latter
opposed the pursuit of a Jewish state, seeing it as a sacrilege since it was

aimed at hastening the end of time and forcing the coming of the Kingdom of God. The former, on the other hand, pursued the idea of 'an organic link between the land of Israel and the Jewish people through the mediation of the Torah'.[10] Religious Zionism obtained from twelfth and thirteenth centuries Jewish traditions the sanction for the settlement of the land of Israel by Jews: settling in Israel 'was a solemn duty, for it alone made possible an encounter between the two holinesses, of the land and the people'.[11]

While Religious Zionism did set up an opportunistic, tactical alliance with secular Zionists in the pursuit of the 'Israel' enterprise, it continued to see itself as 'the sole authentic representative of Judaism as a whole'.[12] Its leaders saw in Zionism, even in its secular manifestation, the hand of divine providence that enabled the oppressed Jews to return to the Promised Land.[13] Dieckhoff refers to this approach as 'nationalised messianism', which saw in the nascent Israeli State a deep religious significance, while affirming the active role of human effort in its achievement.[14] The coming together of the secular and divine in the realization of the state of Israel was given its most influential expression by Rav Abraham Yitzhak Kook, who later became the first Chief Rabbi (Ashkenazi) of Palestine.

Rav Kook saw Zionism as a response to the divine call and not a result of human effort, and thus as the first step in a messianic process; he said:[15]

This wonder is performed before our eyes, not by the work of man or by his machinations, but by the miraculous ways of Him who is perfect in knowledge, the Lord of War, who bringeth forth salvation. This is certain – the voice of the Lord is heard. This is not a hastening and premature anticipation of the time; it is the fortunate moment, the hour of grace, of 'the revealed signs of the End'.

This messianic process, according to Rav Kook, was the commencement of an inevitable 'revealed signs of the End'.[16] The end was certain, though not the pace: that would result from the realization of a 'complete religious consciousness'; this would depend on human effort which could hasten or delay it, but had no power to negate it;[17] as a student of Rav Kook clarified:[18]

We are living in the last phase of history ... the Redemption of Israel in our days is not dependent on Israel's deeds ... Divine guidance in our time does not reckon with the deeds of Israel in general, but is in accordance with the plan of the world ... None of the processes of Redemption in our days – true and faithful Redemption from which there is no return – are dependent on our deeds.

Rav Kook affirmed that redemption was linked to the divine purpose:[19]

Only on the quality of the entire nation's link with the source of life, with the Torah of the Lord, does the success and strength of Zionism depend, now and in generations to come. But if we abandon the Torah there is no hope, and every flower will wither and every root will turn into dust.

Rav Kook applauded the role of the secular pioneers in the Zionist movement as pursuing the creation of a 'holy nation':[20] even though they may not be aware of it or even if they were to deny it, they were certainly instruments of God's will. Secular Zionism, like other atheist ideologies, had a 'temporary legitimacy' till it was possible, in Rav Kook's words, to 'purge the impurities that have become attached to religion to get rid of the dross which hides the face of God from man'.[21] Taking this concept further, Rav Kook insisted that Zionism could not be complete without addressing the spiritual needs of the Jewish people, bringing together the secular vital forces of society and its spiritual energy, so that, 'faith could light up the whole of social existence'.[22] Rav Kook's idea of the Jewish state (twelve years from realization at the time of his death) was: 'The foundation of God's throne on earth – a state whose sole aspiration is that the Lord must be one and His name must be one, which constitutes in truth, the supreme bliss.'[23] With the setting up of the state of Israel in 1948, Religious Zionism, in line with Rav Kook's thinking, saw in it the 'dawn of redemption'.[24]

Religious Zionism never lost sight of the supremacy of the messianic ideal in the Zionist movement for Israel even when its votaries explained the role of the secular strand of the movement as an expression of divine will. It was matched in zeal by another strident Right-wing element in the Zionist movement – the Union of Zionists – Revisionists, led by Vladimir Zeev Jabotinsky (1880–1940). The Revisionists accorded primacy to the political sphere and the exercise of power in it: i.e. the realization of a Jewish majority state in the 'historic space of the Hebrews' (i.e. on both sides of the Jordan river).[25] In Jabotinsky's exaltation of the Israeli state, Dieckhoff sees a 'national messianism'[26] and a 'patriotic messianism'[27] with a religious colouring. This is exemplified by the resolution of the New Zionist Organization (set up by Jabotinsky in 1935) that Zionism must ensure that 'the sacred treasures of Jewish tradition' are rooted in the life of the nation. As Dieckhoff explains, Jabotinsky saw religion as having played a historic role in serving the Jewish nation amidst serious difficulties, and believed it would be the same cementing force in the new Jewish state.[28] But, he went beyond this instrumental role for religion: he believed that the religious zeal of the people would serve the immanent nation in creating 'a spiritual principle, a spiritual family' that would imbue the nation with an enduring strength and vitality.[29]

Jabotinsky, like the Religious Zionists, saw a unique and profound link between the Jewish people and the land of Palestine. In fact, in his early writings, he even defined the Jew in terms of his link with Palestine: '[The Jew of biblical times] had begun to exist as a member of a nation because he had taken root in the earth, the land, the soil of Palestine; he was the fruit of the womb of the motherland.'[30] Later, he described Jewish identity in racial/ethnic terms:[31]

> Territory, language, religion, common history do not form the substance of a nation, they are only its attributes ... The substance of a nation, the first and last fortress of the uniqueness of its form, is found in its specific physical character, in the 'recipe' of its racial composition ... all said and done, when all sorts of coverings due to history, climate, the natural environment, external influences are removed, the nation is reduced to its racial hard core.

Unlike other Zionists, particularly the Religious Zionists, Jabotinsky was deeply conscious of the Palestinians' presence in the 'Promised Land'; he saw them as a nationality and not as a mere component of the Arab nation.[32] He believed in the inevitability of a violent encounter between them and resurgent Zionism.[33]

While Jabotinsky himself maintained a strong ideological distance from the ultra-nationalist fascism of the times, his exaltation of the Jewish nation founded through violence inspired the next generation of Israeli Right-wing extremists who made Revisionism 'a movement of revolt' against the Arabs, the British, and even moderate Jews in Palestine.[34] The most important movement was Irgun, which, from 1937, carried out a campaign of violence against the Palestinians and, from 1944, against the British. As Dieckhoff has noted, Irgun saw this violence in 'metaphysical' terms: as a necessity for the creation of the Jewish nation, recalling the savage encounters of the Jewish people with different enemies throughout their history, as also the violent wars that led to freedom for the Americans, the Poles, the Serbs and the Irish.[35]

Beyond Irgun, other movements emerged on the hardline nationalist Right, such as a new Revisionist movement led by Abba Ahimeir (1897–1962) and Uri Tzevi Greenberg (1897–1981) that came very close to fascism.[36] In 1928, Ahimeir published a series of articles praising fascism as an authentic national revival movement which alone was able to overcome democratic degeneracy and defeat communism.[37] Ahimeir called for a Jewish state based on 'instinct and senses', and for Zionism 'to appear as the expression of the "eternal soul" of the Jewish people, and to make real the promise of salvation contained in messiamism'.[38]

Greenberg, the poet of the extreme Right, saw 'the unchangeable and perfect biological unity' of the Jewish people, and the 'absolute difference' between them and non-Jews which made all understanding between them impossible, the only dialogue possible being the clash of arms.[39] The nation state of Israel was to be achieved through war marked by extreme violence: the enemies were all Christians (due to their anti-Semitism) and Muslims (for they stood for gory brutal anti-Semitism, and were imbued with murderous violence against Jews). Jewish victories would herald Greenberg's 'era of redemption' which would be marked by an all-conquering Israel, recovering through arms the Kingdom of David and subordinating all others to maintain Israel's supremacy.[40]

As Deickhoff has noted, Ahimeir and Greenberg exemplify 'Jewish Fascism', making Zionism into a movement wedded to sustained violence.[41] They inspired the split in the Revisionist military organization to separate from Irgun and set up the 'Stern Gang' headed by Avraham Stern. During the Second World War, while other Jewish leaders in Palestine, socialist and Rightwing, backed the British war effort against Nazi Germany, Stern focused entirely on anti-British activity, seeing in Britain the 'real enemy of the Jewish people', while Nazism was seen as a movement driven by 'reasonable anti-Semitism' with which some understanding was possible.[42]

Impelled by anti-British hatred and attracted to Italian and German Fascism due to kinship based on mindset and approach, defined by Dieckhoff as 'totalitarian messianism', Stern pursued cooperation between his group (described 'as the resurgent Jewish popular – national movement') and the two Fascist states.[43] Killed by the British in February 1942, his followers in the newly-named group, Lehi, indulged in a protracted violent campaign against the British between 1944 and 1948. Dieckhoff suggests that Lehi's top leaders who had been attracted, first to Fascism and, later, for a while, to the Soviet Union, had been irresistibly drawn to the idea of total revolution. It may be noted in parenthesis that, after the emergence of Israel, Lehi's three top leaders pursued different paths – one moving to the far Left, the other to the far Right, while the third, Yitzak Shamir, joined mainstream politics and became Prime Minister in 1983.[44]

In his brilliant reflections on the place of Zionism in the continuum of Jewish history, Alain Dieckhoff has pointed out that all strains of Zionism, including secular Zionism, were linked to Jewish heritage by the 'continuation of the messianic impulse'.[45] He notes in this context that even the premier Socialist Zionist, David Ben Gurion, while setting up a state on modern Western lines, did not reject the uniqueness imparted to the nascent state by the Jewish identity of its nationals; Dieckhoff explains it thus:[46]

> It was simply that in modern times Jews were no longer to be made 'a dynasty of priests and a holy nation', but given a model state which would be an example to edify the whole human race. So it was now through the political sphere that the Jews were called to accomplish their destiny as a chosen people, bringing about the era of universal brotherhood promised by the prophets. The messianic dynamic was not abandoned, but reformulated and placed under control ..... The influence of the messianic theme showed that it was impossible for Zionism to break free from Judaism, and signaled the real if partial continuity between the two phenomena.

As Dieckhoff completed his survey of Zionist thought with the founding of Israel in 1948, he instinctively anticipated a sustained tension between the imperatives of the state order and the 'messianic impulse' that informed the nation state and gave it its unique character, wherein an 'excessive invocation of the messianic vision' would severely constrain the political sphere in the state and subordinate the latter to its utopian vision.[47]

His concerns materialized with the expansion of Israel's territories after the 1967 war to the West Bank, seen as the 'sacred spaces' of Judea and Samaria by Israel's Right-wing movement exemplified by the Gush Emunim [Bloc of the Faithful] and the ideology of 'neo-Zionism' that inspires and motivates this movement. Gush Emunim is in the tradition of the religion-based ideology of Religious Zionism and the xenophobic National Zionism of Revisionism and its ideological successors.

Israel's Messianic Politics After 1967

The wellsprings of contemporary Israeli extremism and violence lie in the Jewish messianic tradition that goes back several thousand years which has been reinvigorated in the country after 1967. Jewish messianic discourse 'with strong fundamentalist bases' is little known and less understood. This has been a matter of concern to liberal Israeli writers: Israel Shahak has noted that 'hardly anybody speaks of Jewish fundamentalism, which is growing in Israel and in the US even more';[48] he goes on to elaborate:

> I do not mean by that the negligible splinters of Kahanism, but the much more influential and dangerous messianic ideology of the religious settlers in the occupied territories, organizationally represented by the Gush Emunim. Unlike the Kahanist splinters, Gush Emunim is considered perfectly respectable. On some important issues, it is supported by the entire opposition in Israel, both right wing and religious, as well as by some influential Jewish and Christian groups in the U.S. Although it has organised demonstrations against Yitzhak Rabin, some of its leaders remain his closest friends. Contrary to what is usually believed, *the ideology of Gush Emunim is, in my view, even more extremist than those attributed to the extremes of Islamic fundamentalism.* [Emphasis added.]

After analyzing the ideology and the beliefs of Gush Emunim, Shahak concluded: 'All this resembles the ideology of the most extremist Islamic organizations, except that one would not find it mentioned in the *New York Times*.'[49] Israeli writers have repeatedly pointed out that Israeli extremist organizations have powerful religious personalities with elaborate belief systems behind them; neither the organizations nor the religious figures are marginal figures but organizations and individuals who play a significant role in Israeli religious and political discourse.

Gush Emunim emerges from the tradition of Religious Zionism, and thus, as Israel Idalovichi has pointed out, its roots are 'deeply anchored in Jewish tradition and religion'.[50] It draws its spiritual inspiration and ideological belief-system from the writings of the late Rabbi Avraham Yitzchak Kook and the discourses of his son, Rabbi Zvi Yehuda Kook (1891-1982), commenting on the beliefs and writings of his father. In line with Rav Kook's thinking, the central belief of the

Gush Emunim is that the Jewish people today are in an era which heralds the beginning of the redemption process. This is confirmed by the rise of modern Zionism and the political gains of the movement such as the Balfour Declaration and the Zionist enterprise that led to the setting up of the state of Israel. Since Israel's victory in the Six-Day War of 1967, the country has become a political reality that is transcendental. As Idalovichi has noted, Rabbi Zvi Yehuda Kook and his school see the Land of Israel as 'possessing unique mystical characteristics, which correspond to the unique traits of the Jewish people. The land is not only the substratum that sustains the existence of the people, but is a value in and of itself.'[51] The land of Israel has been liberated not only from a political adversary, but also from the *sitra ahra* (the 'other side', the 'devil's camp'), that is, from a mystical force which embodies evil, defilement and moral corruption. By virtue of the 1967 war, the Divine presence (*Shekhina*), which has rested upon the Zionist enterprise from its inception, arises from the dust, and is saved from the existential exile in which the Jew had languished. Having raised the Shekhina from its debasement, the return of even an inch of land, would be surrender to the rule of the *klipa*, the concept of Jewish mysticism which symbolizes the forces of evil in the cosmos; in this situation, the sitra ahra would regain sovereignty.[52]

Gush Emunim has described itself as a 'movement for the renewal of Zionist fulfillment';[53] it defines its role thus:

> Our aim is to bring about a large movement of reawakening among the Jewish people for the fulfillment of the Zionist vision in its full scope, with the recognition that the source of the vision is Jewish tradition and roots, and that its ultimate objective is the full redemption of the Jewish people and the entire world.

Gush Emunim, styling itself as the 'Zionism of Redemption', emerged from the Six-Day War, as, in Lustick's words, 'a redemptionist, visionary and territory centered' movement,[54] though it acquired its formal character only after 'the earthquake' of the 1973 war. As Lustick has noted, young religious students had participated in the 1973 war for the first time, thus acquiring a moral standing equal to that of their secular compatriots. They believed Israel's setbacks in the war were the result of Israel's 'demonstrated weakness' after the glorious victory of 1967, particularly its willingness to retreat from occupied territories.[55] Thus, the state had deviated from its messianic development. They called for 'a spiritual rejuvenation of (Israeli) society whose most important expression and source of strength would be settlement and communion with the greater, liberated land of Israel'.[56] Gush Emunim, as the spiritual and ideological successor of Rav Kook's messianism and Jabotinsky's attachment to the 'Revived Land', gave expression to this Messianic vision with the single-point programme to extend Israeli sovereignty across the entire 'Promised Land', commencing with the territories occupied in 1967; the setting up, expansion and consolidation of settlements across the occupied territories was the instrument utilized by the movement to realize its vision. Hanan Porat, a Gush Emunim leader, set out the organization's position thus:[57]

> For us the Land of Israel is a Land of destiny, a chosen Land, not just an existentially defined homeland. It is the Land from which the voice of God has called to us ever since that first call to the first Hebrew: 'Come and go forth from your Land where you were born and from your father's house to the Land that I will show you.'

As Sprinzak has noted, Gush Emunim saw itself as a movement to revitalize historic Zionism, which in its view, had died out in Israel in the 1950s and 1960s.[58] It sought to achieve this by reviving the pioneering spirit of the founders of Israel, exhorting its followers to eschew short-term interests in pursuing a larger course. Jewish Messianism, as elaborated by the religious figures behind Gush Emunim, is founded on three broad beliefs:

(*i*)   the Jewish people are unique, distinct and separate; they have been divinely chosen and constitute a religious nation;

(*ii*) the land of Israel is the land promised to the Jewish people by God and they control this land and live on it by divine command; and,

(*iii*) after a long night of darkness, the era of redemption for the Jewish people has already commenced and will achieve its full realization, with divine blessing, guidance and support.

Gush Emunim asserted that its claim to the land of Israel was founded on divine sanction as set out in the Old Testament and elaborated by Jewish Rabbis over the centuries. Rabbi Zvi Yehuda Kook, the son of Rabbi Kook, became the principal spiritual leader of Gush Emunim. Recalling the writings of Rabbi Moshe Nachmanides (1194–c. 1270), he asserted that the destined borders of the Jewish state, the 'Land of

Israel', would include: Transjordan, the Golan Heights and the 'Bashan' (the Jabal Druze region in Syria).[59] As Sprinzak has noted:[60]

> When Gush ideologues speak about the complete [whole] Land of Israel they have in mind not only the post-1967 territory, but the land promised in the Covenant (Genesis 15) as well. This includes the occupied territories—especially Judea and Samaria, the very heart of the historic Israeli nation, and vast territories that belong now to Jordan, Syria and Iraq.

Occupation of this land, according to Rabbi Zvi Kook, was a divine injunction:[61]

> We are commanded both to possess and to settle [the land]. The meaning of possession is conquest, and in performing this mitzvah, we can perform the other – the commandment to settle ... We cannot evade this commandment ... Torah, war, and settlement – they are three things in one and we rejoice in the authority we have been given for each of them.

However, Gush Emunim and its religious mentors have regularly re-defined Israel's territorial claims in accordance with the prevailing military situation. Thus, following Israel's 1982 attack on Lebanon, a number of prominent Right-wing rabbis declared Southern Lebanon as part of the historic 'Land of Israel'.[62] Another rabbi, Yisrael Ariel, went further: he asserted that the boundaries of the Land of Israel included Lebanon up to Tripoli in the north, Sinai, Syria, part of Iraq and even part of Kuwait.[63] Later, in the same month, he called for the annexation and settlement of most of Lebanon, including its capital Beirut, to Israel, at any price:[64]

> Beirut is part of the Land of Israel—about that there is no controversy, and being that Lebanon is part of the Land of Israel we must declare that we have no intention of leaving. We must declare that Lebanon is flesh of our flesh, as is Tel Aviv and Haifa, and that we do this by right of the moral power granted to us in the Torah.

In 1984, Yaacov Feitelson, a prominent Right-wing politician, set out Israel's imperial vision thus:[65]

> I am speaking of a tremendous vision. We are only in the infancy of the Zionist movement ... Israel must squarely face up to the implementation of the Zionist movement ... a vision that has not changed since the days of Herzl. As is known, Herzl never indicated what the borders of the state were to be ... in his time the settlement [by Jews] of the Syrian desert was

discussed. I say that Israel should establish new cities throughout the entire area. I mean really the whole area of the Middle East, without limiting ourselves: we should never say about any place: "here we stop".

Armed with these divine sanctions, modern-day Israeli rabbis have issued halakhic rulings (rulings made by priests on the basis of religious texts) pertaining to the sanctity of these territories occupied by Israel, enjoining upon the Jewish people to continue to hold these territories as a religious duty. Thus, the Chief Rabbinate stated the following in respect of Temple Mount [the Al-Aqsa Mosque]: [66]

> The Temple Mount is Mt. Moriah, the site of the Temple and of the Holy of Holies, the place where the Lord God of Israel chose to house His Name, which was sanctified by ten holy blessings by David, King of Israel: the Jewish people's right to the Temple Mount and the site of the Temple is an eternal and inalienable divine right, over which there can be no concessions.

The divinely ordained claims to the 'Land of Israel' of Gush Emunim and its religious leaders have placed before them the challenge of how to define and deal with the native Palestinians. The Gush view has been to see them as temporary-alien residents. As a Gush spokesman said in 1980:[67]

> The Arabs must know that there is a master here, the Jewish people. It rules over Eretz Yisrael ... The Arabs are temporary dwellers who happened to live in this country. There are commandments in the Bible concerning such temporary dwellers and we should act accordingly.

Rav Zvi Kook provided a clear rabbinical injunction:[68]

> We find ourselves here by virtue of our forefathers' inheritance, the foundation of the Bible and history, and there is no one that can change this fact. What does it resemble? A man left his house and others came and invaded it. This is exactly what happened to us. *There are those who claim that these are Arab lands here. It is all a lie and falsehood. There are absolutely no Arab lands here.* [Emphasis added.]

Not surprisingly, the concept of 'transfer' of the Palestinian population (voluntary, agreed or compulsory) has been central to mainstream Zionist thinking. It preoccupied Zionist leaders before 1948 and became even more important after 1967 when Israel occupied large territories which had no Jewish population. As Nur Masalha has noted, 'Use of force and coercion formed an important element in Israel's policy towards the

Palestinians in the post 1967 period.'[69] In fact, a major Gush Emunim spokesman publicly advocated that 'the best course of action would be to bring about large-scale Arab emigration through the deliberate creation of economic hardship in the West Bank and Gaza'.[70]

This approach was given religious sanction with the assertion by rabbinical authorities that expulsion of the Palestinians was necessitated by divine commandment. Thus, Rabbi Yisrael Ariel stated:[71]

> On the one hand there is a commandment of settling Eretz-Yisrael, which is defined by our sages of blessed memory also as the commandment of 'inheritance and residence' – a commandment mentioned many times in the Torah. Every young student understands that 'inheritance and residence' means conquering and settling the land. The Torah repeats the commandment 'You shall dispossess all the inhabitants of the land' tens of times, and Rashi [Rabbi Shlomo Yitzhaki, a paramount Bible and Talmud commentator in the eleventh century] explains that 'You shall dispossess – You shall expel.' The Torah itself uses the term 'expulsion' a number of times such as: 'Since you shall expel the inhabitants of the country with my help.' The substance of this commandment is to expel the inhabitants of the land whoever they may be.

He again asserted:[72]

> Doesn't granting of 'autonomy'... to the Arabs of Judea and Samaria contravene a Torah commandment? Is the prohibition 'they shall not dwell in your land' no longer a prohibition? Is the Gentile suddenly permitted to reside in Jerusalem? And has the ban already been lifted on Gentiles entering a place whereof it is said: 'And the stranger who approaches shall be put to death'? And is control of the Temple Mount no longer a duty and an imperative?

Armed with such solid religious support and with the full cooperation of Right-wing governments, the Israeli establishment, as Masalha has pointed out, sanctified the use of violence against Palestinians to 'forestall any moves that might retard the messianic process of territorial redemption and land conquest'.[73] The state apparatus provided weapons and training to Jewish settlers and sanctioned attacks on Arabs and their property. The settlers organized themselves into a well-disciplined militant private army subject not to state law but divine law.[74]

Under the Gush Emunim umbrella, a number of violent and extremist organizations emerged to pursue the organization's territorial agenda and attack Arabs. Many of them attempted to destroy the Al-

Aqsa mosque so that the construction of the Jewish temple could begin. However, most of the extremists apprehended by the security forces for murder and other serious crimes were treated with considerable leniency, particularly following the intervention of prominent religious leaders.[75] The prominent Israeli military leader and academic, General Yehoshafat Harkabi, described these extremists and their activities thus:[76]

> [they are] serious people who occupy high positions among their public ... they have a rational state of mind and their chief motivation stems apparently from the awareness that annexation of the West Bank together with its Arab population would be disastrous and tantamount to national suicide – unless that population were thinned out and made to flee by terrorism. This reasoning is not moral, but it stems from the rational conclusion of the policy that aims at annexation. Such terrorism is neither a 'punishment' nor a deterrent; it is a political instrument.

The Palestinians are routinely compared by Gush Emunim rabbis and their ideological popularizers to ancient Canaanites or ancient Amalekites whose extermination or expulsion by ancient Israelites was, according to the Bible, predestined. Thus, Rabbi Zvi Kook, on the basis of the authority of Maimonides (1135–1204), stated that Canaanites had three choices: to flee, to accept Jewish overlordship, or to fight and thus face extermination.[77] Again, to see the Palestinians as the 'Amalek' is even more invidious. In the Old Testament, the Amalek were a nomadic people living in Sinai and Southern Palestine. They are referred to as the arch-enemies of the Jews against whom war should be waged as a sacred duty so that their 'memory (is) blotted out' forever.[78] Though the Old Testament states that the Amalek were wiped out in the eighth century BC, traditional Jewish writings continue to depict the Amalek as the Jews' arch-foe against whom the Jews will struggle until the coming of the Messiah, when God will destroy the last remnants of the Amalek.[79]

Uriel Tal has pointed out that, on the basis of biblical sources, three positions have emerged in Jewish religious writings with regard to the human and civilian rights of non-Jews. These are: (*i*) the restrictions of rights; (*ii*) the denial of rights; and (*iii*) the call for genocide based on the Torah.[80] With regard to the restrictions of rights, Jewish religious leaders have rejected the principle of equality of the rights of all persons as a foreign democratic principle which has no place in the holy land. Following from this, the principle of equal rights is not binding on

Israel's dealings with Arab residents in the country, and the latter can only have certain partial rights.

The position relating to the denial of the rights is based on the conviction that there can be no place for Arabs in the holy land; and that, in due course, they should be totally expelled from the land of Israel. The argument in support of this is as follows: The commandment to conquer the land 'is above the human and moral considerations of the national rights of the gentiles to our land', Rabbi Shlomo Aviner, a student of Rav Zvi Yehuda Kook, claims in his articles, 'The Messianic Realism', *(Morasha,* Vol. 9); he adds: 'Indeed, Israel was commanded in the Torah that "thou shalt be holy," but we were not commanded to be moral; and the general principles of morality which have been accepted by mankind, in principle at least, do not commit the Jew for he was chosen to be beyond them (Nekuda, No. 43).'[81]

The third position relating to genocide of the non-Jews is again based on the Torah. Uriel Tal notes with concern that, with very few exceptions, the call for eradication of the Amalek (= Arab) from the holy land has not been rejected by Rabbinical teachers in Israel. Rabbi Israel Hess, in his article, 'The Commandment of Genocide under the Torah', published in 1980, asserted:[82] 'The day is not far when we shall all be called to this holy war, this commandment of the annihilation of Amalek' –that is, the commandment of genocide. The manner of carrying this out is described in I Samuel 15.3: 'Go now, attack Amalek, and deal with him and all that he has under the ban. Do not spare him, but kill man and woman, child and infant, ox and sheep, camel and ass.'[83] Rabbi Hess went on to say:[84]

Against this holy war God declares a counter-jihad ... in order to emphasize that this is the background for the annihilation, and that it is over this that the war is being waged and that it is not a conflict between two peoples ... God is not content that we annihilate Amalek – 'blot out the memory of Amalek' – he also enlists personally in this war ... because, as has been said, he has a personal interest in this matter, this is the principal aim.

The prominent Israeli journalist and academic, Danny Rubinstein, has pointed out that this equation of the Palestinians with the Amalek permeates Gush Emunim's writings.[85] Another Israeli academic, Yoram Peri, pointed out in an article in 1984:[86]

The solution of the transport and the trucks is not the end of the story. There is a further stage which the proponents of racist Zionism do not usually refer to explicitly, since the conditions for it are not ripe. But the principles are there, clear and inevitable. *This is the stage of genocide, the annihilation of the Palestinian people.* [Emphasis added.]

Gush Emunim's rabbinical supporters have actively advocated a widespread campaign of violence against the inhabitants of the occupied territories. Rabbi Yisrael Ariel has argued that the killing of Arabs was not murder:[87]

> Anyone who searches through the code of Maimonides, which is the pillar of the halacha in the Jewish world, [and searches for] the concept 'you shall not murder' or the concept 'holy blood' with regard to the killing of a non-Jew – will search in vain, because he will not find [it] ... It follows from the words of Maimonides that a Jew who kills a non-Jew ... is exempt from the prohibition 'you shall not murder'. And so Maimonides writes in the halachas of murder: 'An Israelite who kills a resident alien is not sentenced to death in the court of law.'

Professor Amnon Rubinstein, citing several occasions when Gush writers have referred to Arabs as the 'Amalek of today', commented on Gush's activities thus:[88]

> *We are dealing with a political ideology of violence. It is needless to show how this ideology is expressed in the way the Arabs are treated.* The Rabbis of Gush Emunim – except for the few brave ones ... publicly preach incitement to kill Arab civilians, and those who kill civilians, and are caught and brought to court, are later amnestied by the Chief of Staff *[General Raphael Eitan], who believes in the use of violence that the Arabs 'understand'. Those who think that it is possible to differentiate between blood and blood are wrong. The verdict on 'Amalek' can easily be extended to the enemies within, the traitors.* [Emphasis added.]

In his book, *Reckless Rites*, Elliott Horozwitz has referred to a report in the *New Yorker* of early 2004 where the writer, Jeffrey Goldberg, quoted Israeli settlers in the West Bank and Gaza speaking of the Palestinians as 'Amalek'. The Chairman of the Council of Settlements said: 'We will destroy them. We won't kill them all. But we will destroy their ability to think as a nation. We will destroy Palestinian nationalism.' A leading Likud activist, Moshe Feiglin, told Goldberg: 'The Arabs engage in typical Amalek behaviour. I can't prove this genetically, but this is the behaviour of Amalek.'[89]

The Messianism of Success

As Aviezer Ravitzky has noted, Rav Kook and his son represent the messianism of success which historically has shared space with the messianism of despair and catastrophe in Jewish tradition, with rabbis from each tradition giving respectively optimistic or pessimistic interpretations of historical events.[90] The latter tradition 'originates in disaster and distress' and seeks to move away from current reality; the former sees signs of hope and redemption in historical events. Thus, Rav Kook saw even in the Holocaust a healing process, a 'surgery' and 'treatment' to prepare the Jewish nation for its salvation.[91] It therefore followed that the success of the Zionist enterprise and the setting up of the state of Israel were interpreted by him and his followers as 'redemptive awakening that is ... exclusively based on sensations of success and divine favour'.[92] Rabbi Menahem Brod expressed this sense of optimism and success most eloquently:[93]

> All the great events that have been happening in recent times prepare the climate for the idea of Messiah. For example, the ingathering of exiles. Suddenly, we see a tremendous revolution, that the country [the former Soviet Union] which forcibly held in all of the Jews is beginning to release them at a tremendous pace ... The messianic period is manifested also by 'beating their swords into plowshares', and what do we see before our very eyes if not the cessation of the arms race, with tanks being turned into tractors? One more point: in messianic times, the whole world will unite in faith in the Creator of the World. And behold, you see that communism, which was a big stumbling-block to faith, has collapsed, and there is a renewed flocking toward religion.

Alain Dieckhoff has referred to Gush Emunim's activities as 'true territorial messianism'.[94] He is concerned that the neo-Zionism of the movement's adherents serves to restrict the autonomy of the political sphere in Israel as it derives its absolutist agenda from divine law, ruling out Politics as a space for freedom, negotiation and deliberation. Drawing from the extremist ideology of Jabotinsky and his successors, Israel's Right-wing groups are veering towards the 'totalitarian temptation', seeking to impose homogeneity through force on a fundamentally varied society.[95] Dieckhoff goes on to say:[96]

> This reduction of the political sphere to pure force is characteristic of the far Right in Israel today, when it sees political action only as pitiless confrontation with its adversaries – first, Arabs 'irreducibly hostile to an

Israel in the Middle East'; secondly the nations of the world that are 'anti Semitic by nature'; and, in addition, Jewish left wing opponents accused of treating with the enemy. In the name of ideological coherence (preserving the integrity of the country), all compromise is instantly rejected as an unacceptable surrender.

According to Dieckhoff, since 1977, when Begin became Prime Minister in Israel, 'neo-Zionism has been a potent force in Israel'.[97] He notes in this context that the strength and allure of neo-Zionism emerges from the fact that it represents 'a modern revival of permanent Zionist motives' of the Religious Zionists pertaining to the messianic vision of the redemptive value of the Jewish nation-state.[98] The coming together of a number of religion-oriented parties with the secular Right-wing parties has imparted a strong political support to the neo-Zionist ideology. This process had commenced even before 1977. In 1974, Shimon Peres had initiated the policy of 'functional compromise': working closely with Gush Emunim, he ordained that all land inside the West Bank and the Gaza Strip not being used by anyone could be confiscated and provided to the Jews for their exclusive use.[99] Thus, Gush Emunim succeeded in changing Israel's settlement policy, enabling settlements to spread throughout the West Bank and to occupy large areas of Gaza Strip.

Later, after Begin came to power in 1977, 'a holy alliance' was set up between the Gush Emunim and successive secular Israeli Governments which remains in place to this day.[100] In this way, Religious Zionism allied with the 'secular' right to set up 'an association of religion with hawkishness in foreign policy'.[101] This was further solidified when Benjamin Netanyahu became Prime Minister in 1996: he put in place 'the most religiously dependent and Right-wing government in Israel's history', till then.[102] Since then, the ultra-Orthodox, who had remained aloof from the Zionist state, have moved closer to the Religious Zionists, with the latter in turn increasingly adopting the rigorous religious practices of the former. These developments have served to reduce the representation in the Knesett of the two mainstream parties —Labour and Likud; the latter, under Sharon, had responded to these developments by moving close to the neo-Zionist groups.[103]

Successive Israeli political leaders from different parties have allied themselves with messianic Rabbis and the organizations inspired or led by them. This has led to a remarkable expansion of Israeli settlements in occupied territories even when the governments of the day have criticized them. Ariel Sharon, as a member of the first Likud Government in 1977, initiated a significant settlement effort in the occupied territories: earlier, between 1967 and 1976, Israel had built twenty settlements in the West Bank and around East Jerusalem; after this, under Sharon, in less than four years, sixty-two new settlements were constructed, significantly changing the landscape on the West Bank and in the Gaza strip.[104] As Neve Gordon has noted, the Gush Emunim:[105]

> provided the cadres for new Jewish settlements, and Mr. Sharon provided both the military justification and, at various points in his career, the authority to seize lands owned by the occupied Palestinians. Not surprisingly, every time the legality of the settlements has been challenged before Israel's High Court of Justice, 'security concerns', not religious edicts, have been used to justify the disposition of the indigenous inhabitants.

Gush Emunim's partnership with Ariel Sharon in the settlement enterprise was remarkably successful: if in the early 1970s there were no more than a few hundred Jewish settlers living in a handful of settlements, today 'one cannot travel more than a few kilometers within the Occupied Territories without running into a settlement. Taken together, the settlements house about 400,000 settlers.'[106]

Gordon has pointed out that the success of the settlement policy is based on the policy of Gush Emunim to secularize and militarize its messianic inspiration which has enabled it to change 'Israel's collective consciousness in attaining both cultural and political hegemony'; Ariel Sharon's role was to 'link the Messianic ideology of Greater Israel with the militarist ideology of Greater Israel'.[107] The settlement policy is crucial to realize the Jewish messianic ideology, since Jewish messianism requires not the appearance of a messiah but the control of the land of biblical Israel.

Liberal Israeli writers have noted how Israeli messianism and the inspiration and motivation derived from it by Gush Emunim and its various followers encouraged considerable violence against the Arabs. In April 1984, an attempt to blow up six Arab buses full of passengers was exposed and prevented: the perpetrators were from the Gush Emunim settlement. It was later learnt that these suspects had indulged in other acts of terror such as the assassination attempt on Arab Mayors in June 1980, and the murderous attack on the Islamic College in Hebron in July 1983. Various other acts of terror have been attributed to the followers of Gush Emunim, including a possible proposal to blow up the two mosques at Al-Aqsa. Sprinzak admitted ruefully that it was clear that a small but significant number of hardcore Gush Emunim members either participated in the terrorist activities, supported them indirectly or lent them at least a spiritual legitimacy.[108]

Sprinzak, as early as 1985, regretted the fact that Israeli political parties and Government Ministers and officials tended to ignore the ugly side of the settlement process and focused attention only on Arab violence and terrorism.[109] Due to this silence and inaction, the settlers built up their armed strength and, through the 1980s, pursued a number of private operations. They rejected the term 'terrorist' and saw themselves as the 'true' defenders of the settlements.[110]

Israel Shahak has drawn attention to the apocalyptic implications of the messianic beliefs of the followers of Gush Emunim.[111] He refers in this regard to the remarks of a member of the Jewish underground who was caught in 1984 while laying bombs under Arab buses and planning to blow up the mosque at Al-Aqsa; the man had stated:[112]

> the demolition of these mosques would have infuriated the hundreds of millions of Muslims in the entire world. Their rage would inevitably lead to a war which, in all likelihood, would escalate into a world war. In such a war, the scale of casualties would be formidable enough to promote the process of Redemption of the Jews and of the land of Israel. All the Muslims would by then disappear, which means that everything would be ready for the coming of the Messiah.

The man had also referred to the tight control the Gush Emunim rabbis exercised over the organization and their contempt and hatred for secular Jews who dared to disobey the divine will.[113]

Sprinzak has attempted to explain the political effectiveness of Gush Emunim on the basis of what he refers to as the 'Iceberg Model' of political extremism.[114] His contention is that Gush Emunim is only the tip of an iceberg of a broader religious subculture which started its meteoric development in the 1950s. It is the support of this social and political subculture which made Gush Emunim so effective and irresistible. Again, according to him, Gush Emunim is the tip of a serious cultural and social iceberg which grew quietly over many years until circumstances shaped its extremist tip.[115] For Gush Emunim, the setting up of the settlements is aimed at absorbing the secular population of the State of Israel into their concept of Jewish identity as religious, ethnocentric and anti-liberal and anti-universalist. To illustrate this, Shahak and Mezvinsky have quoted a number of Gush Emunim ideologues. Rabbi Shmaryanu Arieli, a disciple of the two Kooks, said of the 1967 war that a 'metaphysical transformation' had taken place in that the Israeli conquests had transferred land from the power of Satan to the divine spheres, proving that the 'messianic era' had arrived.[116] Rabbi E. Hadaya spoke of the 1967 conquests thus:[117]

> [The conquests of 1967] liberated the land from the other side [a polite name for Satan], from a mystical force that embodies evil, defilement and moral corruption. We [the Jews] are thus entering an era in which absolute sovereignty rules over corporeality.

Rabbi Yehuda Amital, a prominent Gush leader, had this to say about the 1973 Yom Kippur War:[118]

> The war broke out against the background of the revival of the kingdom of Israel, which in its metaphysical (not only symbolic) status is evidence of the decline of the spirit of defilement in the Western world ... The Gentiles are fighting for their mere survival as Gentiles, as the ritually unclean. Iniquity is fighting its battle for survival. It knows that in the wars of God there will not be a peace for Satan, for the spirit of defilement, or for the remains of Western culture, the proponents of which are, as it were secular Jews.

Finally, Rabbi Benny Alon, leader of the extremist group, Emunim, within the Gush Emunim, said in 1992:[119]

> Security considerations in favour of the settlements are not the point. As I see it, politics rest upon spirituality. A body politic needs a soul. Israel's security and even the survival of the Jewish nation are no more than material dimensions of the spiritual Jewish depth. When we say that we must prevent the formation of a Palestinian state in order to save the Jewish state from extinction, we are not taking about spiritual things.

The messianic movement has not just sponsored extremist movements among Gush Emunim and its various followers, but it has also encouraged ultra-extreme organizations beyond Gush Emunim. During the 1980s, the best representative of this tendency was the Right-wing political party, Kach, headed by the radical, Rabbi Meir Kahane. Kahane and his movement originated in New York where, as the Head of the

Jewish Defence League, he set up a vigilante movement in Jewish neighbourhoods and also led attacks against Soviet entities.

He came to Israel in September 1971 and soon plunged into extremist activities. Initially, he targeted the Christian missions and a Black American sect; then his focus turned to the Arabs. He and his group were involved with planning and executing a number of terrorist acts against Arabs. He was jailed briefly in 1980, possibly while preparing an act of sabotage against the Al-Aqsa Mosque. His political strategy was, through acts of violence and intimidation, to create conditions that would impel the Arabs to leave the holy land. Through the 1970s, even as Israeli society moved increasingly towards the right, Kahane's popularity increased accordingly. Sprinzak, writing in 1987, noted that the Kach headed by Kahane was the 'most extreme violent of the present radical right in Israel and was a quasi-fascist movement'.[120] Kahane believed in Israel's messianic destiny:[121]

> It is crystal-clear that Almighty God is prepared, on this day, to lead us to the full and final redemption, and that the initial phase of this redemption is already in full swing.

However, the realization of this moment of redemption required the Jews of Israel to perform their duty, that is the cleansing of the Holy Land by the removal of all gentiles:[122]

> The redemption could come upon us at once, and in shining glory, if we act in accordance with what we have been commanded by God; or else it may come in the wake of a terrible tragedy, if we refuse [to so act]. A major criterion for true Jewish faith in this decisive era is our willingness to set aside our fear of man in favor of the fear of God and the removal of the Arabs from Israel ... *Let us remove the Arabs from our midst, so as to bring about the redemption.* [Emphasis added.]

Conclusion

Messianism in Jewish tradition was most dramatically exhibited in the Jewish uprisings against Romans two millennia ago, when the Jews, convinced of the support of the Lord, confronted powerful Roman armies. The catastrophe that overwhelmed the Jewish people, including the destruction of their temple in Jerusalem, the killing of thousands of Jews, and the exile of the entire community into a worldwide diaspora, led Jewish religious leaders, in subsequent years, to play down the messianic impulse among their communities. However, messianic belief was never extinguished from Jewish tradition and, several centuries later, asserted itself as 'religious Zionism', in tandem with 'secular Zionism' that emerged towards the end of the nineteenth century in Europe and was focused on realizing a homeland for the Jewish people.

Religious Zionism was strongly advocated by Rav Avraham Kook and his son who saw the establishment of a Jewish homeland in the promised land of Israel as part of the realization of the messianic destiny of the Jewish people. Such a concept was not merely confined to the religious tradition; it was also at the core of secular Zionism as represented by the labour/socialist movement that provided Israel's political leadership in the first thirty years of its statehood.

After victory in the 1967 war, when Israel substantially expanded its territories in the 'promised land', the messianic destiny of the Jewish people acquired an even deeper significance. This was represented most robustly by the Gush Emunim movement, which was a redemptionist, visionary and territory-centred movement, articulating forcefully a strong belief in Jewish messianism founded on the conviction that the Jewish people are unique; that the land of Israel is the land promised to the Jewish people by divine command, and that the era of redemption of the Jewish people has now commenced.

The precise extent of the 'promised land' continues to remain flexible, with different leaders articulating an ever-expanding vision of the territories embraced by divine sanction. However, central to Jewish messianic belief is the conviction that this 'promised land' cannot and will not be shared with another people since that would constitute an obstruction to the messianic process of territorial redemption and land conquest. In keeping with this belief, the native Palestinian population has frequently been identified as Canaanite or Amalek, ancient enemies of the Jewish people, with traditional texts being quoted to sanction expropriation of their land, murders of these aliens, and their ultimate expulsion from the Promised Land.

The Jewish messianic movement has over the last 30 years acquired a strong influence over Israeli politics across the political spectrum, with successive governments supporting Gush Emunim in expanding Jewish settlements across the occupied territories. Messianism is the central influence in Israeli politics and provides no scope for compromise with the Palestinians or dilution of the messianic impulse. We look at this aspect in greater detail in the next chapter.

NOTES

1. Alain Dieckhoff, *The Invention of a Nation-Zionist Thought and the Making of Modern Israel* (Cape Town: David Philip, 2003) p. 248.
2. ibid., p. vii.
3. David Hazony, 'Virtually Normal: Is Israel like any other country?', *The New Republic*, 3 June 2008; downloaded from: www.lebanonwire.com/ 0806/MLN/08060314NR.asp;

    The Dreyfus Affair refers to a scandal in France at the end of the nineteenth century. A young French military officer, Captain Alfred Dreyfus, of Jewish descent, was convicted for treason in November 1894, and sent to the French penal colony on Devil's Island in French Guiana. Though later evidence suggested that he might be innocent, the evidence was suppressed and Dreyfus was further accused on the basis of new fake documentation. His cause was taken up by the eminent French writer, Emile Zola, in January 1898, as a result of which, the case was reopened and Dreyfus was brought back to France for a fresh trial. He was found innocent and reinstated in the French army in 1906.

    This case, a dramatic example of anti-Semitism, polarized French society and led to legislation, in 1905, separating church and state in France. The Hungarian-Jewish journalist, Theodor Herzl, reported on the trial. He later wrote *The Jewish State* in 1896, and founded the World Zionist Organisation.
4. Dieckhoff, p. 11.
5. ibid., p. 131.
6. ibid., p. 132.
7. Quoted in: Eliezer Schweid, 'Jewish Messianism: Metamorphoses of an Idea,' *The Jewish Quarterly*, No.36, Summer 1985; downloaded from: www.theunjustmedia.com/Jewish%20Zionists/Jewish% 20Messianism%20Metam-orphoses.
8. Martin L.Gordon, 'Messianism: Conflicting Conceptions,' Department of the World Zionist Organisation, 10 June 2003; downloaded from: www.wzo.org.il/en/resources/print. esp?id=1436
9. ibid.
10. Dieckhoff, p. 150.
11. ibid., p. 155.
12. ibid., p. 159.
13. ibid., p. 160.
14. ibid., pp. 160–1.
15. Aviezer Ravitzky, 'Religious Radicalism and Political Messianism in Israel', in Emmanuel Sivan and Menachem Friedman (Eds), *Religious Radicalism*

and Politics in the Middle East, State University of New York Press, Albany, 1990, p. 21; henceforth respectively Ravitzky and Sivan and Friedman.
16. Ravitzky, p. 23.
17. ibid., p. 22.
18. ibid., p. 23.
19. ibid., p. 25.
20. Dieckhoff, p. 162.
21. ibid., p. 170.
22. ibid., p. 170.
23. ibid., p. 171.
24. ibid., p. 173.
25. ibid., p. 177.
26. ibid., p. 190.
27. ibid., p. 193.
28. ibid., p. 191.
29. ibid., p. 192.
30. ibid., p. 200.
31. ibid., p. 202.
32. ibid., p. 220.
33. ibid., p. 221.
34. ibid., p. 225.
35. ibid., p. 226.
36. ibid., p. 231.
37. ibid., p. 235.
38. ibid., p. 236.
39. ibid., p. 237.
40. ibid., p. 239.
41. ibid., p. 240.
42. ibid., p. 243.
43. ibid., p. 244.
44. ibid., pp. 246–7.
45. ibid., p. 263.
46. ibid.
47. ibid.
48. Israel Shahak, 'The Ideology of Jewish Messianism', from *Race and Class, A Journal of Racism, Empire and Globalisation*, Vol. 37, No. 2, 1995; downloaded from: www.geocities.com/alabasters_archive/ shahak_messianism.html?200623, p. 2.
49. Shahak, p. 7.
50. Israel Idalovichi, 'Cultural-Religious Sources of Messianic Extremism

and its Evolution in Post-colonial Times', May 2006; downloaded from: www.inst.at/trans/16nr/02_2/idalovichi16.htm.

51. ibid.
52. Uriel Tal, 'Foundations of a Political Messianic Trend in Israel', *The Jerusalem Quarterly*, No. 35, Spring 1985; downloaded from: www.geocities.com/a/alabaster_archive/messianic_trend.html? 200623; p. 2.
53. Ehud Sprinzak, 'The Iceberg Model of Political Extremism,' from David Newman (Ed.), *The Impact of Gush Emunim- Politics and Settlement in the West Bank*, Croom Helm Publishers, 1985; downloaded from: www.geocities.com/alabaster_archive/iceberg_model.html? 200222;.
54. Ian S. Lustick, 'The Evolution of Gush Emunim', in: *For the Land and the Lord: Jewish Fundamentalism in Israel*, New York: Council for Foreign Relations, 1988.
55. Yehiel Harari, 'Notions of Messianism and their Influence on Israel's Prospects for Peace,' Association for Israel Studies, 2004 Conference Papers; downloaded from: www.aisisraelstudies.org/2004papers/Harari,Yehid.doc.
56. Lustick.
57. Nur Masalha, *Imperial Israel and the Palestinians – The Politics of Expansion* (London: Pluto Press, 2000) p. 106.
58. Sprinzak, p. 5.
59. Masalha, p. 107.
60. ibid.
61. Masalha, p. 110.
62. ibid., p. 108.
63. ibid.
64. ibid.
65. ibid., p. 109.
66. Tal, p. 8.
67. Masalha, p. 114.
68. ibid., p. 115.
69. ibid., p. 24.
70. ibid., p. 115.
71. ibid., p. 127.
72. Charles S. Liebman, 'The Jewish Religion and Contemporary Israeli Nationalism', in Sivan and Friedman, p. 83.
73. Masalha, p. 121.
74. ibid., p. 122.
75. ibid., pp. 125–6.
76. ibid., p. 126.

77. ibid., p. 129.
78. ibid.
79. ibid., p. 130.
80. Tal, pp. 9–11.
81. ibid., p. 10.
82. Masalha, p. 130.
83. Tal, p. 11.
84. Masalha, p. 130.
85. ibid., p. 131.
86. ibid., pp. 131–2.
87. ibid., p. 132.
88. ibid., p. 133.
89. Elliott Horowitz, *Reckless Rites*, (Princeton, NJ: Princeton University Press, 2006) p. 1.
90. Aviezer Ravitzky, 'The Messianism of Success in Contemporary Judaism', in Bernard J. McGinn, John J. Collins and Stephen J. Stein (Ed), *The Continuum History of Apocalypticism*, (New York: Continuum, 2003) pp. 573–4; henceforth, Aviezer Ravitzky.
91. Aviezer Ravitzky, p. 577.
92. ibid., p. 574.
93. ibid., p. 573.
94. Dieckhoff, p. 265.
95. ibid., p. 267.
96. ibid.
97. ibid., p. 272.
98. ibid.
99. Israel Shahak and Norton Mezvinsky, *Jewish Fundamentalism in Israel*, (London: Pluto Press, 2004) p. 56; henceforth Shahak and Mezvinsky.
100. ibid.
101. Shmuel Sandler, Robert O. Freedman, Shibley Telhami, 'The Religious-Secular Divide in Israeli Politics', *Middle East Policy Council Journal*, Vol. VI, No. 4 June 1999; downloaded from: www.ncpc.org/journal_vol6/9906_sandler.asp
102. ibid.
103. Dieckhoff, p. 288.
104. Neve Gordon, 'The Triumph [of] Greater Israel: militarism v/s messianism is at stake in Sharon's plan to exit Gaza', *National Catholic Reporter*, 12 November 2004; downloaded from: www.findarticles.com/p/articles/nic_m114/ai_n9522571/print, p. 1.
105. Gordon, p. 3.
106. ibid.

107. ibid.
108. Sprinzak.
109. ibid.
110. Shahak, p. 5.
111. ibid.
112. Shahak, p. 6.
113. ibid.
114. Sprinzak.
115. ibid.
116. Shahak and Mezvinsky, p. 64.
117. ibid.
118 Shahak and Mezvinsky, p. 63.
119. ibid, p. 74.
120. Sprinzak.
121. Ravitzky, p. 35.
122. ibid., p. 36.

4

Messianism and Contemporary Israeli Politics

'Our right to defend ourselves against destruction
does not give us the right to oppress others
Occupation results in foreign control
Foreign control results in opposition
Opposition results in suppression
Suppression results in terror and terror against terror ...'

Ad in *HAARETZ*, 22 September 1967
(Quoted in: Shlomo Swirsky, '*The Cost of Occupation—The Burden of the
Israeli Palestinian Conflict*', 2008 Report, June 2008, Adva Centre, Tel Aviv)

Shahak and Mezvinsky have drawn attention to the very limited attention
paid to Jewish fundamentalism, particularly to messianism, in Western
writings on Israel to the extent that even translations from Hebrew into
English deliberately play down or entirely omit references to its role in
shaping Israeli society and politics.[1] In this context, they have particularly
highlighted the role of the 'messianic tendency' in Jewish fundamentalism, believing it to be 'the most influential and dangerous'.[2]

According to surveys in Israel, 25–30 per cent of the Israeli
population is secular, 20 per cent is religious, while 50-55 per cent is
traditional; the latter include both 'Left' and 'Right' elements.[3] However,
the influence of religious Jews and their movements (and political parties)
far exceeds the number of members they command.[4] They are most
influential in regard to the principles of Israel's state policies, besides
the great influence they bring to bear on the Jewish Diaspora, particularly
in the USA.[5]

The religious Jews of Israel belong to two distinct groups–the
Haredim (or Haredi), who are religious extremists, and the religious-

nationalists who are more 'moderate' in religious matters but more extreme in the political domain.[6] The Haredim belong to two political parties – Yahadut Hatorah (Judaism of the Law) and the Shas, which represents the Oriental or Middle Eastern Jews. The religious-nationalist Jews belong to the National Religious Party (NRP), the party most closely affiliated with the Gush Emunim.[6] In the 1996 elections, the Haredi parties got 14 seats, while the NRP got nine. It is estimated that the Haredim constitute 11 per cent of the Israeli population and 13.4 per cent of the Israeli Jewish population, while NRP constitutes 9 per cent of the Israeli population and 11 per cent of the Israeli Jewish population.[7]

The issue that divides the NRP from the Haredim parties is that of redemption: the NRP, in line with the thinking of the two Rav Kooks, believes that redemption has begun and will soon be completed with the imminent coming of the Messiah. The NRP maintains the rigid position that no portion of land in the land of Israel can be given to non-Jews, but allows for some deviation from strict Talmudic injunctions in other matters (such as entering the Army and giving positions to women in the party), believing this is required by the 'special circumstances' prevailing at the beginning of the redemption process.[8] In this, it follows its 'patron-saint' Rabbi Moshe Nachmanides (1194– c.1270) who said that when 'a cosmic process called the beginning of redemption has begun', some of the religious laws should be disregarded, while others should be changed.[9]

On the other hand, the Haredim insist that these are 'normal' times and the messianic era has not yet arrived. Following from this, they reject any deviation from Talmudic requirements. As Shahak and Mezvinsky have noted, 'the aim of Haredi practices has been and still is to preserve the Jewish way of life as it existed prior to modern times'.[10] Thus, Rabbi Ovadia Yoseph, leader of the Shas, agreed with NRP that, in messianic times, the Jews would be stronger than the non-Jews and would have an obligation to conquer the land of Israel and destroy idolatrous Christian churches in the Holy Land; however, as the messianic time of redemption had not yet arrived:[11]

> The Jews are not in fact more powerful than the non-Jews and are unable to expel the non-Jews from the land of Israel because the Jews fear the non-Jews ... God's commandment is then not valid ... Even non-Jews who are idolaters live among us with no possibility of their being expelled

or even moved. The Israeli government is obligated by international law to guard the Christian churches in the land of Israel, even though those churches are definitely places of idolatry and cult practice.

However, the Haredi position is most non-compromising when it comes to the enforcement of *Halacha* (traditional Jewish law) as the law of the state of Israel; its position may be summarized as follows:[12]

God's political authority must be formally and juridically recognized. Ordained rabbis, God's certified agents, must be the decision makers.

Rabbis must oversee all social institutions, adjudicate all issues that arise, make final judgments about all social services and censor all printed, pictorial and sound matter.

Sabbath, other religious laws, physical separation of women from men in public places, and 'modesty' in female conduct and dress must be enforced by law.

Individuals must be obligated legally to report all noticed offences of others to rabbinical authorities.

The messianic worldview of the NRP and its impact across different sections of the Israeli political structure have caused considerable concern to a number of moderate Israeli scholars. Uriel Tal has pointed out that we are not dealing with a band of crazy prophets, nor with an extreme minority on the fringe of society, but with a dogmatic school of thought and methodical doctrine, which inevitably leads to a policy which cannot tolerate the concept of human and civil rights.[13] Tal concludes that, with regard to the structure of the NRP's messianic conception—as distinct from its content—it is impossible not to notice an analogy to totalitarian movements of this century.[14] Shahak and Mezvinsky have elaborated on this point thus:[15]

The similarities between the Jewish political messianic trend and German Nazism are glaring. The Gentiles are for the messianists what the Jews were for the Nazis. The hatred for Western culture with its rational and democratic elements is common to both movements. Finally, the extreme chauvinism of the messianists is directed towards all non-Jews. The 1973 Yom Kippur War, for instance, was in Amital's view not directed against Egyptians, Syrians and/or all Arabs but against all non-Jews. The war was thus directed against the great majority of citizens of the United States, even though the United States aided Israel in that war. This hatred of non-Jews is not new but, as already discussed, is derived from a continuous Jewish cabbalistic tradition. Those Jewish scholars who have attempted to hide this fact from non-Jews and even from many Jews have not only done a disservice to scholarship; they have aided the growth of this Jewish analogue to German Nazism.

Such fascist trends in extremist Jewish thinking are present in the writings of the US-born Rabbi Yitzhak Ginsburgh, which bring together different strands in traditional Jewish theology and reveal his view of the Jewish redemption and the coming of the Messiah; Yehiel Harari has summarized it thus: [16]

> In the heart of every Jew there is a sparkle of the Messiah. Integrating all these sacred sparks, together with the act of the self-suppressing of every Jew in front of the potential king, will cause the natural appearance of the Messiah. This process will be started by a large popular movement of believers that will be led, first by a group of advocate Rabies, and later on by the King of Israel, who will gain control and replace the Israeli government. The king, prior to being revealed as the real Messiah, will fulfill the two main commandments that are imposed on him. First, he will eliminate the 'Amalek', referring to all enemies of Israel, who are also perceived as the enemies of God – the Arabs of course. And second, he will build the third temple in Jerusalem. After building the temple, it will be clear that the king is the real Messiah. The God, in his turn, will establish his written promises, concerning mainly the revival of the dead and afterwards, at the final stage, full integration of the Jewish People in Divinity.

In an interview in 1996, Rabbi Ginsburgh spoke of the Jews' genetic-based spiritual superiority over non-Jews. In the eyes of the Torah, it was superiority that, he asserted, invested Jewish life with greater value: 'If you saw two people drowning, a Jew and a non-Jew, the Torah says you save the Jewish life first. If every single cell in a Jewish body entails divinity, is a part of God, then every strand of DNA is part of God. Therefore, something is special about Jewish DNA.' Later, Rabbi Ginsburgh asked rhetorically: 'If a Jew needs a liver, can you take the liver of an innocent non-Jew passing by to save him? The Torah would probably permit that Jewish life has an infinite value', he explained. 'There is something infinitely more holy and unique about Jewish life than non-Jewish life.' Shahak and Mezvinsky believe that changing the words 'Jewish' to 'German' or 'Aryan' and 'non-Jewish' to 'Jewish' turns the Ginsburgh position into the doctrine that made Auschwitz possible in the past. [17]

The neo-Zionism of the settler movement was energized by the first Intifada (December 1987): while objective observers would suggest that a large part of the blame for the violence and the deteriorating security situation lay with Israel's hard-line policies against the Palestinians in the occupied territories, concerns relating to security continue to encourage the coming together of neo-Zionist groups, as exemplified by the formation of the Sharon-led Government of National Unity in February 2001.[18] At the same time, the sense of being beleaguered by hostile countries bent on Israel's destruction has also encouraged the development of 'civilian militarism' in the country:[19] the nation in arms has militarized Israeli society, promoting state-sponsored violence and in general convincing the populace that all issues need to be viewed through the prism of security.[20]

Allan Brownfeld has suggested that extremism in Israel is actually being fuelled by the growth of the ultra-orthodox movement in the United States.[21] After 1945, about a hundred thousand orthodox European Jews came to the USA. As a consequence, for the first time in modern American history, the secular humanistic belief-system of American Jewry faced the challenge of a vibrant, charismatic and almost completely opposite belief-system, with institutions and a mindset of its own. It is important to note that, while the orthodox in the USA constitute less than 10 per cent of the Jewish population, their impact is disproportionate to their numbers. This impact is particularly felt in so far as the interests of Israel are concerned, since they are the segment of American Jewry most involved with Israel, and most committed to it in concrete actions. This group has played a particularly significant role both in the United States of America and in Israel in favour of not surrendering the lands won in 1967.

Brownfeld has pointed out that, while the Right-wing of American Jewry has expressed itself primarily through political activity, its fringe elements have repeatedly turned to inflammatory rhetoric and violent acts both in the US and Israel. Thus, hatred of Rabin after the Oslo Accord was preached by a number of extremist Rabbis in New York: 'Yigal Amir's trail to the murder of Yitzhak Rabin, it might be said, was one partly blazed by American Jews.'[22]

The Settler Movement in the 1990s

In the 1990s, after the signing of the Oslo Accords and the

commencement of the peace process, the issue of land became a central divisive issue in Israeli politics.[23] The NRP and Gush Emunim saw in it a betrayal of the messianic process of redemption, recalling the Jewish tradition that, often in the past, redemption had been prevented because a majority of the Jews had decided to follow a heretic or traitor: hatred of Arabs was now extended to hatred of secular Jews. A commentator described the agony of the religious elements thus:[24]

> the personal, ideological and religious crisis in which the national religious Jewish community in Israel has found itself generated doubts about the very foundations of religious Zionism: namely, its historic alliance with secular Zionism and its wholehearted acceptance of the State of Israel. In the past that alliance revolved around the perception that the secular State of Israel was the first stage in the process of redemption. At present, even the moderates question this assumption.

An NRP Rabbi, Azriel Ariel, said:[25]

> The religious settlements were established not only to create facts on the ground but also to affect the hearts and minds of the Jewish people. We believed that, by encountering the holy parts of the land as if they were alive, the hearts of the Jewish masses would be united with the heart of the land. We envisaged the process as reconnecting the national Jewish consciousness with its spiritual roots.
>
> For a majority of Jews the settlements have failed to restore that sacred linkage. The majority of Jews have renounced the Jewish roots present in their souls, profaning themselves by [committing the] sin of choosing the so-called 'majority' of Western culture instead of their own moral values. In the state of that grave sin their hearts have remained unaffected by the land of Israel ...

Rather than agitate their concerns and interests from within, as the Haredim have generally done, the NRP has utilized the flexibilities available to it by its religious position to seek to influence the Israeli state from without: this has been done by the entry of NRP adherents into the Israeli armed forces.[26] The army has agreed to be flexible with these religious recruits in regard to the schedule of their participation in the training and fighting programmes in order to accommodate their religious studies. Shahak and Mezvinsky have noted that 'the NRP fighters have distinguished themselves in the suppression of the Intifada, being particularly noted for their cruelty to Palestinians ... When the army commanding officers have wanted to inflict especially cruel punishment upon Palestinians or others, they have most often relied upon and used religious soldiers.'[27]

After Rabin's assassination at the hands of a Jewish religious fanatic, there were concerns in Israel about the penetration of the extreme religious elements into the armed forces. In this context, one commentator, looking at the general aims of the 'messianic religious right', noted:[28]

> Their institutions have the stamina of a long-distance runner since they believe in the eternal survival of the Jewish nation; in this framework they prepared four approaches for the battle of the land of Israel: settlements, financial support, education and promotion of their men in the army to achieve domination of a future General Staff. It is not a case of good and bad but a struggle about the character of the State of Israel.

Shahak and Mezvinsky have discussed in detail the response of different sections of the Israeli population to the massacre of twenty-nine Muslim worshippers at the Patriarch's mosque in February 1994. The murderer, Baruch Goldstein, was a Right-wing religious zealot with a long record of anti-Arab and anti-Muslim hatred. In spite of his heinous crime, the influence of the religious Right on mainstream secular politics in Israel is exemplified by the elaborate arrangements made for his funeral with high-level state support and participation.[29] Rabbi Azriel Ariel expressed the feelings of the overwhelming majority of the religious establishment thus:[30]

> The holy martyr, Baruch Goldstein, is from now on our intercessor in heaven. Goldstein did not act as an individual; he heard the cry of the land of Israel, which is being stolen from us day after day by the Muslims. He acted to relieve that cry of the land.
>
> The Jews will inherit the land not by any peace agreement but only by shedding blood.

His tomb has since become a place of pilgrimage for thousands of Jews from within Israel as also from the USA and France. Describing him as a 'holy saint and martyr', they seek his intercession to obtain benefits.[31]

The Government that came to power in 1991, led by Yitzhak Rabin, was the first Israeli government since 1977 that did not include any representative of the settler movement. In addition, the fact that it was supported by Arab parties condemned it in the eyes of the settlers who saw it as 'a declaration of war on religious Zionism and the settler movement'.[32] Rabbi Shlomo Aviner, spiritual leader of the Gush Emunim, said of this government:[33]

> [These] enemies of Zionism and settlement must be stricken from the blessing [of the state] ... Even though it [the Rabin government] is honoured by the presence of the liberators of Jerusalem, Holocaust survivors and the like, [this government] cannot atone for its negative intentions ... The nihilist forces in the nation, together with our Arab enemies, [are members of the government]. And if we count the Arab Knesset members who support this government, even you will see that this government does not have a majority among the nation in Israel...

The settlers' media depicted the government and Rabin personally as dangerous to their cause and called for a struggle against 'a malevolent and treacherous government'.[34] Their concern was that the government, pursuing the 'peace process' with the PLO, would restrict if not halt the expansion of settlements in the occupied territories that had been taking place briskly and with full government support since 1967 but particularly when the Likud and Likud-led governments ruled from 1977 to 1990.

After the Hebron massacre, there was considerable pressure on Rabin to uproot and relocate the small 400-strong Jewish settlement in Hebron (Kiryat Arba) from where Baruch Goldstein had emerged. This set the stage for a confrontation between the government and the settlers. The settlers' rabbis' committee called on soldiers not to obey the evacuation order, saying that refusal to obey was a divine commandment.[35] The settlers threatened to inundate Hebron with 10,000 supporters, with another 50,000 coming in to replace them if they were arrested. A petition signed by 1002 rabbis from Israel and the diaspora was submitted to the Prime Minister. Security officials and academics familiar with Right-wing movements warned the government about the violence that would engulf the state if Kiryat Arba was forcibly evacuated.[36] The distinguished scholar of Israeli extremism, Ehud Sprinzak, told Rabin that the crisis was a matter of:[37]

> a terrible cleavage, the collapse of an entire world that was built with great faith, great love, and great hope ... This is one of the greatest crises that the State of Israel and the Zionist movement have ever faced, if not the greatest. Those who are going to pay the highest price, ought to be given the full opportunity to convince the nation with their arguments. If there is no peace at home, any peace outside is worth nothing.

In the event, Rabin decided it would be politically unwise to uproot the Hebron settlement: though he is said to have loathed the settlers' movement, and thought Gush Emunim was 'a cancer in the body of Israel's democracy', he was also reluctant to confront it.[38]

This pusillanimity on the part of Israel's leaders has been a recurring pattern in the country's politics from 1967, enabling the settler movement to continue to establish 'a number of solid facts on the ground'.[39] In fact, under the Rabin government, settlement activity continued to flourish, with the fig leaf of 'natural growth' leading to further expansions of Jewish settlements and further confiscation of Palestinian land. All this was done with considerable funding from the government and supply of equipment for construction activity and, ironically, for anti-government activity as well by demonstrators (in the shape of generators, sound systems and vehicles!).[40]

However, the settlers' attacks on the Rabin government for its participation in the peace process continued unabated, it being referred to as the 'evil government' and 'the traitorous government'.[41] Rabin was warned:[42]

> ... If, heaven forbid, the disaster that you are planning for us occurs, you will not be absolved! You will face justice and be put on trial ... Parallel to the internal protest, the ugly face, the monstrous face of the false peace that is purchased by national betrayal will become increasingly clear.

Since the Hebron massacre had lifted all restraint from the Hamas, the Islamist movement indulged in a series of violent actions, including suicide attacks, against the Israeli population, with harsh retaliatory actions from the Israeli forces. Amidst this violence, the settlers were able to broaden and strengthen their base of support in the Israeli population, so that Palestinian violence was able to transform 'the [occupied] territories and Israel into one entity'.[43] Rabin's attempt to enter into dialogue with the settlement leaders did little to enhance his status in their eyes; it was instead seen as 'a sign of his weakness and an invitation to further pressures'.[44]

On 28 September 1995, Rabin signed the Oslo II agreement. In a public demonstration in Jerusalem, in October, Rabin was depicted in an SS officer's uniform. On 4 November 1995, he was assassinated at a peace rally in the main square of Tel Aviv by Yigal Amir, a young student known to be an admirer of Goldstein. Though the Right-wing rabbinical and settler leadership condemned the murder, it also condemned the victim; Hannan Porat said:[45]

> A person who lifts his hand to uproot Jewish settlements from their land ... is not raising his hand against Hannan Porat and Rabbi Druckman; he is raising his hand against the word of God that ordains 'that thy children shall come again to their own border' (Jeremiah 31.17) ... anyone who wants to do a reckoning of conscience must stand in that place, regard the dark abyss and say: 'Anyone who walks in this abyss, and anyone who thinks that in this way he can save the people, is simply stupid and wicked.'

There was also some honest soul-searching among a few settler leaders. Thus, Yehuda Amital, one of the founders of Gush Emunim, said:[46]

> This assassin came from our midst ... Those rabbis who are not beating their breast have not thus far evinced the courage to face their public ... In educational institutions and in yeshivas the students are exposed to the atmosphere created there by the religious and political leadership, with the help of the media and public opinion ... It is not that an authority in religious law came and said to the murderer that it was necessary to murder Rabin according to that law. It is extremism that brought this about. The deterioration began when many chose to ignore, or close a blind eye to, the harassment of Arabs that in the end also led to an act of murder.

In their book, *Murder in the Name of God: The Plot to Kill Yitzhak Rabin*, the authors Michael Karpin and Ina Friedman have described Rabin's assassin, Yigal Amir, as one who:[47]

> believed that there is only one guideline for fixing the borders of the Land of Israel: the Divine Promise made to the Patriarch Abraham, 'to your descendants I give this land, from the river of Egypt to the great river, the river Euphrates' (Genesis 15.17). Today these borders embrace a large part of the Middle East, from Egypt to Iraq ... zealots read this passage as God's Will and God's will must be obeyed, whatever the cost. No mortal has the right to settle the borders any narrower than these. Thus, negotiating a peace settlement with Israel's neighbours is unthinkable. After all, the manifest destiny of the Jewish people has not been realized, say the zealots, so what is the basis for making peace.

However, instead of taking a tough line with the settlers, Rabin's successor, Shimon Peres, guided by electoral considerations, sought the support of the settlers by promising new housing projects, particularly in the Jerusalem area, undertaking not to dismantle any settlements as part of the peace process, maintaining Israeli sovereignty over the occupied territories, and keeping Jerusalem undivided.[48]

The Netanyahu government that took over in 1996, while sympathetic to the settlers, could not satisfy 'the settlers' entire appetite'.[49] The settlers closely monitored his role at the Wye River peace talks (October 1998). On learning that Netanyahu was in the process of making territorial concessions to the Palestinians, a fusillade of attacks on him commenced; Hannan Porat said: 'Netanyahu has experienced an abject failure in the test of his loyalty to the security of Israel and the land of Israel.'[50] Another settler, Zvi Hendel, a leader of the Gaza Strip settlers, declared that 'Netanyahu is about to sign the Declaration of Independence of the Palestinian state.'[51] Zertal and Eldar have pointed out that the settlers were following the same 'crash trajectory' with Netanyahu as they had done with previous Israeli governments, that is, pressing for their maximalist demands in the most uncompromising terms; in this context, the authors noted:[52]

> ... perhaps their [the settlers'] rich experience taught them that there was no politician who would dare to grapple with them. And yet, their belief that the concrete facts that they were establishing day in and day out were resistant to any government and would last longer than any political process proved them right.

Prime Minister Ehud Barak (1999–2001) had the same problems with the settlers as Netanyahu. Though his period in office witnessed the greatest settlement construction activity since the signing of the Oslo Accords, he was 'unable to reach their ideological hardcore and satisfy them'.[53] The settlers' leaders closely monitored Barak's role at the Camp David talks, threatening him with dire consequences including fighting him to 'the last drop of blood' were he to make territorial concessions.[54] The failure of the Camp David conference was thus 'a political and psychological victory for the settlers'.[55]

Sharon and the Settler Movement

Sharon dominated the Israeli political scene between 2000 and 2006. He commenced this period of his political life with the visit to the Al-Aqsa Mosque/Temple Mount in September 2000, initiating the second Intifada in which 1200 Israelis and 4500 Palestinians were killed.[56] Zertal and Eldar have described this period of Sharon's leadership thus:[57]

The continuing malignant occupation; the suffering and injustice entailed in it; the encircling of Israel by a gigantic barrier, in an era when walls of this sort are tumbling down, in a unilateral and illegal effort to draw the permanent border of a country that has lived for almost sixty years with blurred, unfixed boundaries; and the improbable attempt to dismantle some settlements while keeping, even expanding, most of the others—all of this bears Ariel Sharon's fingerprint and was carried out under his inspiration.

In response to the Intifada, the Israeli army 'followed an unprecedented and disproportional military action', using tanks, missiles, helicopters and air force jets.[58] According to Zertal and Eldar, the army acted as 'an agent of a terrible lesson, as an educator, as an organization that waged its own campaign of etching into the minds and souls of the Palestinians, once and for all, who has the power and who is in charge'.[59] This, the authors believe, was the 'war of the settlers ... a relentless war for the preservation of the occupation, the containment of the Palestinian civil uprising against it, and the eradication of the rebellious Palestinian elites'.[60]

It was in this context that the project of the barrier wall was taken up and implemented with full enthusiasm from June 2002. Initially, the settlers opposed the barrier wall project, believing that it would serve to specify Israel's borders in regard to which Israel had, since 1967, maintained a 'deliberate vagueness'.[61] However, amidst increasing Palestinian attacks, the settlers came to support the project, while ensuring they would 'navigate the ship' by determining the route of the barrier.[62] The project enabled them to increase the territories to be brought under Israeli control by expanding the settlements and expelling the Palestinians from their ancient villages. A senior settlement leader explained the settlers' strategy thus:[63]

> It appears that it is not possible to fight against the construction [of the fence]. It is thus necessary to put up a fight so that the side that will remain under Israeli rule will include maximum portions of the Land of Israel, maximum settlements, maximum settlers and maximum strategic depth, in order to prevent the danger of their abandonment ... It is necessary to concentrate forces for a public and vocal battle for the route of the eastern fence ... At a difficult hour of surgery, sometimes it is necessary to harm one organ in order to save another organ, as long as it is possible to do this, as long as it is not too late.

Zeltar and Eldar have explained that the barrier wall project is the concrete realization of Sharon's much earlier project to set up Palestinian 'Bantustans' in the occupied territories so as 'to take hold of as much West Bank territory as possible and block the establishment of a viable Palestinian state'.[64] Sharon's game-plan appears to have been realized; a World Bank report of May 2007 has noted:[65]

> Israel has restricted Palestinian access to more than 50% of the West Bank. This fragmentation not only does not allow the inhabitants to lead normal lives with respect to their economy, education, health and culture but also prevents them from shaping the institutions of an active and cohesive democratic society. Israel's lofty demands that Palestinians strengthen their democracy and impose control on extremist organization is thus nothing but deceptive talk covering its own deeds, which are aimed at achieving exactly the opposite – of eroding Palestinian society.

The Cost of Occupation

On the 60th anniversary of the establishment of the State of Israel, Shlomo Swirski published his report titled: *The Cost of Occupation—the Burden of the Israeli–Palestinian Conflict, 2008 Report*, in which he sought to correct the widespread impression in Israel that 'not only does Israel have nothing to lose from the situation [that is, occupation of Palestinian territories since 1967] but that it actually benefits from it'.[66] Swirsky pointed out:

> The truth is that the conflict with the Palestinians is like a millstone around the neck of Israel: it undermines economic growth, burdens the budget, limits social development, sullies its vision, hangs heavy on its conscience, harms its international standing, exhausts its army, divides it politically, and threatens the future of its existence as a Jewish nation-state. It also kills and injures thousands of Israelis. In short, Israel is paying a heavy price for the continuation of the conflict and for the absence of a fair and agreed-upon partition.

He has illustrated these contentions with the following facts and figures:

- The Israeli economy was adversely affected by the Israeli-Palestinian conflict: during the period 1997-2006, the economy grew by 43%, as against the world average of 67%; growth rates of others were: USA - 68%; EU - 68%; India - 139%; China - 193%.
- Between 1989and 2008, *additions* to the Israeli defence budget to pay for increased military activity in the Palestinian territories amounted to NIS 36.6 billion [$ 10 billion] (2007 figures).

- These additions in the defence budget included NIS 9 billion [$ 2.6 billion] to pay for the disengagement from Gaza; this was more than the budgetary outlay for: Agriculture; Transport; Communications; National Infrastructure; Industry, Trade and Employment; and other departments dealing with the economy.
- The Defence budget also included NIS 13 billion [$ 3.8 billion] for the setting up of the 790 km long 'separation wall'; if the wall had followed the 'Green Line', its length would have been 313 km.
- To pay for the defence outlays, between 2001 and 2005 there were cuts in the civilian parts of the budget amounting to NIS 65 billion [$20 billion] affecting all of Israeli's social services: health, social welfare, education, higher education, housing, and, above all, the social security system.
- Today, one out of every five Israeli families is poor, compared with one out of every ten in the 1970s.
- Over half of Israeli youth (54%) do not receive high school matriculation certificates.
- The majority of young people educated in Israel (70% in 2006) do not go in for higher education.
- On the basis of recommendations of different commissions, the defence budget is expected to *increase* by NIS 4.6 billion [$1.4 billion], on average per year, for the subsequent 10 years, nearly equal to the *total* of the annual budget for higher education.

Shlomo Swirski has also commented on the impact of the Israeli Army's sustained conflict with the Palestinian uprisings on its preparedness for war, its diminishing status in the public eye, and, above all, its increased politicization. With regard to the general preparedness of the Israeli army for war, he quotes the Brodel Commission which said:

> Since 2000, when the Palestinian arena became so dominant, the defense system has lacked a sufficient general organization or the creation of the right balance between the preparedness of the combat units and operations in the framework of routine defense. This defect constitutes a strategic short-sightedness, which contributed to the fact that routine defense lowered the level of [the IDF's] preparedness and the readiness for war. The absence of expertise in the allocation of manpower damaged the general preparedness and led to both insufficient professionalism in routine defense matters and damage to the level of skills, the level of training and the preparation required to maintain combat units of the quality required by the threats.

Given the fact that the Israeli army's fight in the two Intifadas is to sustain occupation of land on behalf of the settler movement, the army has not been able to 'disengage itself from political and ideological considerations' and is increasingly seen as 'operating as an army for the defence of the settlements'.

The expert on the Israeli military, Yoram Peri, published a monograph in November 2002, which looked at the evolution of civil—military ties in Israel. The report pointed out that, at the beginning of the 21st century, there was a 'weakening of civilian control over the military, along with a rather high level of influence of the military over policy',[67] and that Israel's foreign policy has increasingly become 'the servant of security policy, rather than the other way around'.[68] In recent years, this has been most apparent in regard to the Army's response to the second Intifada. The Army opted in favour of 'a real show of strength', hoping that this would induce the rioters to 'understand the heavy price they would have to pay for the continued violence'.[69] In the event, this had the opposite affect, as Palestinian anger led to an escalation of violence.[70]

The Army had adopted the hard-fisted approach in order to improve its image after what it felt had been an ignominious withdrawal from Lebanon in 2000. As Yoram Peri has pointed out:[71]

> The need to restore Israel's deterrent power in the eyes of its enemies and equally to restore the honour of the military in the eyes of the Israeli public and in its own estimation would henceforth be factors that would have considerable impact on Israeli military policy against the Intifada.

Peri has also noted that the sustained conflict with the Palestinians from 1987 required the Israeli army to participate actively in policy-making, as a result of which 'it become increasingly infected by politics and thus became more and more politicized'.[72] Thus, in response to Palestinian violence and suicide bombings, the Israel Defence Force (IDF) launched 'Operation Defence Shield' in March 2002. This operation was aimed, inter alia, at undermining the Oslo Accords (which was the Sharon Government's policy), with Israel directly assuming a security role in the territories governed the Palestine Authority, so that in due course the Palestine Authority would be discredited and would ultimately collapse.[73]

However, after enjoying wide support initially, the operation and the Israeli military came in for unprecedented criticism:[74]

At the military level, the criticism focused on the futility of the war and the fact that it could not bring an end to terror. Added to this was the political criticism. The IDF was accused of waging a political war designed to protect the settlements sand not to safeguard the security of the state, and of maneuvering the political leadership into a battle with the Palestinians.

On the retirement of General Shaul Mofaz, the Israeli Chief of General Staff [CGS] during the Prime Ministership of Ehud Barak and responsible for the harsh military response during the Intifada of 2000, an Israeli journalist said:[75]

> To his discredit it will go on record that there has never been a CGS during whose term the IDF so much resembled the military arm of a political ideology rather than a national military.

State Terrorism

The academic discourse on 'terrorism' has been as much divided on the issue of state terrorism as it has been in regard to the terrorist *versus* freedom-fighter debate, with the Israel-Palestine conflict at the heart of both issues. In regard to the former issue, both the Palestinian and Israeli sides have felt the need to emphasize the distinction between 'civilian' and 'military' in their respective claims to legitimacy for their actions. Israel's use of its armed forces against Palestinian 'freedom fighters' and the collateral damage caused to Israeli non-combatants during Palestinian offensives against Israeli military targets, especially when the Palestinians do not have an internationally recognized 'state', have been significant factors in the debate around the use of military force by a state against what it perceives, or chooses to label, as 'terrorist' activities on the soil of what it claims to be its 'territory'. It is in this context that the Israeli–Palestinian confrontation and the consequent strong disagreement with regard to addressing the issue of State-sponsored in terrorism has to be understood.

The Israeli authority on terrorism, Boaz Ganor, accepts that States can be involved in 'terrorism' in various ways: from various levels of general support for terrorist organizations, through operational assistance, initiating or directing of attacks, up to the perpetration of terrorist attacks by official state agencies.[76] When it comes to violent activity committed by a State against civilians, Ganor refers to various international conventions: he points out that acts forbidden by international conventions are defined as 'war crimes' when they occur in the context of a war situation, and as 'crimes against humanity' in other situations. Having set out this general principle, Ganor, presumably anxious to protect Israel's violent activities in Palestine from the label of 'terrorism', notes that various countries have engaged in attacks against leading activists of terrorist organizations—-planners and initiators of attacks, commanders of operational units, saboteurs and even the organizations' leaders—as a result of which these countries are often accused of engaging in terrorism.

However, Ganor firmly asserts that actions by a state against terrorists cannot be defined as 'terrorism', if only because the latter are not actually civilians. He argues that individuals engaging in terrorist activities, even if not wearing a uniform, exclude themselves from the civilian community, and rules protecting civilians no longer apply to them. Thus, just as the definition views decision-makers as 'legitimate' targets in guerrilla warfare, so targeting terrorists who head operational, administrative or political branches in a terrorist organization should not in itself be considered a terrorist activity, since these are the people responsible for policy formulation and decision making in the terrorists organization.[77]

Bruce Hoffman echoes this approach. He points out that 'even while national armed forces have been responsible for far more death and destruction than terrorists might ever aspire to bring about', their actions are circumscribed by 'rules and accepted norms of behaviour' which prescribe limits on the nature of weapons they may use, the tactics they may utilize and the victims they may target.[78] These 'rules of war' are also codified in international conventions, such as the Geneva and Hague Conventions, which, inter alia:

- prohibit taking civilians as hostages;
- impose regulations governing the treatment of captured on surrendered soldiers (POWs);
- outlaw reprisals against either civilians or POWs;
- recognize neutral territory and the rights of citizens of neutral states; and,
- uphold the inviolability of diplomats and other accredited representatives.

Violations of these norms are punishable under national and international law. Terrorists, on the other hand, have no such constraints on their conduct. Following from this, Hoffman defined terrorism as 'the deliberate creation and exploitation of fear through violence or the threat of violence on the pursuit of political change'.[79] Terrorism has the following characteristics that distinguish it from other forms of crime; it is:

- ineluctably political in aims and motives;
- violent or, equally important, threatens violence;
- designed to have far-reaching psychological repercussions;
- conducted by an organization with an identifiable chain of command or conspirational cell structure (whose members wear no uniform or identifying insignia); and,
- perpetrated by a sub-national group or non-state entity.

In recent years, a number of voices have been raised in support of a more 'neutral' approach to defining terrorism, with particular attention being paid to state terrorism. This has primarily emerged from the atrocities that have taken place as a result of Israeli actions against the Palestinians since 2000 and, later, in Lebanon, which have been documented by human bodies such as Amnesty International and Human Rights Watch. In April 2002, the Israeli academic, Lev Grinberg, wrote an article titled 'Israel's State Terrorism', in which he pointed that, while US and Israeli officials were making frequent references to Palestinian terror, Israel's state terrorism was described as 'self-defence'; he went on to say:[80]

> At the same time, Sharon's responsibility for Israeli war crimes is being completely ignored. Who should be arrested for the targeted killing of almost 100 Palestinians? Who will be sent to jail for the killing of more than 120 Palestinian paramedics? Who will be sentenced for killing of more than 1,200 Palestinians and for the collective punishment of more than 3,000,000 civilians during the last 18 months? And who will face the international Tribunal for the illegal settlement of occupied Palestinian Lands, and the disobedience of UN decisions for more than 35 years?
>
> I want to ask: Who will arrest Sharon, the person directly responsible for the orders to kill Palestinians? When is he going to be defined a terrorist too? How long will the world ignore the Palestinian cry that all they want is freedom and independence? When will it stop neglecting the fact that the goal of the Israeli Government is not security, but the continued occupation and subjugation of the Palestinian people?

The British journalist, John Pilger, writing under the headline, 'Time to Recognize State Terror', wrote in September 2004:[81]

Only by recognizing the terrorism of states is it possible to understand, and deal with, acts of terrorism by groups and individuals which, however horrific, are tiny by comparison. Moreover, their source is inevitably the official terrorism for which there is no media language. Thus, the State of Israel has been able to convince many outsiders that it is merely a victim of terrorism when, in fact, its own unrelenting, planned terrorism is the cause of the infamous retaliation by Palestinian suicide bombers.

On September 7, a Palestinian suicide bomber killed 16 Israelis in the town of Beersheba. Every television news report allowed the Israeli government spokesman to use this tragedy to justify the building of an apartheid wall – when the wall is pivotal to the causes of Palestinian violence. Almost every news report marked the end of a five-month period of "relative peace and calm" and "a lull in the violence". *During those five months of relative peace and calm, almost 400 Palestinians were killed, 71 of them in assassinations. During the lull in the violence, more than 73 Palestinian children were killed.* A 13-year-old was murdered with a bullet through the heart; a 5-year-old was shot in her face as she walked arm in arm with her 2-year-old sister. The body of Mazen Majid, aged 14, was riddled with 18 Israeli bullets as he and his family left their bulldozed home. [Emphasis added.]

In August 2006, a few days after the Israeli assault on Lebanon ended, Amnesty International published a detailed report on the death and destruction wreaked by Israel on Lebanon during its thirty-four day assault. According to the report,[82] between 12 July and 14 August the Israeli air force conducted more than 7,000 air strikes in Lebanon, supplemented by 2,500 naval bombardments and an unknown number of artillery barrages. An estimated 1,183 people were killed, about one-third of whom were children, 4,054 were injured and 970,000 people, or 25 per cent of the total population, were displaced. Half a million people sought shelter in Beirut, many in parks and public spaces without basic facilities.

The report quoted senior Israeli officials as suggesting that civilians and civilian infrastructure were deliberately targeted as collective punishment for the entire Lebanese people. Israeli Chief of Staff, Lt. Gen. Dan Halutz, was quoted as saying that the Lebanese Government was responsible for Hezbollah's actions. Israeli Justice Minister Haim Raimon, said: 'All those now in South Lebanon are terrorists who are related in some way to Hezbollah.'[83] Kate Gilmore, the Deputy Secretary General of Amnesty International, concluded:[84]

Many of the violations identified in our report are war crimes, including indiscriminate and disproportionate attacks. The evidence strongly suggests that the extensive destruction of power and water plants, as well as the transport infrastructure vital for food and other humanitarian relief, was deliberate and an integral part of a military strategy.

Jessica Stern has said that 'States can and do unleash terrorist violence against their own civilians'; again, 'States have also used terrorism as an instrument of war, by deliberately attacking civilians in the hope of crushing enemy morale.'[85] On similar lines, James Rinehart has preferred to focus on the 'acts of terrorists' rather than on the actors of terrorism, noting in this regard the oft-occurring reality, that states themselves embark on activities that any analyst could reasonably call 'terrorist'. Rinehart then went on to identify different elements of terrorism; these included:[86]

(*i*) terrorism must have a political agenda;

(*ii*) it seeks to evoke an emotional response;

(*iii*) it is a tool of communication from the perpetrators to members of the larger community targeted; and,

(*iv*) terrorism is a "group phenomenon" which involves larger units working together, with an even broader base providing material, financial, logistical, ideological, and emotional support.

Based on these considerations, Rinehart put forward the following definition:[87]

Terrorism is limited, organized, premeditated violence, carried out by both state and non-state actors, that is calculated to instill a sense of instability, disorder, and, most importantly, a fear of future, greater violence, in an attempt to achieve specific and, purposeful political goals.

Bruce Hoffman's definition of terrorism includes all the elements contained in Rinehart's definition, with one exception: Hoffman insists that terrorism is perpetrated by 'a subnational group or non-state entity', that is, 'an organization with an identifiable chain of command as a conspiratorial cell structure'.[88]

Neve Gordon has pointed out that the response to questions pertaining to the definition of terrorism in terms of its actors and their actions often 'reflects political alliances and has specific political implications'.[89] He notes that the United States Department of State's definition of terrorism is divided into three clauses, the first of which reads: 'The term "terrorism" means premeditated, politically motivated violence perpetrated against non-combatant targets by sub-national groups or clandestine agents, usually intended to influence an audience.'[90] In the context of the Israeli–Palestinian conflict, Palestinian terrorism corresponds with this part of the definition as it is 'violent, premeditated, and usually perpetrated against non-combatant targets'. Again, the terrorist acts are politically motivated. This clause of the definition also includes the identity of the actor insofar as only 'sub-national groups or clandestine agents' are the perpetrators of terrorism; a state, as such, cannot practise terrorism. Gordon argues that by identifying the actor in the definition of terrorism, the Department of State's definition of terrorism circumscribes the meaning of terrorism such that, within the context of the Israeli–Palestinian conflict, only Palestinians, as stateless people, can be perpetrators of terrorism. Thus, the definition gives a clean chit to Israel.[91]

However, Gordon is not satisfied with this approach. He notes that, in terms of the State Department definition, it is not so much the actor (state/non-state) that defines terrorism but 'what the actors' specific relation to the existing system is'; once this is accepted, it follows that 'at least theoretically, *terrorism can always be attributed to the state's official enemies and never to the state itself or its allies.*' [Emphasis added.][92]

Gordon then examines the Israeli-Palestinian conflict on the basis of the definition of political terrorism by the academic George Lopez, which reads as follows:[93]

> Terrorism is a form of political violence that by design violates some of the society's accepted moral and legal codes, is often ruthlessly destructive, and is somewhat unpredictable in who will be its instrumental targets. Terrorism hardly constitutes mindless violence. Instead, it reflects a detailed strategy that uses horrific violence to make people feel weak and vulnerable, often disproportionate to either the terrorist acts or to the terrorists' long-term power. This fear seeks to promote concrete political objectives.

This definition of terrorism, as against the earlier one of the State Department, enables us to treat Israel and the Palestinians, at least initially, as having an equal capacity to employ terrorism. Although Lopez's definition captures all the incidents of Palestinian terrorism described above, yet it does not identify the perpetrator of the act and, therefore, does not determine in advance that non-state actors are the sole agents of terrorism. Once the actor is considered to be an insignificant variable, it becomes easier to judge the act itself.[94]

Scrutiny of Israel's actions in Lebanon indicates that it has often used methods of terror. Gordon cites a report of Human Rights Watch (HRW) on Israel's 'Operation Accountability' which took place in Lebanon in July 1993, which states:[95]

> While Israel has claimed that broadcast warnings to the civilian population in southern Lebanon were made with a view to protecting civilians from collateral injury in attacks on strictly military objectives, a number of factors make it reasonable to assume that the intention was in fact to sow terror among the civilian population. As the pattern of physical damage showed, the Israel Defense Forces and its mercenary South Lebanese Army subjected entire villages to area bombardment. The threats and the nature of the attacks make it clear that in significant areas in southern Lebanon whole populations, indeed anyone who failed to flee by a certain time, were targeted as if they were combatants.

As per the estimates of HRW cited by Gordon, 120 civilians were killed and about fifty injured during this operation. The bombing by Israel resulted in the immediate displacement of people estimated to be between 150,000 and 200,000. Not only that, less than three years later, Israel launched another operation, titled: 'Grapes of Wrath': 300 sites in Lebanon were air-bombed, causing displacement of about 400,000 civilians and the demolition of over 200 houses. It was estimated that some 198 civilians, including the ninety-seven refugees in the village of Qana, were killed in the operation.[96]

Israel has inflicted considerable damage in the West Bank and the Gaza Strip as well. During the first Intifada, Israeli undercover units penetrated Palestinian settlements, killing Palestinians by means of summary executions: the unit located the victim, and without attempting to arrest him, shot in order to kill. According the HRW, more than 110 Palestinians were killed from the beginning of the Intifada until November 1992.[97]

Gordon argues the actions and methods used by the undercover units and the objectives Israel wanted to achieve by these killings correspond well with the definition of terrorism given by Lopez. Thus, they violate some of society's accepted moral and legal codes; they are ruthlessly destructive, and unpredictable in regard to who will be targeted. The Israeli generals who planned the operations knew, in advance, that innocent people would surely die as a result of the bombing and, in line with the definition, the generals contrived a detailed strategy that used horrific violence in order to make people feel weak and vulnerable. The resulting fear sought to promote concrete political objectives exceeding the violent act, Israel terrorized the population of southern Lebanon, so that it, in turn, would pressure the Lebanese government to clamp down on Hizbullah.[98]

Thus, Lopez's definition accepts that states utilize methods of terror against their enemies in order to reach a particular premeditated political goal. The character of the perpetrator does not determine the nature of the act, or conversely, the character of one act does not necessarily predict the type of perpetrator. Accordingly, the means applied can vary: an aerial bombing in southern Lebanon or a suicide bomber can achieve similar results. The State Department's definition of terrorism, on the other hand, clearly takes into account the US's alliance with Israel; as Gordon notes, if the State Department were to adopt Lopez's definition of terrorism: [99]

> it would have had to indict Israel as a terrorist state. Then, according to U.S. law, Israel would no longer be able to trade with the U.S., nor would Israel be eligible for the $3 billion annual aid. In addition, the Pentagon would not be allowed to provide weapons to the Israeli army.

The Mystique of the Land

The ideology of Zionism and the history of the Israeli State are deeply linked with what Zeev Sternhell has called the 'mystique of the land', which attaches a special meaning and value to the 'Land of Israel' as defined in the Old Testament.[100] As noted earlier, this mystique has been shared in equal measure by the 'secular' Israeli leadership of the left and the religious Zionists for whom it is a central tenet in their belief-system. Though the Israeli leaders of the labour movement, who dominated the nation's politics from its founding up to 1977, were avowedly socialist, they drew from Jewish tradition and history the same attachment of the biblical 'Land of Israel' that the religious Zionists did. Thus, David Ben-Guiron, labour leader and Israeli's first Prime Minister, asserted that the Bible is the 'Jews sacrosanct title-deed to Palestine,with a genealogy of 3500 years'.[101]

Even as early as 1938, Ben-Guiron had made it clear that he was accepting a limited part of the holy land for the Jewish state only as an interim measure: he was not 'satisfied with part of the country, but on the basis of the assumption that after we build up a strong force following the establishment of the state, we will abolish the partition of the country [between Jews and Arabs] and we will expand to the whole Land of Israel'.[102] He also made clear his understanding that the proposed expansion would entail use of force:[103]

> This is only a stage in the realization of Zionism and it should prepare the ground for our expansion throughout the whole country through Jewish-Arab agreement ... the state, however, must enforce order and security and it will do this not by moralising and preaching 'sermons on the mount' but by machine-guns, which we will need.

On similar lines, Moshe Dayan, another stalwart of the labour movement, on reaching the Wailing Wall in Jerusalem after its capture by him in 1967, said: 'We have returned to all that is holy in our land. We have returned never to be parted again.'[104] Later, at the burial ceremony for those killed in the 1948 war, Dayan set out his vision of greater Israel thus:[105]

> We have not abandoned your dream and we have not forgotten your lesson. We have returned to the mountain, to the cradle of our people, to the inheritance of the Patriarchs, the land of the judges and the fortress of the Kingdom of the House of David. We have returned to Hebron and Schem [Nablus], to Bethlehem and Annatto, to Jericho and the fords of the Jordan at Adam Ha'ir.

Sternhell has pointed out that Israel's labour movement was imbued not so much with socialism, with its universalist appeal, as with 'nationalist socialism', the Central and East European ideology of the early twentieth century (where Zionism also took birth), which gave primacy to the nation and subordinated the values of socialism to the service of the nation; socialism was thus 'an essential tool in the process of building the nation-state'.[106] The 'secular' Zionism of the Israeli labour movement was, thus, in reality, a 'tribal nationalism", and was steeped in history, religious and semi-religious values.[107] Zeev Sternhell has elaborated this point thus:[108]

> *The difference between religious and secular Zionism, between the Zionism of the Left and the Zionism of the Right, was merely a difference of form and not an essential difference.* Its adherents unanimously viewed Zionism as an enterprise for the rescue of the Jews and their transfer en masse to Palestine

and, later, to the State of Israel. They all believed that, as far as circumstances permitted, the whole land had to be conquered and settled by all possible means. They all recognized that Zionism's task was to bring about a cultural revolution such as the Jews had not experienced since the conquest of Canaan. And all, finally, held the Bible to be the deed to the land, the entire land of their forefathers.

> For all of them, Zionism was defined in terms of culture, history, religion, and even mysticism. The Jewish people were regarded as a tribe, a tribe that should unite and take its place behind the pioneers who led the enterprise of re-conquest and re-settlement. [Emphasis added.]

This 'historical alliance' between secular and religious Zionism has led to what Zertal and Eldar have called the 'malignancy of occupation' in Palestine.[109] This is most poignantly exemplified by the proliferation of Jewish settlements in the occupied territories: during its occupation, Israel has built 120 legal settlements and numerous 'illegal outposts'.[110] At the end of 2006, the number of settlers was 270,000 (with another 220,000 settlers in neighbourhoods around Jerusalem built in the occupied areas); a further 20,000 were added to the West Bank settlement after the withdrawal from Gaza in September 2005.[111] However, the settlers still constitute less than 5 per cent of the Jewish population in Israel and just 10 per cent of the Palestinian population in the territory.[112]

All the settlement activity has been carried out with the full coopera-tion of the State of Israel and its institutions; in the words of Zertal and Eldar: 'Deception, shame, concealment, denial, and repression have characterized the state's behaviour with respect to the flow of funds to the settlements'.[113] While the settlers have pursued their 'sacred national-religious mission', Israel has simultaneously witnessed 'the gradual collapse of the states institutions, whether by choice or out of weakness in the face of the messianic zeal' in the public sphere since 1967.[114]

It is ironical that, as pointed out by Zertal and Eldar, the settlement activity has evoked very little concern in Israel about the erosion of the authority of the state and the dire implications it has had for the Palestinian community: more than 40 per cent of the settlements land had been privately owned by Palestinians.[115] The steady expansion of the settlements, the annexation of additional land to accommodate the separation wall and the several hundred road blocks, all of these have severely restricted Palestinian movement, and separated them from their fields, relatives neighbours and schools.[116] Zertal and Eldar have concluded ruefully:[117]

To this day, no one has assumed responsibility or has been called to account for his part in the settlement project. Perhaps Israeli society has been relatively silent about it because, even as it has become less democratic, less humane, less rational, and at the same time poorer, more divided, and more hateful, the *lives of most Israelis have continued unhindered while the settlements have been conquering Israel and destroying the lives of the Palestinians.* [Emphasis added.]

Allan Brownfeld has drawn attention to the increasing difficulty in reconciling Israel's democratic and its Jewish characteristics. For instance, he notes with concern that the teachings of Judah Halevi, a twelfth century Jewish poet and philosopher, are standard texts in Gush Emunim schools where he is revered as a great prophet. Halevi had spoken disparagingly of Abraham's son, Ishmael, as containing the former's 'bad elements', thus, giving Talmudic sanction to a racist division between the Jews and the Arabs who are believed to have descended from Ishmael. He quotes first-hand reports that young children of Gush Emunim parents are taught that 'the Arab is Amalek, the enemy tribe that God instructed the Jews to fight eternally and destroy'.[118]

Similarly, Roni Gechtman has noted:[119]

In theory, the principles of a Jewish and a democratic state might coexist in harmony. In practice, in Israel these two conceptions—the Jewish state and the democratic regime—are in a state of constant contradiction. In concrete, everyday situations, political decisions must be taken on specific issues by privileging either one or the other of these two principles. The contradictions are especially intensified in the case of the Israeli Palestinians, who represent one out of every five citizens of Israel.

[Non-Jewish Israelis] receive a clear message that the country belongs more to the Jews than to them, and not only to the Jews who are actual citizens of Israel, but also to every other Jew in the world, even if the Palestinians have been living in what is now Israeli territory for generations. [Emphasis added.]

The distinguished Israeli intellectual, Ilan Pappe, should have the last word on this subject:[120]

'Jewish democracy' is not only an oxymoron that fuses a religious outlook with the secular worship of individual freedom; it is an impossibility, given Israel's history and its bi-national, or, for that matter, multicultural-reality ... 'Jewishness' as a state identity is not just a slogan; it is primarily an exclusionary line that denies full citizenship to non-Jews and to Jews who would not be defined as such by the Orthodox rabbinate ...

A political system with such a powerful exclusionary element can only be a pro forma democracy going through the motions of democratic rule but essentially being akin to apartheid or Herrenvolk ('master race') democracy. The fact that this preclusive power is exercised on an indigenous minority - in addition to foreign workers and 'heterodox' Jews - only accentuates the absurdity of the claim that a Jewish state can be a democracy. Israel must move on to become a true liberal democracy by defining itself as a state of all its citizens. [Emphasis added.]

Conclusion

The Israeli religious movement can be broadly divided into religious-extremists and religious-nationalists. While the former pursue a rigid, fundamentalist religious discourse, they tend to play a relatively low-key role in politics. Religious-nationalists on the other hand, while relatively moderate in the religious area, maintain rigid political positions in regard to questions of land. The powerful Messianism-driven settler movement in Israel has come in regular conflict with successive Israeli governments that have attempted to pursue policies of accommodation with the native Palestinian population, particularly from the Oslo Accords in the 1990s. The settler movement has produced zealots who have strongly opposed all compromise and have periodically indulged in violence against Palestinians as also Jews—who support compromise. Their violence culminated in the assassination of Prime Minister Rabin in November 1995.

Successive Israeli governments, both from the Left and the Right, have consistently compromised with the most extreme demands of the settler movement, systematically subverting the peace process and the setting up of a viable Palestinian state. These policies have been pursued at considerable cost to Israel, itself, in economic terms as also in terms of the increasing militarization of its society and the politicization of its armed forces, even as Israeli settlements have continued to expand across the occupied territories in fulfilment of the settlers' sacred 'national-religious mission'. Such policies have raised questions about the serious difficulties Israel faces in reconciling its 'Jewish' character with its political status as a democratic state which gives equal rights to its non-Jewish population.

During the Cold War, when world politics enjoyed a certain dichotomous clarity, the 'we' versus 'they' situation obviously simplified matters in regard to defining terrorism since all organizations and their actors on our side were good and their actions laudable, while all organizations and their actors on the other side were evil and their actions despicable. Today, after the end of the Cold War, it is the Israel—Palestinian dispute which provides the dichotomous framework within which issues relating to the definition of terrorism have come to be situated. Thus, the United States, which is otherwise a lead role player in the 'global war on terror', is extremely accommodative in respect of actions by Israel against the Palestinians which, in the eyes of most other centres of international public opinion are definitely acts of terror. By the same token, actions by Palestinian groups against Israel are invariably described as acts of terror even if, in terms of their numbers and impact, the victims of Israeli actions overwhelm those resulting from Palestinian actions.

The Israel–Palestinian issue is also central to disputes relating to 'State terrorism': Israel and its apologists strongly argue that state actions cannot fall within the definition of terror even as they admit that Israeli actions have caused victims that are disproportionately higher in numbers than those of their enemies, which are invariably 'terrorist' organizations.

The triumph of Jewish messianism has a strong echo amongst large sections of the Christian community in the USA with whom it has built strong bonds of mutual support. The character of the Christian community that espouses the Israeli cause so fervently is examined in the next chapter.

NOTES

1. Israel Shahak and Norton Mezvinsky, *Jewish Fundamentalism in Israel*, New Edition (London: Pluto Press, 2004) p. xvi.
2. Shahak and Mezvinsky, p. xvii.
3. ibid., p. 7.
4. ibid., p. 6.
5. ibid., p. 152.
6. ibid., p. 7.
7. ibid., p. 8.
8. ibid., p.10.
9. ibid., p. 19.
10. ibid., p. 17.
11. ibid., p. 20.
12. ibid., p. 43.
13. Uriel. Tal, 'Foundations of Political Messianic Trends in Israel', *The*

Jerusalem Quarterly, No. 35, Spring 1985; downloaded from: www.geocities.com/a/alabaster_archieve/messianic_ trend.html

14. ibid.
15. Shahak and Mezvinsky, p. 65.
16. Yehiel Harari, 'Notions of Messianism and their Influence on Israel's Prospects for Peace', *Association for Israel Studies*, 2004 Conference papers; downloaded from: www.aisisraelstudies.org/2004papers/ Harari,Yehiel.doc.
17. Shahak and Mezvinsky, p. 62.
18. For instance, Claudia Baumgart has pointed out: 'Without denying Israel its right to protect itself against terror attacks carried out by Palestinian terrorists – it is clear that Israel has repeatedly contributed to the violent escalation of the Israeli–Palestinian conflict by measures such as military retaliation, targeted killings, curfews, house demolitions, and collective punishment. And, last but not least, the illegal occupation and settlement of Palestinian territory by Israel constitutes one of the major obstacles to peace in the Middle East.' [Claudia Baumgart, 'Religious Zionism and Israeli Foreign Policy', Occasional Paper# 30–1, Peace Studies Programme, Cornell University, Ithaca, December 2006, p. 11; downloaded from: http://www.einaudi.cornell.edu/peaceprogram/ publications/occasional_papers/Baumgart-final.pdf.]
19. Alain Dieckhoff, *The Invention of a Nation – Zionist Thought and the Making of Modern Israel* (Cape Town David Philip, 2003) p. 289.
20. Dieckhoff, p. 279.
21. Allan C. Brownfeld, 'Extremism in Israel is Fueled by a Growing Ultra-Orthodox Movement in the US', *Washington Report*, Jan-Feb 2001; downloaded from: www.themodernreligion.com/jihad.com/jihad/us-movement.html.
22. ibid.
23. Shahak and Mezvinsky, p. 86.
24. ibid, p. 87.
25. ibid.
26. ibid., p. 89.
27. ibid., p. 91.
28. ibid., p. 92.
29. ibid., p. 102.
30. ibid.
31. ibid., p. 111.
32. Idith Zertal and Akiva Eldar, *Lords of the Land – The War Over Israel's Settlements in the Occupied Territories, 1967-2007* (New York: Nation Books, 2007) p. 129.

33. ibid., p. 130.
34. ibid., p. 131.
35. ibid., p. 124.
36. ibid., p. 125.
37. ibid., pp. 125–6.
38. ibid., pp. 127–8.
39. ibid., p. 132.
40. ibid., p. 133.
41. ibid., p. 135.
42. ibid., p. 136.
43. ibid., p. 148.
44. ibid., p. 151.
45. ibid., pp. 154–5.
46. ibid., p. 155.
47. Allan C. Brownfeld, 'Fear of Ultra-Orthodox Violence Threatens Israeli Political Process, Withdrawal Prospects,' *Washington Report on Middle East Affairs,* October 2004; downloaded from: www.wrmea.com/archives/October_2004/0410073.html.
48. Zertal and Eldar, pp. 156–9.
49. ibid., p. 168.
50. ibid., p. 169.
51. ibid., pp. 169–70.
52. ibid., p. 171.
53. ibid., p. 172.
54. ibid., p. 177.
55. ibid., p. 179.
56. ibid., p. 403.
57. ibid.
58. ibid., p. 413.
59. ibid., p. 414.
60. ibid., p. 413.
61. ibid., p. 415.
62. ibid., p. 421.
63. ibid., p. 422.
64. ibid., p. 423.
65. ibid., p. 429.
66. Shlomo Swirski, *The Cost of Occupation—The Burden of Israeli–Palestinian Conflict, 2008 Report,* Adva Centre, Tel Aviv, June 2008; downloaded from: www.adva.org/userFiles/File/costofoccupation-2008 fullenglish(1).pdf
67. Yoram Peri, *The Israeli Military and Israeli's Palestinian Policy – From*

Oslo to the Al-Aqsa Intifada, United States Institute of Peace, Washington DC, Nov. 2002, p. 6; downloaded from: www.usip.org/pubs/peaceworks/ pwks 47.pdf.

68. ibid., p. 9.
69. ibid., p. 31.
70. ibid., p. 32.
71. ibid., p. 33
72. ibid., p. 41.
73. ibid., p. 42.
74. ibid., p. 43.
75. ibid., p. 42.
76. Boaz Ganor, 'Defining Terrorism: Is one Man's Terrorist Another Man's Freedom Fighter?', 1997; downloaded from: http:// www.israelactivism.com/article.php?articleid= 298table= factsheets.
77. ibid.
78. Bruce Hoffman, *Inside Terrorism,* (New York: Columbia University Press, 1998), Chapter One downloaded from: http://www.nytimes.com/books/ first/h/hoffman-terrorism.html.
79. Ibid.
80. Lev Grinberg, 'Israel's State Terrorism', *Tikkum Magazine,* 1 April 2002; downloaded from: http://www.commondreams.org/views02/0401-04.htm
81. John Pilger, 'Time to Recognise State Terror', *Antiwar.com,* 17 September 2004; downloaded from: http://www.antiwar.com/orig/ pilger.php?articleid=3592
82. Peter Symonds, 'Amnesty International Details Israeli War Crimes In Lebanon', *World Socialist Web,* 25 August 2006; downloaded from: http:/ /www.countercurrents.org/leb-symonds250806.htm
83. ibid.
84. ibid.
85. Stern, p. xxi.
86. Rinehart, pp. 14–16.
87. ibid., p. 16.
88. Hoffman.
89. Neve Gordon, 'Defining Terrorism and Assigning the Label', 90 Sep. 2001, downloaded from: http://oznik.com/words/010923.html
90. ibid.
91. ibid; the definition of terrorism as set out by the US Department of State reads as follows:
    (*i*) The term 'terrorism' means premeditated, politically motivated violence perpetrated against noncombatant targets by subnational

groups or clandestine agents usually intended to influence an audience.

(*ii*) The term 'international terrorism' means terrorism involving citizens or the territory of more than one country.

(*iii*) The term 'terrorist group' means any group practising, or which has significant subgroups that practise international terrorism.

92. ibid.
93. ibid.
94. ibid.
95. ibid.
96. ibid.
97. ibid.
98. ibid.
99. ibid.
100. Zeev Sternhell, *The Founding Myths of Israel—Nationalism, Socialism, and the Making of the Jewish State,* (Princeton, New Jersey: Princeton University Press, 1999) p. 337l.
101. Nur Masalha, *Imperial Israel and the Palestinians—The Politics of Expansion* (London: Pluto Press 2000) p. 3; henceforth Masalha.
102. ibid., pp. 6–7.
103. ibid., p. 7.
104. ibid., p. 15.
105. ibid., p. 16.
106. ibid., p. 7.
107. Sternhell, p. 320.
108. ibid, pp. 340–1.
109. Zertal and Eldar, p. x.
110. ibid., p. xv.
111. ibid., p. xiii.
112. ibid., p. xv.
113. ibid., p. xxi.
114. ibid., p. xvii.
115. ibid., p. xiii.
116. ibid., p. 425.
117. ibid., p. xviii.
118. Brownfeld.
119. Roni Gechtman, 'The Israeli Right: Nationalism, Militarism and Messianism', *Journal of Social and Political Thought,* Vol. One, No. One, New York; downloaded from www.yorku.ca/jspot/1/gechtman.ht.
120. Brownfeld.

5

Christian Messianism in the USA

> We Americans are the peculiar, chosen people, the Israel of our time;
> we bear the ark of the liberties of the world ... Long enough have we
> been skeptics with regard to ourselves, and doubted whether, indeed,
> the political Messiah had come. But he has come in *us*, if we would
> but give utterance to his promptings.
>
> Herman Melville

American messianism began with its earliest European settlers and has
ebbed and flowed through its history. Puritans in seventeenth century
New England saw themselves as refugees from a sinful world, preparing
to build in their new American home a millennial kingdom as prophesied
in the Bible. Framers of the US Constitution believed they were engaged
in a divinely supported enterprise, with significant consequences for
the whole world. They inserted evidence of that into the Great Seal of
the United States printed on the back of each dollar bill. The reverse of
the seal bears two significant Latin phrases: the first is *'Annuit Coeptis'*,
interpreted loosely as 'Providence has favoured our undertakings'. The
other is *'Novus Ordo Seclorum'*, meaning, 'A new order of the ages'. As
Donald Jarvis has said:[1]

> Religion has always been a major force in U.S. politics, policy, identity,
> and culture. Religion shapes the nation's character, helps form Americans'
> ideas about the world, and influences the ways Americans respond to
> events beyond their borders. *Religion explains both Americans' sense of
> themselves as a chosen people and their belief that they have a duty to spread
> their values throughout the world.* [Emphasis added.]

Early nineteenth century Americans were seen by contemporary foreign
observers as exhibiting considerable religiosity, which was natural for
the various Christian denominations that had fled persecution in Europe.

At the same time, the absence of an established national Church and the multiplicity of denominations and sects also ensured tolerance amongst these various groups. But, what was unique about America was that the pervasive tolerance and absence of a state religion encouraged these early American Protestants, already 'among the world's most Bible reading', to be attracted 'to the sort of individualist and anti-hierarchical faith that emphasized a personal relationship with God'.[2]

This tendency had the effect of increasingly moving adherents from mainline Protestantism to 'sectarian emotion and revival', so that, by the end of the twentieth century, once peripheral sects were taking over the centre stage.[3] Phillips has pointed out that, at century-end, the USA had 'a superabundance of denominations and sects compared to Europe, as well as a far, far higher ratio of church-goers'.[4] Rough estimates indicate that about 25 per cent of Americans are affiliated with a church that is in a network of conservative Protestant churches, while only about 15 per cent are affiliated to a mainline Protestant church.[5]

Among the US's Protestant denominations, the Southern Baptist Convention (SBC), with 40 million members, is the largest group.[6] In a public discussion on evangelical influence on US politics, a senior SBC figure said about 15-20 per cent Southern Baptists could be classified as fundamentalist, while about 15 per cent would be in the liberal category.[7]

The depth of religious belief among Americans is provided in a variety of polls set out in Phillips' book; some of the important results are:[8]

I.   Is the Bible literally accurate?
a) National sample: Yes,   55%
b) Evangelical Protestants: Yes,   83%

II. Do you believe in:	Affirmative Responses	
	Newsweek (2000)	Fox News (2004)
a) God?	94%	92%
b) Miracles?	84%	82%
c) Satan?	75%	70%

Central to American religiosity is the notion of the 'fundamentalist apocalyptic' in terms of which the Bible's key prophetic and apocalyptic passages:[9]

are viewed not as allegorical representations of spiritual realities, or as a record of apocalyptic expectation at the time the works were composed, but as a guide to God's plan for human history, verbally dictated and inerrant in every detail.

Contemporary Right-wing Christian thinking in the USA draws on the religious debates in different parts of the country in the nineteenth century pertaining to Christian eschatology and the 'second coming' of the Messiah (Jesus Christ), that is, the study of the end of history on the basis of religious scriptures. Christian eschatology predicts four events:[10]

(*i*) **The Millennium:** Revelation describes an important interval lasting for 1,000 years when Christ will rule; this is a golden era, a time of universal peace heralded by the bodily return of Jesus Christ to Earth.

(*ii*) **The Tribulation:** This is a seven-year interval when a world religious-political leader called the Antichrist takes power.

(*iii*) **Armageddon:** is a terrible war provoked by the Antichrist in which most people on Earth will die. God's anger, hatred, and wrath are poured out over mankind and the Earth at this time. A series of violent events, as prophesied in Daniel 9, Matthew 24, and Revelation 4–19, will occur.

(*iv*) **The Rapture:** 1 Thessalonians 4.16–18 describes a *miraculous event* when Christ will descend from the heavens. Conservative Protestants believe that faithful '*born again*' Christians who had died earlier will be resurrected, rise from their graves, and ascend to meet Jesus in the sky. Immediately afterwards, '*born again*' Christians who had not died will also ascend into the air. Since the vast majority of humans are not '*born again*', most people will remain behind on Earth.

Given the obscure nature of the texts, there are disputes among scholars and their adherents about the meaning of the predicted events and their timing and sequence. This has led to the emergence of different denominations and sub-groups among American Protestants. Mainstream thinking in this regard goes as follows: The central narrative of Revelation is that righteous Christians will be tricked and betrayed by trusted political and religious leaders who are secretly conspiring with Satan. It goes on to describe in graphic detail what will happen when an angry God finally intervenes in human affairs at the 'end of time'. (The narrative describes the end-times as a period of widespread sinfulness, moral depravity, and crass materialism.) The Four Horsemen of the Apocalypse ride in, bringing God's wrath in the form of wars, disease, civil strife and natural disasters. Satan's chief henchman appears in human form as the Antichrist, a popular world leader who secretly sympathizes with the Devil. He promises peace and unity of all nations under one world government—but this is a conspiracy. His agents are tracking down and punishing Christians who refuse to abandon their faith. Satan's allies receive a mark—the Mark of the Beast—represented by the number '666'. This period of hard times is called '*the Tribulations*' and culminates in a final cataclysmic doomsday confrontation of massed armies in the Middle East, at a place named Armageddon. Good triumphs over evil at the battle of Armageddon, ushering in a *Millennium* of rule by Jesus Christ.[11]

Among Protestants there are three principal views pertaining to the 'second coming' of Jesus Christ and his thousand-year rule; these are:[12]

(*i*) **Amillenialism**: This tradition believes that the 1,000-year reign of Jesus Christ will be entirely spiritual and not geographical or physical.

(*ii*) **Premillenialism**: It believes that the coming reign of Jesus Christ will be literal: He will return premillenially, that is, before the end of the world, and set up His kingdom in triumph for 1,000 years, and personally administer His kingdom. This tradition has two viewpoints:

    (a) **Historic Premillenialism**: This believes there will be a "Great Tribulation" of the church just prior to Jesus's return.

    (b) **Dispensational Premillenialism**: This believes that, just before the Great Tribulation, Jesus will return secretly, resurrect dead Christians, and raise all living Christians to the sky in an event called the *Rapture*. Those left behind will then go through a war when the Antichrist will lead the world's armed forces against helpless Israel: the Great Tribulation will be a disaster for the Jewish people in which two-thirds of Jews will die. Seven years after the Rapture, Jesus will return with the resurrected and "raptured" Christians with sinless and indestructible bodies, and rule from Jerusalem.

(*iii*) **Postmillennialism**: According to this tradition, some time in the future, a great period of evangelical success will occur, when billions of people will accept Christ as the Saviour; this will be a truly blessed period. After the world has experienced a long period of Christian culture, Jesus Christ will come postmillennially to end history and judge mankind.

Most American Protestants subscribe to the Dispensational Premillenialist tradition: in a 1987 survey, 63 per cent of the Southern

Baptist Ministers indicated 'premillenialist' in regard to their beliefs about Biblical prophecy; only 0.7 per cent of the respondents chose the 'postmillenialist' option. Again, 30 per cent described themselves as 'Dispensationalists'.[13]

Dispensational Premillenialism was brought to the USA by a British preacher John Nelson Darby (1800-82), who toured the USA six times between 1859 and 1877. His doctrine replaced the then prevalent Postmillennialism by preaching that Christ would return to Earth *before* commencing his 1,000-year reign and 'save' the believers, thus promising a reward for faith and piety.[14] Darby preached that history consisted of distinct preordained periods or 'dispensations', with each dispensation being brought to an end when human beings became so wicked that God was forced to punish them. Previous dispensations had ended with such catastrophes as the Fall, the Flood and the crucifixion of Christ.[15]

We are presently living in the Sixth Dispensation of 'grace' in which people are judged according to their relationship with Christ. Satan, represented by the Antichrist, will lead mankind astray. During seven years of Tribulation, a period of total evil, the Antichrist will wage war and massacre numerous people. After this, Christ will appear, defeat the Antichrist, and finally meet Satan at the Battlefield of Armageddon, and inaugurate the Seventh Dispensation that would bring peace and harmony for one thousand years.[16] According to Darby, true believers in Christ will be saved from this calamity: just before the beginning of the Tribulation, there will be a 'Rapture' in which 'born-again' Christians, (that is, Christians who had died) as also these who were alive will be taken up to heaven and thus avoid the suffering of the Last Days.[17]

Through much of the early twentieth century there was considerable difference of opinion between the liberals and the conservatives within US Protestantism. Publicly, the former seemed to be dominant since the conservatives withdrew from the public arena and confined themselves to their own churches and places of study, where they affirmed their commitment to the 'fundamentals' of their faith. By 1930, there were fifty fundamentalist Bible colleges in the USA; during the Depression years, twenty-six more were added. With the arrival of television in the 1950s, the traditional revivalist preachers were replaced by 'televangelists'.[18] During this period, fundamentalist Protestants also moved to the political Right in defence of the 'American way of life' as a sacred duty.[19] This specifically meant agitating against all perceived infiltration by communists into the media, education and the judiciary, as also the mainline denominations.

The Premillenialists and the evangelicals were united in their belief in the end-times, the Rapture, the Antichrist and Armageddon, that is, in the inevitability of war and widespread death and destruction. They saw signs confirming their dire visions all around them: the atom bomb that would totally annihilate the world; the United Nations that would evolve into the dictatorship of the Antichrist; and the setting up of the State of Israel in 1948: John Darby's premillennial vision provided that the Last Days could not begin unless the Jews were living in the 'Holy Land'.[20]

According to modern-day believers, human history is nearing its climax, with contemporary events corresponding to the 'end-signs' foretold in the Bible; these include: increase in apostasy, wickedness, warfare, famine and natural disasters. These will culminate in the seven-year Great Tribulation, when the Antichrist will rule the earth, thus initiating the series of end-times events such as: Christ's return to earth; His battle with the Anti-Christ at Armageddon; His 1,000-year rule from the restored Jewish temple in Jerusalem; the Last Judgment when all living persons will be consigned eternally to heaven or hell; the last uprising of the Antichrist and his final defeat; and finally, the emergence of 'new heaven and new earth when history gives way to eternity'.[21]

Protestant fundamentalism witnessed a significant growth in the 1960s and 1970s. In 1980, a Gallup poll showed that 85 per cent of Americans regarded the Bible as divinely inspired; 40 per cent believed that the Bible was inerrant and had to be taken literally word for word.[22] According to a 1983 Gallup poll, 62 per cent of Americans had 'no doubt' that Jesus would return to Earth.[23] The USA then had 1,300 evangelical Christian radio and TV stations with an audience of 130 million.[24] Today, there are about 80 million evangelical Christians in the USA.[25] (The term 'evangelical' refers to the eagerness of the doctrine's followers to share the 'good news' (the coming of Christ) and win converts.) This conservative trend was a reaction to the perceived excesses of the permissive society as also the activism of the Supreme Court, which, in its robust pronouncements, was seen as intruding into the areas of belief and faith prized by the fundamentalists, particularly in the South. As Karen Armstrong has pointed out:[26]

> Reforms that seemed just and moral to liberals in San Francisco, Boston or Yale seemed sinful to religious conservatives in Arkansas and Alabama

... They did not feel liberated by the permissive society ... they could only conclude that America was falling under the influence of Satan.

Fundamentalists saw US society as dominated by the atheist beliefs and mindset of 'secular humanism', which Tim LaHaye described as 'anti-God, anti-moral, anti-self-restraint and anti-American'.[27] They yearned instead for the political order of the Pilgrim Fathers, that is, 'a republic in which the will of the majority and all egalitarian tendencies would be controlled by biblical law'.[28]

Evangelicals have consolidated their following and obtained new converts through charismatic preachers such as Billy Graham and Jimmy Swaggart; leaders of evangelical movements such as Pat Robertson of the Christian Coalition and Jerry Falwell of the Moral Majority; and extraordinarily popular writers, such as Hal Lindsey, author of *Late Great Planet Earth* (1970), and Tim LaHaye, who has authored the *Left Behind* series of books that have sold over 50 million copies. These and other American millennialist writers have focused on end-signs that herald Christ's return to Earth, such as increasing wickedness and conflict and impending environmental catastrophe, the centrality of the prophetic role of the Jewish people and the role of the Arabs, and Islam generally, in the end-times.[29]

These evangelical preachers have regularly predicted the apocalyptic end of the world: in 1950, Billy Graham set a date, when he said: 'I sincerely believe that the Lord draweth nigh. We may have another year, may be two years to wait for Jesus Christ, and (then) ... it is all going to be over'.[30] In 1965, Graham did not set a date, but still conveyed the same message of the Apocalypse: 'Secular history ... is doomed ... The whole world is hurtling forward a war greater than anything known before.' A nuclear holocaust, he believed, would be God's chosen instrument for the earth's purification.[31]

Both radio and television are powerful tools for charismatic preachers to mobilize their flock and keep it in a divinely empowered state of enthusiasm and excitement. Televangelists such as Billy Graham, Jimmy Swaggart, Jim and Tammy Bakker, and Pat Robertson with his CBN stations, have made millennialism a living experience for their adherents, besides ensuring millions of dollars in their movement's coffers.

The Christian Right in US Politics

Students of US history have noted that a religious mentality, particularly Protestant millennialism, is deeply rooted in the American psyche. The

English Puritans had originally thought of England as the 'New Jerusalem'. After the end of Cromwell's revolution, they replaced it with 'New England'. In due course, as John Judis has noted, America's founders 'translated Protestant millennialism into the language of American nationalism and exceptionalism', seeing the Americans as a 'chosen people'.[32] The religiosity of the Americans has also instilled in them an 'apocalyptic outlook' which emerges from their millennialism.[33] This, as Judis points out, has not only made Americans perceive national and world events in good *vs.* evil terms, it has also meant that they believe in 'cataclysmic transformation' rather than gradual or subtle charge; according to Judis:[34]

> This apocalyptic mentality gravitates toward absolute dichotomies and revolutionary change. It discourages a complex appreciation of differences and similarities in favour of a rush toward generalities and simple polarities. It looks toward immediate resolution of conflict ... and eschews the postponement or modification of ultimate objectives.

Though America's Founding Fathers were staunchly religious, the US Constitution framed by them was based on a strict separation between Church and State. In 1776, Thomas Jefferson confirmed this with his well-known remark: 'Every man's soul belongs to himself ... the evil occurs when man is forced to abandon care of his salvation to another. No man has the power to let another prescribe his faith.'[35] James Madison justified this separation as being good for religion and faith: disestablishing religion, he argued, does not demote religion but rather protects it from exploitation by political authority, from 'an unhallowed perversion of the means of salvation'.[36]

Religion, however, has been invoked in almost all significant national debates. Abraham Lincoln, while campaigning for the presidency, in 1860, in Trenton, New Jersey, made the following statement: 'Americans are the chosen people, and I hope that I might become the humble servant of the Almighty and of his chosen people.'[37] During the First World War, President Woodrow Wilson claimed that the war 'showed America marching to heights upon which there rests nothing but the pure light which came at Calvary, the first dawn which came with the Christian era'.[38] During the Cold War, President Harry S. Truman referred to Communism as 'godless' so many times that 'godless Communism' became a catchphrase.[39]

Adherents of Protestant millenialist belief systems have traditionally belonged to two groups: those who remain aloof from sinful secular society and passively await salvation, while others who seek to intervene in public life to assert their beliefs and world view. Propagated by philosopher Francis Schaeffer and theologian Cornelius van Til, who advocated a 'muscular' and interventionist form of Christianity, the activist approach entered the public domain in the 1950s under the influence of the evangelist preacher, Billy Graham, and become widespread in the 1970s.[40] Believers were then encouraged to participate in electoral and legislative matters, since fundamentalist leaders realized that their cause would not be served unless they intervened in the political process; Hal Lindsey called for activism in the public arena thus:[41]

> We need to get active, electing officials who will not only reflect the Bible's morality in government, but will shape domestic and foreign policies to protect our country and our way of life.

From the early 1980s, different strands of Protestantism increasingly came together to assert 'the theocratic idea that, regardless of religious views or eschatological timetable, Christian men are called by God to exercise dominion over secular society by taking control of political and cultural institutions'; they represented, in Chip Berlet's view, an 'exclusionary Christian nationalism'.[42] Present-day American Right-wing consists of three movements:[43]

   (i)   *the Christian Right*, made up of Christian evangelical denominations and groups such as the Christian Coalition and Moral Majority;
   (ii) *the Right-wing Populists*, which include gun-right activists and armed militant movements, which work closely with the Christian Right; and
   (iii) *the Far Right*, which includes the Ku Klux Klan, and extremists adhering to xenophobic and racist Christian groups such as the Christian Identity Movement, which work with the neo-Nazis on a common anti-government and anti-Jewish platform: the Movement sees Jews as descendants of Satan and its own members as the descendants of the biblical tribes of Israel; they see themselves as 'apocalyptic agents' and believe they have been chosen to use force against the enemies of God.[44]

Berlet believes these three movements had set up a broad 'New Right' coalition in the 1970s, whose rhetoric:[45]

is rooted in historic and contemporary constructs of Biblical Literalism articulated through recurring, polarizing themes of good and evil, personal salvation, evangelism, and the inevitability of apocalypse, among others.

The foundational impulses of the Christian Right-wing in the USA, Berlit believes, emerge from its belief in a 'Liberal secular humanist conspiracy'. He quotes George Marsden to explain this:[46]

> Fundamentalists always had been alarmed at moral decline within America but often had been vague as to whom, other than the Devil, to blame. The 'secular humanist' thesis gave this central concern a clearer focus that was more plausible and of wider appeal than the old mono-causal communist-conspiracy accounts. Communism and socialism could, of course, be fit right into the humanist picture; but so could all the moral and legal changes at home without implausible scenarios of Russian agents infiltrating American schools, government, reform movements, and mainline churches.

Secular humanism, 'epitomising all aspects of liberal Godlessness, including abortion, anti-family feminism, homosexual activists, "pagan" environmentalists, as also "big government" and "globalists"', has among its enemies some of the leading lights of the Christian Right, such as Pat Robertson and Tim LaHaye. Chip Berlit expresses concern about the long-term impact of Right-wing populism that feeds the apocalyptic fears of its adherents:[47]

> Right-wing populist movements can cause serious damage to a society because they often popularize xenophobia, authoritarianism, scapegoating, and conspiracism. This can lure mainstream politicians to adopt these themes to attract voters, legitimize acts of discrimination (or even violence), and open the door for revolutionary right-wing populist movement, such as fascism, to recruit from the reformist populist movements.

He notes further that apocalyptic fears include the denomination of a number of different hate-figures as 'the search for the Devil's partners is continuously updated'.[48] Paul Boyer points out that, in prophetic literature, the identity of Satan's allies in the Battle of Armageddon has shifted seamlessly over time, circumstance, and political interest from the Soviet Union to Chinese communists to Islamic militants; he warns of an increasing level of anti-Muslim bigotry in some contemporary apocalyptic subcultures.[49] Robert Fuller has noted the following targets:[50]

Today, fundamentalist Christian writers see the Antichrist in such enemies as the Muslim world, feminism, rock music, and secular humanism. The threat of the Antichrist's imminent takeover of the world's economy has been traced to the formation of the European Economic Community, the Susan B. Anthony dollar ... and the introduction of universal product codes.

The defeat of Barry Goldwater in 1964, though an 'electoral catastrophe' for the Right-wing, was a watershed event in that it encouraged the Christian Right to pursue the systemtic mobilization of grass roots political support for Right-wing interests which, sixteen years later, would ensure the election of Ronald Reagan.[51] This Right-wing coalition was brought together by a number of shared concerns: erosion of moral and religious values; the expansion of civil rights; the 'banning of God from our schoolrooms'; and widespread interest in reducing the role of national government and taxes, what Stephen Bates refers to as 'a pool of discontent to fish from'.[52] In due course, a number of influential conservative think tanks, religious and secular, emerged, such as the Heritage Foundation, the American Enterprise Institute, Conservation, Political Action and Concerned Women for America, focusing on different interests, but 'sharing personnel, personal ties and a common world view'.[53] In 1979, the Christian Right-wing leaders, headed by Jerry Falwell, set up the Moral Majority.[54]

However, even with the Reagan Presidency, the Moral Majority did not obtain the expected results in respect of their agenda. Pat Robertson, seeking the Republican nomination for the 1988 Presidential election, attempted to correct this. Emerging from an impeccable Christian Right background and nationally influential as the owner of a television station, Christian Broadcasting Network (CBN), Robertson faltered in the campaign after some initial successes against Bush senior, not least because voters, while concerned about the erosion of oral values, were not keen to see the country run by the Religious Right.[55] Later, Robertson set up a more effective body at the grass roots called the Christian Coalition. This body sought power for the Christian Right at the local level, that is, school boards, local councils, etc. Robertson clearly foresaw the need for a theocratic order in the USA:[56]

> When the Christian majority takes over this country, there will be no satanic churches, no more free distribution of pornography, no more abortion on demand and no more talk of rights for homosexuals. After

the Christian majority takes control, pluralism will be seen as immoral and evil and the state will not permit anybody to practise it.

The Christian Coalition was active 'in stirring up a permanent sense of outrage' against organizations that did not conform to its rigid requirements.Its strength also grew significantly: from 125 chapters and 57,000 members in 1990, it went to 2000 chapters and 1.9 million members by 1997.[57] Its political impact was also considerable: 114 members of the House and 26 senators had received perfect approval ratings from the Coalition, and an additional 58 Congressmen voted for Coalition positions at least 85 per cent of the time. In all, 60 per cent of victorious Congressional candidates had the backing of the Christian Coalition.[58]

After 1997, the Coalition went into decline, losing members, contributions and staff. As Falwell and Robertson waned in influence due to age and illness (Jerry Falwell died in May 2007), Dr. James Dobson, founder of the 'Focus on the Family' organization, emerged as the leading light of the Christian Right. *Focus* has a mailing list of six million, with a radio show aired over 4000 radio stations and Dobson's syndicated column published in 500 local newspapers per week. His political support is for Republicans and those candidates who are from the Christian Right; in 2004, he supported Bush.[59] One of Dobson's close associates has this to say about him:[60]

> I believe it is accurate and justified and reasonable to say that Jim wants theocracy ... his perfect president would be someone with a law book in one hand and a Bible in the other, someone who defers to the fundamentalist interpretation. Jim really believes that until that happens, America is on its last legs and is gasping its last breaths. Jim is desperate and fearful and he really believes that only a theocracy can save us.

The avowed separation between Church and State in the USA and the absence of any obvious religion-oriented contentions or conflicts in US public life had lulled scholars, American and foreign, into believing that religion was, perhaps, a less important a factor in determining national affairs as compared to, say, race, education, income, etc. Ronald Reagan's presidency firmly corrected this impression: a 1990 British study ruefully noted that 'it took the surge of the Religious Right to alert academics to the continued salience of religion in political life'.[61] The Presidential elections of 2000 and 2004 have emphasized the extraordinary electoral power of this hitherto neglected force.

The party political implications of the religion-secular divide in US politics have been clearly apparent since 1972 when the 'irreligious' bloc constituted most of McGovern's supporters, while 86 per cent of white southern regular church-goers (many of them registered Democrats) voted for Nixon.[62] The futurist, Herman Kahn, described this development as a 'counter-reformation', and noted that 'the United States is the only Western country that seems to be going through this counter-revolution on a large scale'.[63]

Kevin Phillips has pointed out that, 'well before September 11, 2001, religion and intensity of faith and worship were emerging as the principal dividing lines in national politics,' with the Democrats and Republicans increasingly polarized on 'moral issues' such as abortion, gay marriage and prayer in schools.[64] However, this American religiosity in the later part of the 20th century was different from earlier times in that it had neither the missionary zeal of the earlier decades nor the social concerns pertaining to the disadvantaged; it focused instead on the 'individual pursuit of salvation through spiritual re-birth based on adherence to millennial-affiliated groups which saw the Bible as inerrant, drew the most dubious prophecies from Biblical scriptures, and indulged in bizarre practices including quaking and shaking and speaking in tongues.'[65] The Religious Right, as Phillips noted, had also 'embraced cultural anti-modernism, war hawkishness and Armageddon prophecy.'[66] These trends have caused concern among liberal theologians who are appalled at what they see as 'half-baked preaching' pertaining to 'rapture' and 'end-times': one of them has described such religion as 'a toxin that would harm the health—even the life—of Christian churches and American society.'[67]

The book, *A Matter of Faith*, edited by David E. Campbell, published in 2007, re-confirmed that, in the 2004 election, 'religion took center stage', with Evangelical Protestants constituting the crucial support base for the Bush vote.[68] The book notes that Evangelical Protestants constitute just over 25 per cent of the US population, while mainline Protestants constitute 16.4 per cent.[69] Both groups can be divided into four subgroups: Traditionalist, Centrist, Modernist and Nominal. Among Evangelical Protestants, 93 per cent of Traditionalists believe in a personal God, as do 69.3 per cent of the Centrists; figures for Mainline Protestants are 73 per cent and 32 per cent respectively.[70] In the 2004 election, 88 per cent of Traditionalist Evangelicals gave their votes to Bush, having had a turnout of nearly 71 per cent. Evangelicals taken together had a turnout of 63 per cent, with 77.5 per cent of them being Bush voters. Bush also got 70.4 per cent of the vote of the Centrist Evangelicals, though their turnout was a relatively low 56.3 per cent. Taken together, the two largest evangelical groups made up 35 per cent of the Bush vote; if the modernists and nominals are taken into account, the Evangelical Protestants provided 40 per cent of the Bush vote in the election.[71]

It is important to note that while committed evangelicals have been consistent supporters of the Republican Party since 1980, Bush's significant achievement was his ability 'to attract the less committed evangelicals to the Republican fold',[72] with the proportion of evangelicals voting for the President rising from 68 per cent in 2000 to 78 per cent in 2004,[73] even as nominal evangelicals nearly tripled their vote for the Republican party from 1992 to 2004.[74]

From the analysis of the 2004 election, the following broad conclusions have been drawn by David Leege:[75]

(*i*) there was substantial affinity between President Bush and all types of evangelicals;

(*ii*) the evangelicals are forming a 'group identity' and being Republican is part of their group identity; and,

(*iii*) ideology among Republicans 'has come to be connected more strongly to traditional religious values than to economic interests.'

The Religious Faith of George Bush

Stephan Mansfield, in his book, *The Faith of George W. Bush*, has confirmed that Bush approached the 2000 election as a biblical mission. On the eve of announcing his candidacy, Bush told a Texan evangelist:[76]

I feel like God wants me to run for President. I can't explain it, but I sense my country is going to need me. Something is going to happen. I know it won't be easy on me or my family, but God wants me to do it.

In fact, I really don't want to run. My father was president. My whole family has been affected by it. I know the price. I know what it will mean. I would be perfectly happy to have people point at me some day when I am buying fishing lures at Wal-Mart and say, "That was our governor." That's all I want. And if I run for president that kind of life will be over. My life will never be the same. But I feel God wants me to do this and I must do it.

In the 2004 election, 'reasonably religious' voters cast about half of the US votes; of them, 70–75 per cent backed Bush, the largest portion of his electoral coalition. In this context, it is important to note that Bush won both the 2000 and 2004 elections with very narrow margins; in fact, his 50.7 per cent share of the vote in 2004 'was the weakest for an incumbent President since Woodrow Wilson in 1916.'[77] This confirmed, as Phillips has pointed out, that the Bush presidency rested on a very narrow base, so that, 'religious conservatives were absolutely critical' to his re-election.[78]

Bush, in his presidency, consistently reflected the pervasive US view of its unique, God-given exceptionalism, and that liberty and democracy had been bestowed upon the country 'as a special gift first to the Americans.'[79] This was also the President's explanation for his various foreign policy and military actions; thus, in 2004, he said in a debate with John Kerry:[80]

> I believe that God wants everybody to be free. That's what I believe. And that's one part of my foreign policy. In Afghanistan I believe that the freedom there is a gift from the Almighty. And I can't tell you how encouraged I am to see freedom on the march. And so my principles that I make decisions on are part of me. And religion is part of me.

He was convinced that he was the instrument of God's will; he said in May 2004:[81]

> Our part, our calling, is to align our hearts and actions with God's plan, in so far as we can know it ... we cannot be neutral in the face of injustice or cruelty or evil. God is not on the side of any nation, yet we know he is on the side of justice. And it is the deepest strength of America that from the hour of our founding, we have chosen justice as our goal.

He also believed in the divine force behind America's destined role in world affairs:[82]

> We can also be confident in the ways of providence, even when they are far from our understanding. Events aren't moved by blind change and chance. Behind all of life and all of history, there's a dedication and purpose, set by the hand of a just and faithful God. And that hope will never be shaken.

Stephen Mansfield pointed out that, 'No one in recent memory has pounded that pulpit for religion's role in government quite like the forty-third president.'[83] Bush's 'unapologetic religious tone' and his willingness to 'speak of being called to the presidency, of a God who rules in the affairs of me', and of the United States 'owing her origin to Providence', also distinguished him from his predecessors.[84] 'One of the most unique characteristics of the Bush presidency and very possibly one of the most defining issues of our time,' Mansfield said, is that 'Bush daily puts faith to work'. Mansfield claimed that, in addition to having his legacy established by being President on 9/11, 'another likely pillar of George W. Bush's legacy ... is that matter of his religious faith and his attempts to integrate faith as a whole into American public policy.'[85]

Andrew Austin has also given a succinct account of Bush's deep religious faith. He recalled Bush's remarks in his State of the Union message of 20 January 2001, when he said: 'We are not this story's author, who fills time and eternity with His purpose. Yet His purpose is achieved in our duty ... This work continues. This story goes on. And an angel still rides in the whirlwind and directs this storm.'[86] Bush's religious faith led him and members of his Administration to believe that the September 11 attacks were signs from God that Bush is ordained to lead a crusade against evil.

Ronald Reagan had been the first US President to publicly articulate such sentiments; as Governor, he had said, in 1971:[87]

> In the 38th chapter of Ezekiel, it says that the land of Israel will come under attack by the armies of the ungodly nations and it says that Libya will be among them. Do you understand the significance of that? Libya has now gone communist, and that's a sign that the day of Armageddon isn't that far off ... Everything is falling into place ... Ezekiel tells us that Gog, the nation that will lead all of the other powers of darkness against Israel, will come out of the north ... now that Russia has become communist and atheistic, now that Russia has set itself against God. Now it fits the description of Gog perfectly.

President Bush was not only in line with these sentiments, he also, according to Austin, 'form[ed] his policies around extremist interpretations of Christian doctrine'.[88] A particular understanding of Christian eschatology directed his political decisions. Such beliefs, coupled with the conviction that God chose him to fulfill a part of God's plan, 'represent a frightening political-ideological combination'.[89]

Bush, even before he became President, had already made clear his strong religious convictions, commencing with the reference to his own personal redemption in 1984 (or 1985) and his sense of divine mission as US President. However, the events of September 11 most effectively and dramatically brought forth Bush's deep religious beliefs, particularly his sense of performing God's mission; hence, references to God and the Bible came to inform every one of his pronouncements. Bush's remarks were in the Christian evangelical tradition of linking *us* and *them* with good *vs.* evil, as Bruce Lincoln has noted.[90] These included references to American courage *vs.* cowardly terrorist attacks; American goodness and compassion *vs.* blind hatred and resentment; true American piety *vs.* self-deluded fanaticism; and modern civilization *vs.* medieval resistance to progress. Towards the end of the Afghan war, Bush told the United Nations: 'History has an Author who fills time and eternity with His purpose. We know that evil is real, but good will prevail against it.'[91]

When the time came to make his case for the Iraq war, Bush displayed an apocalyptic mentality, describing Saddam Hussein as 'evil' and as a 'mad man' who could unleash considerable violence upon the United States.[92] The apocalyptic belief that a good future inevitably succeeds an evil past strengthened Bush's conviction that war in Iraq would inevitably set up a chain reaction of democratic reform across West Asia. In his third State of the Union address, after setting out the charges about weapons and terrorist ties and portraying Saddam Hussein as evil incarnate, the President presented his argument thus:[93]

> [W]e go forward with confidence, because this call of history has come to the right country ... Americans are a free people, who know that freedom is the right of every person and the future of every nation. The liberty we prize is not America's gift to the world; it is God's gift to humanity. We Americans have faith in ourselves – but not in ourselves alone. We do not claim to know all the ways of Providence, yet we can trust in them, placing our confidence in the loving God behind all of life, and all of history.

Bruce Lincoln concluded that Bush's theology rested on five principles:[94]

(1) God desires freedom for all humanity;
(2) This desire manifests itself in history;
(3) America is called by history (and thus, implicitly by God) to take action on behalf of this cause;
(4) To the extent America responds with courage and determination, God's purpose is served and freedom's advance is inevitable;
(5) With the triumph of freedom, God's will is accomplished and history comes to an end.

Phillips has robustly argued that Bush used the events of 9/11 to sew together a political set-up that was founded on religious fundamentalism and was giving the shape of a 'theocracy' to the United States.[95] In this context, he recalled Charles Kimball's five principal 'perverse fundamentalist tendencies':[96]

(*i*)   claiming absolute truth,
(*ii*) seizing upon an 'ideal moment', e.g. apocalyptic events or approaching 'end times';
(*iii*) fostering blind obedience;
(*iv*) using ends to justify the means; and,
(*v*)   pursuing a 'holy war', such as the Crusades.

Phillips believes that all these constituted 'traits of the Bush administration, that were magnified' after the 9/11 events.[97] These, in his view, were 'abetting far-reaching ideological change and eroding the separation of powers between church and state',[98] while the Republican Party was 'on the road to a new incarnation as an ecumenical religious party'.[99]

The events of 9/11 and the subsequent war in Iraq were seminal moments for the Christian Right and the Bush Presidency. The former saw in the assaults a fresh justification for the demonization of Islam and specifically to see in Saddam Hussein the prophesied Antichrist. Bush used the events to engage with the American people, particularly his Christian Right constituency by espousing 'a religious fundamentalist world view with political language to create a political fundamentalism' which he rightly believed would be acceptable to Americans traumatized by September 11.[100] His remarks were replete with biblical references ('double-coding', as Bruce Lincoln called them)[101] familiar to his core audience; these included describing his wars as holy and a fulfilment of Divine wishes:[102] Kevin Phillips concluded that Bush's America:[103]

> has taken up the war whoops of militant Protestantism, the evangelical Christian missionary hopes and demands, the heady talk about bringing liberty and freedom to new shores, the tingle of the old Christian-Muslim blood feuds, the biblical preoccupation with Israel, and the scenarios of the end times and Armageddon – the whole entrapping drama that played in British political theatre a century ago.

Conclusion

The American people in general have deep religious convictions. For many of these believers, biblical passages are not allegorical but literal expressions of divine plans and intentions. Central to such religious convictions are those that pertain to the coming of the Messiah and the tradition associated with end-times. The dominant tradition in the USA is that of dispensational premillennialism which came to the USA in the nineteenth century. It provides that true believers will be saved in a *rapture* during end-times and, thus, able to escape the calamities that will attend the 'tribulations' and the 'last days'.

American religiosity has been refreshed and strengthened not just through the proliferation of churches but also through Christian radio and TV stations, charismatic preachers and popular writers focusing on end-times. These religious leaders have been active participants in American politics, constituting a significant presence on the right of the US political spectrum, and generally supportive of Republican Party candidates.

The influence of the Christian Right is primarily felt in the area of domestic politics, where religious leaders ensure that their concerns pertaining to the erosion of moral and religious values, religious education in schools, expansion of civil rights, and role of government and its institutions, are heard and given due consideration. Issues pertaining to religion have emerged as a principal dividing line in national politics, with Democrats and Republicans on different sides in regard to principal moral issues. In the presidential elections of 2000 and 2004, religion was centre-stage in the national debate, with the Christian Right providing a crucial support base for the Bush candidacy and ensuring his success in the two elections.

While successive American presidents since Jimmy Carter regularly manifested personal religious convictions, President George Bush was the most robust in articulating his personal religious convictions and manifesting the influence of these convictions in his political positions and actions. In this sense, President Bush personally assumed the leadership of the Christian Right even as he pursued policies that his followers believed were a fulfilment of divine mandate. This had particular resonance in regard to US policies in West Asia, which are examined in the next chapter.

NOTES

1. Donald K. Jarvis, 'United States and Russia: Parallels Past and Present', *Bridges*, David M. Kennedy Center for International Studies, Brigham Young University, Provo, UTAH, Spring 2005, p. 4; downloaded from: http://kennedy.byu.edu/bridges/pdfs/BridgesSpr2005.pdf
2. Kevin Phillips, *American Theocracy*, (New York: Penguin Books, 2007), p. 104.
3. ibid., p. 107.
4. ibid., p. 105.
5. ibid.
6. ibid., p. 107.
7. Richard Land, 'God's Country: Evangelicals & US Foreign Policy', Pew Research Center Publications, 26 September 2006; downloaded from: pewresearch.org/pubs/70/ gods.country.
8. Phillips, p. 102.
9. Paul Boyer, 'The Growth of Fundamentalist Apocalyptic in the United States', in Bernard J. McGinn et al. (Ed.), *The Continuum History of Apocalypticism* (New York: Continuum, 2003) p. 516.
10. B.A. Robinson, 'Eschatology, End Times, And Millennialism: Competing Theories,' Ontario Consultants on Religious Tolerance, 18 August 2006; downloaded from: www.religioustolerance.org/millenni.htm.
11. Boyer, p. 517.
12. Gary North, 'Millennialism and the Progressive Movement,' *Journal of Libertarian Studies*, 12:1, Spring 1996, pp. 123-28; downloaded from: http://www.mises.org/journals/jls/12_1/12_1_6.pdf.
13. Boyer, p. 534.
14. North, p. 124; Robinson.
15. Karen Armstrong, *The Battle for God – Fundamentalism in Judaism, Christianity and Islam* (London: HarperCollins Publishers, 2000) p. 138.
16. ibid.
17. ibid., p. 139.
18. ibid., p. 214.
19. ibid., p. 216.
20. ibid., p. 217.
21. Boyer, p. 517.
22. ibid., p. 534.
23. ibid.
24. Armstrong, pp. 266–7.
25. Barbara Victor, *The Last Crusade – Religion and the Politics of Misdirection* (London: Constable, 2005) p. 51.

26. Armstrong, p. 269.
27. ibid., p. 272.
28. ibid., p. 273.
29. Paul Boyer, 'The Middle East in Modern American Popular Prophetic Belief,' in: Abbas Amanat and Magnus T. Bernhardsson (Ed.), *Imaging the End-Visions of Apocalypse from the Ancient Middle East to Modern America* (London: I.B. Tauris Publishers, 2002) pp. 317-23.
30. Boyer, p. 534.
31. ibid.
32. John B. Judis, 'The Chosen Nation: The Influence of Religion on US Foreign Policy', Policy Brief, Carnegie Endowment for International Peace, No. 37, March 2005, p. 2-3; downloaded from:http://www.carnegieendowment.org/files/PB37.judis.FINAL.pdf.
33. Judis, p. 3.
34. ibid.
35. Victor, p. 41.
36. ibid., p. 42.
37. ibid., p. 43.
38. ibid.
39. ibid.
40. Chip Berlet and Nikhil Aziz, 'Culture, Religion, Apocalypse, and Middle East Foreign Policy' Right Web of the Interhemispheric Resource Center, Silver City, NM, 5 December 2003, p. 3; Chip Berlet, 'Dances with Devils: How Apocalyptic and Millennialist Themes Influence Right Wing Scapegoating and Conspiracism', revised 15 April 1999, Policy Research Associates, Somerville, MA; downloaded from: www.publiceye.org.
41. Armstrong, p. 274.
42. Berlet.
43. ibid.
44. Stephen J. Stein, 'American Millennial Visions: Towards Construction of a New Architectonic of American Apocalypticism', in: Amanat and Bernhardsson, p. 209.
45. Quoted in Berlet.
46. ibid.
47. Berlet.
48. ibid.
49. Boyer, pp. 325–7.
50. Berlet.
51. Stephen Bates, *God's Own Country—Tales from the Bible Belt*, (London: Hodder & Stoughton, 2007), p. 238.
52. ibid., pp. 238–43.

53. ibid., p. 243.
54. ibid., p. 249.
55. ibid., pp. 253–4.
56. ibid., p. 256.
57. ibid., p. 257.
58. ibid., p. 258.
59. ibid., pp. 262–3.
60. ibid., p. 265.
61. Phillips, p. 122.
62. ibid., p. 184.
63. ibid., p. 185.
64. ibid., p. 192.
65. ibid., p. 100.
66. ibid.
67. Ibid., p. 101.
68. David E. Campbell (Ed), *A Matter of Faith-Religion in the 2004 Presidential Election* (Washington, DC: Brookings Institution Press, 2007) p. 3.
69. ibid., p. 18.
70. ibid.
71. ibid., pp. 22–5.
72. ibid., p. 182.
73. ibid., p. 261.
74. ibid., p. 265.
75. ibid., pp. 265–6.
76. Bates, p. 274.
77. Phillips, p. 193.
78. ibid., p. 195.
79. Bates, p. 275.
80. ibid.
81. Bates, pp. 2756.
82. ibid., p. 276.
83. Quoted in: Bill Berkowitz, 'Bush's Faith-Filled Life', *WorkingForChange*, 11 May 2003; downloaded from: http://www.workingforchange.com/article.cfm?itemid=15937
84. ibid.
85. ibid.
86. Andrew Austin, 'Faith Matters: George Bush and Providence', *The Public Eye Magazine*, 18 March 2003; downloaded from: http://www.publiceye.org/apocalyptic/bush-2003/austin-providence.html.
87. Quoted in Austin.

88. ibid.
89. ibid.
90. Bruce Lincoln, 'The Theology of George Bush', *Christian Century*, Mt. Morris, IL, 5 October 2004; downloaded from:http://marty-center.uchicago.edu/webforum/102004/commentary.shtml.
91. ibid.
92. Judis, p. 6.
93. Lincoln.
94. ibid.
95. Phillips, pp. 204–7.
96. ibid., p. 205.
97. ibid.
98. ibid., p. 208.
99. ibid., p. 182.
100. ibid., pp. 206.
101. ibid., p. 206.
102. ibid.
103. ibid., p. 259.

6

The Christian Right, the Neocons and US Policy in West Asia

'We support Israel because all other nations were created by an act of men, but Israel was created by an act of God!'
John Hagee, Founder, Christians United For Israel (CUFI)

It was the disobedience and rebellion of the Jews, God's Chosen people, to their covenantal responsibility to serve only the one true God, Jehovah, that gave rise to the opposition and persecution that they experienced beginning in Canaan and continuing to this very day ... Their own rebellion had birthed the seed of anti-Semitism that would arise and bring destruction to them for centuries to come ... it rises from the judgment of God upon his rebellious chosen people.
John Hagee

'I've toured Judea and Samaria, and I've stood on the Golan Heights. I didn't see occupied territory. I saw Israel.'
Tom DeLay, House Majority Leader (2002)

By providing financial support to the settler movement and by publicly inveighing against territorial concessions, the Christian Zionists have reinforced hard-line attitudes in Israel and the United States and have made it more difficult for American leaders to put pressure on Israel. Absent their support, settlers would be less numerous in Israel, and the U.S. and Israeli governments would be less constrained by their presence in the Occupied Territories as well as their political activities.
John Mearsheimer and Stephen Walt,
The Israel Lobby and US Foreign Policy

Beyond the shores of the United States, the impact of the American Christian Right has been most acutely felt in the area of foreign policy in regard to West Asia. This theological influence has linked together 'the war on terror, the rapture, the end times, Armageddon, and the thinly disguised US crusade against radical Islam'.[1] For, the American evangelical movement, allied first with the Zionist movement and later the State of Israel, has increasingly come to see Muslims as 'the modern-day equivalent of the Evil Empire'.[2] Paul Boyer believes that in a 'shadowy but vital way that belief in biblical prophecy is helping mold grassroots attitudes toward current US foreign policy'.[3]

Christian evangelists supporting Israel, particularly its Right-wing parties and militant leaders, are called Christian Zionists. Their support is founded on the Dispensational Premillennianist belief system as articulated originally by John Nelson Darby (1800-82), set out in recent years in the hugely popular books, such as Hal Lindsay's *The Late Great Planet Earth* and the *Left Behind* series of Reverend Tim LaHaye, and fervently advocated by popular American evangelists such as Pat Robertson and Jerry Falwell. According to their doctrine, once the Jewish State is reconstituted in the 'Promised land', and the Temple, destroyed in AD 70, rebuilt as the Third Temple of Solomon, the Antichrist will emerge to destroy the Temple, ushering in a seven-year period of tribulation, as set out in the Book of Revelation. This will set the stage for the 'Second Coming' of Jesus Christ: all Jews will either become Christians or perish violently. Christ will then usher in a 1,000-year reign of perfect justice and happiness.[4]

As noted in the previous chapter, millions of Americans see the prophetic scriptures as 'familiar trusted guides to current events'.[5] Given the pervasive influence of dispensational premillennialism, these fervent believers have been interpreting events in West Asia through the prism of their belief-system. This discourse in popular millennial writings commenced with the emergence of the Zionist Movement and the Balfour Declaration, and continued with the setting up of the Jewish state of Israel in 1948 and the subsequent Israeli capture and occupation of Jerusalem in 1967. All these events had a crucial resonance for millennial writers since the return of the Jews to Palestine, is the first step in the series of events culminating in the return of Christ to Earth.

The Christian Zionist belief system encompasses the following specific tenets in so far as the Jewish role in end-times is concerned:[6]

(*i*) Christian Zionists insist that all of historic Palestine including all land west of the Jordan which was occupied by Israel after the 1967 war-must be under the control of the Jewish people, for they see that as one of the necessary stages prior to the second coming of Jesus.

(*ii*) God's covenant with Israel is eternal and exclusive and will not be abrogated.

(*iii*) The Bible speaks of two distinct and parallel covenants, one between God and Israel, and one between God and the Church. The latter covenant is superseded by the covenant with Israel. The Church is a 'mere parenthesis' in God's plan and, as such, it will be removed from history during the 'Rapture'. At that point, Israel, the nation, will be restored as the primary instrument of God on earth.

(*iv*) Genesis 12.3 ('I will bless those who bless you and curse those who curse you') should be interpreted literally: this means maximum political, economic, moral and spiritual support for the modern state of Israel and for all the Jewish people.

(*v*) Apocalyptic texts like the Book of Daniel, Zechariah 9-12, Ezekiel 37-8, I Thessalonians 4-5 and the Book of Revelation refer to literal and future events: the establishment of the state of Israel, the rebuilding of the Third Temple, the rise of the Antichrist and the buildup of armies poised to attack Israel are among the signs leading to the final battle and Jesus' return for his thousand-year reign.

The prominent journalist and commentator on evangelical Christians, Bill Moyers, has explained the end-times of the latter thus:[7]

> Once Israel has occupied the rest of its 'biblical lands', legions of the anti-Christ will attack it, triggering a final showdown in the valley of Armageddon. As the Jews who have not been converted are burned, the Messiah will return for the rapture. True believers will be lifted out of their clothes and transported to heaven, where, seated next to the right hand of God, they will watch their political and religious opponents suffer plagues of boils, sores, locusts, and frogs during the several years of tribulation that follow. ... It's why the invasion of Iraq for them was a warm-up act, predicted in the Book of Revelation ... A war with Islam in the Middle East is not something to be feared but welcomed – an essential conflagration on the road to redemption.

Millennial writers not only celebrated Israel's creation and its expansion but also drew from biblical sources its ultimate boundaries 'from the river of Egypt unto the great river, the river Euphrates'; they also anticipated the construction of the Jewish temple (on the site of the Al-Aqsa Mosque and the Dome of the Rock) from where Christ would rule during the Millennium.[8] However, premillennialism also predicts the absolute annihilation of the Jews during the seven-year Great Tribulation: according to one interpretation, two-thirds of the Jews will be killed by the Antichrist; this is prophesied in the Bible (Zech. 13.7–8) which says:[9]

> [S]mite the shepherd, and the sheep shall be scattered: and I will turn mine hand upon the little ones. And it shall come to pass, that in all the land, saith the Lord, two parts therein shall be cut off and die; but the third part shall be left therein.

While Islam and Muslims have been consistently portrayed in the most negative light in Christian writings over the last several centuries, they used to be grouped with the Jews and both were seen 'as equally loathsome manifestations of the evil, Anti-christian element in the world whose final extermination is pre-told in scripture'.[10] However, while writings after the Second World War continue to be anti-Arab and anti-Islam, the Jews are now portrayed in Christian Right writings as 'divinely ordained' and as the 'chosen people whose ultimate redemption is assured'.[11] The holocaust is recalled as a 'lamentable consequence' of the Jews' failure to accept Christ as the Messiah and of their continued unbelief. Writers, particularly in the 1990s, emphasize the Jews' central role in the fulfilment of biblical prophecy and express full support for Israel and its 'sacred destiny'; Israel's history since 1948 is seen as a 'remarkable record of divine providence'.[12] On the other hand, Islam is presented as embodying the 'evil' that in the Cold War years had been represented by the Soviet Union, with increasing emphasis on the threat that Islam and Muslims pose today;[13] thus, the prophecy writer, Dave Hunt, wrote in 1995:[14]

> Islam is fighting a *holy war* for control of the world! That war was begun by Mohammed himself ... and is still carried on today by his faithful followers through terrorism. The terrorists are not *radicals* or *extremists,* as the media continually labels them. Instead, these are Islamic *fundamentalists* who are true to their religion and the teachings of the Koran and who follow faithfully in the footsteps of their great prophet, Mohammed ... [V]iolence and terrorism have been the means of spreading Islam from the very beginning.

In the same year, the popular millennial writer, Hal Lindsey, confirmed that Islam had replaced communism as the evil 'other':[15]

> Today, Communism appears to be on its way to the ash heap of history. But a greater threat – a more evil empire – is quietly, without fanfare, filling the void left by the breakup of the Soviet Union. *This movement seeks not only to destroy the state of Israel but also the overthrow of Judeo-Christian culture – the very foundation of our western civilization* ... The name of this movement - the greatest threat to freedom and world peace today – is Islamic fundamentalism ... More than at any time since the Crusades, Islam is posing a serious threat to the Western world. It now possesses the wealth and *the modern lethal weaponry* (sic) to supplant the Soviet Union as the greatest challenge to the Judeo-Christian based Western world order ... What started as a sibling rivalry [i.e., Ishmael and Isaac] and evolved into a racial blood feud has escalated into a deadly religious war that threatens the whole planet. [Emphasis added.]

At the same time, Lindsey portrayed the Jews as 'divinely blessed, though rebellious':[16]

> While God has a special place in His heart for the Jews, He has also allowed a national spiritual blindness to come upon them, [leading to their] worldwide dispersion and persecution ... [But] God kept his promise of external blessings and will someday restore the Jews to a position of special favor.

US Evangelican Support for the Israeli Right-wing

While there is a long history of Christian evangelical interest in Palestine and the Zionist cause, the strong links between the US Christian Right and the Israeli Right were forged in the 1970s when five trends came together:[17]

(*i*) the rapid expansion of the evangelical movements in the US at the expense of mainline Protestant and Catholic churches;

(*ii*) the election of Jimmy Carter, a Southern Baptist, brought the till then marginalized evangelical movement to the national centre;

(*iii*) Israeli military victory in 1967 that significantly expanded its territories and united Jerusalem: even as Israeli expansionist and settlement policies alienated the mainline American churches, US evangelicals saw in the territorial expansion the first steps in the realization of their messianic vision; this

encouraged the American pro-Israel lobby groups to expand
and deepen their links with the Christian Right-wing groups;

(*iv*) the election of Begin in 1977 replaced the secular Labour Party
and brought to power the Israeli Right-wing, linked with figures
like Ariel Sharon, as also a government that was backed by the
messianic settler movement and the religious parties supporting
it; the evangelicals supported the settler movement and the
Likud's hard line agenda; and,

(*v*) in response to Carter's remarks in favour of Palestinian rights
and right to a homeland, Likud reached out to the evangelicals
while seeking to split the evangelical movement by isolating
the liberals represented by Jimmy Carter in its fold. Likud's
tactics paid off immediately, with full-page advertisements
issued by the Christian Right, affirming their messianic beliefs
and Israel's divine right to the 'Promised Land'; the
advertisements said:[18]

> We affirm as evangelicals our belief in the Promised Land to the
> Jewish people ... We would view with grave concern any effort to
> carve out of the Jewish homeland another nation or political entity.

In the 1980 US election, the evangelicals, the major American Jewish
organizations and the pro-Israel lobby got together to defeat Carter and
take Ronald Reagan to victory. Begin, during this period, built up close
ties not only with Reagan but also with leaders of the Christian Right
such as Jerry Falwell. The Reagan administration, in its mobilization of
its Christian Right constituency through briefings and seminars, also
ensured that pro-Likud lobbies were invited to them. Present at such
events were the stalwarts of the US Christian Right such as Hal Lindsey,
Jimmy Swaggart, Jim and Tammy Bakker, Pat Robertson and Tim and
Bev LaHaye.[19]

Netanyahu's election in 1996 initiated the next stage in the
consolidation of ties between the US Christian Right and Likud.
Netanyahu set up the Israel Christian Advocacy Council made up of
prominent US evangelical leaders, which pledged full support to the
Likud agenda. More important in this regard was the support for Likud's
position on Jewish sovereignty over Jerusalem: the full page
advertisements of the Christian Right claimed that: 'Jerusalem has been
the spiritual and political capital of only the Jewish people for 3,000
years. [Israel should] not be pressured to concede on issues of Jerusalem

in the final status negotiations with the Palestinians.'[20] Again, Likud turned to the evangelical organizations for financial support when non-Orthodox American Jews reduced their financial support for Israel to convey their unhappiness at Likud's increased dependence on Orthodox parties at home.[21] Thus, by the end of the twentieth century, the hard-line Likud position had the backing of both Houses of the US Congress, the major Jewish lobbies and the Christian Right. As a consequence, the Christian Zionists support the most extreme Israeli policies in Palestine and actively oppose any territorial and political concessions to the Palestinians. Yaakov Ariel describes this unique alliance thus:[22]

> Christian Zionism has been an extraordinary development in the history of the relationships between religious communities. In no other case have members of one religious community considered members of another religious tradition to hold a special role in God's plans for human redemption and to be God's first nation.

The Right-wing writer, Daniel Pipes, has noted that Christian Zionists are 'increasingly the bedrock of Israel's support in the United States, more solidly pro-Israel and more robustly Zionist than many in the Jewish community'.[23] Paul Merkely, who has written extensively on Christian-Zionism and the history of Christian Zionism relations, has encapsulated the Christian Zionist view of the West Asian situation succinctly:[24]

> The Christian Zionist is not knocked off his perch when Israel is denounced for rough treatment of the Palestinians, or when the Mossad carries off a dirty trick, or when instances of brutality occur in her prisons, etc. The Christian Zionist does not have to rework the ethical arithmetic when bad news appears, in order to reckon whose side he is on. *To the Christian Zionist, it is a requirement of faith to prefer the blessing of Israel above all passing things. Doing this, he believes, cannot, by definition, ever be incompatible with the will of God.* [Emphasis added.]

This alliance between the Christian and Israeli Right-wings is obviously opportunistic and tactical, but both sides focus primarily on the immediate political advantage accruing to them and play down the contradictions at the core of their positions.

Still, given the highly emotive character of their differing belief-systems and messianic visions, serious differences do emerge in public from time to time. Thus, in 1985, Jerry Falwell described himself as 'the most outspoken [Christian] supporter of Israel and the Jewish people the world over'.[25] However, five years earlier, he had predicted the conversion of the world's Jews to Christianity at the 'end-times', seeing this as 'the most dramatic and glorious event ever'. In 1991, speaking at an evangelican conference, Falwell said that the Antichrist was alive, and was likely to appear in the next decade, 'and, of course, he'll be Jewish'.[26]

While their messianic vision informs the position of the US Christian Zionists vis-à-vis Israel and the politics of West Asia, the Jewish position, in Israel and in the USA, is influenced by pragmatic considerations, primarily the need to ensure the continued influence of the Christian Right on the White House and support for the most extreme of Israeli policies and actions in Palestine. The Jewish position appears to be: 'At this point in History, when those same evangelicals come out in support of Israel, many Jews are happy to conclude: "we'll take our chances on the Apocalypse" '.[27] The American Jewish writer, David Brog, author of *Standing with Israel,* has ridiculed the secular Jewish critics of Christian Zionism thus:[28]

> There is a wonderful irony in secular critics of Christian Zionism, typically Jewish, complaining about the great disasters that will befall them upon Christ's Second Coming. These critics, of course, don't actually believe that there will be a Second Coming of Christ. If there will be no Second Coming, then there will be no mass conversion or death [of the Jews]. So what exactly are these critics worried about?

Examples of the efficacy of this opportunistic but mutually advantageous position are several: the Christian Zionists have supported Israel's policy of expanding settlements in the occupied territories; the Israeli attack on Iraq's nuclear plant in 1981; the Israeli invasion of Lebanon in 1982, and continued opposition to the two-state plan as also to the 'road-map' that calls upon Israel to make territorial concessions. In 1998, Jerry Falwell promised to mobilize millions of Americans to ensure that Netanyahu was not compelled to trade land-for-peace.[29] In April 2002, when the Israeli forces were carrying out a destruction programme in Jenin (in retaliation for a Palestinian attack), President Bush demanded that Israeli tanks be withdrawn immediately; the White House then received 100,000 emails from Christian conservatives protesting against the President's demand. The President then maintained silence on the subject and the offensive continued.[30]

Yaakov Ariel has noted the irony inherent in this cooperation:[31]

> In no other realm has the paradoxical nature of the relation of Christian Zionists to Jews demonstrated itself as in the Christian attempts to help traditionalist Jews rebuild the Temple. Christians expecting the Second Coming of Jesus have formed historically unprecedented friendships and alliances with Jews that would have been difficult to imagine at other times and places. Although each of the groups has had a different vision for the messianic times, they have both shared the same agenda for the near future.
>
> ... the Christian interest in the Jewish resettlement of Palestine in the nineteenth and twentieth centuries and their support of the Jewish Zionist cause have derived first and foremost from their messianic hope and their mode of interpreting biblical passages. Christians advocating and acting on such views see themselves as supporting and working toward a great cause, the greatest of all, the unfolding of the messianic age and the establishment of the kingdom of God on earth.

A moderate Baptist minister has pointed out that the Christian Right's position that 'calls for a cataclysmic resolution of the conflict in the Middle East in order for Christ to return' is not so much a position supportive of Israel as 'supportive of the conversion [to Christianity] of Jews who live in Israel'. They do not see Jerusalem as the international capital of Judaism 'but as the centre for realising the sovereignty of Christ'.[32]

Not all groups representing the two sides in this alliance are comfortable with this arrangement. Gershom Gorenberg notes that Christian Zionist Messianism, in its final act, means that Jews must either convert to Christianity or perish. He finds this 'a strangely exploitative relationship', posing problems of principle for Jews in return for an 'illusory short-term pay-off'.[33] Other moderate Jewish leaders note that Jewish alliance with the Christian Right serves to strengthen the political and social agenda of the latter which many Jews find unacceptable, particularly with regard to church–state separation, gun control, Darwinism *vs.* creationism, and the status of women and their reproductive rights.[34]

Finally, several moderate leaders, both Christian and Jewish, reject the extremist policies of successive Israeli governments that exacerbate the Israeli–Palestinian conflict, make reconciliation impossible, and, indeed, bring the Jews and Arabs nearer to the messianic Armageddon envisaged in the traditions of the three Semitic religions. Other dissenting voices have expressed concern about the proselytizing activities of the evangelicals among the Jewish community, the obstructions to the Israel–Palestinian peace process encouraged by them, and the attempt being made to wean American Jews towards the Republican Party.[35] Even evangelical Christians have some dissent in their fold: a letter sent to President Bush from 40 evangelical Christian leaders [in 2002] called upon him to employ an even-handed policy toward Israeli and Palestinian leadership, and noted that the 'American evangelical community is not a monolithic bloc in full and firm support of present Israeli policy'.[36]

The Neo-conservatives (Neocons)

In contrast to mainstream American Jews who have traditionally been associated with liberalism and the Democratic Party, the Neo-conservatives (neocons) represent American Jewish conservatism and are closely associated with the Republican Party.[37] Prominent Jewish neo-conservatives played a central role in the Bush administration, such as: the Pentagon's Paul Wolfowitz and Douglas Feith; the National Security Council's Elliott Abrams; and Richard Perle, formerly of the Defence Policy Board.[38]

These influential policy makers were ably supported by a galaxy of conservative Jewish intellectuals, such as William Kristol, editor of the Washington-based *Weekly Standard*; columnists David Brooks and Charles Krauthammer; Robert Kagan, an international affairs specialist and political scientist; Joshua Muravchik, a frequent contributor to *Commentary;* and Norman Podhoretz, longtime editor of *Commentary,* the neocon bible.[39] This neocon cabal has been credited with shaping the robust foreign policy of the Bush administration (the 'Bush Doctrine') and specifically advocating the assault on Iraq.

The neocons, as Micklethwait and Wooldridge have noted, sprang from the very heart of Democratic America.[40] Most of them were Jewish, nearly all of them were children of migrants; many of them were even Marxists. However, as they grew older, they embraced 'old fashioned liberalism' (meritocracy, high culture and mixed economy), which led them to be increasingly estranged from the far Left.[41] Drawing inspiration from the writings of the philosopher, Leo Strauss (1899-1973), the neocons asserted the importance of individual virtue over individual liberty and saw in religion a 'noble myth', i.e., religion might not be true, but it can serve a useful purpose in keeping society in order.[42]

Murray Friedman saw their rise in the broad framework of growth in conservatism in the USA as a whole, with 41 per cent Americans describing themselves as 'conservative' as against only 19 per cent seeing themselves as 'liberals'.[43] Conservative Jews were generally at the margins of their community up to the 1980s. This changed when conservative Jewish intellectuals raised their voice against the 'counterculture'; in 1993, Irving Kristol, who later emerged as the doyen of the neocons, had this to say:[44]

> There is no 'after the Cold War' for me. *So far from having ended, my Cold War has increased in intensity, as sector after sector has been ruthlessly corrupted by the liberal ethos.* Now that the other Cold War is over, the real Cold War has begun. We are far less prepared for this Cold War, far more vulnerable to the enemy, than was the case with our victorious war against a global Communist threat. [Emphasis added.]

The main issue that agitated the neocons (and most Americans) was the breakdown of the American family.[45] Analyzing the problem, Kristol believed that, as societies become wealthier, they:[46]

> seem to breed all sorts of new social pathologies and discontents ... Crime and other forms of delinquency increase with increasing prosperity. Alcoholism and drug addiction also rise. Civic mindedness and public spiritedness are corroded by cynicism ... The emphasis is placed on the pleasures of consumption rather than the virtues of work. The ability to defer gratification ... is scorned ...

Norman Podhoretz, who was also to become a major neocon ideologue, saw US radicalism as a 'spiritual plague', and began his attacks on the counterculture in 1970, with severe criticisms of leftwing writers, the Black Panthers and women's lib.[47] Through the 1980s and 1990s, a number of Jewish conservative intellectuals began attacking the excesses of US society and seeking re-affirmation of traditional values, mainly through neocon publications such as *Commentary, National Review,* the *Public Interest* and, later, the *National Interest* and the *New Republic.*[48] The neocons decried the domination of liberals on US campuses, and severely criticized campus rebellions, multiculturalism, political correctness and racial preferences in university admissions and hiring of staff.[49]

As the neocons found a congenial space for themselves in the conservatism that was increasingly sweeping across the USA, they had to work on their ties with their Christian counterparts, the Christian Right. Not surprisingly, such encounters often left the neocons uneasy. On the positive side were their similar concerns relating to morality and the American family and the robust support for Israel articulated by the Christian Right.[50] However, what troubled the neocons were the frequent remarks of evangelical leaders that seemed to be anti-Jewish. Neocon intellectuals tended to downplay the significance of the anti-Semitic remarks of Christian theologians, emphasizing that their being 'vigorously pro-Israel' was more important.[51] Kristol made this position clear:[52]

> The fact that the Moral Majority is pro-Israel for theological reasons that flow from Christian belief is hardly a reason for Jews to distance themselves from it. Why would it be a problem for us? It is their theology, but it is our Israel.

Recognizing the increasing importance of the Christian Right, conservative Jews worked actively to cooperate with them in support of Israel's interests. In 1983, the International Fellowship of Christians and Jews (IFCJ) was set up by an Orthodox rabbi to promote ties with evangelicals.[53] He later also set up the Center for Judeo-Christian Values in Washington DC, dedicated 'to finding common religious ground in order to establish moral standards and a greater sense of personal accountability in society'.[54] Positive results were quickly apparent: in 1998 and 1999, the IFCJ was the largest donor to the United Jewish Appeal, giving $6.5million for Israel in 1999. By 2002, according to one report, American evangelicals had given about $100 million over the previous seven years for humanitarian assistance to Jews worldwide.[55]

Problems between the conservative Jews and Christians remained: in 1994, the Jewish civil rights group, the Anti-Defamation League (ADL), published a report criticizing conservative Christians for their 'sectarian, absolutist declarations', and referring to the Christian Right as an 'exclusionist religious movement'.[56] It castigated the latter for seeking to destroy the wall between Church and State, and at times expressing 'conspirational, anti-Jewish and extremist sentiments'.[57] The report specifically attacked Jerry Falwell and Pat Robertson. While the Christian Right vigorously defended itself, a surprising response was the sharp attack on the ADL by prominent Jews, including a number of neocons: seventy-five Jews signed an advertisement in the *New York Times* in August 1994 criticizing the ADL for using 'marginal extremists to impeach individuals and groups who acted out publicly their Christian beliefs'; the advertisement concluded: 'Judaism is not, as the ADL seems to suggest, co-extensive with liberalism'.[58]

The first term of the Bush Presidency marked the apogee of neocon influence in US politics when this band of till-then marginal intellectuals was actually able to exercise influence and power in the country, with the full support of the President. This was the period when they could put in practice the ideas and policies they had been developing (and discussing primarily in small journals and seminar rooms) over the previous decade, but which had been ignored both by Bush Sr. and the Clinton administration.

Persons who were seen as neocons vehemently denied there is a neoconservative movement: Irving Kristol, referred to as the 'Godfather' of the neocons, saw it as a 'persuasion', 'one that manifests itself over time, but erratically, and one whose meaning we clearly glimpse only in retrospect'.[59] Other neocons referred to it as 'a distinctive neoconservative sensibility' (Joshua Muravchik), and a 'neoconservative tendency' (Norman Podhoretz).[60]

Neocons argued that they are not a 'movement' since they had not aspired to 'the kind of central organization characteristic of a movement'.[61] They, however, admitted, even if reluctantly, that there were enough common beliefs and policy affinities among their most prominent adherents to warrant publishing *The Neocon Reader,* edited by Irwin Stelzer, which conveniently brought together the principal aspects of their thinking and explained the wellsprings of their policies.

When the *Reader* was published in 2005, the neocons were anxious to address some of the main criticisms directed at them. The timing of their riposte was significant: the setback in the Iraq enterprise had suggested that neocon influence had climaxed and there would be a diminution in its impact on the Bush Presidency in its second term, accompanied by an increasing disenchantment with the Bush policies among the American people. Hence, the *Reader* served several purposes: first, it addressed some of the general misgivings about neocons articulated by critics, particularly over the previous four years. Second, it attempted to assert that the neocon world view was not novel, by placing neocon policies in the broad context of US and British history. Third, it clarified that neo-conservatism, though it had a number of Jews in its fold, was not an exclusive Jewish preserve. Fourth, it asserted that the setbacks in Iraq were not the result of anything wrong with neocon policies or belief system, but were due to poor execution by the Bush administration. Finally, the neocons wished to authoritatively point out that, the criticisms and setbacks notwithstanding, theirs had been a 'policy triumph', even if a limited one,[62] and that the ideas espoused by neocon thinkers 'will probably have an enduring place in American policies'.[63]

It is interesting to note that a group that denied it was a movement but a mere persuasion or tendency was able to put together a fairly coherent statement of values, principles, visions, policies and action plans on a number of foreign, economic and domestic policy matters, bringing together a number of neoconservatism's principal ideologues who remained convinced of the enduring value and validity of their contribution to the US national interest.

Neocon Foreign Policy

At the commencement of the Bush Presidency, the neocons were 'junior members' of the Bush team: 'they were usually Jews in a party that had traditionally been a bastion of gentiles. They were intellectuals and professionals ... they were not natural comrades of a President who judged people by the content of their hearts rather than the quality of their minds'.[64] Within two years after September 11, the neocon agenda saw itself implemented in full not just through war on Afghanistan and Iraq and the free hand provided to Sharon in Palestine, but also through the proclamation of the National Security Strategy of 2002 which provided for pre-emptive arms strikes and for active encouragement to 'free and open societies of every continent'.[65] Micklethwait and Wooldridge have described the neo-conservatives as 'a cabal with a mission', and go on to say:[66]

> At home, they want to reform welfare and get rid of affirmative action. Abroad, it comes down to two things: asserting American power in a more unilateral way, shorn of the pragmatic (and, in their view, enfeebling) entanglements of multilateralism, and using that power to redraw the map of the world and spread liberal democracy – particularly in the Middle East.

Ideologues William Kristol and Robert Kagan set out the contours of a neocon foreign policy in July 1996 in a joint article in *Foreign Affairs*, titled: 'Towards a Neo-Reaganite Foreign Policy'; these ideas were elaborated in 2000, when they wrote the 'Introduction' to a book, *Present*

Dangers: Crisis and Opportunity in American Foreign and Defense Policy.[67] Their principal ideas may be summarized as follows:

(*i*) The 1990s was a 'squandered decade' and successive US administrations failed to use untrammeled US power for 'preserving and reinforcing America's benevolent global hegemony' and convert what was a 'unipolar' moment into a unipolar era.[68]

(*ii*) There was need to move away from concerns relating to better management of the status quo towards a 'fundamental change' in the way US leaders and public think about America's role with world: the US should not wait for the arrival of the next threat, but rather 'shape the international environment to prevent such threat from arising in the first place.' In short, US foreign policy should preserve and extend an international order that is in accord with both its interests and principles.[69]

(*iii*) To effectively implement this foreign policy, the USA should 'create a force that can shape the international environment', putting in place the substantial defence spending required for the effort.[70]

(*iv*) The USA should seek to work with allies in different parts of the world to the maximum extent possible, seeing threats to allies as also instability in important regions as if they 'are threats that affect us', and address them 'with almost the same immediacy as if they were occurring on our doorstep.'[71]

(*v*) The USA should be willing to and should be seen as capable of projecting force quickly and with devastating affect so as to pre-empt likely challengers to regional instability.[72]

(*vi*) The USA should be prepared to pursue policies to effect regime change in regard to tyrannical regimes, though the tactics actually adopted would vary according to circumstances.[73]

Kristol and Kagan were at pains to point out that the proactive, robust foreign policy set out by them had precedents in US history. Thus, Theodore Roosevelt had declared: 'A nation's first duty is within its borders, but it is not thereby absolved from facing its duties in the world as a whole; and if it refuses to do so, it merely forfeits its right to struggle for a place among the people that shape the destiny of mankind.'[74] Irwin Stelzer went beyond Kristol and Kagan to point out that neocon foreign policy 'is less radical and certainly less novel, than is widely thought';[75] he argued that it had deep roots in early American and British history, embracing Presidents John Quincy Adams and Theodore Roosevelt and British Prime Minister Margaret Thatcher and Tony Blair.[76] In fact, in terms of 'ends' they were Wilsonion, though in 'means' they were 'hard Wilsonians', placing their faith 'not in pieces of paper but in power, specifically US power'.[77]

In a postscript to the 2000 'Introduction' summarized above, written in June 2004, William Kristol confirmed that the neocon foreign policy advocated by him and Kagan was a direct result of 9/11, which created 'a lot more receptivity to the argument that the world was more dangerous than it seemed in the 1990s'.[78] Kristol conceded that 'the difficulties and troubles in Iraq have damaged neoconservative advocates of the war'. However, he argued, the setbacks were due to 'the Bush administration's poor performance' in implementing the war, 'by trying to will the ends without the means'. He stated specifically:[79]

> There was no big increase in the size of the military, no overhaul of our political, diplomatic, and intelligence institutions, no suitable commitment of resources, no radical adjustments of government bureaucracy and mindset needed to adjust to the post-9/11 world.

The most significant achievement of the neocons after 9/11 was to ensure the passage of the National Security Strategy [NSS] in September 2002, one year after the 9/11 events.[80] This document encapsulated the foreign policy principles of the neocon ideologues, specifically those advocated by Kristol and Kagan in their writings. In her comment on the NSS, included in the *Neocon Reader*, Condoleeza Rice, then the President's National Security Advisor, said that the period from the fall of the Berlin Wall to the fall of the World Trade Centre had been 'a long transition period' during which US policy makers had 'searched for an overarching, explanatory theory or framework that would describe the new threats and the proper response to them'. The events of 9/11 had confirmed that the USA faced an 'existential threat': the National Security Strategy was 'a bold vision for protecting our nation that captures today's new realities and new opportunities'.[81]

The US National Security Strategy (the 'Bush Doctrine')

The central feature of the 'Bush Doctrine' was the clear shift from the traditional US national security policy of deterrence and containment to an aggressive unilateral approach based on global military supremacy and pre-emptive militay strikes. The document noted:[82]

> Rogue states and terrorists do not seek to attack us using conventional means. They know such attacks would fail. Instead, they rely on acts of terror and, potentially, the use of weapons of mass destruction – weapons that can be easily concealed, delivered covertly, and used without warning...
>
> The United States has long maintained the option of preemptive actions to counter a sufficient threat to our national security. The greater the threat, the greater is the risk of inaction – and the more compelling the case for taking anticipatory action to defend ourselves, even if uncertainty remains as to the time and place of enemy's attack. *To forestall or prevent such hostile acts by our adversaries, the United States will, if necessary, act preemptively.* [Emphasis added.]

In respect of military pre-eminence, the Doctrine stated:[83]

> The United States must and will maintain the capability to defeat any attempt by an enemy—whether a state or non-state actor-to impose its will on the United States, our allies, or our friends. We will maintain the forces sufficient to support our obligations, and to defend freedom. Our forces will be strong enough to dissuade potential adversaries from pursuing a military build-up in hopes of surpassing, or equaling, the power of the United Sates.

The various aspects of the Bush Doctrine may be summarized as follows:

(*i*) The world order that had emerged after the Second World War and which was maintained for over 40 years through the Cold War now has to be reworked taking into account the following new realities:

(*a*) the United States is the world's sole super-power;

(*b*) the threat faced by the USA and the world from terrorism, armed, violent and messianic, and capable of acquiring WMD, is unprecedented, and requires new rules of engagement and new alliances;

(*c*) a number of states have emerged, particularly in East Europe, that have shed their communist past, have a certain latent political and economic value, and are anxious to engage with the United States; and,

(*d*) US's ties with the principal states of continental Europe will have to be reviewed and adjusted to new realities.

(*ii*) On the world scene, the United States will assert its interests, political and economic, robustly and unilaterally.

(*iii*) In the promotion of its interests, the United States will pursue a policy of **pre-emptive action**, including through the use of force.

(*iv*) The United States will abridge where necessary the traditional norms of state sovereignty and will not hesitate to effect '**regime change**' whenever it is convinced that its interests are threatened by a particular leader or regime.

(*v*) In order to **maintain the unipolar world**, the United States will pursue a policy of maintaining military superiority over all potential rival countries or combinations thereof. This military superiority will be maintained through a technology gap which will be overwhelmingly in favour of the United States.

(*vi*) The United States will take particular care to protect its interests in the **energy sector**. Beginning with domination over Iraqi oil, the United States will pursue policies that will ensure free flow of oil at reasonable prices. In the medium to long-term, US control over crude flows will give the United States an overwhelming advantage vis-à-vis potential strategic rivals such as Europe, China and Japan.

(*vii*) The United States will actively engage with the **Arab and Islamic world** to root out all manifestations of Islamic extremism and violence as also anti-Americanism and anti-Westernism. Towards this end, it will actively promote domestic political, economic, religious and socio-cultural reform, with a view to nudging these countries towards freedom, democracy and free markets.

(*viii*) The United States will **intervene actively** in different parts of the world (not necessarily only in areas where its strategic interests are involved) to prevent disputes from getting out of control, and will use its full force to ensure that disputes are seriously addressed and quickly resolved.

(*ix*) In regard to Iraq, the United States believes the **United Nations** did not fulfill its mandated role. Obviously, this body to be reworked so that it can play its proper role or else it should face marginalization and irrelevance.

(x) US interests will not necessarily be defined only in terms of political or strategic interest, but will have a long-term idealist content of promoting freedom, democracy and free markets.

US Policy in West Asia

In his article titled 'The Neoconservative Persuasion', Irving Kristol had made a brief reference to neocon foreign policy: he had said: 'there is no set of neoconservative beliefs concerning foreign policy, only a set of attitudes derived from historical experience'.[84] While setting out his 'theses' pertaining to these so-called attitudes, Kristol had noted that large nations, like the former Soviet Union and the USA, inevitably have 'ideological interests in addition to more material concerns'; he had then gone on to elaborate:[85]

> Barring extraordinary events, the United States will always feel obliged to defend, if possible, a democratic nation under attack from non-democratic forces, external or internal. That is why it was in our national interest to come to the defense of France and Britain in World War II. That is why we feel it necessary to defend Israel today, when its survival is threatened. No complicated geopolitical calculations of national interest are necessary.

Thus did the 'godfather' of neoconservatism very briefly, even casually, refer to Israel in the context of neocon foreign policy, which, in the view of the observers (and critics) of neoconservatism, in fact lay at the centre of neocon foreign policy in West Asia and which impacted on nearly every aspect of US foreign and domestic policy. Indeed, it was the overwhelming importance given to Israel's interests (especially those articulated by its most extreme elements) that led critics to take note of the Jewish identity of several of the top votaries of the neocon 'persuasion' (or 'tendency'), and even to suggest that the neocons, in their support for Israel's most extreme positions had tended to place Israeli interests above those of the USA.

The Bush 'vision' for West Asia, developed in the immediate aftermath of 9/11 and heavily influenced by neocon thinking, was founded on 'the determination to use America's unprecedented power to reshape the Middle East, supporting America's friends in the region, opposing its enemies and seeking to promote democracy and freedom'.[86] This vision was based on four assumptions.

First, the status quo in West Asia was no longer acceptable: while for several decades America had substantial ties with repressive regimes in the Arab world, this arrangement was no longer tenable primarily because, as 9/11 has shown, it had become a problem for America itself. The practice of US's principal allies, the regimes of Saudi Arabia and Egypt, to maintain themselves in power by using 'Islam' and tolerating/encouraging anti-American and anti-Israel positions in their population had, in the Administration's view, culminated in the attacks of 9/11, and threatened US and Western security.

Second, the approach to Iraq needed to be reviewed. The policy followed till then by the West towards Iraq has itself fomented anti-Westernism in West Asia and encouraged terrorism. The argument was as follows: so long as Saddam Hussein was in power, Iraq would threaten its neighbours, as a result of which economic sanctions, no-fly zones, and US armed-presence in neighbouring countries world have to be maintained. However, these policies, in turn, contributed to anti-American and anti-Western sentiments and fuelled Islamic extremism.

Third, in regard to the situation relating to Israel and Palestine, the Administration believed that, at Camp David in December 2000, in spite of the major and unprecedented concessions the Israeli side had made, the Palestinians, led by Arafat himself, had responded with terrorist violence. The Administration now believed that peace would come to the region only when the Palestinian people had an alternative leadership that unambiguously gave up terrorism and was willing to make difficult compromises.

Fourth, in the long run, peace and stability and an end to anti-Westernism would not be possible until the region's regimes become more democratic. While the Bush officials accepted that such a task would be difficult and time-consuming, they were convinced that the process should be begun and pursued through muscular diplomacy, containment and, where necessary, use of force. Bush had articulated his position in this regard in his State of the Union Address in January 2002 when he had said:[87]

> America will lead by defending liberty and justice because they are right and true and unchanging for all people everywhere ... America will always stand firm for the non-negotiable demands of human dignity: the rule of law; limits on the power of the state; respect for women; private property; free speech; equal justice; and religious tolerance. *America will take the side of brave men and women who advocate these values around the world, including the Islamic world,* because we have a greater objective than

eliminating threats and containing resentment. We seek a just and peaceful world beyond the war on terror. [Emphasis added.]

The Bush Administration believed that history was on its side: Reagan, with his references to the 'evil empire' and calls for democracy and freedom, had finally achieved liberty throughout Eastern Europe; it followed that regime change in Iraq would be the first step in this process in West Asia: Iraq would emerge as a model Arab country that was free, democratic and prosperous. The success of this model, as also the reduced US dependence on Saudi oil, would enable the Americans to vigorously address such issues as human rights, anti-Americanism and corruption. Over time, the people of the Arab world would come to see that free, liberal democracy and capitalism were the best principles on which to organize their society.

The Neocons and US Policy in West Asia

The pro-Israel lobby that dominated the Bush Presidency and influenced its policy in West Asia was made up of an alliance of pro-Israel Jewish organizations, the Christian Right and the neocons who held senior positions in the first term and the Bush administration, particularly in the State and Defence Departments. Michael Lind has pointed out that, while the neocon cabal had a number of prominent Jewish adherents, there were also non-Jews within the group, such as former Defence Secretary Rumsfeld, Vice-President Cheney and his daughter Lynne Cheney. In fact, according to him, the Jewish neocons do not speak for the majority of Jews: 'in a survey of US Jewish opinion in 2003, 54 per cent of American Jews surveyed disapproved of the war in Iraq, while a similar 54 per cent also criticized the way Bush was handling the campaign against terrorism'.[88]

Hugh Urban astutely pointed that Bush Jr. 'represents a crucial link' between the two powerful groups that support his administration—the neocons and the Christian Right; he went on to say:[89]

> Bush presents the Neoconservatives' radical foreign policy in a guise that is acceptable to his large base of support in the Christian Right, even as he reassures his Christian base that their moral agendas (anti-abortion, anti-gay marriage, faith-based initiatives, etc.) will be given powerful political support. In Bush, America as the benevolent hegemon of the Neocons and the American-led 'Tribulation Force' of LaHaye's novels, comes together in a disturbing, yet surprisingly successful way.

Urban went further: he identified a number of areas where the hard-Right neocons and the hard-Right Christians shared common ground.

The first, according to him, is the centrality of religion in their agenda. While this was obvious in regard to the Christian Right, Urban pointed out that the neocons too recognised the importance of religion; he quoted Irving Kristol thus: [90]

> The three pillars of modern conservatism are religion, nationalism, and economic growth. Of these religion is easily the most important, because it is the only power that ... can shape people's characters and regulate their motivation ...
>
> Conservatives and the Republican Party must embrace the religious if they are to survive. Religious people always create problems since their ardor tends to outrun the limits of politics in a constitutional democracy. But if the Republican Party is to survive, it must work on accommodating these people.

More interestingly, Urban saw an affinity between the evangelical vision of the 'New Millennium' and the neocon ideal of a 'New American Century'.[91] Melani McAlister explained it thus:[92]

> The Neoconservatives and the Christian Right may not be conspiring together secretly behind the scenes, but they do need each other to promote their respective agendas, *and they overlap on certain key issues, such as their focus on the Middle East, and specifically Israel, as the epicenter of the coming New Millennium/New American Century.* [Emphasis added.]

Urban concluded: 'it is difficult not to see striking reflections of the Neoconservative agenda in the *Left Behind* narrative. Indeed, these novels provide a striking kind of fictional, evangelical, and astonishingly popular counterpart to the Neoconservative's rather elite and intellectual geo-political vision'.[93]

West Asia and the place of Israel in it had been a principal preoccupation of the neocons. In 1996, Richard Perle and Douglas Feith (later both senior policy-makers in the Bush Jr. Presidency) had authored a paper for then Israeli Prime Minister Netanyahu, titled 'A Clean Break: A New Strategy for Securing the Realm', in which they had advised the Prime Minister to abandon the Oslo Peace Process and return to military repression of the Palestinians.[94] The paper had advocated that Israel devote 'every possible energy on re-building Zionism' and reduce its political and economic dependence on the USA, as greater self-reliance would give it greater freedom of action and remove a significant level of US pressure. The writers had seen a threat to Israel from Iraq and Syria, and had advocated the removal of Saddam Hussein and his replacement by a malleable monarchy. They had seen in the ouster of the Iraq leader 'an important Israeli strategic objective', noting that 'Iraq's future could affect the strategic balance in the Middle East profoundly'.

Another neocon intellectual, David Wurmser, also wrote about 'the battle to dominate and define Iraq (which) is, by extension, the battle to dominate the balance of power in the Levant over the long run'. The USA and Israel, in alliance with Turkey and Jordon, were to fight this battle together against a 'Saudi–Iraqi–Syrian–Iranian–PLO axis'.[95] In 1997, Douglas Feith, not yet an administration official, in an address in Jerusalem, condemned 'those Israelis [who] contend that Israel like America should not be an ethnic state – a Jewish state – but rather a state of its citizens'.[96]

In 1998, the eighteen neocon associates at their think tank, *Preparing for the New American Century* (PNAC), addressed a letter to President Clinton in which they warned of the need to secure 'the significant portion of the world's oil supply' in Iraq, and advised the President that the only acceptable strategy was to 'undertake military action' and 'remove Saddam Hussein and his regime from power.'[97] In September 2000, PNAC issued a report titled 'Rebuilding America's Defenses: Strategy, Force and Resources for a New Century'. Its authors regretted the lack of effort to 'preserve American military preeminence in the coming decades' and criticized Clinton for squandering his opportunity to make the US the sole, indomitable superpower. They contended that the removal of Saddam Hussein and the US occupation of Iraq would provide both the crucial justification and the ideal precondition for this larger global agenda. Achieving this goal of undeniable US power, the authors suggested, would require a radical transformation in public opinion and government policy. But they also cautioned that 'the process of transformation, even if it brings revolutionary change, is likely to be a long one, absent some catastrophic and catalyzing event—like a New Pearl Harbor'.[98]

Hugh Urban has quoted David Henry, author of *The New Imperialism*, as pointing out that Bush's response to 9/11 provided the ideal rationale for pursuing the neocons' larger agenda of 'establishment of and respect for order, both at home and upon the world stage'. On the domestic front, 9/11 provided the excuse to impose an extremely invasive new measure like the *USA Patriot Act*, championed by conservative Christian, Attorney General John Ashcroft. On the international front, it provided the ideal motivation—and spiritual justification—for the neocon's plans for Iraq, dating back to the early 1990s.[99] Henry believed that the neocon strategy for occupying Iraq had behind it a much larger and more disturbing global agenda: with Iraq as its base of operation, and Saudi Arabia, Syria, and Iran close at hand, the US would be uniquely placed to dominate the flow of oil from the Middle East and, by extension, the flows of capital throughout the world in an age still fuelled by oil and petro-dollars; Henry concluded:[100]

> The U.S. will be in a military and geo-strategic position to control the whole globe militarily and, through oil, economically ... The neo-conservatives are, it seems, committed to nothing short of a plan for total domination of the globe.

Looking at the West Asia situation in September 2004, former CIA analysts Kathleen and Bill Christison could not but note that several of the ideas and arguments presented by neocon intellectuals in support of Israel's interest had actually came to pass in the four years they had dominated the Bush administration. These had included the war on Iraq and the ouster (and later execution) of Saddam Hussein; a complete halt in the Israel-Palestine peace process; no forward movement in respect of any Arab-Israeli peace; and continued confrontation with Iran and Syria, with sporadic threats of armed assault.[101]

The Christisons and Michael Lind saw in the implementation of the neocon-inspired Bush foreign policy in West Asia an extraordinary and pervasive zealotry. According to the Christisons, neocon zealotry has meant a 'zealous advocacy' of Israel's interests: this has included 'extreme action' to sustain policies including manipulating intelligence data to reach pre-determined conclusions; support for the most extremist of Israel's interests, and absolutely no role in pursuing a peace process that would reduce violence in the region. They pointed out that the affiliation of the neocons with the Christian extremists had encouraged the growth of the messianic strain of the latter, including their 'crazed' view that warfare between Jews and Arabs was a divinely ordained prelude to Armageddon. They concluded:[102]

> These right-wing Christian extremists have a profound influence on Bush and his administration, with the result that the Jewish fundamentalists

working for the perpetuation of Israel's domination in Palestine and the Christian fundamentalists working for the Millennium strengthen and reinforce each other's policies in administration councils. The Armageddon that Christian Zionists seem to be actively promoting and that Israeli loyalists inside the administration have tactically allied themselves with, raises the horrifying but very real prospect of an apocalyptic Christian—Islamic war. The neo-cons seem unconcerned, and Bush's occasional pro forma remonstrations against blaming all Islam for the sins of Islamic extremists do nothing to make this prospect less likely.

These two strains of Jewish and Christian fundamentalism have dovetailed into an agenda for a vast imperial project to restructure the Middle East ...

Michael Lind took a similar view of neocon zealotry: he saw the neocons as working on behalf of a 'crusading, messianic ideology', both Christian and Jewish; it was articulated in terms of promoting democracy, but actually ended up supporting Israel's Likud Party and the Christian Zionists of the Southern religious Right.[103]

Contrary to the suggestion from prominent neocons that they were not even in touch with each other, a number of observers set out substantial details of the familial, educational and institutional ties that bound most of the prominent neocons. Thus, Kathleen and Bill Christison, in their paper, 'Dual loyalties, the Bush neocons and Israel', identified the ways in which the 'who's who' of the Bush administration was linked and the ties they had with pro-Israel lobby groups and think tanks.[104] They pointed out that the neocon promoters of Israel's interests in the Bush administration had 'long records of activism on behalf of Israel in the United States, of policy advocacy in Israel, and of promoting an agenda for Israel often at odds with existing US policy'.[105] They raised the question of the possible 'dual loyalties' of these officials:[106]

> The issue we are dealing with in the Bush administration is dual loyalties – the *double allegiance of those myriad officials at high and middle levels who cannot distinguish U.S. interests from Israeli interests*, who baldly promote the supposed identity of interests between the United States and Israel, who spent their early careers giving policy advice to right-wing Israeli governments and now give the identical advice to a right-wing U.S. government, and who, one suspects, are so wrapped up in their concern for the fate of Israel that they honestly do not know whether their own passion about advancing the U.S. imperium is motivated primarily by America-first patriotism or is governed first and foremost by a desire to

secure Israel's safety and predominance in the Middle East through the advancement of the U.S. imperium.

Michael Lind and Edward Said noted how the pro-Israel elements in the USA had almost entirely stifled all objective discussion and debate about the situation in West Asia. Lind said that though the Middle East was becoming 'the centre of US foreign policy', 'an uninhibited debate is not taking place because of the disproportionate influence of the Israel lobby'.[107] He noted that this lobby was an 'ethnic donor machine' that provided funds across the US political system from local to national levels to candidates sympathetic to Israel. It was thus able to mobilize huge political support in Congress.[108] Again, it was able to place a number of pro-Israel officials at high levels in the administration, the neocons in the Bush set-up being the most obvious presence. Finally, it enjoyed near-total media support not just through prominent columnists (many of them from the Christian and Jewish Right) but also through news reports that had a built-in pro-Israel bias and/or failed to provide the historical or political context in regard to Palestine-Israel differences or conflicts.[109] Lind also noted with deep concern that Israel's occupation of Palestinian territories had led to the 'moral coarsening' of sections of the Jewish–American community, which consisted of frequent use of racially abusive language against Arabs.[110]

Edward Said echoed the points made by Lind. He saw the American supporters of Israel, both settlers in Israel or leaders of extremists groups in the USA, as exhibiting a 'frightening mixture of vicarious violence against Arabs and a deep fear and hatred of them'.[111] He noted that, in the USA itself, the official discourse relating to West Asia was 'totally dominated by Zionism'.[112] He also expressed astonishment at the arrogance exhibited by American Zionists vis-à-vis Israeli leaders and their policies when the latter were seen to pursue a moderate or conciliatory course in the region.[113] Said concluded:[114]

> American Zionism has now reached the level of almost pure fantasy in which what is good for American Zionists in their fiefdom and their mostly fictional discourse is good for America and Israel, and certainly for the Arabs, Muslims and Palestinians, who seem to be little more than a collection of negligible nuisances. Anyone who defies or dares to challenge them (especially if he/she is either an Arab or a Jew critical of Zionism) is subject to the most awful abuse and vituperation, all of it personal, racist

and ideological. They are relentless, totally without generosity or genuine human understanding.

The working of the Israel lobby in the USA to control the discourse relating to the Bush Administration's policies relating to Israel came to light most clearly in connection with the controversies surrounding the publication of a paper by two prominent American academics, John J. Mearsheimer and Stephan M. Walt, titled 'The Israel Lobby and US Foreign Policy'.[115] The paper was first submitted to the American journal, the *Atlantic Monthly*, in January 2005. After being kept for several months, the paper was returned to the authors. A few months later, a shorter version was published in the *London Review of Books* issue of 23 March 2006.[116] (The full original text was available only on the Internet.)

The publication of the shorter version outside the USA unleashed a storm of protest and abuse against the two writers, effectively confirming the principal point made in the paper that the Israel lobby deliberately restricted discussion relating to USA's policies in West Asia. The Jewish civil rights group, the Anti-Defamation League, described the paper as 'a classical conspiratorial anti-Semitic analysis invoking the canards of Jewish power and Jewish control'.[117] Professor Daniel Drezner called it 'piss-poor, monocausal social science'.[118] The well-known Harvard Law Professor, Alan Dershowitz, said the authors had 'destroyed' their professional reputations.[119]

The authors were criticized from the Liberal and Left as well. Daniel Fleishler said the issue of Jewish influence was 'so incendiary and so complicated' that it could not be discussed in the public sphere without causing rancour.[120] Michelle Goldberg said the authors had 'blundered forth' into the issue in 'clumsy and crude' ways.[121]

The two writers were defended by a number of prominent personalities as well. The liberal intellectual, Tony Judt, criticized the US media for its fear in refusing to discuss the main ideas set out in the paper.[122] Former Secretary of State Colin Powell's Chief of Staff, Col. Lawrence Wilkerson, praised it for conveying 'blinding flashes of the obvious', ideas 'that were whispered in corners' rather than stated in public.[123] Robert Pape noted that his research into suicide bombers had indicated they were not religiously motivated but acting against occupation.[124]

Two distinguished American intellectuals from the Right who backed the writers were Anatol Lieven and Francis Fukuyama. In 2004, Lieven had published a book, *America Right or Wrong* in which he had indicated that the USA had subordinated its interests to a tiny militarized state, Israel; for this, he was attacked as an anti-Semite.[125] Anatol Lieven said:[126]

> It's self-evidently true that other interests and ambitions are involved in the war with Iraq ... Oil is very much-imperial ambitions are very much there. [But], it is crazy to suggest on the one hand that the neoconservatives had a great influence on the Bush Administration and to say that it didn't play out in terms of a hard interest for Israel. If you think the neocons were not running the whole show but had a definite impact, then you can't possibly suggest that Israeli interests were not involved.

Francis Fukuyama, till the early years of the twenty-first century, was one of the most prominent neocon ideologues. He moved away from the neocons from 2004, and wrote in *The National Interest* that the neocons were harming American and Israeli interests; he said: 'Are we (Americans) like Israel, locked in a remorseless struggle with a large part of the Arab and Muslim world, with few avenues open to us for dealing with them other than an iron fist? ... I believe there are real problems in transposing one situation to the other.'[127]

In 2007, Mearsheimer and Walt expanded their paper and published a book titled *The Israel Lobby and US Foreign Lobby*.[128] This 484-page tome, alongside former President Jimmy Carter's book, *Palestine—Peace Not Apartheid*, published in 2006,[129] was a major critique of US policy in West Asia and the disproportionate influence wielded in this areas by the 'Israel Lobby'. The principal points made by Mearsheimer and Walt earlier in their paper and then elaborated in their book may be summarized as follows:

(i) There is a 'remarkable level of material and diplomatic support that the United States provides to Israel'; 'this support could not be fully explained on either strategic or moral grounds ... it was due largely to the political power of the Israel lobby, a loose coalition of individuals and groups that seeks to influence American foreign policy in ways that will benefit Israel.'[130]

(ii) Many of the policies pursued by the US government as a result of the influence of the Israel lobby 'were not in the US national interest and were in fact harmful to Israel's long term interests as well.'[131]

(iii) The Israel lobby is 'not representative of mainstream opinion in the American Jewish community or the US more broadly.'[132]

(*iv*) 'The Israel lobby has successfully convinced many Americans that American and Israeli interests are essentially identical', when, in fact they are not.[133]

(*v*) It is difficult to talk about the lobby's influence on American foreign policy, at least in the mainstream media in the United States, without being accused of anti-Semitism or labeled a self-hating Jew.[134]

(*vi*) The Israel lobby is 'now led by hardliners who support the positions of their hawkish counterparts in Israel'; [... they have become] 'voices for the Likud half of the government ...'[135]

Mearsheimer and Walt have examined in detail the role of the Israel lobby in influencing US policy in four specific areas of West Asia, and concluded that, but for the pernicious role of the lobby, US's (and Israel's) interests would have been better served in all cases if the US had followed alternative policies.[136] The Israel lobby played a major role in influencing the Bush administration's approach to the Palestinian issue by ensuring that the Government supported the most extreme of Israeli actions in Palestine. As Mearsheimer and Walt noted, after September 11, President Bush did express, from time to time, a genuine interest in addressing the Palestinian issue by supporting the idea of a Palestinian state and calling for a halt to Israeli settlements in the Occupied Territories. In order to thwart these initiatives, the Israel lobby projected to the administration and in the US media that the US and Israel faced a common threat from terrorism and that there was no real difference between Yasser Arafat and Osama bin Laden.[137] Within a few days after September 11, the neocon-dominated 'Project for the New American Century' published an open letter to President Bush in which it described Israel as 'America's staunch ally against international terrorism' and called on the President to 'fully support our fellow democracy'.[138]

After September 11, Israel carried out numerous attacks on Palestinian territories in Gaza and the West Bank, often in the face of US opposition, but was invariably able to ensure that it was the US Administration that climbed down in support of Israeli actions. Describing the situation in early 2004, *New York Times* columnist Thomas Friedman said:[139]

> Mr. Sharon has the Palestinian leader Yasir Arafat under house arrest in his office in Ramallah, and he's had George Bush under house arrest in the Oval Office. Mr. Sharon has Mr. Arafat surrounded by tanks, and

Mr. Bush surrounded by Jewish and Christian pro-Israel lobbyists, by a vice president, Dick Cheney, who's ready to do whatever Mr. Sharon dictates, and by political handlers telling the President not to put any pressure on Israel in an election year—all conspiring to make sure the president does nothing.

Mearsheimer and Walt came to the obvious conclusion that Israel leaders, including Sharon and his successor Olmert, had little interest in a peace process with the Palestinians 'because it would require Israel to give up almost all of the West Bank and create a viable Palestinian State on that territory'.[140] In this position, Israel obtained the full support of its lobby in the US whose members, both inside and outside the Administration, were able to ensure that no US-sponsored peace initiative was ever successful. In fact, according to the two authors, certain neocon members of the White House, such as Elliott Abrams, had actively worked with senior Israeli officials to subvert the policies of the Bush Administration.[141]

Mearsheimer and Walt examined the role of the Israel lobby in the US in encouraging the Bush administration to go to war in Iraq. They pointed out that, in initiating this war, the Bush administration invaded 'a deteriorating country that had nothing to do with the attacks on the World Trade Centre and the Pentagon and was already effectively contained'.[142] Till before the events of September 11, neither Bush nor Vice President Cheney had been planning a war against Iraq.[143] On the other hand, even before 9/11, neocon intellectuals had been pushing for a US assault upon Iraq and, ultimately, were a 'critical element' in the US's decision to go to war.[144] While the idea of the war originated with the hardliner members of the Israeli lobby in the USA, by August 2002, they had succeeded in also bringing Israeli leaders on board, so that the latter added their voice in urging the Administration and the US public to accept the neocon position that Saddam Hussein was a threat to Israel and a war should be launched to remove him from power.[145] While there was little support for war in the State Department, the CIA or the Pentagon, war was encouraged by 'mainly high-level civilians in the White House and the Pentagon, almost all of whom were neoconservatives'.[146] These neocon advocates of war within the Administration were provided strong support by neocon intellectuals such as Charles Krauthammer, Robert Kagan, William Kristol and also neocon academics such as the historian Bernard Lewis.[147]

According to the neocon vision, regime change in Iraq was to be the first step in a plan to reform the West Asia in support of long term American and Israeli interests. According to this vision, a democratic Iraq under US influence would become a model for the reform of the rest of the authoritarian countries in the region.[148] An Israeli journalist reported on this thinking in the following terms:[149]

> Senior IDF officers and those close to Prime Minister Ariel Sharon, such as National Security Adviser Ephraim Halevy, paint a rosy picture of the wonderful future Israel can expect after the war. They envision a domino effect, with the fall of Saddam Hussein followed by that of Israel's other enemies: Arafat, Hassan Nasrallah, Bashar Assad, the Ayatollah in Iran and maybe even Muammar Gadaffi. Along with these leaders will disappear terror and weapons of mass destruction.

Mearsheimer and Walt have also pointed out that the Israel lobby, in support of Israeli hawks, was a strong advocate of an aggressive US policy against Iran, including the use of military force to destroy Iran's nuclear facilities. The authors argued that Israel and its lobby were encouraging the USA 'to pursue a strategically unwise policy' towards Iran.[150] They believed that the Israel lobby undermined the recommendation of the Iraq Study Group that the Bush Administration negotiate with Iran, and concluded that, were it not for the lobby, the United States would almost certainly have a different and more effective Iran policy.[151] Mearsheimer and Walt also provided details of the Israel lobby and Israeli hawks working in tandem in support of the war option against Iran. For instance, Douglas Feith, the neocon Undersecretary of Defence for Policy until August 2005, was said to have developed plans for attacking Iran in cooperation with Israeli planners and consultants.[152] The authors strongly advocated a US–Iran engagement, pointing out that a pre-emptive US assault on Iran would not serve US interests: not only would an attack encourage Iran to re-build its nuclear facilities, but Iran would also ensure that its future programme would not be vulnerable to such attacks. Again, Iran, in all likelihood, would retaliate with attacks on other targets in the region, including oil shipments.[153]

The fourth area of US policy in West Asia looked at in considerable detail by Mearsheimer and Walt was the Lebanon war of July 2006. They pointed out that Israel had planned this assault upon Lebanon to destroy Hezbollah several years earlier, and was only awaiting an opportune moment to implement it.[154] Israel's war plans were actually discussed with the US Administration in advance and full support was obtained with the help of neocons in the Government, including Elliott Abrams in the National Security Council and David Wurmser, who was Vice-President Cheney's adviser on the Middle East.[155]

What Israel unleashed upon Lebanon was a 'classic punishment campaign', inflicting the maximum possible pain upon the civilian population by destroying their homes and their country's infrastructure,[156] besides killing over eleven hundred persons, a third of them children.[157] In spite of the Israeli violence, the war failed in its objective of destroying the Hezbollah or even diminishing its support-bases. Instead, it enhanced Hezbollah's influence and prestige in Lebanon and the Arab world, increased anti-Americanism and de-moralised the Israelis on account of the failure of their leaders and the army in realizing their proclaimed aims.[158] It also served to damage Israel's (and by extension, the US's) image in international opinion on account of the severe indictment of Israel's violence in the non-partisan reports of Amnesty International and Human Rights Watch.[159] These reports revealed the deliberate and callous harm done to civilians and their property even when no military objectives were involved.[160] The reports also exposed the wanton use of cluster bombs by the Israeli forces: four million bomblets were fired over the entire war, with one million of them fired in just the last three days when it was known that cease-fire was imminent. About one million bomblets are believed to be lying unexploded in the southern part of the country.[161]

As in other Israel-related matters, in this conflict, too, the Israel lobby assiduously mobilized political and popular support in the USA on behalf of Israel, projecting the war as part of the US-led war on terror, and ensuring that even the most muted criticism was not articulated by Congressmen and Senators.[162] Amnesty International and Human Rights Watch were criticized for unfairness and charged with anti-Semitism.[163] An American academic, Rosa Brooks, rejected these charges as 'savage, unfounded and fantastical'; she went on to say:[164]

> What's most troubling is that it's typical. Typical, that is, of what *anyone* rash enough to criticize Israel can expect to encounter. In the United States today, it just isn't possible to have a civil debate about Israel, because any serious criticism of its policies is instantly countered with charges of anti-Semitism. [Emphasis in original].

Levelling charges of anti-Semitism against all critics of Israel is the principal weapon in the armoury of the Israel lobby in the USA. Even as early as November 2002, when Richard Perle, the author of the neocon manifesto, *An End to Evil*, was asked to explain why the American neo-conservative hawks were mainly Jewish, and whether there was a hidden agenda in his call for the overthrow of Saddam Hussein, Perle, instead of giving a straight answer, said that the first query had an undertone of anti-Semitism, while the second 'gave off the same aroma'. [165]

In attempting to highlight how the neocons have made US and Israeli interests congruent, Thomas Powers has pointed out that Perle, in his book, bunched together Al Qaeda, Hizbullah and Hamas, even though the latter two consider themselves to be at war with Israel but not the US; Powers noted:[166]

> President Bush seems to have adopted Perle's inclusive definition of terror, possibly without understanding quite how clearly it commits the United States to support Israel's continuing occupation of the West Bank and Gaza.

Powers further said: 'In the world according to Richard Perle, everything is clear and all choices are stark—except when it comes to the West Bank and Gaza. There he grows vague.' Perle in his book presents the standard Israeli argument that the Arab-Israeli conflict is not a cause of Islamic extremism; instead, 'the unwillingness of the Arabs to end the quarrel (with Israel) is a manifestation of the underlying cultural malaise from which Islamic extremism emerges'. [167]

It is interesting to note that in May 2004, two prominent Americans who publicly discussed the role of the neocons in pushing America to war in Iraq were both branded 'anti-Semitic'. Senator Earnest Hollings of South Carolina, in an article published in a local newspaper, under the headline: 'Bush's Failed Mideast Policy is Creating More Terrorism', had attempted to answer his constituents' question: 'why are we in Iraq?' He had said: 'President Bush's policy is to secure Israel.' Recalling Wolfowitz's call for the spread of democracy across the Arab world, Hollings went on to say:[168]

> Led by Wolfowitz, Richard Perle and [columnist] Charles Krauthammer, for years there has been a dominant school of thought that the way to guarantee Israel's security is to spread democracy in the area.
>
> He [Bush] came to office imbued with one thought – re-election. Bush felt tax cuts would hold his crowd together and spreading democracy

in the Mideast to secure Israel would take the Jewish vote from the
Democrats. You don't come to town and announce your Israel policy is to
invade Iraq.

And, without any Iraq connection to 9/11, within weeks he had the
Pentagon outlining a plan to invade Iraq.

For these views, Senator Hollings was labeled anti-Semitic by the
American Board of Rabbis, whose President has called him a 'disgrace
to the Senate and a disgrace to our Nation'. Another Rabbi said of the
Senator's remarks: 'It makes him anti-Israel. It's anti-Semitic ... It is
dangerous.'[169] A senior Rabbi warned the Senator:[170]

> Hollings is an unpatriotic disgrace to the American Flag and if he does
> not immediately resign, he should be impeached. Further more, in Genesis,
> God tells Abraham, the founder of the Jewish people, 'I'll bless those who
> bless you [Israel] and him who curses you [Israel], I will curse.' *And by
> cursing the Jewish people, Hollings has invoked the wrath of God upon himself.*
> [Emphasis added.]

Again, in a TV interview, retired Major General Anthony Zinni, who
had opposed the Iraq war, said he had been labelled 'anti-Semitic' because
he named certain neocons who, he had said, are 'political ideologues
who have hijacked American policy in Iraq'. The journalist, Joel
Mowbray, took Zinni severely to task for this assertion on the basis that
'today that term ['neo-conservative'] has become synonymous with Jews'!
Mowbray went to say:[171]

> It is well-known that those who are labeled 'neocons' within the
> administration – whether the number-two official at the Pentagon, Paul
> Wolfowitz, or Under Secretary of Defence Dough Feith – are almost always
> Jews.

The deteriorating situation in Iraq and mounting US casualties; the
revelations of the Abu Ghraib abuses, and the apparent continued
allurement, capability and reach of Islamic extremism, all of these have
led to a strengthening of the criticism from mainstream commentators
of US policy vis-à-vis the Middle East and 'Islam' in general, and of
US's ties with the Israeli hawks. Thus, Nicholas Kristoff, in an article in
the *New York Times,* in May 2004, noted that:[172]

> It is our Israel-Palestine policy which has become so unbalanced that it is
> now little more than an embrace of the right-wing jingoist who Bush
> unforgettably labelled a man of peace: Ariel Sharon.

Similarly, the former CIA official and commentator on Gulf and Middle East affairs, Anthony Cordesman, in May 2006, said: [173]

— no issue drives Arab and Islamic perceptions of the United Stated as much as the Israeli-Palestinian conflict. US peace efforts are perceived as weak and dishonest, and the United States is viewed as having become little more than Israel's proxy. This perception alienates regional moderates and reformers, aids Islamists and terrorists and undermines pro-US governments.

Echoing this view, former US President Jimmy Carter pointed out:[174]

Two other interrelated factors have contributed to the perpetuation of violence and regional upheaval: the condoning of illegal Israeli actions from a submissive White House and U.S. Congress during recent years, and the deference with which other international leaders permit this unofficial U.S. policy in the Middle East to prevail. There are constant and vehement political and media debates in Israel concerning its policies in the West Bank, but because of powerful political, economic, and religious forces in the United States, Israeli government decisions are rarely questioned or condemned, voices from Jerusalem dominate in our media, and most American citizens are unaware of circumstances in the occupied territories ...

The United States has used its UN Security Council veto more than forty times to block resolutions critical of Israel. Some of these vetoes have brought international discredit on the United States, and there is little doubt that the lack of a persistent effort to resolve the Palestinian issue is a major source of anti-American sentiment and terrorist activity throughout the Middle East and the Islamic world.

Such observations, however muted and well-reasoned they might be, have inevitably been responded to with strident accusations of anti-Semitism, the kiss of death for US politicians, academics and journalists! Carter himself was lambasted by the Israel lobby as anti-Semitic and a 'Jew-hater'; some even suggested that he was sympathetic to the Nazis.[175]

Conclusion

Outside domestic politics, the principal influence of the Christian Right has been in regard to US policies in West Asia. Over the years, the US Christian Right has set up a strong alliance, first, with the Zionist movement, and later with the state of Israel. This is an opportunistic relationship on both sides since it brings together two peoples whose messianic beliefs are fundamentally contradictory in that Christian redemption ultimately involves the annihilation of the Jewish people or their conversion to Christianity. However, the two movements seem to agree that consideration of issues pertaining to end-times can be postponed in favour of matters that have more contemporary urgency.

For the Christian Right, referred to as Christian Zionists on account of their strong support for Israel, biblical prophecy requires full support to Israel's aspirations to conquer and occupy all the lands that constitute historic Palestine. Thus, Christian Zionists have not only celebrated the setting up of the Israeli state, they have also supported Israel's control over the occupied territories and the settlements movement as part of biblical prophecy. Not surprisingly, in the eyes of Christian Zionists, Arabs/Muslims are increasingly seen as the biblical Antichrist.

Successive government leaders of Israel and members of groups that espouse Israeli interests in the USA maintain strong personal links with Christian movements in the USA and their Right-wing leaders to the extent of even accommodating the Christian end-times prophecy of Jewish annihilation and tolerating occasional anti-Semitic remarks uttered by Christian leaders. This has also meant that Jews, many of them liberal in so far as domestic social issues are concerned, find themselves supporting the conservative social agenda of the Christian Right on matters such as Darwinism, status of women, abortion, gay rights, etc. The Christian Right are thus active role-players in the Israel lobby in the United States.

The Israel lobby is a loose group of individuals and associations that robustly articulate and pursue Israel's interests and actions in American political circles and public opinion in general. Members of the American neoconservative movement, referred to as neocons, have, in recent years, emerged as influential members of the Israel lobby. In President Bush's first term, they were responsible for envisioning and implementing a robust American foreign policy, particularly a West Asia policy that strongly supports Israel's interests. Within two years of September 11, they were able to realize their foreign policy vision and agenda in West Asia through wars on Afghanistan and Iraq, the free hand provided to Sharon in Palestine to crush Palestinian resistance against Israeli occupation, and, above all, the proclamation of the National Security Strategy of 2002, which provides for unchallenged US military supremacy and the right of pre-emptive military action in support of US interests.

The failure of the US to successfully implement its agenda in Iraq as a result of the prolonged and lethal insurgency has now increasingly encouraged commentators in the USA and abroad to focus greater attention on the shortcomings of neocon policies, particularly in respect of Palestine and the broader global war on terror, which includes US complicity in regard to the abuses of Guantanamo and Abu Ghraib, and the sense that the Islamic extremist movement have gained in terms of strength and credibility as a result of these policies, pursued primarily in Israel's interest.

Having analyzed different aspects of Jewish and Christian messianism and their deep collaboration in pursing policies hostile to the Muslim 'other', we now turn to look at various aspects of resurgent Islam and Islamic messianism, and its confrontation with the Jewish and Christian messianic forces that are arrayed against it.

NOTES

1. Kevin Phillips, *American Theocracy* (New York: Penguin Books, 2007) p. 259.
2. Phillips, p. 251.
3. ibid., p. 253.
4. Paul Boyer, 'The Growth of Fundamentalist Apocalyptic in the United States', in: Bernard J. McGinn et al. (Ed), *The Continuum History of Apocalypticism* (New York: Continuum, 2003) p. 517.
5. Paul Boyer, 'The Middle East in Modern American Popular Prophetic Belief', in: Abbas Amanat and Magnus Bernhardsson (Eds.), *Imaging the End: Visions of Apocalypse from the Ancient Middle East to Modern America* (London: I.B. Tauris Publishers, 2002) p. 312.
6. Donald Wagner, 'Evangelicals and Israel: Theological Roots of a Political Alliance', *Christian Century*, No.4, 1998; downloaded from: http://www.religion-online.org/showarticle.asp?title=216.
7. Quoted in Dr. Lieven De Cauter, 'The Tyrant as Messiah – Messianism and Anti-Nomianism in the Neoconservative Theology', 9 September 2006; downloaded from: http://www.williambowles.info/empire/tyrant_as_messiah.html
8. Boyer, p. 319.
9. Stephen J. Stein, 'Apocalypticism Outside the Mainstream in the United States', in McGinn, p. 539.
10. Boyer, p. 323.
11. ibid., pp. 321–2.

12. ibid., p. 322.
13. ibid., p. 326.
14. ibid., p. 328.
15. ibid., p. 329.
16. ibid.
17. Wagner.
18. ibid.
19. ibid.
20. ibid.
21. ibid.
22. Yaakov Ariel, 'An Unexpected Alliance: Christian Zionism and its historical significance,' *Modern Judaism*, Vol. 26, No. 1, 2006, p. 94.
23. Daniel Pipes 'Christian Zionism: Israel's Best Weapon?' *New York Post*, 15 July 2003; downloaded from: http://www.israelnationalnews.com/ Articles/Article.aspx/2514.
24. Paul C. Merkley, 'Christian Attitudes Towards the State of Israel: A Bird's-Eye View', *IsraPundit*, 9 December 2003; downloaded from:http:// christianactionforisrael.org/attitudes.html.
25. Daniel Levitas, 'A Marriage Made for Heaven', *Reform Judaism Magazine*, Summer 2003; downloaded from: http://www.reformjudaismmag.net/ 03summer/focus.shtml.
26. ibid.
27. ibid.
28. Quoted in Spengler, 'You Don't Need To Be Apocalyptic, But It Helps', *Asia Times Book Review*, 20 June 2006; downloaded from: www.atimes.com/atimes/middle_East/HF20Ak02html.
29. Wagner.
30. ibid.
31. Ariel, p. 95.
32. Levitas.
33. Quoted in Chip Berlet & Nikhil Aziz, 'Culture, Religion, Apocalypse, and Middle East Foreign Policy,' *IRC Right Web*, Silver City, NM, Inter-hemispheric Resource Center, 5 December 2003; downloaded from: rightweb.irc_online.org/andysis/2003/0312apocalypse.html.
34. Levitas.
35. ibid.
36. Margot Patterson, 'Will Fundamentalist Christians and Jews ignite apocalypse?', National Catholic Reporters, 11 October 2002; downloaded from: http://www.natcath.com/NCR_Online/archives/101102/ 101102a.htm
37. Murray Friedman, *The New Conservative Revolution – Jewish Intellectuals*

and the Shaping of Public Policy (New York: Cambridge University Press) p. 1.
38. ibid.
39. ibid.
40. John Micklethwait and Adrian Woodridge, *The Right Nation – Why America Is Different* (New York: Penguin Books, 2005) p. 72.
41. ibid.
42. Micklethwait, p. 75.
43. Friedman, p. 7.
44. ibid., p. 185.
45. ibid.
46. ibid., p. 186.
47. ibid., p. 187.
48. ibid., p. 191.
49. ibid., pp. 196–7.
50. ibid., pp. 207–8.
51. ibid., p. 209.
52. ibid.
53. ibid., p. 210.
54. ibid.
55. ibid.
56. ibid., p. 215.
57. ibid.
58. ibid., pp. 216–17.
59. Irving Kristol, 'The Neoconservative Persuasion – What It Was, and What It Is', in Irwin Stelzer (Ed.): *The Neocon Reader* (New York: Grove Press, 2005) p. 33.
60. Neocon Reader, p. 4.
61. ibid.
62. ibid., p. 17.
63. ibid., p. 23.
64. Micklethwaith, p. 200.
65. ibid., p. 203.
66. ibid., p. 205.
67. Included in *Neocon Reader*, pp. 57–74.
68. ibid., pp. 57–8.
69. ibid., pp. 61–4.
70. ibid., p. 66.
71. ibid., p. 67.
72. ibid.
73. ibid., pp. 69–70.

74. ibid., p. 73.
75. Neocon Reader, p. 3.
76. ibid., pp. 3–4.
77. ibid., p. 10.
78. ibid., p. 75.
79. ibid., p. 76.
80. *The National Security Strategy of the United States of America,* September 2002; downloaded from: http://www.whitehouse.gov/nsc/nss.pdf; henceforth *NSS* .
81. *Neocon Reader*, p. 81.
82. *NSS,* p. 15.
83. ibid., p. 30.
84. *Neocon Reader*, p. 35.
85. ibid, p. 36.
86. Phillip Gordon 'Bush's Middle East Vision', *Survival,* Vol. 45, No. 1, Spring 2003, pp. 155–65; downloaded from: http://www.brookings.edu/ views/articles/gordon/20030301.pdf.
87. *The President's State of the Union Address,* Washington DC, 29 January, 2002; downloaded from: http://www.whitehouse.gov/news/releases/ 2002/02/print/20020129-11.html
88. Michael Lind, 'A Tragedy of Errors', *The Nation,* 23 February 2004; downloaded from: http://www.thenation.com/docprint.mhtml?i= 20040223&s=lind
89. Hugh B. Urban, 'America, Left Behind: Bush, the Neoconservatives, and Evangelical Christian Fiction', *Journal of Religion and Society,* The Kripke Centre, Vol.8 (2006), p. 2; downloaded from: moses.creighton.edu/JRS/2006/2006-2.html.
90. Urban, p. 6.
91. ibid., p. 10.
92. Quoted in Urban, p. 10.
93. Urban, p. 5.
94. Kathleen and Bill Christison, 'Dual Loyalties – The Bush Neocons and Israel', *CounterPunch,* 6 September 2004: downloaded from: http:// www.counterpunch.org/christison09062004.html.
95. ibid.
96. ibid.
97. Urban, p. 7.
98. ibid.
99. ibid., p. 9.
100. ibid.
101. Christisons.

102. ibid.

103. Lind, 2004, p. 6.

104. Christisons on links among the neocons: An examination of the cast of characters in Bush administration policymaking circles reveals a startlingly pervasive network of pro-Israel activists, and an examination of the neo-cons' voluminous written record shows that Israel comes up constantly as a neo-con reference point, always mentioned with the United States as the beneficiary of a recommended policy, always linked with the United States when national interests are at issue. First to the cast of characters. Deputy Secretary of Defence *Paul Wolfowitz* leads the pack. He was a protégé of *Richard Perle,* who heads the prominent Pentagon advisory body, the Defense Policy Board.

Wolfowitz in turn is the mentor of *Lewis 'Scooter' Libby,* now Vice President Cheney's chief of staff who was first a student of Wolfowitz and later a subordinate during the 1980s in both the State and the Defense Departments. Another Perle protégé is *Douglas Feith,* who is currently undersecretary of defense for policy, the department's number-three man, and has worked closely with Perle both as a lobbyist for Turkey and in co-authoring strategy papers for right-wing Israeli governments. Assistant Secretaries *Peter Rodman* and *Dov Zackheim,* old hands from the Reagan administration when the neo-cons first flourished, fill out the subcabinet ranks at Defense. At lower levels, the Israel and the Syria/Lebanon desk officers at Defense are imports from the Washington Institute for Near East Policy, a think tank spun off from the pro-Israel lobby organization, AIPAC.

Neo-Cons have not made many inroads at the State Department, except for *John Bolton,* an American Enterprise Institute hawk and Israeli proponent who is said to have been forced on a reluctant Colin Powell as undersecretary for arms control. Bolton's special assistant is *David Wurmser,* who wrote and/or co-authored with Perle and Feith at least two strategy papers for Israeli Prime Minister Netanyahu in 1996. Wurmser's wife, *Meyrav Wurmser,* is a co-founder of the media-watch website MEMRI (Middle East Media Research Institute), which is run by retired Israeli military and intelligence officers and specializes in translating and widely circulating Arab media and statements by Arab leaders.

In the vice president's office, Cheney has established his own personal national security staff, run by aides known to be very pro-Israel. The deputy director of the staff, *John Hannah,* is a former fellow of the Israeli-oriented Washington Institute. On the National Security Council staff, the newly appointed director of Middle East affairs is *Elliott Abrams,* who came to prominence after pleading guilty to withholding information from Congress during the Iran-contra scandal (and was pardoned by President Bush the elder) and who has long been a vocal proponent of right-wing Israeli positions. Putting him in a key policymaking position on the Palestinian-Israeli conflict is like entrusting the henhouse to a fox. [Italics added.]

105. Christisons.
106. ibid.
107. Michael Lind, 'The Israel Lobby', *Prospect*, 1 April 2002; downloaded from: www.newamerica.net/index.cfm?sec= Documents & pg. =article & Doc/D=779 & T2=Arti....
108. ibid.
109. ibid.
110. ibid.
111. Edward Said, 'American Zionism – The Real Problem', published in three parts in *Al-Ahram Weekly*; posted on *Media Monitors Network* on 14 March 2001; downloaded from: www.mediamonitors.net/ edward12.html.
112. Said, part I, p. 4.
113. ibid., part II, p. 3.
114. ibid.
115. John J. Mearsheimer and Stephen M. Walt, 'The Israel Lobby and US Foreign Policy', *CSG Faculty Research Working Paper Series*, Harvard University, March, 2006, downloaded from: http:// ksgnotes1.harvard.edu/Research/wpaper.nsf/rwp/RWP06-011.
116. John Mershimer and Stephen Walt, 'The Israel Lobby', *London Review of Books,* Vol. 28, No. 6, 23 March 2006; downloaded from: www.Irb.co.uk/v28/no6/print/mear01_html
117. Quoted in: Philip Weiss, 'Ferment Over 'The Israel Lobby', *The Nation*, 15 May 2006; downloaded from: www.thenation.com/doc120060515/ weiss/4.
118. ibid.
119. ibid.
120. ibid.
121. ibid.
122. ibid.
123. ibid.
124. ibid.
125. ibid.
126. ibid.
127. ibid.
128. John J. Mearsheimer and Stephen W. Walt, *The Israel Lobby and US*

Foreign Policy (London: Allen Lane/Penguin Books, 2007).
129. Jimmy Carter, *Palestine-Peace Not Apartheid*, (New York: Simon & Schuster, 2006).
130. Mearsheimer, p. viii.
131. ibid.
132. ibid., p. ix.
133. ibid., p. 8.
134. ibid., p. 9.
135. ibid., p. 126.
136. ibid., pp. 5, 8.
137. ibid., pp. 204–5.
138. ibid., p. 206.
139. ibid., p. 218.
140. ibid., p. 223.
141. ibid., pp. 223–4.
142. ibid., p. 229.
143. ibid., p. 245.
144. ibid., p. 230.
145. ibid., p. 235.
146. ibid., p. 247.
147. ibid., pp. 246–9.
148. ibid., p. 255.
149. ibid., p. 257
150. ibid., p. 282.
151. ibid.
152. ibid., p. 296.
153. ibid., pp. 301–2.
154. ibid., p. 308.
155. ibid., pp. 309–10.
156. ibid., p. 313.
157. ibid., p. 306.
158. ibid., pp. 315–17.
159. ibid., pp. 320–5.
160. ibid., pp. 323–5.
161. ibid., p. 322.
162. ibid., pp. 326–30.
163. ibid., pp. 328–9.
164. ibid., p. 329.
165. Thomas Powers, 'Tomorrow the World', *New York Review of Books*, Vol. 51, No. 4, 11 March 2004, p. 5.
166. ibid.

167. ibid.
168. Quoted in: Said Arikat, 'Bush's Iraq, Mideast policy critics called anti-Semitic', *Gulf News*, 26 May 2004.
169. 'The American Board of Rabbis Condemns SC Senator Ernest Hollings', *PRWeb*, 29 May 2004, downloaded from www.prweb.com
170. ibid.
171. Joel Mowbray, 'General Zinni, What a Ninny', *townhall.com*, 31 December 2003; downloaded from www.townhill.com
172. Nicholas, Kristoff, 'US Mideast Policy Adrift', *New York Times*; reproduced in the *Saudi Gazette*, 27 May 2004.
173. Anthony, H. Cordesman, 'Bush Needs to Drop US-led Initiative for Middle East Reform,' *The Baltimore Sun*; reproduced in *Arab News*, Jeddah, 9 May 2006; downloaded from www.tompaine.com
174. Carter, pp. 209–10.
175. Mearsheimer, p. 9; p. 193; The Israeli lobby obtained considerable international attention in the early days of the Obama regime when its sustained efforts in opposing the appointment of Mr. Charles Freeman as Chairman of the National Intelligence Council (NIC) resulted in the candidate withdrawing his name from the appointment. [See Andrew Sullivan, 'First Blood in the War for Obama's World-view', *The Sunday Times*, London, 8 March 2009; Joseph A. Kechichian, 'Freeman is Nothing More Than a Sideshow', *Gulf News*, Dubai, 19 March 2009; Uri Avnery, 'Obama Blinks In First Test With Israeli Lobby', *Gulf News*, Dubai, 16 March 2009; Tony Karon, 'Chas Freeman Won't Be the Israel Lobby's Last Victim', *The National*, Abu Dhabi, 15 March 2009.] The American commentator Robert Dreyfuss has suggested that the Freeman episode might 'have helped to change the very nature of Washington politics.' He believes that this episode has 'already sparked a new more intense mainstream focus on the [Israel] lobby', and that such scrutiny would bring increased attention on the functioning of this lobby and in time diminish its effectiveness. The author concludes:
> 'the recent three-week Israeli assault on Gaza had already generated a barrage of headlines and television images that made Israel look like a bully nation with little regard for Palestinian lives, including those of women and children. According to polls taken in the wake of Gaza, growing numbers of Americans, including many of the Jewish community, have begun to exhibit doubts about Israel's actions, a rare moment when public opinion has begun to tilt against Israel.' [Robert Dreyfuss, 'Is the Israel Lobby Running Scared?', *Asia Times*, 17 March 2009; downloaded from:http://www.atimes.com/atimes/printN.html.]

7

Resurgent Islam:
The Intellectual Narrative

Islam is not merely a religious creed or a name for a collection of a few acts of worship. It is a comprehensive system which seeks to annihilate all evil and tyrannical systems in the world, and enforce its own programme of reform, which it deems best for the well-being of mankind.

...

Therefore, in order to eradicate evil and prevent wrong, Islam has prescribed that by systematic endeavour, jihad – and if the necessity should befall, by war and bloodshed – all such governments should be wiped out. In their place a just and equitable system of government should be erected which is founded upon the fear of God and based upon the canons He ordained.

Maulana Abul Ala Maududi

'Islam' in its political, religious, cultural and intellectual dimensions was dramatically thrust upon global consciousness in February 1979, by the spectacle of the bearded cleric, Ayatollah Ruhallah Khomeini, slowly descending the steps of his aircraft at Tehran airport in the aftermath of the abrupt departure into exile of the Shah of Iran. This sudden reversal of Western political fortunes in West Asia caused a robust revival in the study of Islamic groups and movements, defined as those that are 'active in the political arena and call for the application of Islamic values and laws in the private and public spheres'.[1] The terms used by scholars to define and describe these movements have been variously: Islamic Fundamentalism, Islamic Revivalism, Militant Islam, Political Islam, Islamism, the Rage of Islam, the Islamic threat, and Islamic Resurgence.

The term 'Islamic Fundamentalism' was in vogue after the Iranian Revolution through much of the 1980s, and was used extensively by Western and Islamic commentators. However, it slowly fell into disuse since:

(*i*) the term's origin in Protestant fundamentalism of late nineteenth century USA led many scholars to doubt the appropriateness of its use in a completely different political and cultural context;

(*ii*) its allusion to adherence to the 'fundamentals' of one's faith reflected an archaic scholarly position which, mainly in Western discourse, tended to contrast 'fundamentalism' with the 'other', modernism, and thus saw human progress in unilinear terms, moving inevitably towards a modern, secular society; and,[2]

(*iii*) the term 'fundamentalism since it referred to an 'anti-modern 'other' ', suggested that it was a marginalized phenomenon in a society; it thus, failed to take account of religious movements which reflected the socio-cultural mainstream in a particular country or society.[3]

Hence, scholars felt the need to use a more neutral but comprehensive term that would do justice to the various aspects of contemporary Islamic consciousness and Islamic response to the situations in the Islamic world and in the West. 'Islamic Movements' is a value-neutral term which, while adequately describing the rise of Islamic consciousness, fails to do justice to its dramatic character which flows from its sudden claim to global attention from the Islamic Revolution in Iran in 1979, and its subsequent radical and militant manifestations in different parts of the world.

In this study, the term 'Resurgent Islam' has been used to describe the phenomenon of Islamic consciousness over the last one hundred years during which Muslim intellectuals and political leaders have attempted to understand and respond to the experience of Muslim defeat and despair. This commenced with the rapid success of Western colonialism over Asia and Africa, followed by the consolidation of imperialist domination and control after World War I and through the twentieth century, and the attendant sense of loss of control over their destiny that has been the reality of the Muslims' experience the world over. While emphasizing the pervasive strength of Islamic consciousness, the term 'Resurgent Islam' includes the various aspects of the emergence of the phenomenon in Islamic discourse, covering its political, social, cultural, religious, intellectual and militant aspects. It avoids the limited connotations of the other descriptions and does justice to the robust and dramatic value of the movement while, at the same time, avoiding the polemical connotations of other terminologies.

'Political Islam' and 'Islamism' are also used quite extensively in scholarly writings. However, they have a purely *political* connotation and do not embrace the Islamic movements' religious, social and cultural agenda. In this work, 'Islamism' has been used when the reference is primarily to the *political* aspects of the movements, with the attendant use of 'Islamist' to describe the protagonists of such movements.

Aspects of Resurgent Islam

The roots of resurgent Islam may be traced to the nineteenth century, when the bulk of the Islamic world, for the first time, found itself defeated and dominated by non-Islamic Western forces. This situation was unique in Islamic history since it was pervasive and, more importantly, not just a temporary setback but a total defeat, with no indication when the subjugation would come to an end. Again, an analysis of this serious setback revealed that the factors that contributed to Western success were not merely superiority of weaponry or tactics or even strategy; it was an all-comprehensive superiority that emerged from the development of science and technology in the West which were then little known and less assimilated in the Islamic world.[4]

Not surprisingly, as Muslims delved deep into themselves, an explanation for their present predicament that was most convincing was that they had deviated from the path set out in the Koran and the ideal lifestyle of pristine Islam. David Cook has explained the Muslim predicament thus:[5]

> For the contemporary Muslim, the present world is a world turned upside down. Everywhere his faith has lost ground as a result of colonial conquests and Christian missionaries, as well as representatives of cultural imperialism, such as the media (they are frequently all grouped together). God has promised to Muslims that they are not only the recipients of the final abrogating revelation to the Prophet Muhammad, but that they will be crowned with worldly success and dominion as well.

For over a thousand years (from the perspective of the Muslim) this was true. It was the Arabs and the Turks who dominated the world scene, in accordance with God's promise, from 630 to 1688. However, not even the most hardened traditionalists can deny the second or even third-class status of the Muslim today.

Obviously God cannot be at fault for this situation—the Muslims themselves must be. The perception is that God is testing the chosen few just before the end of the world. They must prove their faith to God through worldly domination and the reestablishment of the God-ordained Muslim superiority.

In their response to this malaise, votaries of contemporary resurgent Islam assert four basic principles: *first*, that 'Islam' is self-sufficient: it provides a blueprint for a perfect way of life, that is, the ideal community of pristine Islam of Prophet Mohammed made up of the spirit of compassion, solidarity, paternity and social justice. *Second*, the existing political, economic, and social systems tried out in different parts of the Islamic world have failed because they were based on alien Western models. *Third*, the West connotes materialism, licentiousness and godlessness, and thus cannot provide a model for an Islamic state or the Muslim person. *Finally*, Islam provides the basis for the assertion of an authentic personal identity on the basis of one's *own* cultural and religious roots.

In their analysis of the Islamic world, leaders of resurgent Islam see a pervasive social and cultural abasement of the Muslim people, accompanied by a sustained economic failure which has led to rising levels of poverty and privation for the mass of the people, amidst high levels of consumerism and gross self-indulgence of a small elite. They ascribe this to the absence of an effective Islamic polity based on Islamic principles and, in its place, the presence of regimes that lack all political legitimacy, are totalitarian and tyrannical, and are allied with the West against the legitimate interests of the Muslim people.

Accordingly, the agenda of the Islamist movement includes: first, opposition to all foreign domination and hegemony in its political, economic and cultural aspects; second, it opposes the internal repression of authoritarian Muslim rulers, be they traditional monarchies or secular ideologues; and, third, the movements seek the liberation of all Muslim lands from foreign occupation and the assertion of the freedom, identity and progress of the Muslim people.

The Muslim Polity and Islam-West Ties

The American theo-conservative movement that has emerged in the United States as a result of the pragmatic alliance between the neocons and the Christian Right, has an essentialized broad-brush view of Islam and Muslims, and believes, on Huntingtonian lines, in the inevitability of a clash with 'Islam'. In so doing, the American theo-conservative movement, while demonizing the 'other', is denying the complexity, variety and colour that are based on its rich history and cultural evolution over 1,400 years.

The general tendency is to see 'Islam' as a monolithic entity with a polity dominated by religion. Thus, Bernard Lewis has said:[6]

> In classical Islam there was no distinction between Church and state. In Christendom, the existence of two authorities goes back to the founder, who enjoined his followers to render unto Caesar the things which are Caesar's and to God the things which are God's ... each with its own laws and jurisdictions, its own structure and hierarchy. In pre-Westernised Islam, there were no two powers but one ... in classical Arabic, as well as in other languages which derive their intellectual and political vocabulary from classical Arabic, there were no pairs of words corresponding to spiritual and temporal, lay and ecclesiastical, religious and secular.

Such a view echoes a wished for ideal of the ulema but was never actually realized in such absolute terms in Islamic history. The central trend in Islam's history has been for the Amir, the political leader, to dominate the ulema and not the other way round. As Mamoun Fandy has said:[7]

> This interaction between state and Islam brought about certain adjustments to Islam rather than the other way round; the state was not adjusted to become Islamic; rather, Islam was adjusted to support the state. In this arrangement, the state has used the 'ulema to justify the policy choices of the ruling elite. The function of the 'ulema is thus to establish the hegemony of the ruling Amir and his family.

At the same time, the caveat that the Amir rule according to the law retained its resonance, and, as in the case of the Magna Carta, its specific provisions could be invoked at various times to restrain a capricious ruler. Thus, up to, say, two centuries ago, in the tension between politics and religion, between law and caprice, between the Amir and the ulema, the situation in the Islamic world replicated to a considerable extent the order that prevailed in Europe. This situation, as in Europe, also enabled the development of considerable space in the polity that was outside the grip of religion. From its inception, Islam the religious faith entirely embraced neither the political ethos of the Muslim state nor the full personality of the Muslim person.

In fact, the Islamic state from its earliest times was dominated by non-state structures playing an important role in religious and secular life.[8] In all cultures, it lived side by side with inherited traditions that pre-dated it and continue to influence contemporary life in Muslim societies. The two most important influences on the Muslim person were *ailiyya*, translated as familialism, and *asabiyya*, loosely referred to as tribalism, or more accurately, as tribal solidarity. *Qaraba*, or closeness, binds the extended family in a political economy context, providing for abiding social solidarity.[9]

The pattern of societal/political structure in most West Asian Islam has been to provide 'Islamic familialism' a central role, this being defined as 'the dominant ethos that results from the interaction between general Islamic values and familial and Qaraba customs, habits and values'.[10] The ethos of familialism 'permeates the political system', providing the polity with protection (or sponsorship), inter-dependence and accountability.[11] Fandy has noted that Islam historically has been secondary to the *aila* (family), playing the role of supporting the cultural domination of the ruling tribe or dynasty.[12] Islamic history, thus, is a narrative of a vibrant civil society *outside* state control, which made itself felt mainly in the intellectual arena.[13] Civil society jealously guarded its autonomy, so that Muslim solidarity, as Effendi has noted, manifested itself chiefly in 'opposing oppression not in suppressing individuals'.[14]

While Islamic theory demanded that the Islamic state be governed by recognized law derived from revelation, the *sharia*, contrary to what Bernard Lewis has said, was, in reality, neither universal nor inflexible. As Hourani has noted, the sharia 'did not in fact cover the whole range of human activities': it was most dominant in areas of personal status, less on commercial matters, and least on penal or constitutional questions.[15] In fact, criminal justice was generally administered by the ruler himself or his officials, not by the *qadi*.

Again, the administration of sharia in practice was quite flexible, with the qadi seeking conciliation to promote social harmony rather than insisting on the strict application of the law. The concepts of *qiyas* (precedent) and *ijma* (consensus), to which the ulema referred while pronouncing on specific cases, provided them with remarkable flexibility.[16] Law remained under the sway of the ulema, and it was consensus amongst them (and not the whims of rulers) that laid the foundations of formal Islamic law. This meant that the Islamic state was not a religio-political monolith; as Ira Lapidus has pointed out:[17]

> In the development of Islamic institutions we have come from an early identification of politics and religion to a differentiation of political and religious life into organized and partly autonomous entities ... Though the modalities of 'state' and 'religion' in the Islamic world are quite different from those of 'state' and 'church' in the west, *Islamic society, in fact, if not in its own theory, is one of those societies in which religious and political institutions are separate.*[Emphasis added.]

Thus, there was space in the Islamic polity where *secular* interests had full play, such as: the military, commerce, the arts and foreign affairs, which remained the prerogative of the Amir, as they did in the European context. This enabled the evolution of a variety of political cultures in the Islamic world, that, while based on a commonality of faith, still allowed scope for the development of a robust state (under a strong ruler) and a flourishing civil society. Civil society provided both resilience and continuity to the political order, particularly during times of crisis or national calamity, such as during the devastating foreign invasions and during political uncertainties such as wars of succession. Thus, on the eve of imperialist inroads, in the Islamic world, as Olivier Roy has noted, 'secularization in Muslim countries had taken place routinely', as it had done in Europe; he explains:[18]

> Islam has, in fact, experienced secularization, from both the political and the sociological point of view . All authorities in Islam were secular in the sense that they were not determined by religious criteria. Except for the period of the Prophet, there was never a theocracy. Sultans, emirs, generals, and presidents took power (and continue to take it) following perfectly temporal processes (force, dynastic succession, coup d'etat, or even election) and were content with negotiating their legitimacy with a body of more or less domesticated ulema ...

The roots of contemporary radical Islam lie in imperialism when, for the first time in over one thousand years, Muslim lands and peoples found themselves under the hegemony of alien, non-Muslim rulers, who made an impact on every aspect of traditional life, including religious life, and threatened to uproot it fundamentally. It is, therefore, not surprising that present-day Muslim identity, as Roy has noted, should be tinged with anti-imperialism.[19]

Change in power equations between Islam and the West became apparent from the last quarter of the eighteenth century,[20] while the cultural impact of the West came to be felt from the mid-nineteenth century.[21] Under Western influence, a new educated class emerged in the Arab world, nurtured under the influence of Western teachers who brought new perspectives to the traditional Arab societies. Obviously, this raised questions about personal identity that needed to be looked at in the new political and cultural context. Educated Muslims saw in Europe a challenge, as Hourani has noted, and an attractive one at that, particularly in regard to science and technology, modern political institutions and the social morality of the new societies.[22]

There was early recognition that the challenge posed by the West would have to be met by the reform of native institutions, particularly in the areas of law, administration, armed forces and political order. Naturally, this raised questions about the place of religion—Islam—in this new order; more importantly, about what that 'Islam' would be. Clearly, traditional Islam would have to be re-interpreted in light of contemporary needs: it would have to be 'modernized'. Thus, 'Islamic modernism', that would make Islam compatible with reason, progress and social solidarity, became the central pursuit of educated Muslims. The debates in the Muslim world were comprehensive and covered: religion and reason; nobility and modernity; religion and the state, and religion and knowledge.[23]

Resurgent Islam

In considering present-day Islamic resurgence, it is useful to recall Abdulwahhab El-Affendi's important point that resurgence, renewal and revival are recurring themes through Islamic history.[24] In fact, renewal commenced with the advent of Islam, which was an attempt to revive Abrahamic monotheism by rescuing it from the deviations under which it had lain buried for long. John Voll notes that the two concepts in Islam *tajdid* (renewal) and *islah* (reform), together reflect 'a continuing tradition of revitalization of Islamic faith and practice within the historic communities of Muslims'.[25] The central motive force of this effort was to define Islam clearly and explicitly in terms of God's revelation as set out in the Koran and the Hadith. The point of reference in this regard was the period of the Prophet's lifetime, a period of 'righteous excellence'.[26]

Through all of Islamic history, steps were taken by intellectuals, in tandem with rulers where possible, to protect and preserve the core message of Islam through movements of renewal/revival based on such myriad tools as science and learning, self-criticism and introspection, worship and jihad. Intellectual and spiritual movements and setting up of theological and juristic schools, pursuit of Islamic sciences, all of these constitute a continuing pattern in Islamic history.

Even after the advent of colonialism, when Muslim lands and rulers gradually came under alien domination, reform movements continued to make themselves felt in different parts of the Islamic world, such as those of Mohammed ibn Abdul Wahhab in Najd (1703–91), the Dahlawiyya in India (1702–62), the al-Sanusiyya movement in North Africa (1859–78), the al-Mahdiyya in Sudan (1881–98) and the movement of Dan Fodio in Nigeria (1754–1817). These movements, while mainly of a political nature, were preceded and followed by many spiritual and social movements.

However, the completion of the colonial project and the hegemony of the imperialist powers brought about a fundamentally new character to Islam-West relations. The defeat of Islam was recognized as total and complete, and called for a fundamental review of what constituted Islamic belief and practice relevant to these changed times and where Islam, the tradition and way of life, stood in relation to this new, alien force. Central to these concerns was recognition of the obvious backwardness, weakness and poverty of Muslims and their decline in comparison with Western imperialism.[27]

Thus, the Islamic intellectual resurgence that now emerged was at once modern and Islamic.[28] It was modern in that it had recognized the modern environment within which the encounter with the West would be played out; but, it was Islamic in that it turned to and used 'Islam' and Islam-based authority in its response to the challenge of modernity.

The foundations of the twentieth century Islamic consciousness were laid by three great intellectuals who flourished in the late nineteenth century, Jamaluddin Al-Afghani (1838–97), Mohammed Abduh (1850–1905) and Rashid Rida (1865–1935).

Al-Afghani flourished at the height of Western power. He recalled a glorious Muslim past that had gradually come under Western domination since the beginning of the nineteenth century. (The glorious past he recalled included the pre-Islamic past of the ancient Egyptians, the Chaldeans and the Phoenicians.) He analysed Muslim decline in the following terms:[29]

> The Europeans have now put their hands on every part of the World. The English have reached Afghanistan; the French have seized Tunisia. In reality, these acts of usurpation, aggression, and conquest have not come from the French or the English. Rather it is science that everywhere manifests greatness and power. Ignorance had no alternative to prostrating itself humbly before science and acknowledging its submission.

He identified two causes for Islam's political failure: *taasul* (fanaticism) which he explained as misuse and misinterpretation of religion to legitimize the existing social and religious order; the other was *istibdad* (tyranny) which he felt could be ended with the removal of existing governments and their replacement by a parliamentary system.[30] According to Jansen, Al-Afghani's influence on later Islamic intellectuals was significant:[31]

> The influence of Gamal al-Din al-Afghani's teachings led many Muslim thinkers to develop a straightforward theory on the return of the superiority of Islam. They argued that the Muslim community is under an obligation to implement the God-given laws of Islam and that to neglect that supreme duty to carry out God's will causes political misery. Whenever the Muslim community is dominated by non-Muslim powers, it no longer lives in accordance with God's law, either because of widespread religious laxity or because the set of rules that it regards as God's law is in reality at variance with God's law.

Nikki Keddie has pointed out that Al-Afghani's principal contribution was in regard to changing Islam from a religious faith into a 'politico-religious ideology' which could become a source of solidarity against Western encroachment.[32]

Mohammed Abduh was Al-Afghani's principal disciple and pupil. He contrasted Western achievement and Muslim backwardness thus:[33]

> The torrent of science has rushed forth and engulfed the entire globe, drowning the unsuspecting ['ulama] in the process. It is an age which has formed a bond between ourselves and the civilized nations, making us aware of their excellent conditions ... and our mediocre situation: thus revealing their wealth and our poverty, their pride and our degradation, their strength and our weakness, their triumphs and our defeats, etc.

In his view, Muslim backwardness was both due to Western hegemony that threatened the very existence of Muslim societies, as also 'internal realities' that informed the Muslim situation such as their internal divisions, sectarianism and poor political leadership.[34]

He saw early Muslim life at the time of Prophet Mohammed as the 'golden age', but rejected blind imitation of all aspects of the past; he called for a review of all traditional texts against the Koran. In the area of religion, he called for the re-interpretation of Islam for the twentieth century by a new kind of religious leadership: 'one tied neither to slavish imitation of the past nor to the godless interpretations of the West, one able to understand the benefit of modern sciences and the reality of living in the modern world. This leadership must sit in judgment on the politicians and emphasize substance over traditional rituals.'[35] Again, while he argued in favour of an Islamic State, he saw non-Muslims as full citizens, with all rights and privileges. The core values of this state were public welfare (*al-maslaha al-amma*) and consultation (*shura*).

Abduh summarized his life's mission thus:[36]

> I took upon myself to plead the cause of two great issues. The first was the liberation of thought from the shackles of blind imitation, and the comprehension of religion according to the rules laid down, before the emergence of conflict, by the ancestors of the community, and the return, in acquiring religious knowledge, to the original source, considering them in the light of human reason. The second issue was the reform of the Arabic language ...
>
> The other issue that I espoused ... and is the pillar of social life was the differentiation between the entitlement of government to obedience from the people, and the people's right to justice from their government. Yes, I was one of those who called upon the Egyptian nation to recognize its right over its ruler—a suggestion that had not occurred to it for over twenty centuries. We urged it to believe that the ruler, although his obedience is obligatory, is only a human being, liable to err and be overwhelmed by his whims, and that nothing can dissuade him from his error and check the preponderance of his whims except the advice that the nation proffers him by word or deed.

The third pioneer of Islamic resurgence was Rashid Rida (1865–1935), who was among the first modern Islamic intellectuals to see Muslim salvation in the revival of the caliphate (the supreme leadership of Islam), culminating in the application of the sharia. In an interpretation of a Koranic verse, Rida wrote:[37]

... whomsoever thinks it is distasteful to rule in accordance with the just rules which God sent down, does not rule by them because he holds different views, or because he has worldly interests. According to these verses, they are the [apostate] unbelievers; because true faith requires obedience. Obedience requires deeds, and is not consistent with dislike [of the rules of the sharia] and omitting [to apply them].

Writing in 1906, Rida applauded the emergence of constitutional governments in Egypt, Tunisia, Iran and the Ottoman Empire:[38]

> The greatest benefit that the peoples of the Orient have derived from the Europeans was to learn how real government ought to be, as well as the assimilation of this knowledge. They thus surged forward in order to substitute restricted rule based on consultation and the law for one based on the absolute will of individuals. Some, such as Japan, have attained their full objectives, others, such as Iran, have embarked on this task; while yet others, as in Egypt and Turkey, are still struggling, by word and pen, to achieve such an end.
>
> This benefit is not a trivial or facile matter. It is a matchless gain, and the height of human development. Those who are content to let a ruler govern them according to his will and desires have to be classed with grazing livestock. This benefit is then ascension from the abyss of bestiality to the apogee of human civility.

However, he made it clear their origin was not in Islam but in Western influence:[39]

> Do not, O Muslim, say that this type of government [constitutionalism] is one of the basic foundations of our religion, so that we have simply inferred it from the Koran and the life stories of the rightly-guided caliphs, and not as a result of associating with the Europeans and being acquainted with the conditions of Westerns. Had you not reflected upon the state of these people, you, or others like you, would not have considered this to be part of Islam. Had it not been so, the 'Ulama in Istanbul, Egypt and Morocco, would have outstripped all others in calling for the erection of this pillar. Most of these 'ulama are still upholders of tyrannical autocracy and are counted amongst its foremost agents ...

The other contribution that Rashid Rida made in the early era of Islamic resurgence was his role in giving the thirteenth century Muslim scholar, Ibn Taymiyya, a central place in the contemporary debate within resurgent Islam. Today, almost all Islamic movements refer to and draw their inspiration from the writings of Ibn Taymiyya (1263–1328). In his time, Ibn Taymiyya was confronted by one of the greatest tragedies in Islamic history, the destruction of the Abassid Caliphate by the Mongols. Following the Mongols' conversion to Islam, Ibn Taymiyya needed to provide an intellectual justification for the continued confrontation of Arab Muslims with the Mongol Muslims; he utilized the tool of *bid'ah* (innovation), suggesting that the Mongols, although Muslims superficially, still retained many of their pre-Islamic customs, values and practices and, thus, were deviants from the ideal norms of Islam. Ibn Taymiyya idealized a 'pure' Islamic society and argued that *jihad* (holy war) against heretics and apostates was not just permitted in Islam but was indeed obligatory. In this context, Ibn Taymiyya divided the world into two absolute and mutually exclusive spheres—the land of Islam (*dar al-Islam*) and the land of unbelief (*dar al-kufr*), and asserted that the relationship between the two would necessarily have to be hostile.[40]

Ibn Taymiyya further believed that the character of the ruler was decisive in determining whether he was fit to exercise authority in the Islamic realm.[41] He pointed out that an Islamic government had two responsibilities—the upholding and enforcement of Islamic laws and the defence of Muslim lands against invaders. He believed that these two responsibilities could be implemented where necessary through coercion. He clarified his position thus:[42]

> Since lawful warfare is essentially *jihad* and since its aim is that the religion is God's entirely and God's word is uppermost, therefore, according to all Muslims, those who stand in the way of this aim must be fought.

Ibn Taymiyya justified jihad in response to a very broad range of religious infractions:[43]

> It is allowed to fight people for [not observing] unambiguous and generally recognized obligations and prohibitions, until they undertake to perform the explicitly prescribed prayers; to pay *zakat*, to fast during the month of Ramadan, to make the pilgrimage to Mecca and to avoid what is prohibited, such as marrying women in spite of legal impediments, eating impure things, acting unlawfully against the lives and properties of Muslims and the like.
>
> It is obligatory to *take the initiative* in fighting those people, as soon as the Prophet's summons, with the reasons for which they are fought, has reached them. But if they first attack the Muslims, then fighting them is even more urgent, as we have mentioned when dealing with the fighting against rebellious and aggressive bandits.

Ibn Taymiyya also highlighted the importance of martyrdom in the pursuit of jihad: thus he said:[44]

> It is in jihad that one can live and die in ultimate happiness, both in this world and in the Hereafter. Abandoning it means losing entirely or partially both kinds of happiness.

Johannes J.G. Jansen has referred to Ibn Taymiyya's position as a case of 'war theology', with Ibn Taymiyya being a part of the resistance movement against the Mongol invasion of Syria and Egypt.[45] Ibn Taymiyya's struggle against the Mongols *required* him to depict the latter as evil and therefore apostate; as Jansen has said, he wanted to characterize the Mongols of his day as sub-human enemies of Muslims in a credible way.[46] Accordingly, Ibn Taymiyya emphasized that, while the Mongols had apparently converted to Islam, they did not apply the Islamic sharia law but followed their own customary law. Flowing from this, he argued that the Mongol ruler who allowed his followers to practice customary law was guilty of the crime of the apostasy and therefore could be regarded as the enemy of Islam. Ibn Taymiyya said:[47]

> The Mongols and their like are even more rebellious against the laws of Islam than these *khawarig* (or any other group). Whosoever doubts whether they should be fought is most ignorant of the religion of Islam. Since fighting them is obligatory they have to be fought, even though there are among them some who have been forced to join their ranks.

Ibn Taymiyya's conclusion was unambiguous:[48]

> A consensus [ijma] exists that someone who makes it possible to follow another religion than the religion of Islam, or to follow another law than the law of Muhammad, is an infidel [*kafir*]. His unbelief is even explicitly mentioned in the Koran. [It] is like the unbelief of whosoever believes in part of the book and does not believe in other parts.

While Ibn Taymiyya had set out his categorical views in the specific context of the Mongol invasion of Arab lands, his writings were seized upon by Muslim intellectuals in the twentieth century to argue that, in line with the norms set out by Ibn Taymiyya in respect of the Mongols, the present rulers of the Arab world could also be regarded as apostates. It is this argument that is being used 800 years later by Muslim ideologues to advocate a violent confrontation against those Muslims, particularly Muslims leaders, who, in their view, have deviated from the moral codes and practices that informed Islam's first 'pure' society.

Al-Afghani, Mohammed Abduh and Rashid Rida constitute the first generation of modern Islamists. El-Affendi speaks of their contribution thus:[49]

> There is no doubt that the general legacy of this intellectual school, including its main principles and concerns – such as resisting colonialism and regaining the glory of the nation, establishing the basis of the Shura, and the reforming of Government, religious reform and the renewal of religion – constituted the bases for the emergence of the modern Islamic movements.

After this period of the pioneers, the first part of the twentieth century saw the next generation of Islamic scholars whose writings taken together constitute the *oeuvre* of contemporary resurgent Islam. The shining star of these intellectuals was the Indian intellectual and political activist, Sayyid Abul Ala Maududi (1903–79). In his analysis of the Muslim predicament in the early twentieth century, Maududi developed the concept of the 'new *jahiliyya*' in terms of which most of the Islamic world had been alienated from the essential values of Islam, was living in an era of ignorance and had thus effectively become apostate. Islam, he believed, had the capacity to fundamentally alter this life of ignorance of Muslims:[50]

> [Islam] is a revolutionary ideology which seeks to alter the social order of the entire world and rebuild it in conformity with its own tenets and ideals. 'Muslims' is the title of that 'International Revolutionary Party' organised by Islam to carry out its revolutionary programme. 'Jihad' refers to that revolutionary struggle and utmost exertion which the Islamic Nation/ Party brings into play in order to achieve this objective ... There is no doubt that all the Prophets of Allah, without exception, were Revolutionary Leaders, and the illustrious Prophet Muhammad was the greatest Revolutionary Leader of all.

Maududi believed in the unique and exclusive nature of Islam: though 'ignorance' had emerged from time to time in early Islamic history, according to Maudidi:[51]

> it would be wrong to assume that Islam at any time was wholly routed and completely over-powered by this onslaught of 'Ignorance'. As a matter of fact, once a community accepted Islam, the lives of its people ever after bore in some degree the imprint of its reformative influence. It was all due to this imprint of Islam that great tyrants and absolute rulers shuddered, at times, with the fear of God, and were impelled to walk the path of truth

and justice ... On this very account the Muslim people all over the world have always been morally superior to the non-Muslim communities.

Maududi recognized that the Muslims of his times were completely powerless and it was beyond their capacity to effectively confront their external and internal enemies. He pointed out that Prophet Mohammad himself had faced the same situation and that his life from the first revelation to the final establishment of the Muslim State in AD 630 was, for all practical purposes, an 'Instruction Manual' for Islamic revolution. The pattern of Muslim empowerment, according to Maududi, was thus: the first step was the call (*dawa*) which pulls together a small community, the *jamaat*. Initially, this community was weak; in order to develop its internal resources and capacities, this community would separate itself from the pervasive jahiliyya and develop its strength. When it was sufficiently strong, it would engage in jihad and set up an ideal Islamic State, which Maududi referred to as a 'theo-democracy'.[52]

Maududi believed that Muslims would anxiously seek and support the Islamic order once they had been tutored in Islam's true teachings. However, Maududi saw the need for an 'Islamization of society' *before* the setting up of the Islamic State; if the timing were reversed, the Islamic state would have to be autocratic to enforce Islamic law, while Maududi's Islamic state was a democracy, which, because of its Islamic character, had no divisive issues to cope with: 'the population would willingly abide by the demands of Islamic laws. The Islamic state would not be the enforcer of the Sharia, but the implementor of the will of the people.'[53]

Maududi exalted the status of jihad which he declared to be the principal tenet of Islam. Jihad, according to Maududi, was not just self-defence or even a means to convert non-Muslims. In Islam's struggle with the modern jahiliyya of the West, jihad would play the central role: it would be the revolutionary struggle to establish God's just order on earth 'to bring about a revolution and establish a new order in conformity with the ideology of Islam'.[54] This struggle is undertaken not for selfish reasons, but to earn God's pleasure, the aim being not to 'replace Caesar with Caesar' but to establish a 'just and equitable social order among human beings. ... Under an evil government, an evil system takes root and flourishes and no pious order can ever be established. This is why the Islamic party has no option but to wrest the authority of government from wicked hands and transfer it to the hands of true Muslims.'[55]

The next influential ideologue, whose writings resonate powerfully with contemporary resurgent Islamic discourse, was the Egyptian Sayyid Qutb (1906–66). Just as Maududi's thinking emerged from his concerns relating to the fate of Indian Muslims in British India, so also Qutb's thinking was rooted in his personal encounters, first with the 'amoral' West, and later with the 'deviant secularism' of revolutionary Egypt. With his body wracked with pain due to torture in Nasser's prison, Sayyid Qutb wrote *Milestones on the Road* (1964). He also authored several volumes of commentary on the Koran. Qutb believed that there was a real battle in this world between the forces of good and evil and between faith and unbelief. His analysis of the human condition was clear:[56]

> Humanity today stands on the brink of the abyss ... not because of the threat of destruction that hangs over its head (for that is merely a symptom of the evil, not the evil itself), but because of its bankruptcy in the domain of the "values" under which man could have lived and developed harmoniously.
>
> Humanity needs a new direction!

The panacea was also available to mankind:[57]

> Now, at this most critical of times, when turmoil and confusion reign, it is the turn of Islam, of the *umma[h]* [the community of believers] to play its role ... Islam's time has come, Islam which does not renounce the material inventions of this world, for it considers them the first function of man, since God has accorded man his lieutenancy over the world, and as a means—under certain conditions—of worshipping God and of realizing the aims of human existence.

However, present-day Islamic society was ill-equipped to play its historic role. He saw contemporary Islamic society as either *jahili* (ignorant) or *kufr* (made up of disbelievers or infidels); he said:[58]

> Islamic society today is not Islamic in any sense of the word ... In our modern society we do not judge by what Allah has revealed; the basis of our economic life is usury; our laws permit rather than punish oppression ... We permit the extravagance and luxury that Islam prohibits; we allow the starvation and the destitution of which the Messenger once said: 'Whenever people anywhere allow a man to go hungry, they are outside the protection of Allah, the Blessed and the Exalted.'

His critique was unambiguous:[59]

> Any society that is not Muslim is *jahiliyya* ... as is any society in which something other than God alone is worshipped ...Thus, we must include in this category all the societies that now exist on earth!

He adopted Maududi's pattern in regard to evolution towards a true Islamic society with no accommodation being possible between belief and ignorance:[60]

> Islam cannot accept any compromise with *jahiliyya*, either in its concept or in its modes of living derived from this concept. Either Islam will remain, or *jahiliyya*; Islam cannot accept or agree to a situation which is half-Islam and half-*jahiliyya*. In this respect Islam's stand is very clear. It says that truth is one and cannot be divided; if it is not the truth, then it must be falsehood. The mixing and co-existence of the truth and falsehood is impossible. Command belongs to Allah, or else to *jahiliyya*. The *Shari'ah* of Allah will prevail, or else people's desires.

He slightly modified Maududi's demand for a complete separation from a Jahiliyya society by advising that separation should not be complete:[61]

> This [the Islamic world] cannot come about by going along even a few steps with *jahiliyya*, nor by severing relations with it and removing ourselves to a separate corner; never. The correct procedure is to mix with discretion, give and take with dignity; speak the truth with love, and show the superiority of the Faith with humility. If they do not respond to our call, then we shall say to them what Allah commanded His Messenger, peace on him, to say: 'For you your way, for me mine'.

The task before the believer was then set out by him:[62]

> Our first task is to change society in deed, to alter the *jahiliyya* reality from top to bottom ... To start with, we must get rid of this *jahiliyya* society, we must abandon its values and ideology, and must not enfeeble our own values and ideology by even one iota to bring them closer to it! Certainly not! Our paths diverge, and if we took even a single step toward it, our ethics would vanish and we would be lost!

Qutb called for the setting up of a God-centred society since only such a society was capable of giving justice to its members; he said:[63]

> This means that religion is an all-embracing and total revolution against the sovereignty of man in all its type, shape, system and state, and completely revolts against every system in which authority may be in the

hands of man in any form or in other words, he may have usurped sovereignty under any shape. Any system of governance in which the final decision is referred to human beings and they happen to be the source of all authority in fact deifies them by designating "others than God," as lords over men ... In short, proclamation of the sovereignty of Allah and declaration of His Authority connotes the wiping out of human kingship from the face of the earth and establishing thereon the rule of the Sustainer of the world.

Though Sayyid Qutb drew heavily from Ibn Taymiyya in developing his radical vision of Islam and jihad, as Delong-Bas has noted, 'Qutb's experiences of repressive, authoritarianism, imprisonment and torture by his own government led to his radicalization'.[64]

Qutb saw armed struggle as the only hope to free humanity to accept the message of Islam, so that 'we succeed in wiping off the tyrannical powers from the face of God's earth whether they may be of a purely political nature cloaked in the form of radicalism or class distinctions within a race'.[65] His view of jihad was apocalyptic: as David Zeidan has pointed out, for him jihad was an activist movement committed to restoring the Muslims' freedom and destroying the regimes that deny people the freedom to listen to the message of Islam and force them to bow to their own sovereignty rather than to that of Allah. Having annihilated the tyranny, Islam then establishes a new social, economic and political system, in which all men and women enjoy real freedom. The purpose of *jihad bil-saif* (jihad with the sword) is to introduce true freedom for mankind and prepare the way for a free preaching of Islam to all humanity.[66] In Qutb's jihad there could be no compromise:[67]

Islam [submission to God] is a universal truth, acceptance of which is binding on the entire humanity ... If anyone adopts the attitude of resistance, it would then be obligatory on Islam to fight against him until he is killed or he declares his loyalty and submission.

In advocating the concept of global jihad, Qutb saw the conflict between the good and evil as one of cosmic proportions. In his view, there was an inherent conflict between Islam and every other faith. This imbued his concept of jihad with a global perspective; his vision of jihad recognized no boundaries, physical or temporal: this struggle was not a temporary phase but 'a perpetual and permanent war ... Jihad for freedom ... [could not] cease until the Satanic forces ... [were] put to an end and the religion ... purified for God in toto'.[68]

This jihad was all-comprehensive: it was not only a personal effort 'to liberate the individual from his passions'; it was also a weapon to free the individual from those who wished to confine him:[69]

> To establish the reign of God on earth and eliminate the reign of man, to take power out of the hands of those of His worshippers who have usurped it and to return it to God alone, to confer authority upon divine law (*shariat allah*) alone and to eliminate the laws created by man ... all this will not be done through sermons and discourse. Those who have usurped the power of God on earth and made His worshippers their slaves will not be dispossessed by dint of Word alone; otherwise the task of His messengers would be far more easily done.

Sayyid Qutb is regarded as the main contemporary ideologue of resurgent Islam. As Jansen has noted, his writings in the 1950s and 1960s transformed the Muslims from pious civilians into self-conscious conscript soldiers having no choice but to make war against the enemies of Islam.[70]

Hasan Al-Banna (1906–49) was a contemporary and associate of Sayyid Qutb. His significant contribution in the discourse of resurgent Islam was the setting up of the Muslim Brotherhood (1928) in order to: (i) re-Islamize all classes of people; and, (ii) work towards establishing a government that would rule 'on the basis of Muslim values and norms'. He emphasized the role of jihad in the realization of an ideal Islamic state and exalted it as 'supreme martyrdom'.

While Maududi and Sayyid Qutb were intellectuals, Hasan Al-Banna was a political activist who converted the ideas of these intellectuals into a movement. The Muslim Brotherhood set up by him was a response to some local workers in Ismaliyyah who wanted some action that would effect change in their miserable lives. Karen Armstrong describes them as appealing to Al-Banna thus:[71]

> We know not the practical way to reach the glory of Islam and to serve the welfare of the Muslims. We are weary of this life of humiliation and restriction. So we see the Arabs and the Muslims have no status and no dignity. They are not more than mere hirelings belonging to foreigners. We possess nothing but this blood ... and these souls ... and these few coins. We are unable to perceive the road to action as you perceive it, or to know the path to the service of the fatherland, the religion and the ummah as you know it.

When Al-Banna was assassinated in 1949, the Muslim Brotherhood had 2,000 branches in Egypt, with a total membership between 300,000 and 600,000 members. Sayyid Qutb joined the society in 1953.

Among the next generation of militant Islamist thinkers, Shukri Mustafa (1942–78), Mohammed Abdul Salam Faraj (1952–82) and Abdullah Azzam (1941–89) stand out most prominently.

Shukri Mustafa, in his early years, was an activist with the Muslim Brotherhood. He was imprisoned between 1965 and 1971, when he developed his thinking on Islam and Islamic society. In July 1977, soon after his release, he and some of his followers were re-arrested and later executed for the murder of Sheikh Mohammed al Dhahabi, former Minister for Religious Affairs.

While most of his extensive writings are not available in public as they were confiscated by the security forces when he was arrested, some information about his and his group's thinking is available from reports of his trial for the al-Dhahabi murder. Shukri was radical even by Islamist standards for asserting that the decline of Islam started in the fourth century of the Hijri era when Muslims became dependent on the writings of Islamic scholars on what was said and meant in the Koran rather than on the Koran itself. As a former follower of Shukri clarified:[72]

> We do not accept the words ascribed to the Apostle's contemporaries, or the opinions of those versed in Islamic law, the *fuqaha*. We do not accept the opinions of the early jurists, or their consensus *igma*, or the other idols, *asnam*, like analogy, qiyas. How can words of mere humans be a source of divine guidance?

Again, besides rejecting all the commentaries and canonical works of Islam, Shukri at his trial also conveyed that he was not absolutely certain about the historicity of the Koranic stories as also about the infallibility of the process of transmission.[73] Having asserted that there was only one source of divine guidance—the Koran—Shukri Mustafa, at his trial, made three further assertions: (*i*) all present societies are un-Islamic; (*ii*) only members of the Shukri group are true Muslims; and, (*iii*) the classical system of Islamic law must be rejected.[74]

There is some doubt about the name of Shukri Mustafa's organization. Most literature on the subject refers to it as '*Jamaat al-Takfir Wa-al-Hijra*', that is, Movement for Ex-communication and Migration. However, as Jansen has pointed out, the group did not itself choose this name; it was created for it by the Egyptian authorities and the press, though it does refer to certain core tenets of the group: that true Muslims should emigrate to Muslim political communities, away from the day-to-day paganism of secular Egypt; and that people who do not live completely in accordance with the directives of Islam are not Muslims but unbelievers.[75]

The group actually called itself *Jamaat-al-Muslimeen* or *Al-Jamaat Al-Muslima*, that is, Society of Muslims or the Muslim Community, emphasizing Muslim exclusiveness and asserting that it was 'the real community of Muslims'.

Faraj is remembered for his book *The Neglected Duty*, published in 1981, in which he has argued that jihad, the neglected duty of Muslims, was indeed the sixth pillar of Islam. He differed from Maududi and Sayyid Qutb in rejecting the concept of the early 'period of weakness' of the Muslim community as also the need for a physical separation from an apostate society. Faraj, instead, advocated an infiltration by Muslims into the society, Government and armed forces of the apostate state and even a militant engagement with the regime to force radical change.

Faraj argued that jihad was not just the sixth pillar of Islam but was, indeed, the main duty of true Muslims and superior to all other forms of struggle. He criticized other groups who advocated a gradualist approach to Islamic empowerment as a strategy that would only strengthen the apostate ruler, and asserted that active and immediate jihad was the only effective strategy to achieving an Islamic state. Such an Islamic State was absolutely essential because:[76]

> ... to carry out God's prescripts [is] an obligation for the Muslims. Hence, the establishment of an Islamic State is obligatory ... because something without which what is obligatory cannot be carried out, itself becomes obligatory. If such a state cannot be established without war, then this war is an obligation as well ... The laws by which the Muslims are ruled today are [not the laws of Islam but] the laws of Unbelief ... The rulers of this age are [hence] in apostasy from Islam... An apostate has to be killed even if he is unable to carry arms and go to war.

Faraj was very clear who the enemy was:[77]

> In the Islamic countries the enemy is at home; indeed, it is he who is in command. He is represented by those governments that have seized power over the Muslims, and that is why *jihad* is an imperative for every individual (*fard ayn*).

He also had a detailed action plan:[78]

First: the fight against the enemy at home takes priority over the fight against the enemy abroad.

Second: since the blood of the Muslims flows until victory, one may well ask who benefited from this victory. Was it the Islamic state, or the infidel regime, whose foundations were only consolidated by this victory? ... The entire fight must be waged exclusively under Muslim command.

Third: the responsibility for the existence of colonialism or imperialism (*istiʿmar*) in our Muslim countries lies with these infidel governments. To launch a struggle against imperialism is therefore useless and inglorious, a waste of time; we must concentrate on our Islamic problem, namely the establishment of God's law in our own countries.

He also knew that action was more important and the outcome was always uncertain:[79]

> To carry out God's order is to build the Islamic state. We do not insist on this or that result; ... the mere fall of the infidel regime will bring everything within the reach of the Muslims!

Faraj set up the *Jamaat Al-Jihad* in 1981, which was involved with the assassination of President Anwar Sadat. After this, the organization was destroyed by the Egyptian security forces, and Faraj, himself, was executed in 1982.

The next prominent figure in the pantheon of contemporary resurgent Islam is the Palestinian scholar and activist, Abdullah Yusuf Azzam (1941–89). Azzam was nurtured in jihad in the school of Muslim Brothers in Egypt. He found sanctuary in Jeddah after Nasser's crackdown on the Brotherhood but was expelled in 1979, following the occupation of the Makkah Mosque. After his expulsion, Azzam made his way to Pakistan and immersed himself in the jihad against the Soviet occupation of Afghanistan. In Afghanistan, he set up 'Maktab-Al-Khidmaat' or 'Services Office' which provided guest houses and paramilitary training camps for operational units active in the Afghan jihad. In this, he worked closely with Osama bin Laden, the Saudi businessman—billionaire who was the principal coordinator of Saudi relief supplies and other material for use in the *Mujahedeen* struggle.

Azzam broke free from national concerns that had, according to him, limited the vision and approach of earlier jihadi writers, and advocated the setting up of a paramilitary infrastructure for the globalization of Islamist movements. In 1979, he issued a fatwa titled:

'Defence of the Muslim Lands', in which he saw jihad as the first obligation after faith in Allah; Azzam understood jihad as 'God's ordained method for establishing Islam in the world, a battle ... for the formation of mankind that the truth may be made dominant and good propagated'.[80] According to Azzam, jihad comes just after *iman* (faith), which makes it a pillar of Islam. When kuffar (plural of kufr, meaning infidel) occupy Muslim lands, jihad becomes a compulsory individual obligation on every single Muslim (*fard 'ayn*) and remains so until the liberation of the last occupied piece of Muslim land.[81] Jihad is a religious duty first: 'Jihad is the most excellent form of worship, and by means of it the Muslim can reach the highest of ranks.'[82]

Azzam, the chief ideologue of the Arab–Afghans, saw their role in the Afghan jihad in near-messianic terms; on the death of a Saudi 'martyr' in the Afghan jihad, Azzam wrote:[83]

> Everything in your soul used to speak that you were the next to be a martyr. There were your brothers who shared with you the pains of the path of sacrifice, the sweat and blood, under the shower of bullets and the thunder of cannons, to awaken an *umma[h]* whose depths were filled by weakness. I sensed in my depths that you would be a *shahid*.
>
> O Yahya! Your fragrant blood began to flow and not a single person that touched your body or perfumed themselves with drops of your blood remained without the smell of musk filling their noses.
>
> You refused to let the Muslims' honour be violated, their support reduced or their victory be trampled on. You did not sit by patiently while the Muslims were being humiliated ... rather you advanced to Allah, steadfast.

The role he envisaged for this vanguard was very clear:[84]

> Establishment of the Muslim community on an area of land is a necessity, as vital as water and air. This homeland will not come about without an organized Islamic movement which perseveres consciously and realistically upon Jihad, and which regards fighting as a decisive factor and as a protective wrapping. The Islamic movement will not be able to establish the Islamic community except through a common, people's Jihad which has the Islamic movement as its beating heart and deliberating mind. It will be like the small spark which ignites a large keg of explosives, for the Islamic movement brings about an eruption of the hidden capabilities of the Ummah, and a gushing forth of the springs of Good stored up in its depth.

He also saw jihad in Afghanistan as only the first of several other struggles:[85]

> The duty will not end with victory in Afghanistan; jihad will remain an individual obligation until all other lands that were Muslim are returned to us so that Islam will reign again: before us lie Palestine, Bokhara, Lebanon, Chad, Eritrea, Somalia, the Philippines, Burma, Southern Yemen, Tashkent and Andalusia.

Azzam was active and inspirational in the anti-Soviet jihad in Afghanistan, with his fund-raising and consciousness-raising activities taking him across the world, including to the USA. After the Soviet withdrawal from Afghanistan, Azzam proposed that the jihad in Afghanistan be consolidated, while Osama bin Laden suggested, instead, the pursuit of a globalized agenda. Azzam was assassinated by unknown persons in 1989 in Peshawar.

Azzam played a central role in giving primacy to jihad in the Afghan struggle, imparting practical shape to what till then had only been extortions on the pages of manuscripts of ideologues assaulted and beaten by the systems they had attacked. It was Azzam's call to the holy struggle that lured thousands of young men from the ummah to the battlefields of Afghanistan, unleashing a force that forcefully reverberates today in contemporary politics.[86]

Conclusion

Contemporary resurgent Islam has its origins in the early nineteenth century when the Islamic world came under Western military, political economic and cultural hegemony. This total domination, which had no precedent in Islamic history, instigated a pervasive introspection in different centres of the Islamic world. The responses it evoked were varied and complex. The first instinctive reaction in the eighteenth century was to suggest that Muslims had deviated from the true path and thus exposed themselves to defeat at the hands of the non-Muslim West; the panacea then was to hark back to the pristine Islam of the Prophet. These responses were vividly expressed through the Dalhawiyya movement in India and the Wahhabi movement in Najd. However, as Muslim intellectuals got a deeper exposure to Western society and culture, the response to Western domination became more complex and focused increasingly on the various political and cultural implications of Islam's encounter with the West.

Jamaluddin Al-Afghani was a pioneering Islamic intellectual who pointed out that the West's achievements in regard to science as against Islam's fanaticism and tyranny were the central cause of the Muslim malaise. Muhammed Abduh broadly agreed with his mentor, but argued strongly against blind imitation and urged the need for widespread political and cultural change based on indigenous traditions. Rashid Rida, on the other hand, saw Muslim salvation in the revival of pristine Islam. He provided a contemporary resonance to the writings of Ibn Taymiyya who had justified jihad against a Muslim ruler if the latter did not rule in conformity with the sharia. Ibn Taymiyya had argued that jihad was 'lawful warfare' against such rulers, and that martyrdom in pursuit of jihad was the 'ultimate happiness'.

Muslim intellectuals of the twentieth century primarily focused on going back to the fundamentals of Islam, cleansing contemporary belief and practice from 'innovation' that had crept into the faith over the centuries, and imbuing the faith with militant zeal in the face of domestic and foreign antagonists. Maududi and Sayyid Qutb played a pioneering role in giving shape to such militant doctrines, seeing jihad as the instrument to establish God's 'just order' on earth. Both intellectuals saw their struggle in 'cosmic' terms as a conflict between good and evil. Hasan Al-Banna was a political activist who set up the Muslim Brotherhood as the organization that would bring the true message of Islam into the lives of the Muslims and provide them with a political order based on Islamic norms and values.

It should be noted that, with the exception of some radical Islamic stalwarts, the vast majority of Muslims under imperialism did not become wide-eyed *ghazis* (Muslim warriors) or *mujahids* (participants in jihad); in fact, they *adapted* to imperialist rule, becoming, as businessmen, bureaucrats, policemen and soldiers, staunch pillars of the imperial order. Generally speaking, Muslims handled the challenge of imperialism in the normal fashion of initial hostility being followed by adaptation, support, imitation, and, on occasion servility [derisively referred to as 'Westernized Oriental Gentlemen' (Wogs) by racist imperialism], responses that were not different from those in other non-Muslim societies.

In fact, the main narrative of the twentieth century is of considerable give-and-take and cooperation between 'Islam' and the West. Muslims from India fought in the British Indian armies against Turkey and in several other battles in the two World Wars in defence of the Empire. Arabs from the Arabian Peninsula backed the British against Turkey, and, though betrayed after the war, their leaders continued to support British interests in the Gulf and West Asia through the inter-war period.

The Islam-West interaction eventually yielded a novel concept in Islam, that its essential doctrines be separated from its social teachings and laws, so that a social morality would be put in place that was acceptable to modern times. The Egyptian intellectual, Taha Hussain (1889–1973), described himself as made up of three distinct influences—-the Egyptian, the Arab and the Western that came down from the Greeks and encompassed all interactions with the West over the last two millennia.[87] He idealized the Islam of the time of the Prophet, but the dominant principle for him was the collective identity of the Egyptian nation that was independent and strong in the modern world. Hassan Al-Banna, on the other hand, in the face of Western challenge, put his emphasis on Islam—a return to the true Islam—with the Koran interpreted by genuine *ijtihad* (innovation) and the state based on a *reformed* sharia.[88] The appeal of the Muslim Brotherhood, while significant in the 1930s, was primarily among the urban population, but even then it was confined to the strata between the poor and the educated elite.[89]

Similarly, though Sayyid Qutb emerged as a powerful 'Islamist' voice and proclaimed a vision of Islam that was comprehensive and uncompromising, and was articulated in the context of modernity, his impact in his time was limited: the primary trend in political thought consisted of secular perspectives and progammes led by nationalism.[90] Islam was a part of popular nationalism, but it had a subordinate part; the dominant elements were: consciousness about belonging to the Third World as exemplified by membership of the Non-Aligned Movement; Arab unity, and socialism. These were the premier ideologies of reform and protest in the Islamic world, but they emerged not from Islam but from modern democratic, socialist and Marxist perspectives.[91]

The military defeat of 1967 and Nasser's death in 1970 marked the end of this era of hope and fomented a new crisis of identity. In these troubled times, there was a fresh focus on 'inherited beliefs and culture' which would provide guidance and direction.[92] While the Islamists, as we have seen, were strident in their claim that 'Islam' was the only way out of this crisis, theirs was not the sole voice. In fact, there were a wide variety of assertions. Thus, the Syrian philosopher, Sadiq Jalal al-Azm (b. 1934), called for a rejection of religious thought, while the Tunisian scholar, Hisham Djait (b. 1935), called for a separation between social institutions and laws from religion.[93]

The Islamists on the other hand, believed that Islam was sufficient. They believed that Islamic heritage by itself could provide the basis for life in the present, and that it alone could do so because it was derived from the word of God. However, they experienced a schism in their group, with one group suggesting working with the political order hoping to reform it from within, while the other, led by Qutb, felt that the political order was so corrupt (a jahilliyya) that the good Muslim had no chice but to reject all possible interaction with it.[94] Sayyid Qutb was confident that final victory would be his:[95]

> The leadership of Western man in the human world is coming to an end, not because western civilization is materially bankrupt or has lost its economic or military strength, but because the western order has played its part, and no longer possesses that stock of 'value' which gave it its predominance ... *The scientific revolution has finished its role, as have 'nationalism' and the territorially limited communities which grew up in its age ... The turn of Islam has come.* [Emphasis added.]

There was also a middle view that felt that Islam was not just a culture but, still, it needed to be reformed to enable it to fulfill its role as the moral basis of modern society. Most scholars supporting this view called for re-opening the doors of ijtihad, so that the sharia would be adapted to contemporary times.[96]

The tradition of West-Islam political collaboration continued robustly during the Cold War, with the West seeing Islam as a 'natural ally' against godless Communism. The global jihad in Afghanistan in the 1980s, the modern world's first jihad, was the child spawned by this alliance, being put together by the leaders of the West and Islam working in close cooperation, that is, the USA, Saudi Arabia and Pakistan. Abdullah Azzam (1941–89) took the Islamic struggle out of Egypt and pursued a vision of global jihad from his base in Afghanistan. In line with the thinking of earlier radical Islamic intellectuals, Azzam exalted the role of jihad as a compulsory individual duty to obtain liberation of occupied Muslim lands. Jihad in Afghanistan was seen by him as only the first of such struggles which were to be carried out in different parts of the Muslim world that were subjected to apostate or alien domination.

Even as the Egyptian government came down heavily on its Islamic leaders and their movements, the base of radical Islam moved to Afghanistan in a political arrangement, sanctioned by Saudi Arabia, Pakistan and the United States, that promoted global jihad against the Soviet Union as part of the Cold War. How this 'natural alliance' between the West and Islam evolved into a clash of civilizations, with 'Crusader forces' (loosely represented by the West and specifically USA and Israel) on one side and radical Islam emerging as the evil 'other' is examined in the next chapter.

NOTES

1. Abdulwahhab El-Affendi, 'Islamic Movements: Establishment, Significance and Contextual Realities', in *Islamic Movements-Impact on Political Stability in the Arab World* (Abu Dhabi: the Emirates Centre for Strategic Studies and Research, 2003) p. 7.
2. El-Affendi, pp. 10–11.
3. ibid.
4. ibid., pp. 15–16
5. David Cook, 'Islam and Apocalyptic', Position Paper, Centre for Millennial Studies, Boston University, undated; downloaded from: www.bu.edu/mille/scholarship/papers/cookabs.html.
6. Quoted in N. R. Keddie, *Iran and the Muslim World: Resistance and Revolution* (New York: New York University Press, 1995) p. 220.
7. Mamoun Fandy, *Saudi Arabia and the Politics of Dissent* (New York: St. Martin's Press, 1999) p. 25.
8. John L. Esposito and John O. Voll (Eds), *Islam and Democracy* (New York: Oxford University Press, 1996) p. 4, henceforth Esposito.
9. Fandy, pp. 23–4.
10. ibid., p. 30.
11. ibid., p. 24.
12. ibid., p. 25.
13. Abdelwahab El-Affendi, 'Rationality of Politics and Politics of Rationality – Democratisation and the Influence of Islamic Religious Traditions', in John L. Esposito and Azzam Tamimi (ed.), *Islam and Secularism in the Middle East* (London: Hurst & Co., 2000) p. 167.
14. ibid.
15. Albert Hourani, *A History of the Arab Peoples* (Cambridge, MA: The Belknap Press of Harvard University Press, 1991) p. 114.
16. ibid.

17. Quoted in Esposito, p. 48.
18. Olivier Roy, *Secularism Confronts Islam* (New York: Columbia University Press, 2007) p. 53.
19. Olivier Roy, p. 49.
20. Hourani, p. 259.
21. Azzam Tamimi, 'The Origins of Arab Secularism', in *Esposito and Tamini* (Ed), op. cit., p. 17.
22. Hourani, p. 306.
23. Tamimi, p. 17.
24. El-Affendi, p. 12.
25. John O. Voll, 'Renewal and Reform in Islamic History: Tajdid and Islah', in John L. Esposito (ed), *Voices of Resurgent Islam* (New York: Oxford University Press, 1983) p. 32.
26. Voll, p. 34.
27. El-Affendi, p. 17.
28. ibid.
29. Yousef M. Choueiri, *Islamic Fundamentalism* (London: Pinter Publishers, 1990) p. 37.
30. Johannes J. G. Jansen, *The Dual Nature of Islamic Fundamentalism* (London: Hurst & Co. , 1997), p. 27.
31. Jansen, p. 87.
32. Nikki R. Keddie, 'Sayyid Jamal Al-Ain Al-Afghani', in Ali Rehnema (Ed), *Pioneers of Islamic Revival* (Kuala Lumpur: New Updated Edition, SIRD , 2005) p. 23.
33. Choueiri, p. 36.
34. Yvonne Haddad, 'Muhammad Abduh: Pioneer of Islamic Reform', in *Ali Rahnema,* op. cit., p. 35.
35. Haddad, p. 49.
36. Choueri, p. 38
37. Jansen, p. 39.
38. Choueri, p. 54.
39. ibid, p. 55.
40. Natana J. Delong-Bas, *Wahhabi Islam – From Revival and Reform to Global Jihad* (London: Oxford University Press, 2004) p. 248.
41. ibid.
42. ibid., p. 250.
43. ibid., p. 252.
44. ibid., p. 254.
45. Jansen, p. 38.
46. ibid., p. 34.
47. ibid., p. 38.

48. ibid., p. 37.
49. El-Affendi, p. 19.
50. David Zeidan, 'The Islamic Fundamentalist View of Life as a Perennial Battle', *MERIA Journal*, Vol. 5, No. 4, p. 4; downloaded from: meria.idc.ac.il/journal/2001/issue 4/jv5n4a2.htm.
51. Choueri, p. 95.
52. Trevor Stanley 'Maulana Maududi – Radical Islam's Missing Link', *Perspectives on World History and Current Events [PWHCE]*, 2004; downloaded from: www.pwhce.org/maududi.html.
53. Seyyed Vali Raza Nasr, 'Maududi and the Jamaat-i-Islami: The Origins, Theory and Practice of Islamic Revivalism', in *Ali Rahnema*, op. cit., p. 107.
54. Zeidan, p. 17.
55. ibid.
56. Gilles Kepel, *The Roots of Radical Islam*, (London: Saqi, 2005) pp. 41-2.
57. ibid.
58. Quoted in Spenglar, "Crisis of Faith in the Muslim World", *Asia Times Online*, 1 November 2005;downloaded from:www.atimes.com/atimes/ Frong_page/GK01Aaq/html; Kepel, p. 46.
59. Kepel, p. 46.
60. Zeidan, p. 4.
61. ibid., p. 7.
62. Kepel. p. 53
63. ibid., p. 258.
64. ibid.
65. ibid., p. 260.
66. Zeidan, p. 17.
67. Delong-Bas, p. 260.
68. ibid., pp. 263–4.
69. Kepel, pp. 54–5.
70. Jansen, p. 49.
71. Karen Armstrong, *The Battle for God – Fundamentalism in Judaism, Christianity and Islam* (London: Harper Collins Publishers, 2001) p. 220.
72. Jansen, p. 80.
73. ibid.
74. Jansen, p. 93.
75. ibid., p. 91.
76. ibid., p. xvi.
77. Kepel, p. 209.
78. ibid., p. 210.
79. ibid., p. 211.

80. Zeidan, p. 18.
81. Olivier Roy, *Globalised Islam – The Search for a New Ummah* (London: Hurst & Company, 2006) p. 295.
82. Roy, p. 296.
83. Jason Burke, *Al Qaeda – The True Story of Radical Islam* (London: Penguin Books, Third Edition, 2007) p. 2.
84. Roy, p. 296.
85. Burke, p. 73.
86. Jonathan Randall, *Osama – The Making of a Terrorist* (London: I.B. Tauris, 2006) p. 87.
87. Hourani, p. 308.
88. ibid., p. 341.
89. ibid., pp. 348–9.
90. ibid., p. 349.
91. ibid., p. 399; Esposito, p. 5.
92. ibid., p. 401; Esposito, p. 5.
93. ibid., pp. 442–3.
94. ibid., p. 444.
95. ibid., p. 445.
96. ibid., pp. 445–6.

8

Resurgent Islam:
The Political Narrative

'There is no God but Allah, and Mohammed is the prophet of Allah.'
Such is the cry which electrifies 250 millions of the inhabitants of
this globe. Such is the cry which thrills them so that they are ready to
go forward and fight for their religion, and consider it a short road to
Paradise to kill Christians and Hindus and unbelievers. It is that cry
which at the present time is echoing and re-echoing through the hills
and mountain fastnesses of the North-West Frontier of India. It is
that cry which the *mullah* of Afghanistan are now carrying to mountain
hamlets and to towns in Afghanistan in order to raise the people of
that country to come forward and fight. That is a cry which has the
power of joining together the members of Islam throughout the world,
and preparing them for a conflict with all who are not ready to accept
their religion ...
> Dr. Theodore Pennell, Missionary Doctor at Bannu, *Among the*
> *Wild Tribes of the Afghan Frontier, 1909*

The intellectual and ideological wellsprings of resurgent Islam are
intertwined with a series of specific political developments in the Islamic
world which have served to provide Islam's radical ideology with a base,
a focus and a legitimacy, all of which taken together have made 'Islamism'
a potent force in contemporary global affairs.

While Islam's radical ideologues in different parts of the Muslim
world laboured over their writings, drawing on their understanding of
Islam's early texts and attempting to imbue it with a contemporary
resonance in the light of their own thinking and experiences, it was the
series of political developments in the seminal year 1979, that have

provided an effective platform for what otherwise would have been isolated, and possibly, even irrelevant writings.

The year 1979, the commencement of the new Islamic century, witnessed three political events whose implications resonate to this day. The first was the Islamic revolution in Iran which saw, in January 1979, the departure of the Shah of Iran from his country and, in February of that year, the arrival of Iran's new clerical leader, Ayotallah Ruhollah Khomeini. The second event was the occupation of Haram Sharief in Makkah on 20 November 1979, when a group of Islamic zealots, acting in the name of a mahdi, seized the Haram Sharief and issued a political proclamation condemning the corruption and venality of the Saudi royal family and its deep association with the Western powers. The third event was the occupation of Afghanistan by Soviet forces commencing from December 1979.

The Islamic revolution in Iran had ideological, political and strategic implications for West Asia and world affairs. The new regime in Iran was anti-United States and, hence, its emergence deprived the USA of an important and powerful ally in the heart of West Asia. Again, the Islamic revolution was expansionist, ideologically and militarily, and was perceived as constituting a military threat to neighbouring Arab regimes that were either overtly secular or far removed from their nations' Islamic moorings or deeply allied with the West. Besides this, the occupation of the US Embassy on 4 November 1979, and the holding of American diplomats as hostages for 444 days, with the US being repeatedly portrayed as satanic and humiliated on television sets across the world, set the basis for a deep divide between the US and Iran which has not been bridged over the last thirty years.

The occupation of the Haram Sharief was an assault on the very foundation of the Saudi regime, that is, its commitment to Islam and, specifically, its most demanding form—Wahhabi Islam—that had originated in a covenant in 1744, between an ancestor of the Saudi royal house, Mohammed ibn Saud, and his contemporaneous religious reformer, Mohammed ibn Abdul Wahhab. This covenant set -up an alliance between the religious tenets of the Najdi reformer and the nascent political Saudi state. Later, it provided legitimacy and credibility to Saudi claims to rule over the Arabian Peninsula, enabling the Al-Saud to replace Sharif Husain, scion of the Prophet's family, then ruling Makkah, and assuming the guardianship of the two holy mosques in Makkah and

Madinah. This provided the Kingdom of Saudi Arabia with a 'leadership role' in the Islamic world.

Iran's Islamic revolution and the critique of the occupiers of Haram Sharief made it necessary for Saudi Arabia to reaffirm its Islamic credentials and reassert its predominant role in the Islamic world, with the concomitant assertion of its right to guardianship over the two Holy Mosques, which Islamic Iran repeatedly questioned in the early days of the revolution.

The Soviet occupation of Afghanistan brought together an unlikely triumvirate—the USA, Saudi Arabia and Pakistan—which put in place the modern world's first jihad. The motives of the three partners were decidedly opportunistic and impelled by a short-term vision to obtain maximum political and strategic advantage with the minimum effort and in the shortest possible time-frame. The USA saw in the Afghan jihad an opportunity to mobilize its 'natural' Muslim allies in a global effort against the godless communists. US motives in backing the Afghans against Soviet occupation were initially limited to raising the cost of the Soviet occupation, and possibly deterring other Soviet invasions in the Third World.[1] The US involvement would be CIA-led, but 'the agency was to work through Pakistan and defer to Pakistani positions'. In due course, as Steve Coll has noted, '[Pakistani President] Zia-ul-Haq's political and religious agenda in Afghanistan gradually became the CIA's own.'[2]

President Zia-ul-Haq's motives in setting up the jihad in Afghanistan were more complex: he saw in the Islamic struggle an opportunity to assert the Islamic credentials of his military dictatorship. He also feared that the Afghan communists would encourage Pashtun separatism in Pakistan. Thus, as Coll has noted, 'a war fought on Islamic principles could also help shore up a political base at home and deflect appeals to Pashtun nationalism'.[3]

The Pakistani leadership had a strategic agenda as well: it believed that a pro-Pakistan Afghanistan would give Pakistan 'strategic depth' vis-à-vis India,[4] that is, in an armed conflict with India, Pakistani forces would have a deeper hinterland to obtain logistical support, and, in due course, establish 'a new sphere of influence stretching from Kabul to Tashkent'.[5]

Saudi Arabia, through its lead role in the Afghan jihad, saw an opportunity to affirm its Islamic credentials and its premier role in the

Islamic world. It had certain strategic considerations as well: its senior leadership was concerned that the Afghan occupation would be followed by further expansion of Soviet power in the region in its drive to obtain strategic parity with the USA in West Asia.[6]

By the mid-1980s, the motives of the three allies had expanded considerably beyond their modest origins: even as US funding for the Afghan operations continued to increase year after year, merely keeping the Soviets tied down in Afghanistan was not sufficient; now it was necessary not only to drive the Soviets out of Afghanistan, but also to push the Afghan jihad into the Soviet Union itself by bringing into its fold the Muslims of Central Asia.[7]

The jihad in Afghanistan coincided with the Iran–Iraq War, which was an attempt by Iraq to stem the tide of Iran's Islamic Revolution. In this eight-year campaign, Iraq was actively supported by the Arab Gulf sheikhdoms as also the US. The war ended in 1988, after extraordinary destruction and bloodshed, with Iraq claiming a rather dubious victory. However, more seriously, the Iraqi leadership came to believe that the sacrifices it had made to confront the Islamic revolution justified its claim to a substantial price from the world community. It sought to exact this price in the shape of the occupation of Kuwait. The occupation in August 1990 was preceded by a series of aggressive Iraqi postures vis-à-vis Kuwait over the previous weeks, following Iraqi complaints that Kuwait's oil production was far in excess of its OPEC quota which had led to a fall in oil prices. This had increased Iraq's economic concerns, saddled as it was with the burden of reconstruction and foreign debt servicing.

Iraq's aggressiveness was also bolstered by what it saw as the US decision not to get involved in the Iraq–Kuwait dispute. In a meeting with President Saddam Hussein, the US Ambassador, April Glaspie, was reported to have said: 'We have no opinion on the Arab–Arab conflicts, like your border disagreement with Kuwait ... The instructions we had during this period [the 1960s, when she was posted in Kuwait] was that we should express no opinion on this issue [of borders], and this issue is not associated with America.'[8]

Saddam Hussein rebuffed every attempt by regional leaders and the USA to withdraw from Kuwait, thus helping to set up a broad US-led coalition that liberated Kuwait and provided a justification for prolonged US military presence in the region. This presence was institutionalized through a series of measures which included US-sponsored UN economic sanctions against Iraq, UN inspections to detect and destroy weapons of mass destruction (WMD) in Iraq, and two no-fly zones in northern and southern Iraq, which were enforced outside the UN purview by the Anglo–American alliance.

The Afghan Jihad

The Afghan struggle against Soviet occupation acquired the character of a jihad from 1980 itself.[9] The protagonists of the struggle, though divided into several separate and competing groups, were united in seeing their opposition to Soviet occupation in terms of a religious struggle, with the participants being described as *mujahideen*. However, from its very inception, the mujahideen struggle exhibited a cleavage between those parties in Afghanistan that were traditional tribal-based parties and, thus, the representatives of the historic Islamic traditions of Afghanistan on the one hand, and the radical, pan-Islamic groups on the other. The former included the *Harakat Inquilabi-Islami*, headed by Maulana Mohammedi, and the *Hizb-e-Islami* led by Younis Khalis. The radical Islamic mujahideen parties were the *Ittehad-e-Islami* headed by Abdul Rasool Sayyaf, a 'Wahhabi' grouping sponsored and funded by Saudi Arabia, and the other *Hizb-e-Islami* headed by Gulbuddin Hekmatyar.

From the early days of the Afghan jihad, the US–Saudi–Pakistani alliance, which sponsored and sustained the mujahideen struggle, ensured that the bulk of the arms and funds was provided not to the traditional Islamic groups but to the radical parties. These Afghan Islamic radicals had already been living in Pakistan since 1975, following an unsuccessful uprising against President Mohammed Daud; thus, when the Soviets invaded Afghanistan in 1979, Pakistan already had these Islamic radicals under its control. Zia-ul-Haq decided that they would lead the jihad and that the bulk of the CIA military aid would be provided to them.[10] This bias in favour of Afghan radical Islamic groups was to have considerable influence on the flow of Afghan and Islamic politics in the years to come.

It is important to note that the Pakistani leadership of the time was not merely a provider of arms, funding and training to Afghanistan's Islamic radicals; these groups had deep linkages with radical Islamic parties in Pakistan itself, particularly the *Jamaat-e-Islami*, which belonged to the tradition of Sayyid Qutb and Maulana Abul Ala Maududi.[11] Central to the belief and world view of these Islamic radicals was the concept of jihad, seen by them as a 'Holy War' against unbelievers.

From 1980 to 1986, the actual struggle against Soviet occupation in Afghanistan was carried out by the various Afghan groups, albeit funded and trained by the CIA and the Inter-Services Intelligence Directorate (ISI). However, in 1986, a significant transformation was brought about in the struggle: a decision was jointly taken by the United States, Pakistan and Saudi Arabia to convert the Afghan struggle into a global jihad, for which radical Muslims from around the world would be recruited and brought to Pakistan to fight alongside the Afghan Mujahideen.[12] (Even before this decision was formally taken, from 1982 onwards, Pakistan had already directed its embassies to give visas freely to anyone wishing to come to Afghanistan to fight with the mujahideen.)[13]

Ahmed Rashid has described how the jihad was put together: in West Asia, the Muslim Brotherhood, the Saudi-based Muslim World League (MWL) and Palestinian Islamic radicals organized the Islamic recruits and put them into contact with the Pakistanis. The ISI and Pakistan's *Jamaat-e-Islami* set up reception committees to welcome, house and train the arriving militants, and then encouraged them to join the mujahideen groups, usually the *Hizb-e-Islami* of Hekmatyar.[14] The funds for this enterprise came directly from Saudi Intelligence.[15] As Rashid has pointed out: 'Thanks to the CIA–ISI arms pipeline, the engine of the *jihad* was the radical Islamic parties.'[16]

Ahmed Rashid has noted that, between 1982 and 1992, some 35,000 Muslim radicals from 43 Islamic countries in the Middle East, North and East Africa, Central Asia and the Far East would pass their baptism under fire with the Afghan Mujahideen. Tens of thousands more foreign Muslim radicals came to study in the hundreds of new *madrassas* that Zia's military government began to fund in Pakistan and along the Afghan border. Eventually, more than 100,000 Muslim radicals 'were to have direct contact with Pakistan and Afghanistan and be influenced by the jihad'.[17] Participants from Arab countries, primarily Saudi Arabia, Egypt, Jordan, some Gulf States, and Morocco, came to be referred to as 'Arab-Afghans.'

In the early 1980s, the centres for the Arab-Afghans were the offices of the Muslim World League and Muslim Brotherhood in Peshawar, headed by Abdullah Azzam, a Jordanian Palestinian who had studied in Jeddah. Azzam had close ties with Hekmatyar and Sayyaf, whom the Saudis had sent to Peshawar to promote Wahhabi tenets in the Afghan struggle. Saudi funds flowed to Azzam and the Maktab al-Khidmaat or Office of Services, which he set up in 1984 to service the new recruits and receive donations from Islamic charities.[18]

During the 1980s, when the struggle of the Afghan Mujahideen was at its height, Azzam's writings served to justify a clearly defined jihad and attracted to it a host of volunteers. Azzam saw the Afghan jihad in global, trans-national terms. According to Azzam, every Muslim had an obligation to participate morally and financially in jihad. He said: 'If the enemy has entered Muslim lands, the jihad becomes an individual obligation according to all doctors of the law, all commentators of the Sacred Texts, and all the scholars of tradition (those who assembled the words and deeds of the Prophet).'[19]

Again, any Muslim who considered himself capable of participating in the jihad had the right to take up arms without the authorization of any other individual, 'not even the commander of the faithful, if such a one exists'.[20] Obviously, 'impious' leaders of certain Muslim counties had no right to prevent or obstruct an individual's duty to participate in the jihad.

Osama bin Laden (b. 1957), the son of a Saudi construction magnate with close ties to the Saudi royal family, was among the thousands of foreign jihadis who came to participate in the Afghan struggle. Between 1980 and 1982, he visited the region frequently, finally settling in Peshawar in 1982, utilizing the resources of his family company to construct facilities for the struggle. In due course, bin Laden emerged as the principal Saudi representative in Afghanistan, setting up his own training camp for Arab-Afghans at Khost.

In view of his later notoriety, several of bin Laden's associates have attempted to downplay their proximity to him at this time and his significant role in the Afghan jihad. According to Coll:[21]

> Some CIA officers later concluded that bin Laden operated as a semi-official liaison between GID (General Intelligence Directorate of Saudi Arabia), the international Islamist religious networks such as *Jamaat*, and the leading Saudi-backed Afghan commanders, such as Sayyaf. Ahmad Badeeb [senior Saudi intelligence official] describes an active, operational partnership between GID and Osama bin Laden.

About his role in the Afghan jihad, bin Laden himself said: [22]

> To counter these atheist Russians, the Saudis chose me as their representative in Afghanistan ... I settled in Pakistan in the Afghan border region. There I received volunteers who came from the Saudi Kingdom and from all over the Arab and Muslim countries. I set up my first camp where these volunteers were trained by Pakistani and American officers. The weapons were supplied by the Americans, the money by the Saudis. I discovered that it was not enough to fight in Afghanistan, but that we had to fight on all fronts, communist or Western oppression.

Bin Laden had been a former student of Abdullah Azzam in Jeddah. From 1984, the two collaborated closely in recruiting jihadis from the Arab world. Azzam announced that bin Laden would pay the expenses ($300 p.m.) for any Arab volunteer who wanted to fight in Afghanistan.[23]

In 1987, bin Laden was joined by the prominent Egyptian intellectual and activist, Ayman al-Zawahiri (b. 1951). After his release from a brief imprisonment in Cairo, in 1984, following Sadat's assassination, al-Zawahiri came to Peshawar in 1985 as a doctor to treat the mujahideen and the Afghan refugees. While, according to him the basic battle of Islam was being fought in Egypt, he felt that 'a jihadist movement needs an arena that would act like an incubator, where its seeds would grow and where it [could] acquire practical experience in combat, politics and organizational matters'.[24] He saw the Afghan struggle in this light and thus settled in Peshawar in 1986. He met bin Laden in 1987, and heard the latter speak about a 'global jihad' not only against the Soviet Union, but also the corrupt secular governments of the Middle East, the USA and Israel.[25]

The end of the first phase of the mujahideen struggle in 1989-90, following the Soviet withdrawal from Afghanistan, had significant implications for the global jihad, because, in the words of Gilles Kepel:[26]

> The international brigade of jihad veterans, being outside the control of any state, was suddenly available to serve radical Islamic causes anywhere in the world ... They became the free electrons of jihad, professional Islamists trained to fight and to train others to do likewise; they were based in Pakistani tribal zones, in smugglers' fiefdoms over which Islamabad exercised next to no authority, and in Afghan mujahideen encampments. Around the most heavily involved militants gathered crowds of sympathizers, many of whom were in trouble in their own countries and

unable to obtain visas to Western nations. Young Islamists from all over the world came to join these men and learn the terrorist trade from them.

The significance of the Afghan jihad lies in the following factors:

(i) The world's first jihad of modern times had been successfully organized by the triumvirate of the USA, Saudi Arabia and Pakistan. The protagonists of the jihad saw in the Soviet withdrawal from Afghanistan the first significant 'Islamic' victory in several hundred years.

(ii) This jihad had transcended its Afghan moorings and acquired a global character: the principal external element was provided by Pakistanis and Arab-Afghans, predicated on the close ties between the Pakistani political and military leadership, particularly the ISI, with the radical Islamic parties in Afghanistan as also the Arab–Afghans headed by Abdullah Azzam and Osama bin Laden. The jihad was the training ground for thousands of Muslim radicals from across the Arab and Islamic world who were imbued with the belief-system and zeal of radical Islam and, in addition, were provided proficiency in arms and subversion.

(iii) This struggle spawned numerous Islamic organizations across the Muslim world, led by militants with grievances against the West, particularly the United States, but more urgently against their own regimes which they saw as corrupt and betrayers of the true message of Islam: the world witnessed extraordinary ferment and violence led by radical Islamic movements. This was most powerfully felt in Algeria, which went through a veritable civil war from 1992 onwards in which at least 75,000 people were killed, as also in Egypt where a radical Islamic movement took on the state power of the Mubarak regime.

Kepel, along with other commentators like Abdul Bari Atwan, uses the term '*jihadi-Salafism*' to describe the ideology and motive force of these Islamic radicals.[27] These Salafists were different from the traditional Wahhabi ulema in that they perceived the latter as puppets of the oil-rich rulers of the Arabian Peninsula who had exposed their own hypocrisy by allying with the United States, the greatest enemy of the faith, and against Iraq. In intellectual terms, the jihadi-Salafists belonged to the tradition of Maududi, Qutb, Faraj and Abdullah Azzam.

It is not surprising that the mujahideen struggle in Afghanistan provided a powerful boost to Islamic radicals the world over, who drew certain important lessons from this inspirational episode in the modern history of Islam. First, the jihadis noted with satisfaction that, in Afghanistan, they had witnessed the practical implementation of the blue-print for jihad set out by Maulana Maududi and Sayyid Qutb. Thus, there had been an Islamic awakening (*daawat*) against an infidel regime. This had been followed by *hijra*, the movement of Arabs from the Arabian Peninsula to Sudan and then to Afghanistan. In Afghanistan, the small Muslim group had set up its enclave where it built up its strength, defeated a super-power in a jihad, and effectively contributed to its ultimate destruction. In Afghanistan itself, the jihad culminated in the end of the godless (communist) regime and the emergence of an Islamic state under the Taliban.

The second lesson drawn by jihadis from the retreat and ultimate break-up of the Soviet Union was that the destruction of the remaining superpower, the USA, was a necessary pre-condition for an Islamic revolution in Muslim countries; hence, in a reversal of previous jihadi thinking, now the destruction of the USA had to be accomplished first before attempting the overthrow of corrupt regimes within the Islamic world. Olivier Roy had clarified that jihadis who come to Afghanistan did not turn anti-West after 1991—they had always been anti-West, particularly Afghan jihadi leaders such as Hekmatyar and the Arab–Afghans in general.[28]

Third, after the Afghan jihad, while the bulk of the jihadists felt the need to pursue their respective national struggles, albeit with new Islamic fervour, the core group of Islamic radicals around bin Laden and Ayman al-Zawahiri also recognized the need to reject national borders between Muslims (which had in any case been set up by the infidel imperialists) and to work towards greater unity in the pursuit of their jihadi agenda. From this thinking emerged the idea of a trans-national globalized jihad. In fact, Azzam had already prepared the ground for this when he said: 'Unfortunately, when we think about Islam we think nationally. We fail to let our vision pass beyond geographic borders that have been drawn up for us by the kafir.'[29]

This jihadi thinking got further consolidated in the decade of the 1990s since the United States ceased to be an active role-player in Afghanistan once the Soviet troops had withdrawn in 1989, leaving the destiny of this country primarily in the hands of Pakistan. Roy sees this as benign neglect rather than a Machiavellian strategy:[30] during this period, the principal focus of attention of the USA was Europe, where it coped with the consequences of the end of the Cold War, including the unification of Germany as also the break-up of the USSR. Not surprisingly, US's interest in West Asia was relatively marginal, being primarily confined to maintaining a vice-like grip over Iraq while ensuring the containment of Iran.

Pakistan, in alliance with Saudi Arabia, was the US's strategic partner in West Asia and the principal guardian of its interests. US policy itself pertaining to Afghanistan, Pakistan, Iran and Central Asia lacked a cohesive strategic framework, as Ahmed Rashid has noted. First, between 1994 and 1996, it backed Pakistan and Saudi Arabia in building up the Taliban politically and militarily because it was 'anti-Iranian, anti-Shia and pro-Western'.[31] Later, it backed policies to facilitate the Taliban occupation of all of Afghanistan so that UNOCAL, an American company, could tap Central Asian gas resources and build gas pipelines that would take Turkmen gas across Afghanistan to Pakistan and, possibly, India.[32] Even after the August 1998 Al-Qaeda-sponsored bombings of US Embassies in East Africa, US policy was primarily to 'get' bin Laden, without any serious attempt to restrict the support extended to the Taliban by the Pak-Saudi alliance.[33]

The Al-Qaeda

As the Afghan jihad drew to a close, there were increasing differences between Abdullah Azzam and Osama bin Laden.[34] In the early days of the Afghan jihad, bin Laden had been Azzam's student. However, the first gaps between them seem to have emerged after the arrival of Ayman al-Zawahiri into bin Laden's circle in 1987 and his increasing influence on the latter. Al-Zawahiri saw Azzam as part of the Muslim Brotherhood of whom he, as a member of the Egyptian Islamic Jihad, was most critical. As Atwan has noted, Azzam was accused of compromise by al-Zawahiri and his colleagues because he (Azzam) objected to their ideology of *takfir* (accusing fellow Muslims of apostasy) and to their strategic goal of toppling existing regimes by force.[35] Over time, bin Laden came to be surrounded by non-Brotherhood Egyptians such as Mohammed Aref (aka Abu Hafs al-Masri) who was close to al-Zawahiri, and Abu Ubaidah al-Benshiri.[36]

There were other differences between Azzam and bin Laden as well. In keeping with Brotherhood tradition, Azzam recruited jihadis from among the elite while bin Laden brought into his organization (set up in 1988, the precursor of the later Al-Qaeda) persons from all social strata and backgrounds.[37] This is what, perhaps, led to bin Laden emerging as the 'emir' of the Arab-Afghans rather than Azzam who was sixteen years his senior and a greater Islamic scholar.[38]

Their differences came to a head after the Soviet withdrawal. Azzam wanted to consolidate the success of Islam in Afghanistan, particularly by bringing together the various rival factions, chief among which were led by Ahmad Shah Masood and Gulbuddin Hekmatyar. Bin Laden, on the other hand, called for 'a wider war against impious rulers', and refused to focus his attention on Afghanistan to the exclusion of other causes.[39] A journalist familiar with bin Laden's thinking at the time has said: 'He (bin Laden) went to Afghanistan, not for the Afghans alone, but to liberate the ummah.'[40] After the assassination of Abdullah Azzam in 1989, Osama bin Laden took over his organization, Maktab al-Khidmaat, and established bases in different parts of Afghanistan such as, Kunnar, Nuristan and Badakhshan.[41]

The internecine quarrels among the Afghan Mujahideen leaders following the Soviet withdrawal encouraged a frustrated bin Laden to return to Saudi Arabia in 1990. However, within two years, he went into exile in Sudan following differences with the Saudi royal family about the entry of US troops into the Kingdom to evict the Iraqis from Kuwait. His continued criticism of Saudi Arabia and the royal family led to his Saudi citizenship being revoked in 1994.

He remained in Sudan till May 1996, collaborating with Ayman al-Zawahiri in some of the latter's 'jihadi' operations in Egypt and other places. In Sudan, he attracted more veterans of the Afghan war whose anger had increased with the USA after its victory in Iraq as also with the Arab regimes which had allowed USA forces on their soil. Bin Laden returned to Afghanistan in May 1996. In August 1996, he issued his first declaration of jihad against the Americans whom he saw as an occupation force in Saudi Arabia. Western intelligence and political commentators had now come to see bin Laden as 'one of the most significant financial sponsors of Islamic extremist activities in the world', with terrorist training camps set up by him in Somalia, Egypt, Sudan, Yemen and Afghanistan.[42] Egyptian intelligence corroborated this with the report that bin Laden 'was training 1000 militants, a second generation of Arab–Afghans, to bring about an Islamic resolution in Arab countries'.[43]

Jason Burke has thrown valuable light on the evolution of Al-Qaeda, first as a concept and later as an organization. 'Al-Qaeda' in Arabic means a base or a foundation.[44] The word was in use during the early part of the Afghan struggle by Arab-Afghans to describe the base from which they operated.

However, it appears that Abdullah Azzam, the principal ideologue of the Arab–Afghans, started using the term 'to describe the role he envisaged the most committed of the volunteers playing once the war against the Soviets was over'. Thus, in 1987, he wrote:[45]

> Every principle needs a vanguard to carry it forward and [to] put up with heavy tasks and enormous sacrifices. There is no ideology, neither earthy nor heavenly, that does not require ... a vanguard that gives everything it possesses in order to achieve victory ... It carries the flag all along the sheer, endless and difficult path until it reaches its destination in the reality of life, since Allah has destined that it should make it and manifest itself. *This vanguard constitutes the strong foundation (al-qaeda al-sulbah) for the expected society.* [Emphasis added.]

While some commentators believe that 'Al-Qaeda' referred to in Azzam's remarks indicates that a formal organization had already come into being at this time, Burke is of the view that Azzam's reference was to 'a mode of activism', not an organization.[46]

Bin Laden and his associates set up a militant organization in Peshawar, in August 1988, to bring together the disparate militant elements and set up an 'international army' to defend the cause of Islam.[47] Randall, suggests that bin Laden's initial interests may have been to maintain 'a kind of data base to keep track of the comings and goings of the Muslim volunteers he hoped to turn into a international legion for jihad. Its initial importance and influence was as much political as military'.[48] However, there are doubts whether this group called itself 'Al-Qaeda'. Burke refers to a CIA report of 1996 which recalled the setting up of bin Laden's 'Islamic Salvation Front' in 1985 and referred to this body as synonymous with 'Al-Qaeda'.[49] However, it was only in 1998 that the State Department categorically referred to 'Al-Qaeda', describing it not as an organization but as an 'operational hub, predominantly for like-minded Sunni extremists'.[50]

The Taliban-Al-Qaeda Nexus

The Taliban in Afghanistan emerged from madrassas at the Pakistan-Afghan border. The background was as follows: In Pakistan, after Partition, a few students and teachers of the prestigious Darul-Uloom school of Deoband had set up the *Jamiat-ul-Ulema-e-Islam* (JUI) religious movement to propagate their beliefs and to mobilize followers. [Over the years, they came to be referred to as *Deobandis* though their religious and ideological beliefs and agenda had very little in common with the mainstream adherents of their alma mater, Darul Uloom, Deoband.] In 1962, in the NWFP, the JUI became a political party. Through the 1980s, which saw the political ascendancy in Afghan and Pakistan affairs of the *Jamaat-e-Islami* under Zia's patronage, the JUI, till then ignored by the ISI, set up hundreds of madrassas along the Pashtun belt in the NWFP and Baluchistan. These madrassas were sustained by funds from Saudi Arabia and, hence, their teachings conformed to Wahhabi tenets.[51]

In 1993, in a reversal in Pakistani politics, the JUI allied itself with Benazir Bhutto and her political party, the PPP. The Bhutto government, in order to reduce the power and near-autonomy of the ISI, encouraged the JUI to expand its role in Afghan-related matters. Unable to reconcile itself to the ongoing intra-Afghan differences, Pakistan, using the students at the madrassas run by the JUI and its various breakaway groups, mobilized the rank and file of a new military force—the Taliban-led by a till then unknown person, Mullah Omar.[52]

Though the ISI was not involved in the initial stages of the setting up of the Taliban, it, in due course, was given the responsibility to organize and train the Taliban military forces. This it was able to do with generous funding that continued to pour in from sources in the Arabian Gulf, supplemented, when need arose, from the coffers of the Pakistani Government itself. Over 80,000 Pakistani Islamic militants trained and fought with the Taliban from 1994.[53]

While Pakistan made every effort at the time to project the Taliban as an independent fighting force, the factual position was that Pakistani soldiers and officers, led by the ISI, were responsible for the organization, arming and training of those elements, besides providing them with the required logistical support. There is also evidence that Pakistani involvement extended to combat support as well: most of the major successes of the Taliban, such as at Herat (September 1993), Kabul

(September 1996) and Mazar-e-Sharif (August 1998) were due to Pakistani planning, military support in the shape of vehicles, tanks and aircraft, and active participation of Pakistani advisers and even personnel. Indeed, there is also evidence that attacks launched by the Taliban without the involvement of Pakistan elements, such as on Herat in April 1995, were a disaster. A Pakistani commentator has pointed out that the presence of professional Pakistani fighters was most obvious during the Taliban attack on Taloqan, the capital of the Northern Takhor province, in September 2000. There were reports at the time that Pakistani aircraft were used to rotate Taliban troops at the frontline.[54]

In a move that was to have considerable significance for the development of regional and international politics, the Pakistani intelligence agency, ISI introduced Osama bin Laden to Mullah Omar in 1996, and thus set the stage for an intimate symbiotic relationship between the Al-Qaeda and the Taliban.[55] The Taliban gave Osama and the Al-Qaeda sanctuary and protection from the USA, while, in turn, Osama bin Laden brought in 2,500–3,000 Al-Qaeda fighters to buttress the Taliban forces and imbued Mullah Omar and the Taliban with jihadi Omar zeal and deep animosity for the West, particularly the United States.[56]

Taliban's offensives in 1997–98 were supported by hundreds of Arab–Afghans. Arab fighters helped the Taliban carry out the massacres on the Hazaras, and later fought with them outside Kabul against the forces of Ahmad Shah Masood. At this stage, Islamic extremist groups from a number of countries and regions such as Russia, China, Burma, Iran, Central Asia and South-East Asia, fought for the Taliban.

After the Al-Qaeda bombings in August 1998 in East Africa, the Taliban too, under bin Laden's influence began to speak out against the Americans and their Muslim allies, including Saudi Arabia. Thus, at the end of the twentieth century, the jihad sponsored by the USA, Saudi Arabia and Pakistan had spawned in Afghanistan the most obscurantist regime the Muslim world had ever seen, which provided sanctuary to the most radical and militant Islamic movement that the world faced till then. As Ahmed Rashid has pointed out, Afghanistan was now truly 'a haven of Islamic internationalism and terrorism'.[57]

Conclusion

The decision to organize the Afghan jihad was taken by the leaders of Saudi Arabia, Pakistan and United States and given concrete shape by their respective intelligence agencies. Saudi Arabia and United States provided financial support for this enterprise, while US intelligence (CIA) and its Pakistani counterpart, the ISI, provided the weaponry and training. In due course, the lead role in the Afghan jihad enterprise came to be played by Pakistan, and its political head, General Zia-ul-Haq, who saw in the jihad an opportunity to gain credibility for his military dictatorship as also to obtain 'strategic depth' vis-à-vis India.

In the Afghan jihad, the three principal external role-players worked through Afghan radical Islamic groups, whose ideological moorings were derived from Islamic radical writers such as Maududi and Sayyid Qutb. In the early years, a central role in this regard was played by the Palestinian-origin intellectual and activist Abdullah Azzam. The Afghan jihad attracted a number of young Arabs who together constituted a cohesive group generally referred to as Arab–Afghans. They were the instrument that Azzam utilized to give shape to his vision of global jihad against the enemy who had occupied Muslim lands.

Azzam was the mentor of a young Saudi businessman, Osama bin Laden, who involved himself actively in providing logistical and financial support to the Afghan jihad. Towards the end of the 1980s, bin Laden also came to be associated in Afghanistan with the radical intellectual, Ayman al-Zawahiri, another activist from the Egyptian tradition of radical Islam, though at odds with the Muslim Brotherhood with which Azzam was affiliated. As the Afghan jihad drew to a close in 1989, differences became apparent between Azzam and bin Laden in regard to the next steps in the implementation of global jihad, that is, on whether the jihad should be consolidated in Afghanistan, as advocated by Azzam, or it should be expanded into a 'wider war' in other parts of the world, which was bin Laden's proposal. During this period, al-Zawahiri, who had strong ideological and personal differences with Azzam, increased his influence over bin Laden. Azzam's assassination in 1989 left bin Laden as the principal external role-player in Afghanistan. In due course, an organization referred to as 'Al-Qaeda' emerged as bin Laden's principal platform in the struggle of militant Islam to be led by him, with al-Zawahiri as his ideological mentor.

While the US and most of the world lost interest in Afghan affairs after the Soviet withdrawal, Pakistan continued to dominate the country, which was of strategic value to it, by replacing the quarrelsome mujahideen groups with a cohesive and highly motivated organization called the Taliban. In due course, Osama bin Laden and the Taliban leader, Mullah Omar, came close to each other and set up a deep and mutually beneficial relationship, both personal and between their organizations. The stage was thus set for Al-Qaeda to utilize its secure base in Afghanistan to put into action its vision of global jihad, which is examined in the next chapter.

NOTES

1. Steve Coll, *Ghost Wars – The Secret History of the CIA, Afghanistan, and bin Laden, from the Soviet Invasion to September 10, 2001*, (New York: The Penguin Press, 2004) p. 58; US Congressman Charles Wilson, an active supporter of the jihad candidly stated that US support for the Afghan jihad was 'pay back time' for what the Americans had suffered at communist hands in Vietnam. [Richard Bonney, *Jihad-From Qu'ran to bin Laden* (Basingstoke, UK: Palgrave/Macmillan, 2004) p. 328.]

2. Coll, p. 60; there is information now in the public domain that the US had begun assisting the Afghan Mujahideen at least six months before the Soviet invasion and, in fact, could have precipitated the Soviet Invasion. [*Bonney*, p. 326.] Brzezinski, President Carter's National Security Adviser, said in an interview in January 1998: 'According to the official version of history, CIA aid to the mujahideen began during 1980, that is to say, after the Soviet army invaded Afghanistan, 24 Dec 1979. But the reality, secretly guarded until now, is completely otherwise. Indeed, it was 3 July 1979, that President Carter signed the first directive for secret aid to the opponents of the pro-Soviet regime in Kabul. And that very day, I wrote a note to the president in which I explained to him that in my opinion this aid was going to induce a Soviet military intervention [Bonney, p. 529].

3. Coll, p. 62.

4. Ahmad Rashid, *Taliban—The Story of the Afghan Warlords*, (London: Pan Books, 2001) p. 186.

5. Olivier Roy, *Globalised Islam—The Search for a New Ummah*, (London: Hurst & Co., 2004) p. 291

6. Coll, p. 81.

7. Coll, pp. 102–3; Brzezinski, in an interview in January 1998, rejected the longer term implications of US support for an avowedly, 'Islamic Fundamentalist' movement; he said: 'What is most important to the history of the world? The Taliban or the collapse of the Soviet empire? Some stirred-up Muslims or the liberation of Central Europe and the end of the cold war?' [Bonney, p. 337.] On the other hand, the then

Soviet leaders saw US policy in Afghanistan as a case of double standards. The Soviet leader Gorbachev is quoted as saying: 'The impression is being created that the Americans are actually concerned with the danger of the spread of Islamic fundamentalism. They think, and they frankly say this, that the establishment today of fundamentalism in Afghanistan, Pakistan and Iran would mean that tomorrow this phenomenon would encompass the entire Islamic world. And there are already symptoms of this, if you take Algeria for example. But the Americans were, and will remain, Americans. And it would be naïve if one permitted the thought that we see only this side of their policy and do not notice other aspects. It is clear that the U.S. is not opposed to fundamentalism becoming the banner of 40 million Soviet Muslims and creating difficulties for the Soviet Union. They object only to it affecting their own interests.' [Bonney, p. 334.]

Dilip Hiro has commented: 'The main architect of US Policy was Zbigniew Brzezinski, President Carter's National Security Advisor. A virulent anti-Communist of Polish origin, he saw his chance in Moscow's Afghanistan intervention to rival Henry Kissinger as a heavyweight strategic thinker. It was not enough to expel the Soviet tanks, he reasoned. This was a great opportunity to export a composite ideology of nationalism and Islam to the Muslim-majority Central Asian states and Soviet republics with a view to destroying the Soviet order. Brzezinski also fell in easily with the domestic considerations of Gen. Mohammad Zia ul-Haq, the military dictator of Pakistan ... The glaring contradiction of the US policy of bolstering Islamic zealots in Afghanistan while opposing them in neighbouring Iran seemed to escape both Brzezinski and his successors. [Bonney, *p.* 336]

8. Dilip Hiro, *Iraq – A Report from the Inside* (London: Granta Books, 2003) p. 34.
9. Rashid, p. 85; one year before the Soviet invasion of Afghanistan, Jihad had been proclaimed by Qazi Amin, the Amir of *Hizb-i-Islami,* against the Dawood Government. [Bonney, p. 325]
10. Rashid, p. 84; the Pakistani military official, Brigadier Mohammed Yousaf, has provided detailed information about Pakistan's role and responsibilities in the Afghanistan jihad in which he was a lead role-player. [Bonney, p. 329; also see Bonney, pp. 329-30 about the detailed arrangements made on the ground by the Pakistani ISI in support of the Afghan jihad.]
11. Rashid, p. 86.
12. ibid., p. 129.
13. ibid., pp. 129–30.

14. ibid., p. 130.
15. ibid.
16. Rashid, p. 85.
17. ibid., p. 130.
18. Gilles Kepel, *Jihad—The Trail of Political Islam* (London: I.B. Tauris , 2004) pp. 222–6.
19. Kepel, p. 146.
20. ibid.
21. Coll, p. 87.
22. Rashid, p. 132.
23. Coll, p. 155; in regard to Azzam's influence on Osama bin Laden, the Egyptian commentator and biographer of Ayman al-Zawahiri, Montasser al-Zayyat, has said: 'Some people wrongly believe that Osama bin Laden took a *jihadi* approach due to the influence of Shaykh Abdullah Azzam, the leader of the Arab *mujahidin* in Afghanistan. Azzam used bin Laden's financial help to provide relief services to the mujahidin in their war against the Soviets. The impact that Azzam had on bin Laden was limited to political and geographical issues related to *jihad* against the Soviets. Azzam was not interested in clashing with the Arab governments that supported him. Still, Azzam's interaction with bin Laden laid the groundwork for Zawahiri's influence.' [Bonney, p. 356.]
24. Coll, p. 163.
25. ibid.
26. Kepel, p. 219.
27. Kepel, p. 219; Abdel Bari Atwan, *The Secret History of Al-Qaeda* (London: Abacus, 2006) p. 68.
28. Roy, p. 293.
29. Atwan, p. 67.
30. Roy, p. 292.
31. Rashid, p. 175.
32. ibid., p. 176.
33. ibid., p. 180.
34. Coll, pp. 203–4.
35. Atwan, p. 68.
36. Jonathan Randall, *Osama-The Making of a Terrorist* (London: I.B.Tauris, 2006) p. 91.
37. ibid.
38. ibid.
39. Randall, p. 92.
40. ibid.
41. Rashid, p. 132.

42. Ibid., p. 134.
43. ibid.
44. Jason Burke, *Al Qaeda – The True Story of Radical Islam* (London: Third Edition, Penguin Books, 2007) p. 1.
45. ibid., p. 2.
46. ibid.
47. ibid., p. 3.
48. Randall, p. 90.
49. Burke, p. 5.
50. ibid.
51. See Rashid, for a detailed account of the rise of the Taliban; also Coll, pp. 28-39.
52. Rashid, p. 89.
53. Rashid, p. 194.
54. *Human Rights Watch* in its Report: 'Afghanistan – Crisis of Impunity: The Role of Pakistan, Russia and Iran in Fuelling the Civil War', Vol. 13, No. 3(c), July 2001, downloaded from: www.hrw.org/reports/2001/afghan2/afghan 0701 - 02.htm, provides details of direct and indirect Pakistani military support to Taliban forces from 1995 up to late 2000. Its conclusions are based on various newspaper reports of the time as also interviews of its investigators with Taliban and Pakistani officials and diplomats; also Randall, pp. 243–4.
55. Rashid, p. 133.
56. ibid., p. 139.
57. ibid., p. 140.

9

Al-Qaeda and Global Jihad

Never since God made it, created its desert, and encircled it with seas has the Arabian Peninsula been invaded by such forces as the crusader armies that have swarmed across it like locusts, devouring its plantations and growing fat off its riches. All this is happening at a time when nations are attacking Muslims like leeches. In light of increasing dangers and the lack of support, we must face what current events conceal, before agreeing on how to settle the matter.

* * *

All these crimes and sins committed by the Americans are a clear declaration of war on God, his messenger, and Muslims. And the ulema throughout Islamic history have agreed unanimously that jihad is an individual duty [fard 'ayn] if the enemy is destroying Muslim territory.

World Islamic Front's Declaration of Jihad Against Jews and Crusaders,
23 February 1998

In the aftermath of the Gulf War of 1990–1, an alternative Islamist discourse emerged, particularly among disaffected Muslim youth across the world who now turned to violence against the West and its symbols, as also its 'allies' in the Arab world.[1] Many of these Muslim radicals were attracted to the nascent trans-national militant organization, Al-Qaeda, led by Osama bin Laden.

Through the 1990s, bin Laden's central concerns were the 'occupation' by US 'crusader' forces of Saudi Arabia from which emerged his fierce critique of the Kingdom's leaders for permitting the despoiling of Islam's holy land by the non-believers. In October 2002, in his intervention in the debate between American and Saudi intellectuals, Osama bin Laden highlighted the centrality of the Palestine issue in the conflict between 'Islam' and the USA thus:[2]

The British handed over Palestine with your help and your support, to the Jews, who have occupied it for more than fifty years-years overflowing with oppression, tyranny, crimes, murders, expulsion, destruction, and devastation. The creation and continuation of Israel is one of the greatest crimes, and you are the leaders of its criminals. And of course there is no need to explain and prove the degree of American support for Israel. The creation of Israel is a crime that must be erased.

It brings us both laughter and tears to see that you have not yet tired of repeating your fabricated lies that the Jews have a historical right to Palestine, as it was promised to them in the Torah. Anyone who disputes with them on this alleged fact is accused of anti-Semitism. This is one of the most fallacious, widely circulated fabrications in history.

The people of Palestine are pure Arabs and original Semites. It is the Muslims who are the inheritors of Moses and the inheritors of the real Torah that has not been changed. Muslims believe in all of the prophets, including Abraham, Moses, Jesus, and Muhammad. If the followers of Moses have been promised a right to Palestine in the Torah, then the Muslims are the most worthy nation of this.

Between February 1993 and October 2000, the Al-Qaeda and Islamic elements inspired by it were responsible for the following major acts of violence:

(*i*) February 1993: Explosion at the World Trade Centre
(*ii*) November 1995: Bombing at National Guard headquarters in Riyadh.
(*iii*) June 1996: Bombing of US military headquarters in Al Khobar.
(iv) August 1998: Bombing of US Embassies in East Africa
(*v*) October 2000: Attack on *USS Cole,* off the coast of Yemen.

However, the Al-Qaeda attacks on the US on 11 September 2001 constitute the most dramatic assault by the Islamic extremists on the West and are the culmination of the Islamic radical impulse which had been given birth to during the early decades of the twentieth century and had acquired a clear shape and character from 1979 onwards in different parts of the Islamic world.

In attempting to understand the events of 9/11, Lawrence Wright has addressed the question whether 9/11 or some other similar event could have taken place without Osama bin Laden; he answers: [3]

The answer is certainly not. Indeed, the tectonic plates of history were shifting, promoting a period of conflict between the West and the Arab

Muslim world; however, the charisma and vision of a few individuals shaped the nature of this context.

Lawrence Wright believes that the bin Laden–al-Zawahiri relationship lies at the core of the Al-Qaeda and is central to the success of the 9/11 events:[4]

> The dynamic of the two men's relationship made [al-]Zawahiri and bin Laden into people they would never have been individually; moreover, the organization they would create, Al-Qaeda, would be a vector of these two forces, one Egyptian and one Saudi. Each would have to compromise in order to accommodate the goals of the other. As a result, Al-Qaeda would take a unique path, that of global jihad.

Given the importance of bin Laden and Ayman al-Zawahiri in contemporary Islamic radical discourse, their philosophy and ideology is examined in some detail in the following pages.

Osama bin Laden and Ayman al-Zawahiri

Bin Laden's ideological roots lie not so much in the tradition of Mohammed ibn Abdul Wahhab as of Ibn Taymiyya and Sayyid Qutb. However, in his early days as a global jihadi in Sudan, he pursued a rather moderate agenda; the Advice and Reform Committee set up by him had the following goals:[5]

(*i*) to eradicate all forms of Jahiliyya [pre-Islamic or non-Islamic] rule and apply the teachings of God to all aspects of life;

(*ii*) to achieve true Islamic justice and eradicate all aspects of injustice;

(*iii*) to reform the Saudi political system and purify it from corruption and injustice; and,

(*iv*) to revive the *hesba* system [the right of citizens to bring charges against state officials], which should be guided by the teachings of the top ulema.

However, though the tone is moderate, Delong-Bas sees the echo of Qutb in the call to eradicate Jahiliyya and a reflection of Ibn Taymiyya in the right of citizens to bring charges against state officials.[6]

While bin Laden has frequently referred to Ibn Taymiyya in his pronouncements as the 'original inspiration of jihad against a corrupt regime',[7] he has not specifically cited Qutb. However, Delong-Bas notes the impact of Qutb in a number of significant public positions that bin

Laden has taken.[8] Thus, she finds the influence of Qutb in bin Laden's attacks on 'Christian Crusaders and Zionist Jews'. Again, he follows Qutb in justifying violence in pursuit of what is right and rejecting what is wrong. He also sees an irreconcilable division between the world of Muslims and the world of the kuffar, and envisages a cosmic battle between the good and the evil.

Finally, like Qutb, he glorifies martyrdom as is confirmed by these two remarks: 'There is a special place in the hereafter for those who participate in jihad', and 'Being killed for Allah's cause is a great honor achieved by only those who are the elite of the nation'.[9] Again, soon after the 9/11 attacks, bin Laden called on God to accept those killed as martyrs in the fight against the Crusaders and to make the faithful victorious over the 'forces of infidels and tyranny' so as to 'crush the new Christian–Jewish crusade'.[10] He went on: 'We hope that these brothers are among the first martyrs in Islam's battle in this era against the new Christian–Jewish crusade led by the big crusader, Bush, under the flag of the Cross; this battle is considered one of Islam's battles.'

In his first substantial statement issued on 23 February 1998, and generally referred to as the 'World Islamic Front's Declaration of Jihad against Jews and Crusaders', the USA was indicted on three counts:[11]

(*i*) the US has been occupying the lands of Islam in the Arabian Peninsula for over four years;

(*ii*) awful devastations have been inflicted upon the Iraqi people [through the sanctions/inspections regime]; and,

(*iii*) the US agenda for West Asia is primarily to serve the interests of Israel, diverting attention from its occupation of Jerusalem and the murders of Muslims, and pursuing policies to destroy Iraq and to divide other Islamic states in the region such as Iraq, Saudi Arabia, Egypt and Sudan.

The Declaration asserted that jihad 'is an individual duty whenever the enemy enters into the lands of Muslims' and 'after faith, there is nothing more sacred than repulsing the enemy who attack the religion and the life'.[12] The Declaration issued a decree that 'to kill the Americans and their allies, civilians and military, is an individual obligation' upon every Muslim, until the Muslim holy sites of Makkah and Al-Aqsa Mosque in Jerusalem are liberated and the foreign armies withdraw from the lands of Islam.[13]

Later, after September 11, bin Laden personally intervened in an ongoing discussion between Saudi clerics and intellectuals and American scholars and theologians who, while setting out their basic positions, were also attempting to explore ways through which such differences between them could be addressed and, hopefully, resolved. Bin Laden's substantive essay was initially published under the title: 'Al-Qaeda's Declaration in Response to the Saudi ulema: It's Best You Prostrate yourselves in Secret'.[14] This essay is an authentic source on Al-Qaeda's thinking on a number of issues.

The principal point that bin Laden asserted was the centrality of faith in Allah, upholding the doctrine of 'loyalty' and 'enmity' and espousing (offensive) jihad in the path of Allah. Bin Laden rejected any possibility of a compromise on these principles and asserted that 'Muslims and especially the learned among them should spread sharia law to the world, that and nothing else'.[15] A moderate approach that compromises Islam's basic principles particularly in respect of jihad is not acceptable, especially in regard to 'Offensive Jihad' which is one of the exclusive principles of Islam and its rejection implies defeat.[16]

Ayman al-Zawahiri (b. 1951) is the last principal and only surviving jihadi ideologue who, in his person, combines the intellectual wellsprings of Islamic resurgence as also the evolution of the political narrative of resurgent Islam that culminated with the events of September 11. In his early writings in Egypt, al-Zawahiri, in his pamphlet, 'The Road to Jerusalem is through Cairo', argued that it was important to attack the 'near' enemy, that is, the Egyptian Government, before taking on the 'far' or external enemy, meaning Israel and the West.[17]

He was briefly imprisoned in 1981 for possible involvement with Sadat's assassination, but released in 1984, when he set up the Egyptian *Islamic Jihad*. He moved to Afghanistan in 1985 where he revised his earlier views and increasingly advocated the need for the destruction of the USA as a necessary pre-condition for the overthrow of corrupt Muslim regimes. In his model for the realization of the Islamic State, al-Zawahiri combined the thinking of Sayyid Qutb and Faraj, advocating both the physical migration of the Islamic community for its safety and the infiltration of the Eastern and Western infidel societies.

In line with radical Islamist thinking, al-Zawahiri saw a fundamental unbridgeable gap between the Muslim believer and the kuffar and envisaged no compromise or accommodation between them in any set of circumstances: there had to be 'loyalty' to other believers and 'enmity' for unbelievers. In fact, as al-Zawahiri asserted:[18]

> Not only did the Almighty and Exalted One forbid us from befriending the infidels, but he also ordered us to wage jihad against the original infidels [those who never submitted to Islam], the apostates [Muslims who have strayed from the faith], and the hypocrites.

Al-Zawahiri called for jihad not just against the infidel who raid the Abode of Islam, but, more stridently against the apostate rulers who reign over Islamic lands and govern without shariat—the friends of Jews and Christians:

> The most exceptional group deviating from the doctrine of Loyalty and Enmity at this [point in] time—despite their claim that they adhere to Islam—is that clique of [secular] rulers who, while domineering over the lands of Islam, oppose *sharia*.[19]
>
> The danger this clique poses to the Muslim *umma* has become perilous, diverting the umma from the creed and preventing by force the practice of its faith. This is a clique that has utterly deviated from the path of Islam, [while possessing] absolute authority over the affairs, souls, and livelihoods of the Muslims; simultaneously, its [authority] is exceedingly widespread, so that not a single Muslim country has been able to escape the grasp of its evil.[20]
>
> Such, then, is this clique—a clique of rulers that violate Sharia. Their corruption and power to corrupt, crimes against the general Muslim populace, not to mention the elite, and their friendship to Jews and Christians, are evident for all to see. Because of this, they fear an uprising against them from the Muslim umma, and its *mujahid* youth—particularly in light of the rising tide of Zionist–American aggression against Palestine, Iraq, Chechnya and Kashmir. They have utilized a number of groups in order to numb the umma, *ensuring* its continued incapacity, depression, and submission. And the most dangerous of these groups are those that cloak themselves in the garb of Islam and its summons, worming their way into the umma's beliefs, mind and heart. They are like lethal bacteria trying to overcome the human immune system, trying to destroy it to sow corruption in the cells of the human body.[21]

Al-Zawahiri was deeply conscious of the present-day scenario in which Muslims have suffered a series of setbacks. Therefore, he warned both against defeatism and ignoring the dangers that face the community:[22]

> Behold! the Crusader-Jewish military machine occupies exalted Jerusalem!

It crouches a mere ninety kilometers from the shrine in Mecca. It surrounds the Islamic world with a series of bases, armies, and fleets. It gears its aggression against us through a network of submissive rulers.

We do not wish to live as if in another world, behaving as if the danger is yet another thousand years hence. We could open our eyes—any given morning—to discover the Jewish tanks that have destroyed homes in Gaza and Janin [in Palestine].

His response to this challenge was simple and categorical:[23]

We must act and act quickly. Enough time has been lost. *Let the Muslim youth not await anyone's permission*, for jihad against the Americans, Jews, and their alliance of hypocrites and apostates is an individual obligation. ...*Young people of every class must assume responsibility for the umma and make plans to defend it from its foes*. We must set our lands aflame beneath the feet of the raiders; they shall never depart otherwise. [Emphasis in the original.]

In March 1996, after the bombing of the Egyptian Embassy in Islamabad, al-Zawahiri published a treatise titled, *Shifa Sudur al-Mumineen* (The Cure for the Believers' Hearts), in which he attempted to respond to the severe criticism of the operation by setting out in some detail his thinking on 'martyrdom operations' and the killing of innocents in an operation.[24] In the treatise, al-Zawahiri addressed the question of 'innocence'. In this regard, he propounded the thesis of 'personal responsibility' in terms of which persons serving an infidel or apostate regime must accept their personal responsibility and acknowledge their complicity in the crimes of the regime they serve. This, in the Egyptian context, included *all* officials serving the government.[25]

He then went to expound an even more extremist position: that those serving an apostate regime could not be regarded as Muslims. As Maha Azzam has noted, such a position could be applied to the killing of all civilians in an apostate or infidel country (such as the USA or Israel).[26]

The points made in this treatise were later (but before 9/11, when his organization, Islamic Jihad, was still separate from Al-Qaeda) elaborated in a more detailed treatise titled: *Jihad and the Superiority of Martyrdom*.[27] After a detailed survey of the relevant Koranic verses and Hadith, al-Zawahiri pointed out that, as jihad was the highest duty of the Muslim, martyrdom was the highest reward for the jihadi:[28]

All the above demonstrates the greatness of martyrdom and the obligation to fight the imams of infidelity and their aides. Thus abandoning *jihad* and becoming caught up with [the desires of] this world lead to humiliation and the loss of property, honour and land, whereas loving martyrdom and engaging in battle lead to glory and strength.

The dividing line between suicide (which is forbidden) and martyrdom was 'intentions':[29]

... there is no difference whatsoever between the man who kills himself, or who plunges himself into the ranks of the enemy and they kill him, or who commands another to kill him – *provided that this is all done for the good and glory of Islam.* [Emphasis added.]

Al-Zawahiri concluded with these words:[30]

The best of people, then, are those who are prepared for *jihad* in the path of Allah Most High, requesting martyrdom at any time or place. Whenever he hears the call to jihad he flies to it until Allah's authority is established. By way of Abu Hurreira, the Prophet said: 'In order that the people have a livelihood, it is best that they have a man who holds on to the reins of his horse, battling in the way of Allah. He flies upon [his horse's] back every time he hears the call or alarm, wishing for death or expecting to be slain.'

Thus, whoever sacrifices himself on behalf of Allah Most High, submitting himself to the path of Allah, is the best of persons, by witness of the truest of all creation [Muhammad].

Al-Zawahiri then addressed the second question pertaining to the incidental killing of Muslims and innocent women and children in a jihadi operation such as a bombing. After a detailed study of the pronouncements of the ulema, al-Zawahiri concluded that their position varied from total prohibition to permissibility in specific circumstances. He then set out his own views:[31]

(*i*) bombing operations were a necessity in contemporary jihad since the mujahideen were fighting against 'massive and vigilant armies armed to the teeth';

(*ii*) the enemy forces sheltered themselves in armoured vehicles with lots of security measures; and,

(*iii*) enemy forces frequently deliberately located themselves 'among people and populace', hoping thereby to avoid attacks upon them and thus delay the jihad.

Al-Zawahiri pointed out that in no circumstances could jihad be abandoned for 'forfeiting the faith is a much greater harm than forfeiting our money or lives'.[32]

However, his clinching argument was that all the traditional constraints on killing of innocents in an operation pertained to 'offensive jihad', that is, jihad initiated by Muslims to extend the realm of Islam. What Muslims are engaged in now is 'defensive jihad', that is, the defence of Islam under attack. Al-Zawahiri then quoted Ibn Taymiyya's unambiguous position with regard to 'defensive jihad':[33]

> Defensive warfare is the most critical form of warfare [since we are] warding off an invader from [our] sanctities and religion. It is a unanimously accepted duty. After belief, there is no greater duty than to repulse the invading enemy who corrupts faith and the world. There are no rules or conditions for this; he must be expelled by all possible means. Our learned *ulema* and others have all agreed to this. It is imperative to distinguish between repulsing the invading, oppressive infidel [defensive jihad] and pursuing him in his own lands [offensive jihad].

In early 1998, Ayman al-Zawahiri, having been implicated in the murder of 58 Western tourists at Luxor and, rejecting any compromise with the Egyptian government, returned to Afghanistan. In December 2001, he published his book, *Knights Under the Prophet's Banner*. By this time, as Atwan has noted, he was Al-Qaeda's principal theoretician and strategist.[34] This book, most of which was written before 9/11, provides a valuable insight into the thinking of al-Zawahiri and bin Laden on jihad and the future of their organization.

The first point made in the book is the call for unity among the various jihadi groups, dropping their ideological differences (as the Taliban and Al-Qaeda have done). Al-Zawahiri noted in this context that the 'enemies' of Islam had come together:[35]

> The Western forces that are hostile to Islam have clearly identified their enemy. They refer to it as Islamic fundamentalism. They are joined in this by their old enemy, Russia ... The *jihad* movement must realize that half the road to victory is attained through unity.

Second, al-Zawahiri writes of taking the battle to the enemy's home:[36]

> We must move the battle to the enemy's grounds to burn the hands of those who ignite fire in our countries; small groups could bring frightening horror to the Americans.

Thirdly he advocates the use of extreme violence, pointing out that attempts at collaboration or peaceful boycott had been completely unsuccessful in the past; he says:[37]

The West, led by the US, which is under the influence of the Jews, does not know the language of ethics, morality and legitimate rights. They only know the language of interests backed by brute military force. Therefore if we wish to have a dialogue with them and make them aware of our rights we must talk to them in a language they understand.

The violent means used could include human bombs 'to inflict maximum casualties on the enemy at the least cost in terms of casualties for the *mujahedin*'.[38]

The book also outlined Al Qaeda's long-term plans: this was the setting up of an Islamic state based on sharia which would be a caliphate that would regain the 'lost glory' of the Muslims.[39]

Thus, al-Zawahiri, well before 9/11, had set out Al Qaeda's ideological positions in full detail and clarity, which was based on a complete separation between the Al Qaeda adherents on one side and the 'enemy' who included all Muslims connected in some way to non-Islamic regimes and citizens of Western countries that support Israel and are against Islam and Muslims.

Maha Azzam has noted that al-Zawahiri's thinking is 'a completely new departure for the Islamist movement' as it is based neither on the main schools of Muslim theology nor on Ibn Taymiyya nor even on the writings of Mohammed ibn Abdul Wahhab.[40] In spite of this, it was used to justify the carnage of 9/11 and the subsequent acts of Islamist violence. Thus, al-Zawahiri's influence is clearly visible in the remarks made by Ramzi bin Al-Shibh, a leading global jihadist, and bin Laden himself. Thus, Ramzi bin Al-Shibh said about the 9/11 events:[41]

> Concerning the operations of the blessed Tuesday [9/11] ... they are legally legitimate, because they are committed against a country at war with us, and the people in that country are combatants. Someone might say that it is the innocent, the elderly, the women, and the children who are victims, so how can these operations be legitimate according to Sharia? *And we say that sanctity of women, children, and the elderly is not absolute.* There are special cases ... Muslims may respond in kind if infidels have targeted women and children and elderly Muslims, [or if] they are being invaded, [or if] the non-combatants are helping with the fight whether in action, word, or any other type of assistance, [or if] they need to attack with heavy weapons, which do not differentiate between combatants and non-combatants ... [Emphasis added.]

Osama bin Laden provided the following explanation as to why the assault was launched upon the USA rather than on any other target:[42]

> What takes place in America today was caused by the flagrant interference on the part of successive American governments into others' business. These governments imposed regimes that contradict the faith, values, and lifestyles of the people. This is the truth that the American government is trying to conceal from the American people...
>
> Our current battle is against the Jews. Our faith tells us we shall defeat them, God willing. However, Muslims find that the Americans stand as a protective shield and strong supporter, both financially and morally. The desert storm that blew over New York and Washington should, in our view, have blown over Tel Aviv. The American position obliged Muslims to force the American out of the arena first to enable them to focus on their Jewish enemy. Why are the Americans fighting a battle on behalf of the Jews? Why do they sacrifice their sons and interests for them?

Jihad in Iraq

A number of American and other Western commentators have drawn attention to the fact that the American war on Iraq and its continued occupation of the country have strengthened Al-Qaeda and the militant Islamic movement. Soon after the fall of Baghdad, Al-Qaeda, through the Internet, called upon jihadis to confront the Americans in Iraq. Al-Qaeda recommended the advantages of guerilla warfare against conventional enemies; thus it said on 9 April 2003:[43]

> Guerrilla Warfare Is the most Powerful Weapon Muslims have, and It is The Best Method to Continue the Conflict with the Crusader Enemy ... With guerilla warfare the Americans were defeated in Vietnam and the Soviets were defeated in Afghanistan. This is the method that expelled the direct Crusader colonialism from most of the Muslim lands, with Algeria the most well known. We still see how this method stopped Jewish immigration to Palestine, and caused reverse immigration of Jews from Palestine. The successful attempts of dealing defeat to invaders using guerilla warfare were many, and we will not expound on them. However, these attempts have proven that the most effective method for the materially weak against the strong is guerrilla warfare.

Al-Qaeda's strategy in Iraq was then explained by al-Zawahiri himself on the occasion of the second anniversary of the 9/11 attacks:[44]

> We thank God for appeasing us with the dilemmas in Iraq and Afghanistan. The Americans are facing a delicate situation in both countries. If they

withdraw they will lose everything and if they stay, they will continue to bleed to death.

On the attacks' third anniversary, he issued a slightly different version of the same statement, now proclaiming that the US' defeat in Iraq and Afghanistan 'has become just a question of time' and explaining: 'The Americans in both countries are between two fires. If they continue, they will bleed until death, and if they withdraw, they will lose everything.'[45]

The well-known terrorism expert Bruce Hoffman has set out the importance of Iraq in Al-Qaeda's plans thus:[46]

Iraq has figured prominently in Al-Qaeda and jihadist plans and propaganda as a way to reinvigorate the jihadist cause and sustain its momentum as well as engage U.S. forces in battle and thus perpetuate the image of Islam cast perpetually on the defensive with no alternative but to take up arms against American and Western aggressors. In addition, the ongoing violence in Iraq, coupled with the inability of U.S. and coalition and Iraqi security forces to maintain order and the Abu Ghraib revelations along with other disadvantageous developments, have all doubtless contributed to America's poor standing in the Muslim world.

In his testimony before the House Armed Services Committee, on 14 February 2007, Daniel Benjamin pointed out that the invasion of Iraq has given the jihadis 'an unmistakable boost'; he elaborated:[47]

Whatever one thinks of American intentions in going into Iraq, in the context of the culture of grievance that exists in much of the Muslim world, the extremists' narrative has had a profound resonance. Through their violence, the jihadists have also created a drama of the faith that disaffected Muslims around the world can watch on television and the Internet. New areas of the globe are increasingly falling under the shadow of this growing threat. To be sure, the jihadists have not achieved anything like a true mobilization of Muslim opinion, and the overwhelming majority of Muslims will not embrace a vision of their faith that places violence at its very center, but the process of radicalization has gained momentum.

He concluded:

Where the collapsed state of Afghanistan allowed numerous opportunities for bin Laden's endeavors, the ongoing insurgency in Iraq has produced a new type of threat: a real-time, authentic "jihad" experience which is grooming a new generation of committed fighters.

Abdul Bari Atwan has agreed with this assessment, pointing out that [the US]:[48]

> has created the perfect training ground in Iraq for Al Qaeda and any other jihadi group or individual seeking action ... Furthermore, they have provided Al [–]Qaeda and other jihadi groups with new allies in their fight against a common enemy. The new and deadly combination of Islamists and Arab nationalists that we are currently witnessing in Iraq could have very serious implications for the whole region.

From 2007 onwards, even as Osama bin Laden and Ayman al-Zawahiri began to proclaim the 'victory' of the Iraqi insurgency against US occupation, their immediate concern was to maintain the unity and integrity of the Islamist movement. In his taped message of 29 December 2007, bin Laden asserted that the USA knew it had been militarily defeated in Iraq and predicted that US and its allies would leave Iraq (though he did not provide a date for the withdrawal).[49] He was, however, more concerned that the Islamic insurgency should ensure that the Americans and their Arab allies do not put together a national unity government that would enable the US to enjoy the fruits of occupation, particularly free control over Iraqi oil. In the tape, bin Laden spoke about:

> ... the plots that are being hatched by the Zionist-Crusader alliance, led by America, in cooperation with its agents in the region, to steal the fruit of the blessed jihad in the land of the two rivers, and what we should do to foil these plots.

He reminded the Iraqi people about the need to consolidate their victory and recalled, in this context, the failure of the Afghan insurgency after the Soviet withdrawal; he said:

> It would be useful here to recall an effort in the past to unify the leaders of the Afghan mujahideen, which includes important lessons that are related to our topic.

A few months later, al-Zawahiri and the head of the *Al-Qaeda in Iraq*, Abu Hamza al-Mujahir, echoed the same concerns. Thus, on 18 April 2008, al-Zawahiri pointed out that the US and its allies had been defeated and their future was one of 'failure and defeat'.[50] He then went on to say: 'The people of Islam and jihad in Iraq have only to be persistent and remain firm in order to exploit their military success'. While 'the Americans are being routed' and 'they are fighting in Washington over the date of the withdrawal', al-Zawahiri warned that achieving unity must be the mujahideen's principal concern, and that all fighting groups should rally around the Islamic State of Iraq [ISI]. By uniting under the ISI's leadership, al-Zawahiri said, Sunni fighters will be able to prevent the Iraqi Shiites and their Iranian sponsors from achieving Tehran's goal of 'annexing southern Iraq and the eastern parts of al-Jazirah [a region of northwest Iraq between the Tigris and Euphrates Rivers] and expanding to establish contacts with its followers in Lebanon'.

Abu Hamza al-Mujahir expressed the same concerns: 'Let all Muslims know that complete victory [over the US-led coalition] is imminent', and that 'the future will be for this religion [Sunni Islam] ... with our omnipotent God's help'.[51] Al-Muhajir stressed that the Mujahideen 'are not fight[ing] the Crusader occupiers or Arab apostates or for the sake of land, but to exalt God's word on earth'. Al-Muhajir warned the Sunni Mujahideen that 'sincere adherence to God is the most important factor of victory and consolidation', and that only genuine unity can provide 'pride, victory, and consolidation'.

Following the success of the American forces and their allies to win over the Sunni tribal leaders, particularly in the Anbar province, through the setting up of the 'Awakening Councils', from 2006 onwards, besides maintaining the unity of the jihadi forces, Al-Qaeda's strategy in Iraq is to perpetrate widespread destruction and violence in the country to discredit the government of Prime Minister Nuri al-Maliki and his attempts to forge a non-sectarian coalition government. Towards this end, in August 2009, Al-Qaeda carried out coordinated explosions in Baghdad, killing over 120 people. This was followed by two bombings on 25 October 2009, in which 155 people were killed; this was the bloodiest episode since August 2007.[52] Besides the killing of large numbers of peoples, these attacks targeted central and provincial government buildings. Separately, the Al-Qaeda in Iraq have also assassinated local leaders of the 'Awakening Movement' in different parts of the country.

The Iraqi National Security Adviser, Safa Husain, in public remarks at the end of December 2009, said that Al-Qaeda insurgents in Iraq had dropped from a peak of 10,000 to less than 2000, and that the percentage of foreign fighters among them had also fallen to less than 10 per cent.[53] He added that Al-Qaeda in Iraq had come under the influence of hardcore Baathists who had now crept up the leadership ladder after Zarqawi's death in 2006, and were principally responsible for the spate of deadly bombings in the country. He believed that Al-Qaeda's main goal was to disrupt the national elections in March 2010 and discredit Nuri Al-Maliki's government, and predicted some more bombings in the run-up to the elections. He pointed out ominously that the Baathists, by disregarding the main political groups, hoped to reap electoral advantage for themselves by backing certain individuals, groups and parties in the coming elections.

It is noteworthy that, just as the Afghan mujahideen struggle of the 1980s had provided battle-hardened jihadis who were available to inspire, organize and carry out jihadi violence in different parts of the world, so has the Iraqi insurgency not only attracted jihadi warriors from other Arab countries, but it has also provided veterans who have become part of the anti-US/NATO insurgency in Afghanistan. Thus, experienced foreign fighters went from Iraq to Afghanistan in late 2007 and, according to an expert, 'the bleed-out of insurgent tactics and techniques from Iraq ... transformed the Taliban'.[54] According to this expert, under the influence of Al-Qaeda militants coming from Iraq, the Taliban, in their second incarnation in Afghanistan after 9/11, have evolved into a 'bonafide terrorist movement', with importance now being given to lethal suicide bombings.

Several fighters from Iraq have also gone to other fronts such as Lebanon, Yemen, Somalia, Saudi Arabia and North Africa. Michael Scheuer, an expert on radical Islam, has noted Al-Qaeda's ability to 'exfiltrate' fighters from one battlefield to another as an example of its flexibility and focus on longer-term goals; he believes that the American military will not be able to limit this without the deployment of hundreds of thousands of troops in Afghanistan.[55]

The Jihad in Europe

As the Afghan mujahideen struggle came to an end in 1989-90, several of the Arab-Afghan veterans found they were no longer welcome in their home countries. Some of them joined bin Laden in Sudan (from 1992), while others sought asylum in the West and joined the jihad in Bosnia or Chechnya. Thousands of Afghan jihadis also found their way to Europe, particularly London, which was 'the most welcoming and most liberal of the European destinations'.[56]

However, it was the conflict in Bosnia that played a major role in the development of the next phase of the jihad. About 5,000 veterans of the Afghan struggle participated in the war in Bosnia which, between 1992 and 1995, claimed nearly 300,000 lives, mostly of Bosnian Muslims.[57] The Bosnian jihadis had the added advantage of direct contact with the top jihadi leadership from Afghanistan—bin Laden and al-Zawahiri. The latter was in charge of jihadi operations in Bosnia in 1993, while bin Laden visited Bosnia three times between 1994 and 1995.[58] After the Bosnian war was over, many of the veterans settled in different parts of Europe: at least two of the 9/11 suicide bombers were veterans of the Afghan struggle while a third, Abdul Aziz Al-Muqrin, would later head the Al-Qaeda in Saudi Arabia.[59]

The jihadis who came to Europe after the Afghan struggle in the early 1990s and those who came there at the end of the decade after Bosnia have inspired a new generation of West-based jihadis. Now, Islamic militants operating in different parts of the world after September 11 have tended to be located in the West, living away from their families and socializing only with other radicals centred around certain mosques. Olivier Roy has described them as 'cultural outcasts in their home countries and their host countries'.[60] With the exception of persons of Saudi and Yemen origins, they are 'westernized', have not had any formal religious education and have generally trained in technical or scientific disciplines.

These West-based radicals generally belong to three categories:[61]

(*i*) students who came to the West from West Asia;

(*ii*) second-generation Muslims who were either born in the West or came to the West as children; and,

(*iii*) Western converts to Islam.

Based on a detailed study of individuals involved with terrorist activity from 1993, Roy has noted the following three principal characteristics of contemporary Islamic militants:[62]

(*i*) The militants are "de-territorialized" in that they operate globally and settle in countries that have little connection with their homelands and also speak foreign languages.

(*ii*) Many of the militants have been uprooted from their own culture and brought up in a Western milieu where they pursue modern secular education, including engineering, information technology, town planning, architecture, agriculture, electronics, etc.

(*iii*) While in their early years the Islamic militants showed little sign of being religious-minded, they later got "re-Islamized", not as a result of community or family pressure but "as the result of an individual quest which involved interaction with a veteran of the Afghan struggle often in a local radical mosque." At these mosques, charismatic preachers lure them into radicalism by playing on "their sense of being victims of racism exclusion and loneliness in Western society."

The case of Mohammed Bouyeri who murdered the Dutch film-maker, Theo van Gogh, illustrates these aspects of contemporary jihadis in Europe. As Timothy Garton Ash has pointed out:[63]

> Bouyeri's story has striking similarities with those of some of the London and Madrid bombers, and members of the Hamburg cell of al-Qaeda who were central to the September 11, 2001, attacks on New York. There's the same initial embrace and then angry rejection of modern European secular culture, whether in its Dutch, German, Spanish, or British variant, with its common temptations of sexual licence, drugs, drink and racy entertainment; the pain of being torn between two home countries, neither of which is fully home; the influence of a radical imam, and of Islamist material from the Internet, audiotapes, or videocassettes and DVDs; a sense of global Muslim victimhood, exacerbated by horror stories from Bosnia, Chechnya, Palestine, Afghanistan and Iraq; the group think of a small circle of friends, stiffening one's resolve; and the tranquil confidence with which many of these young men seem to have approached martyrdom.
>
> Such suicide killers are obviously not representative of the great majority of Muslims living peacefully in Europe; but they are, without question, *extreme and exceptional symptoms of a much broader alienation of the children of Muslim immigrants to Europe*. [Emphasis added.]

Al-Qaeda's Strategic Vision

Towards the end of his book, *Globalised Islam*, Olivier Roy asserted that 'Al-Qaeda has no strategic vision'.[64] He supported this by pointing out that Al-Qaeda attacks what it sees as evil, that is, the USA and Israel, but in reality its targets have no military or strategic value. This conclusion is strongly contested by a number of other observers. Thus, the former senior US official and present-day academic Bruce Riedel, in an article in *Foreign Affairs* in May 2007, asserted: 'Al-Qaeda is a more dangerous enemy today then it has ever been before.'[65] He pointed out:

The organization now has a solid base of operations in the badlands of Pakistan and an effective franchise in western Iraq. Its reach has spread throughout the Muslim world, where it has developed a large cadre of operatives, and in Europe, where it can claim the support of some disenfranchised Muslim locals and members of the Arab and Asian diasporas. Osama bin Laden has mounted a successful propaganda campaign to make himself and his movement the primary symbols of Islamic resistance worldwide. His ideas now attract more followers than ever.

Echoing this assessment, the well known Arab journalist and commentator, Abdel Bari Atwan has said: [66]

[Al-Qaeda] is not only still in existence, but has a long term strategy and a solid ideological base. At the same time, it is capable of constantly transforming and adapting to changes in circumstances, history and strategy...

All indications confirm that Al-Qaeda is, in fact, growing more powerful. Having transformed itself into an ideology, physical and geographical restrictions no longer apply. It has become a global umbrella for groups and individuals who share its agenda.

Contrary to Olivier Roy's assertion that Al-Qaeda has no strategic vision, in an audio tape dated 30 January 2005, al-Zawahiri had set out the 'three foundations' of Al Qaeda's global ideology, which were as follows:[67]

(*i*) The ultimate aim of the movement was to set up an Islamic state governed solely by sharia law: secular government and man-made laws were unacceptable and rejected.

(*ii*) 'The Liberation of the Human Being': al-Zawahiri articulated a vision of a contractual social relationship between Muslims and their rulers that would permit people to choose and criticize their leaders but also demand that Muslims resist and overthrow rulers who violate Islamic laws and principles. He criticized hereditary government and identified a need 'to specify the power of the Sharia-based judiciary, and ensure that no one can dispose of the people's rights, except in accordance with this judiciary.'

(*iii*) Muslim lands had to be liberated from every aggressor: the Muslim world was 'impotent' and exposed to Israel's nuclear arsenal; there was need to establish control over West Asia's energy resources.

The Al-Qaeda Military Commander, 'Saif Al Adal' set out a detailed strategic framework for the jihadi movement in May 2005.[68] His thinking may be summarized as follows. *Firstly*, the strategic objectives of the jihadist movement should be rooted in and motivated by what Al Adal referred to as 'the clear banner of Islam—the banner of "there is no deity but God and Muhammad is the messenger of God"'. This fundamental statement of Islamic faith is meant to signify the ultimate priority of the principle of *tawhid*, or the unity and authority of God and religion, in Al-Qaeda's ideological framework.

Secondly, jihadist action must have a clear 'thought or idea that outlines its means and objectives'. Al Adal said that the Movement's strategic objective is 'to reintroduce the Islamic way of life by means of establishing the state of Islam that will solve the entire problems of the nation'. This objective should be supported ideologically by 'a circle of judicious men and scholars' and propagated by 'a special *da'wah* [Islamic outreach] authority'. At the same time, the jihadist movement should employ 'the [Islamic] nation's potentials, including human and financial resources' by attracting more supporters.

Thirdly, detailed strategic and operational plans must be developed with short-term and long-term components. Al Adal links the failures of other contemporary Islamic movements to the fact that their 'actions were mostly random'. According to Al Adal, 'mujahidin should have short-term plans aimed at achieving interim goals and long-term plans aimed at accomplishing the greater objective, which is the establishment of a state'.

Fourthly, the jihadist movement should remain flexible enough to take advantage of 'available opportunities' such as the conflict in Iraq. Al Adal underlines the importance of using current developments to widen the movement's appeal and further strengthen the movement's ability to act fluidly across the Islamic world.

In his book, *The Secret History of Al-Qaeda*, Abdel Bari Atwan has published extracts from a document printed in an Arabic newspaper in March 2005 which is titled 'Al Qaeda's strategy to the year 2020'.[69] This was posted on the Internet by Mohammed Ibrahim Makkawi, who is said to be Al-Qaeda's main military strategist. This document sets out details of a long-term jihadi campaign to rid the ummah from all forms of oppressions in five phases.

Firstly, Al-Qaeda would seek to provoke the USA into invading Muslim lands. (This has been achieved by ensuring that the 9/11 attacks led to the invasion of Afghanistan and Iraq.)

Secondly, the Ummah is to be provoked into anger at the presence of foreign soldiers on Muslim soil, against whom a bloody insurgency should be mounted. (This is said to have been achieved both in Afghanistan and Iraq.)

The *third* phase involves engaging the USA in a prolonged war of attrition. (The resurgent Taliban have already met with considerable success in Afghanistan as has the insurgency in Iraq.) The ultimate aim is to create a 'jihadi triangle of terror which will stretch from Afghanistan through Iraq and embrace Lebanon, Syria and Turkey.'

In the *fourth* stage, Al-Qaeda would become a global network with Al-Qaeda itself principally providing the guidance and ideology, while giving local commanders full autonomy in carrying out local operations.

At the *fifth* and final stage, US's military and economic capacities would be fully stretched so that its military budget will crash into bankruptcy, its loss in personnel will become catastrophic, and the superpower will implode. Following the destruction of the far enemy, it will be easy to overthrow the Arab regimes and establish a caliphate across the Islamic world.

The strategy document also envisages, in messianic terms, 'an ultimate definitive military clash' between 'the mighty Islamic army and the non-believers which will end in the victory and global domination of the caliphate'.[70]

Gilles Kepel, in his latest book, *Beyond Terror and Martyrdom—The Future of the Middle East,* has described in considerable detail a debate on future strategy between Ayman al-Zawahiri and Abu Musab al-Suri. Al-Suri, deeply involved in radical Islam in Syria in the 1980s from his late teens, went into exile to France and later, in 1985, married and settled in Spain. He went to Peshawar in 1989 and came close to Abdullah Azzam. After the latter's death, he became associated with bin Laden and al-Zawahiri. In 1992, he returned to Spain and then, from London, supported the Islamic uprising in Algeria in the mid-1990s. With the Taliban conquest of Kabul, he returned to Kandahar in 1996. Even then, he is said to have opposed the Al-Qaeda-sponsored attacks on the US Embassies in East Africa, fearing that the jihadi movement would be greatly harmed by American retaliation.[71]

Later, he also opposed the attacks on the USA on September 11, 2001. In December 2004, he posted his treatise, 'Call to Global Islamic Resistance', on the website, partly as a response to al-Zawahiri's triumphalist publication, *Knights Under the Prophet's Banner*, written in December 2001. Al-Suri pointed out that the 9/11 attacks had not only deprived the Al-Qaeda of its sanctuary and its prominent leaders, they had also not helped the global Islamic movement either. The principal beneficiaries were the nationalist—Islamic Hamas, and the Shia in Lebanon, Iraq and Iran, while there had been no mass uprising in the Islamic world.[72] Al-Suri advocated a 'global Islamic resistance' which would function through quasi-independent cells that would carry out 'harassment operations' against the West and pro-West Islamic countries.[73] The effect of such operations would be to gradually establish sanctuaries of control and wear down the enemy.[74] It would then be a 'leaderless jihad'.[75]

This gradualist approach of 'resistance' contrasted with al-Zawahiri's focus on spectacular 'martyrdom operations' and his insistence that every such operation brought the ultimate victory of Islam closer and constituted 'the grand narrative of triumphant jihad'. Al-Suri was arrested in late 2005, while his associate in Iraq, Abu Musab Al-Zarqawi, was killed in 2006.

Al-Qaeda Today

In his outstanding work on the Al-Qaeda, Jason Burke has been at pains to emphasize that Al-Qaeda is not a rigidly structured organization made up of a network of thousands of trained and highly motivated persons located in different parts of the world, taking instructions from a top leadership headed by Osama bin Laden. He believes that it was only between 1996 and 2001 that Al-Qaeda actually had a relatively coherent structure with a hardcore around bin Laden.[76] During this period, it provided a 'central focus' for many militants. Burke quotes a Pakistani diplomat, who, in January 2001, listed the various groups of militants in Afghanistan thus: 500 Arabs left over from the war against the Soviets, 500 Chechens, 100 Uighurs, 100 Tajiks, 100 Bengalis, 100 Filipinos and 5,000 Pakistanis.[77]

During its most cohesive period between 1996 and 2001, Al-Qaeda had an ideology, a hardcore and network of co-opted groups.[78] The hardcore consisted of senior militants who had been bin Laden's associates in the Afghan Mujahideen struggle in the 1980s. Though most were located in Afghanistan, there were also long-term associates in other places such as in London, Jordan, northern Iraq and Yemen. These associate members constituted a link between the hardcore Al-Qaeda around bin Laden in Afghanistan and the large number of radical Islamist cells, local and national groups and splinter groups in different parts of the world.

Burke describes the hardcore Al-Qaeda as a 'small group of experienced militants who were able to access resources of a scale and with an ease that was hitherto unknown in the Islamic militancy'.[79] Olivier Roy has identified the hardcore around bin Laden who were with him in Afghanistan in the 1980s, and then accompanied him to Saudi Arabia, Sudan and then back to Afghanistan as: Muhammad Atef, Abdulaziz Abu Sitta alias Abu Hafs Al-Misri, a former Egyptian police officer (who would become the father-in-law of bin Laden's son), Sulaiman Abu Ghaith, bin Laden's spokesman, and Ayman al-Zawahiri.[80]

Various Islamic groups and cells in different parts of the world would approach this central authority with proposals for specific jihad-related actions of which some would be approved and funded to a greater or lesser extent. Sometimes personnel would also be provided to implement specific operations.

The organizational structure of Al-Qaeda and its role in global jihad went through a significant change after 2001, when American forces destroyed the Taliban governmental structures and forced the Al-Qaeda cadres out of their sanctuaries and into local hideouts or into exile. From this period on, Burke has noted two trends within Islamic militant violence.[81] The first is made up of operations in different parts of the world carried out by local jihadi networks but with the support of central strategic and logistical resources provided by bin Laden and his immediate associates. However, even in these operations, the role of hardcore Al-Qaeda was limited, and the lead role was played by individuals with some experience from the Afghanistan camps, who in turn, recruited jihadis with little or no previous operational experience. Thus, the bombing of a synagogue in Tunisia in December 2002, the bombing in Istanbul in November 2003, and the attacks in Saudi Arabia, between 2002 and 2004, were all local operations carried out by persons who had not trained in jihad in the Afghanistan camps but were provided resources or guidance by persons linked with Afghanistan and jihad.

The second trend noted by Burke is that in which there are dramatic and violent episodes perpetrated almost entirely by local recruits who have no direct or even indirect connection with the Al-Qaeda hardcore or with Afghanistan.[82] One example of this trend is the bombing in Bali on 12 October 2002 which was carried out by a local radical splinter group broadly connected to the South East-Asian radical Islamic network known as *Jamaa Islamiyya*. The Bali bombers' cell was largely composed of young men who had no previous involvement in terrorism. They were not recruited by bin Laden or anyone close to him but came together of their own accord and appear to have decided to go ahead with a campaign of violence directed at local Western targets despite the opposition of more moderate senior figures within *Jamaa Islamiyya*.[83] Bali, as Burke has noted, was an attack 'in the style of Al-Qaeda',[84] but apparently not directly involving the group itself. The bombing in Casablanca in July 2003 was on similar lines: it was planned by two men who had earlier visited Afghanistan, but was carried out by fourteen suicide bombers recruited locally.

The Madrid bombings on 11 March, 2004 were even more disconnected from the Al-Qaeda hardcore. The bombings did not involve suicide bombers and, on the face of it, could not be justified as having any political, military or commercial significance. The conclusion of the Spanish investigators was that the perpetrators had no links with West Asia or the Al-Qaeda but were in fact 'home grown radicals acting on their own'.[85] Burke has described the general scenario thus:[86]

> ... though united by an ideology and a vision of the world, Islamic militancy was clearly, at least operationally, as fragmented as it had ever been, relying more and more heavily on amorphous, self-forming cells composed of motivated individuals influenced by elements of a common ideology.

Other recent writers on Al-Qaeda have echoed this assessment. Thus, David Cole has noted that, today, the threat of fundamentalist Islamic terrorism is 'not centralised, but globalised and dispersed'.[87] He points out that the Madrid (2003) and London (2005) attacks were not directed or implemented by Al-Qaeda, but were the work of 'small bands of young men with little or no connection to Al-Qaeda, and little or no previous record as terrorists'.[88] He quotes Daniel Benjamin and Steven Simon in describing these attacks as a 'new breed of self-starting terrorist cells', primarily encouraged by the internet, which, in the authors' view, has also encouraged the dramatic increase in suicide bombings.

However, though the radical Islamic movement is now widely dispersed, what it has not lost is its driving force that remains as intense as ever. Jason Burke said in a television interview that, while Al-Qaeda no longer constitutes the central hub of militant Islam, the Al-Qaeda world view or 'Al-Qaedaism' is growing stronger every day.[89] Jonathan Raban has noted that 'the political causes and theological justifications for jihad are as alive as ever', and continue to resonate in 'the minds of well-headed and technologically capable young men outraged by US policies and actions in the Middle East, and impassioned by religious beliefs of fresh and furious vitality'.[90]

Israel and Iraq provide the most powerful motive forces for radical Islam. Abu Musab al Suri, described by the Norwegian scholar, Brynjar Lia, as an Al-Qaeda strategist (now in US custody), is quoted as saying:[91]

> Israel creates a motive for a global Islamic cause, and the American occupation (of Iraq) adds a revolutionary dimension, which is an excellent key to jihad.

He also set out Al-Qaeda's broader agenda which is to drive the Americans from the region, 'to fight the Jews, remove idolaters from the Arabian Peninsula and to free its oil and other resources from the American hegemony' and to remove all the 'injustices and afflictions' caused by the occupation of the Islamic lands by America and its allies.[92]

Through the early part of 2008, a number of American and European commentators began to assert that Al-Qaeda was no longer a formidable threat to the West, and that people in the West had been scared 'into exaggerating the terrorist threat'.[93] One scholar pointed out that Al-Qaeda leaders were 'down to a few dozen people on the run in the troubled areas of North-West Pakistan', and that the religious element motivating the Islamic movement had now been replaced by 'hero-worship'.[94]

These views were even at that time strongly rejected by other terrorism experts who pointed to the regular spate of jihadi violence in different parts of the world as evidence that Islamist extremism remained a grave threat, as also the assertions by Western intelligence sources about the presence of jihadis in different European countries.[95] Lawrence Wright, the well-known expert on Al-Qaeda and the Taliban, and the author of *The Looming Tower*—a book about the 9/11 events—pointed out that, with respect to the Al-Qaeda, 'its leadership is intact, its sanctuaries are unthreatened and the social conditions that give rise to the movement are largely unchanged'.[96] The British journalist, Robert Fisk, explained some basic facts relating to Al-Qaeda which have ensured its longevity and influence:[97]

> Because al-Qaeda is a way of thinking, not an army. It feeds on pain and
> fear and cruelty – our cruelty and our oppression – and as long as we
> continue to dominate the Muslim world with our Apache helicopters and
> our tanks and our Humvees and our 'friendly' dictators, so will al-Qaeda
> continue ...

The well-known authority on strategic affairs, George Freidman, felt
that suggestions relating to the end of Al-Qaeda emerged from the
accurate assessment that Al-Qaeda and its jihadi supporters 'do not
constitute a single organized force with a command structure and staff',
and that the original Al-Qaeda 'is now largely shattered'.[98] However, he
pointed out that, for the Al-Qaeda, such fragmentation was both 'a
strategic necessity and a weapon of war for jihadists'. By not having a
centralized command, the jihadi movement was able to ensure that US
forces would not be in a position to destroy it and thus severely damage
the movement. The jihadis have survived because they are today 'a series
of barely connected pods of individuals scattered across continents [that]
have denied the United States a center of gravity to strike'.

The present situation pertaining to the presence of Al-Qaeda-
oriented elements is summarized in the following paragraphs.

After the death in Iraq of Abu Musab Al-Zarqawi in 2006, the
leadership and some Al-Qaeda-oriented militants have moved their base
of operations to other parts of the Levant such as Gaza, Syria and Jordan.
The Al-Qaeda leadership has particularly sought to attract young
disgruntled Palestinians in Gaza, as also in refugee camps in Lebanon,
Syria and Jordan, to its ideology and to participate in its operations.
Towards this end, in his various taped messages, Osama bin Laden has
regularly referred to the central importance of Palestine in Al-Qaeda's
global struggle. Thus, on 29 December 2007, Osama bin Laden had
this to say about Palestine:[99]

> I assure our kinfolk in Palestine in particular that we will expand our
> jihad, God willing, and we will not recognize the [Anglo-French] Sykes-
> Picot [Treaty] borders or the rulers appointed by the colonialists. By God,
> we have not forgotten you after the 9/11 events. Will anyone forget his
> own family? ... We will not recognize a state for the Jews, not even on one
> inch of the land of Palestine, as did all the rulers of the Arabs when they
> adopted the initiative of the ruler of Riyadh years ago ... Nor will we
> respect the international conventions recognising the Zionist entity over
> the land of Palestine, as the Hamas leadership did, or as stated by some

Muslim Brotherhood leaders. It will be a jihad for the liberation of all of Palestine, from the river to the sea, God willing, joining hands with the sincere Mujahideen there from the cadres of Hamas and other factions, who denounced their leaders for deviating from righteousness.

Recognizing the need to bolster the jihadi cadres in Iraq, bin Laden sought volunteers from the Palestinian refugee camps, promising them that the struggle would move from Iraq to Palestine soon thereafter; Osama bin laden had this to say in March 2008:[100]

> My Islamic nation! You know that the nearest field of jihad today to support our people in Palestine is the Iraqi field, so it is necessary to be concerned with it, focus on it, and support it. The duty of providing support is most urgently needed from Muslims living in neighboring countries. It is necessary for all the people of the Levant, the people of that blessed land to recognize the power which Allah has bestowed upon them, and to support their Mujahideen brothers in Iraq as they are obliged to do. It is a great opportunity and a great duty upon the arriving emigrant brothers from Palestine—who were prevented from waging jihad on the hills of Jerusalem—to shake off the illusions of political parties and other groups which are immersed in deception of the democracy. And they should hasten to take their positions among the ranks of the Mujahideen in Iraq, and through support and trust in Allah ... he will aid them by his will. Then, there shall be a move towards the blessed al-Aqsa (mosque in Jerusalem) and then the Mujahideen coming from outside shall encounter their brothers within – and this moment will remind us of the legacy of Hittin [where Muslim leader Salah al-Din defeated the Crusaders in 1187], and the Muslims shall delight in their clear victory.

In Lebanon, jihad is represented by a new militant group, Fatah Al-Islam, which is seeking to infiltrate into the Palestine refugee camps in Lebanon, and is both contributing to and taking advantage of the increasing radicalization of young Palestinians in these camps as also those in Jordan and Syria.

Again, Al-Qaeda-oriented cadres have found 'safe havens' in Afghanistan, Yemen and Somalia. Observers have noted that Yemen has for long had considerable significance in Osama bin Laden's quest for global jihad.[101] Yemeni nationals had played an important role in the Afghan Mujahideen struggle; later, they attacked American troops on their way to Somalia in Aden in December 1992; again, the persons who had attacked the American warship, *USS Cole,* in Aden, in October

2000, were Saudis of Yemeni origin; and, later, in Iraq, a number of non-Iraqis who participated in the insurgency against US forces were Yemenis. After 9/11, Yemen cooperated with the USA to attack Al-Qaeda strongholds, killing Al-Qaeda's regional head, Qaid Salim Sinan Al-Harethi, in a US drone attack. By early 2004, there was a sense that Al-Qaeda was 'finished' in Yemen as it relocated its operations to Iraq. However, it made a comeback to Yemen from 2007 and succeeded in obtaining considerable support for its local activity as also to expand its operations to Africa, particularly the Horn of Africa.

Towards the end of 2009, Al-Qaeda-oriented militants in Yemen were boosted by the presence of extremists from Saudi Arabia. These included Saudis who had served prison sentences in Guantanamo, rejected the 're-education' programme in Saudi Arabia on their release, and obtained leadership positions as Al-Qaeda militants in Yemen. These leaders have articulated robust jihadi positions from Yemen under the banner of Al-Qaeda in the Arabian Peninsula (AQAP) set up in January 2009; thus, a senior official, Shaykh Abu Sufyan al-Shahri, earlier a prisoner in Guantanamo, said:[102]

> By God, we assert to our leaders and shaykhs – Shaykh Osama bin Laden, God preserve him, and Dr. Ayman [al-]Zawahiri – that we will fulfill our promise, and that we will perform the jihad. By God our detention only made us more insistent and committed to our principles, which we strove for and were detained for.

Another former prisoner at Guantanamo, Ibrahim al-Rubaish, a mufti (religious leader), has emerged as an ideologue of Al-Qaeda in the Arabian Peninsula. Al Rubaish, in a taped statement, justified the assassination attempt on Saudi Assistant Interior Minister, Prince Mohammed bin Nayif, in August 2009, by citing an example from Islamic tradition calling for the assassination of the enemies of Islam; he said:[103]

> We are in dire need of reviving this Sunnah against the enemies of Allah, for it instills terror and fear in the ranks of the enemy. It also is a factor which leads the mercenaries in the ranks of the enemy to re-evaluate their work, for even though they are slaves of money, their lives are more important to them than their salaries. It also makes those giving orders amongst the soldiers think about the assassination team before they think about fulfilling their commands. Through them, the enemies live in fear, even in their own houses amongst their families, for they do not know when they will be attacked by the predator lions.

At the end of 2009, American security experts admitted publicly that Yemen had become a major Al-Qaeda base for operational and training purposes, at par with those in the tribal areas of Pakistan.[104] The Americans have committed themselves to spending $70 million to enhance Yemeni capabilities to combat the Al-Qaeda militants. With intellgence inputs from the USA, Saudi Arabia and other sources, Yemeni forces carried out air strikes against Al-Qaeda camps in which 60 militants were killed. Though the assault was successful, a high-ranking Yemeni official, in the same report, said anonymously:

> They [Al-Qaeda] have been hit hard, but they have not yet been disabled ... The problem is that the involvement of the United States creates sympathy for Al-Qaeda. The cooperation is necessary—but there is no doubt that it has an effect for the common man. He sympathises with Al-Qaeda.

Though the Al-Qaeda jihadis are geographically dispersed today, they are able to maintain close contact with each other through the Internet, counselling each other, boosting morale, and engaging in debates on jihadi philosophy, strategy and tactics. One of the most active Internet users is 'Asad al-Jihad2', believed to be the pseudonym of Mohammed Khalil al-Hakaima, an Egyptian and a former member of Gamaa Islamiyya, who joined Al-Qaeda in 2006. In Internet postings on 11 September 2008, 'al-Jihad2' set out the following principal Al-Qaeda battlefronts:[105]

- *Palestine*: it remains at the core of Islamic issues and provides the motivation for Palestinians to join the jihad,
- *The Arabian Peninsula*: its base is Yemen, with considerable funding coming in from other parts of the Peninsula,
- *Afghanistan*: the present joint Taliban-Al-Qaeda struggle is taking place on many fronts; ultimately, Kabul will be taken and an Islamic Emirate set up in the country,
- *Pakistan*: Al-Qaeda already controls the tribal areas and is confident of setting up an Islamic government with popular support,
- *The Horn of Africa*: the Al-Qaeda base in the region is Somalia, where jihad is led by Al-Shabaab; its Emir is Shaikh Mukhtar al-Zubair, who has been assisted from time to time by military commanders sent by bin Laden, and,
- *The Maghreb*: this is an area of considerable importance to the Islamic movement; the terrain is also most propitious for armed activity.

After playing down the importance of Al-Qaeda in 2008, towards the end of 2009 top American policy makers seemed to recognize the central importance of this organization in fomenting global jihad and particularly the significance of its leader Osama bin Laden. General Stanley A. McChrystal, US/NATO Commander in Afghanistan, said in December 2009:[106]

> I believe that al-Qaeda can be defeated overall but I believe it is an ideology and he [Osama bin Laden] is an iconic leader, so I think to complete the destruction of that organization, it does mean that he needs to be either captured or killed or brought to justice.

Contemporary Debate Within Radical Islam

The near-monopolistic control exercised by Ayman al-Zawahiri on contemporary radical Islamic thinking has been challenged recently by some highly influential sources. First, the distinguished Egyptian Islamist ideologue, Sayyid Imam Al Sharif, popularly known as Dr. Fadl, published articles in Egyptian newspapers in November and December 2007, providing a detailed commentary on jihad which was titled: *Rationalising Jihad in Egypt and the World.*[107] This was a major retraction of his own two earlier writings on the subject, published in 1988 and 1994, which had been titled, respectively, *The Essential Guide for Preparation* [for Jihad] and *The Compendium of the Pursuit of Divine Knowledge.* The first book had become the basic text used by Al-Qaeda jihadis. The second book constituted the full development of Fadl's jihadi thinking in which he asserted that that there was divine sanction for the annihilation of all enemies of Islam, including 'apostate' Arab rulers and all Government officials, uniformed and civil, working under them. According to observers, while cautioning Muslims about castigating other Muslims of *takfir,* Dr. Fadl himself defined Islam so narrowly that a large number of individuals and groups could be among those marked out for annihilation. Al-Zawahiri is said to have described this book as 'a victory from Almighty God'.[108]

Dr. Fadl and Ayman al-Zawahiri had been close associates since 1968 when they were together at medical college.[109] They were senior leaders of the Egyptian Islamic Jihad, and also worked together in the Mujahedeen struggle in Afghanistan in the 1980s. Later, in September 1993, Dr. Fadl joined al-Zawahiri and bin Laden in Sudan, after which, in 1994, Dr. Fadl moved to Yemen, while al-Zawahiri followed bin Laden to Afghanistan.

At this stage, the path of the two jihadi revolutionaries diverged: while al-Zawahiri became bin Laden's closest associate and Al-Qaeda's ideologue and strategist, Dr. Fadl in Yemen distanced himself from jihadi activity. Dr. Fadl is also said to have cut off all ties with al-Zawahiri, blaming him for tampering with the manuscript of his book, *The Compendium*, and making it more radical and uncompromising in tone and content than his original text. Soon after 9/11, Dr. Fadl was imprisoned in Yemen and then extradited to Egypt in February 2004, where he remains in prison till now.

In 2007, while sitting in an Egyptian prison, Dr. Fadl set out new rules for jihad in terms of which most forms of jihadi violence and terror would be illegal under Islamic law, with jihad being sanctioned only in rare situations. For jihad to be legitimate in Islam, Dr. Fadl asserted it should meet the following conditions:[110]

- the enemy should be properly identified in order to avoid harming the innocent;
- the jihadi must obtain the blessings of a qualified imam and the permission of his parents and creditors;
- violence is not the only way to confront the enemies of God; one can isolate oneself from unbelievers;
- jihad is not required if the enemy is twice as powerful: in such situations, peace treaties and ceasefires can be resorted to;
- rulers should be fought only if they are non-believers and then only if the battle will improve the situation of Muslims;
- it is forbidden to kill civilians, including Christians and Jews, unless they are actively attacking Muslims;
- indiscriminate bombings are not permitted because they kill innocents; and,
- no harm should be done to those who are affiliated with Islam even if they belong to a different creed.

Fadl also called for considerable caution in regard to the issue of takfir, that is, the declaration of others as infidels. This matter, according to him, was so complex that it should be left in the hands of competent jurists and ordinary persons should not take it upon themselves to enforce it.

Fadl sanctioned legitimate terror in respect of Muslim communities under hostile foreign occupation such as those in Iraq, Palestine and

Afghanistan. However, he criticized terrorist attacks in the USA, London and Madrid because they were based on 'nationalism' and were a form of indiscriminate slaughter that is forbidden by Islam.

Not surprisingly, Dr. Fadl's views evoked a strong response from Ayman al-Zawahiri. Al-Zawahiri, in March 2008, titled his 188-page rebuttal, *The Exoneration*, in order to 'exonerate' the Muslim people from the insult heaped upon them by Fadl, who was appeasing the US and the West and was propagating the idea of an Islam without jihad.[111] Al-Zawahiri ridiculed Fadl for projecting his own weakness onto the Mujahideen movement as a whole, particularly when jihad had become so much stronger since Fadl had 'deserted' it 15 years ago. Noting that Fadl had written his recantation from an Egyptian prison, al-Zawahiri asked sarcastically whether Fadl's fax machine was connected to the same line as the electric shock machines used to torture prisoners. For the rest, al-Zawahiri, relying on Islamic texts, gave a spirited point-by-point rebuttal of the specific assertions made by Dr. Fadl in support of the moderate discourse presented by him.

Later, in June 2009, another jihadi ideologue, Abu Mohammed al-Maqdisi, who had emerged from a Jordanian prison a year earlier, also presented a moderate approach to jihad, thus inviting the wrath of fellow jihadis in Iraq and Jordan. Al-Maqdisi, a Palestinian and a radical jihadi ideologue, was arrested in Jordan in the 1990s, when he shared a cell block with Abu Musab Zarqawi, who later led the Al-Qaeda in Iraq before being killed in 2006. Al-Maqdisi was said to have been Zarqawi's mentor, though even in 2005, Al-Maqdisi had wanted a reduction in suicide attacks. Al-Maqdisi's fresh views were:[112]

- he questioned the legitimacy of blowing up entire buildings and shedding innocent blood;
- he deplored the kidnapping of neutral representatives of relief agencies who assist Muslims in many countries;
- he opposed the targeting of churches and cinema houses; and,
- with regard to the Shia, he distinguished between the average Shia who do not know anything of their belief and, hence, do not observe apostate practices, and the educated elite Shia who support apostate ideas; flowing from this, he opposed the bombing of Shia mosques because many ordinary men, women and children worship there.

Separate from these individual assertions of moderate jihad, the extremist movement in Egypt headed by the Gamaa Islamiyya also went through a significant change, with renunciation of extremism and violence by its members, many of whom had been arrested in the 1980s and 1990s and had been in prison for about twenty years.[113] This moderate approach evolved in prison itself when Gamaa Islamiyya's leader, Karam Zuhdy, and other senior leaders entered into detailed discussions with their followers and persuaded them that the path of violence chosen by them had been erroneous and contrary to Islam. After his release, Zuhdy publicly apologized to the Egyptian people for the violence perpetrated by his group, beginning with the murder of President Anwar Sadat.[114]

The rejection of violence and calls for a fresh look at jihadi radicalism have set up a deep ideological schism in the global Islamist movements, with moderate commentators increasingly asserting the futility of violence and pointing out that jihadi violence has become 'the beginning and end of all actions' instead of serving any larger Islamic purpose.[115] The mindless violence of the jihadis, in which hundreds of innocent persons, most of them Muslims, have been killed, has served to engender a revulsion against jihadi tactics. Thus, in Algeria, Al-Qaeda-affiliated suicide bombings of 2006 seem to have alienated large numbers of Algerian people from the organization.

In Saudi Arabia, Shaikh Salman Al-Awdah, a prominent radical Islamic cleric and mentor of bin Laden, who had been imprisoned between 1994 and 1999, later became a moderate preacher advocating peace and co-existence of religions. Sometime in September 2007 he read out on television a severe critique of bin Laden, when he said:[116]

> Brother Osama, how much blood has been spilled? How many innocent children, women, and old people have been killed, maimed, and expelled from their homes in the name of 'al[-] Qaeda'? ...
>
> The image of Islam today is tarnished. People around the world are saying how Islam teaches that those who do not accept it must be killed. They are also saying that the adherents of Salafi teachings kill Muslims who do not share their views ...
>
> Many of your brethren in Egypt, Algeria and elsewhere have come to see the end of the road for that ideology. They realize how destructive and dangerous it is. They have also found the courage to proclaim in their writings and on the air that they were mistaken and that the path they had been on was the path of error. They admit that it cannot lead to anything good. They have sought Allah's forgiveness for what has passed and have expressed their sincere regrets for what they had done.
>
> Those with brave hearts need just as much to have courageous minds.

As of now, the overall jihadi intellectual scenario is, on the one side, made up of a fairly strong and influential radical grouping that is Al-Qaeda-affiliated and inspired, and, on the other side, represented broadly by the thinking of Dr. Fadl, which emphasizes harmony and co-existence.

Conclusion

Modern-day jihad has passed through three phases: the first phase was from 1979 to 1989, when the US-sanctioned jihad in Afghanistan provided a cause and a terrain to the radical Islamic movement. It ended with the Soviet withdrawal from Afghanistan. The second phase extended from 1989 to 11 September 2001. During this period, veterans of the Afghan jihad inspired, guided and often actively participated in jihad in their home countries as also in other parts of the world. This period saw serious setbacks to the Islamist cause, with blood defeats in Algeria, Egypt, Bosnia and Chechnya. However, the 'successful' assault of 9/11 ended this phase.

During this period, Osama bin Laden gave final shape to his radical Islamist ideology in the tradition of Ibn Taymiyya and Sayyid Qutb. He became a fervent advocate of the use of violence, and envisaged a 'cosmic war' with the non-Muslim world, particularly the US. In his world view, there could be no compromise with the kuffar (non-believers).

Osama bin Laden's jihadi mindset was considerably influenced by his close associate in Afghanistan, Ayman al-Zawahiri. Al-Zawahiri too saw no scope for accommodation with the *kuffar*, and, indeed, believed there was divine sanction for jihad against infidels, apostates and hypocrites. In defining the enemies of Islam, al-Zawahiri went well beyond Islamic tradition in advocating that, in 'martyrdom operations', innocents could be killed. Again, in his view, 'innocents' did not include officials who served an apostate government. In fact, al-Zawahiri even approved of the accidental killing of Muslims and of innocent women and children in bombing operations on the ground that the jihadis were fighting a formidable foe, who had access to powerful weaponry and who frequently sheltered himself among the general population. The pursuit of jihad was more important and could not be obstructed by the possible death of a few innocent people. He was a strong advocate of martyrdom which he distinguished from suicide on the basis of 'intentions'. The influence of al-Zawahiri's thinking is apparent in the Al-Qaeda-led carnage of September 11.

After 11 September 2001, the third phase of contemporary global jihad commenced. As a result of US assaults, Al-Qaeda lost its bases in Afghanistan, with its top leadership either annihilated or dispersed across Afghanistan or sheltered in sanctuaries in the mountains on the Pakistan-Afghanistan border. The continued Israeli assaults on Palestinians and US policies in support of Israel, now supplemented by the US occupation of Iraq and the abuses perpetrated on the Iraqi population, all of these strengthened the Muslim sense of grievance and victimhood and enhanced the appeal of the radical Islamic movement. Now, Al-Qaeda's influence is apparent in different parts of the world where various Islamic groups and cells carry out terrorist actions without necessarily involving Al-Qaeda leaders in their operational aspects. A new area of Al-Qaeda-related violence has also emergedin Europe where the radicalization of the expatriate Muslim population has been led by veterans of the Afghanistan war and the Bosnian struggle.

This phase of jihad has also generated a public debate on jihadi tactics and strategy between Ayman al-Zawahiri and his young Syrian colleague, Abu Musab al-Suri. While the former has focused on spectacular 'martyrdom operations' to carry forward the 'grand narrative of triumphant jihad', al-Suri has favoured the gradualist option of resistance through quasi-independent cells which would conduct harassment operations which would wear down the enemy and slowly create enclaves of freedom. Today, both approaches are in favour.

At present, Al-Qaeda lacks a cohesive global structure. Its vision, involving the setting up of a globalized Islamic state in place of the present tyrannical apostate leaders, and its agenda to liberate Muslim lands occupied by foreigners, are being pursued by a number of different individuals and groups inspired by an Islamic messianic vision, whose writings confidently anticipate the ultimate and inevitable triumph of Islam. This is examined in the next chapter.

NOTES

1. Gilles Kepel, *Jihad – The Trail of Political Islam.* (London: I.B. Tauris, 2004) p. 208.
2. Raymond Ibrahim (Ed), *The Al Qaeda Reader.* (New York: Doubleday, 2007) pp. 197–8.
3. Lawrence Wright, *The Looming Tower—Al Qaeda and the Road to 9/11.* (New York: Alfred A. Knopf, 2006) p. 332.

4. Wright, p. 127; in regard to the bin Laden-al-Zawahiri relationship, Montasser al-Zayyat, al-Zawahiri's biographer and critic, has pointed out that each influenced the other:

   "[al-]Zawahiri convinced bin Laden of his *jihadi* approach, turning him from a fundamentalist preacher whose main concern was relief, into a *jihadi* fighter, clashing with despots and American troops in the Arab world. [Al-]Zawahiri gave bin Laden some of his closest confidants to help him. They became the main figures in bin Laden's al-Qaeda ... Not only did [al-]Zawahiri influence bin Laden, the latter [had an impact on] the philosophy of [al-]Zawahiri and of Islamic Jihad. For example, bin Laden advised [al-]Zawahiri to stop armed operations in Egypt and to ally with him against their common enemies: the United States and Israel. His advice to [al-]Zawahiri came upon their return to Afghanistan, when bin Laden ensured the safety of [al-]Zawahiri and the Islamic Jihad members under the banner of the Taliban ... [al-]Zawahiri's alliance with Osama bin Laden changed his philosophy [that is, [al-]Zawahiri's] from one prioritizing combat with the near enemy to one of confronting the far enemy: the United States and Israel." [Richard Bonney, *Jihad - From Qu'ran to bin Laden* (Basingstoke, UK: Palgrave/Macmillan, 2004) pp. 358–9.]

5. Natana J. Delong-Bas, *Wahhabi Islam – from Revival and Reform to Global Jihad,* (New York: Oxford University Press, 2004) p. 269;

6. Delong-Bas, pp. 269–70.

7. ibid., p. 273.

8. ibid., pp. 274–5.

9. ibid., p. 275.

10. ibid.

11. Ibrahim, pp. 11–12.

12. ibid., p. 13.

13. ibid.

14. ibid., p. 284.

15. ibid., p. 33.

16. ibid., p. 56.

17. Khalil Gebara, 'The End of Egyptian Islamic Jihad?', *Global Terrorism Analysis,* Vol. 3, Issue 3 (10 February 2005); downloaded from: jamestown.org/terrorism/news/article.phd? issue – id = 3228.

18. Ibrahim, p. 93.

19. ibid., p. 101.

20. ibid.

21. ibid., pp. 103–4.

22. ibid., p. 114.

23. ibid.
24. Maha Azzam, 'Al-Qaeda: The Misunderstood Wahhabi Connection and the Ideology of Violence', Briefing Paper No. 1, Royal Institute of International Affairs, London, February, 2003, p. 3.
25. Azzam, p. 4.
26. ibid
27. Ibrahim, p. 294.
28. ibid., p. 145.
29. ibid., p. 156.
30. ibid., pp. 145–6.
31. ibid., p. 169.
32. ibid., p. 170.
33. ibid.
34. Abdel Bari Atwan, *The Secret History of al-Qaeda* (London: Abacus, 2006), p. 76.
35. ibid.
36. ibid., p. 77.
37. ibid.
38. ibid.
39. ibid.
40. Azzam, p. 4.
41. Alan Cullison, 'Inside Al-Qaeda's Hard Drive', *The Atlantic Monthly*, September 2004; downloaded from: www.theatlantic.com/doc/print/2004-09/cullison.
42. ibid.
43. Quoted in Bruce Hoffman: 'Terrorism Today and Tomorrow', Chapter excerpted from his book, *Inside Terrorism* (New York: Columbia University Press, 2006); downloaded from: www.columbia.edu/cu/cup/publicity/hoffman excerptrev.html; Henceforth Hoffman.
44. ibid.
45. ibid.
46. ibid.
47. Daniel Benjamin, 'The Nature of the Terrorist Threat'; Testimony before the House Armed Services Committee: Terrorism, Unconventional Threats and Capabilities Sub-committee, 14 February 2007; downloaded from: www.brookings.edu/views/testimony/benjamin/20070214. pdf; henceforth Benjamin.
48. Atwan, p. 213.
49. Michael Scheuer: 'Bin Laden Identifies Saudi Arabia as the Enemy of Mujahedeen Unity', *Terrorism Focus*, vol. 5, Issue 1, 9 January 2008;

downloaded from: http://www.jamestown.org/programs/gta/archivesgta/
2008/?tx_publicationsttnews_pi2%5Bissue%5D=1

50. Michael Scheuer: 'Al-Qaeda in Iraq: Still Striving to Undo al Zarqawi's Damage to Mujahedeen Unity', *Terrorism Focus*, Vol 5, Issue 7, 30 April 2008; downloaded from: http://www.jamestown.org/programs/gta/archivesgta/2008/?tx_publicationsttnews_pi2%5Bissue%5D=17.

51. ibid.

52. Ramzy Mardini: 'Al-Qaeda in Iraq Operations Suggest Rising Confidence Ahead of US Military Withdrawal', *Terrorism Monitor*, Vol. 7, Issue 36, 25 November 2009; downloaded from: http://www.jamestown.org/programs/gta/archivesgta/gta2009/?tx_publicationsttnews_pi2%5Bissue%5D=36.

53. 'Depleted Al Qaeda ranks still a threat, *Gulf News*, Dubai, 30 December 2009, p. 12.

54. Michael Bonner: 'Al-Qaeda's Migrant Martyrs, *Vanity Fair*, Web Exclusive, 16 December 2009; downloaded from: http://www.vanityfair.com/politics/features/2009/12/iraqi-terrorists-2...

55. ibid.

56. Atwan, p. 222.

57. ibid, p. 223.

58. ibid.

59. ibid., p. 224.

60. Roy, p. 302.

61. ibid., p. 303.

62. Roy, pp. 304–13.

63. Timothy Garton Ash: 'Islam in Europe', *The New York Review of Books*, Vol. 53, No. 15, 5 October 2006.

64. Roy, p. 292.

65. Bruce Riedel: 'Al Qaeda Strikes Back', *Foreign Affairs*, New York, May 2007, downloaded from:www.brookings.edu/views/articles/riedel/20070501.htm;

66. Atwan, p. 250.

67. Christopher M. Blanchard: 'Al Qaeda: Statements and Evolving Ideology, Congressional Research Service, The Library of Congress, updated 20 June 2005; downloaded from: www.history.navy.mil/library/online/al-qaeda%20evdre.htm (sic)..

68. ibid.

69. Atwan, p. 252.

70. ibid., p. 254.

71. Gilles Kepel, *Beyond Terror and Martyrdom – The Future of the Middle*

East. (Cambridge MA and London, UK: The Belknap Press of Harvard University Press, 2008) p. 113.

72. ibid., p. 117; Montasser al-Zayyat is also a critic of the 9/11 attacks; he says:

> Islamists across the globe were adversely affected by the September 11 attacks on the United States. Even Islamic movements that did not target the United States are paying the price for this folly…Bin Laden's desire to take revenge heedless of the American and international response, and its effect on the future of the Islamic movements in the world, has given the Americans and other governments the power to destroy the Islamists before our eyes…bin Laden and al-Zawahiri lost the Taliban, a government that had protected Islamists for many years. [Bonney, p. 361.]

73. Gilles Kepel, p. 118 .
74. Gilles Kepel, p. 119.
75. Gilles Kepel, p.170.
76. Jason Burke, *Al-Qaeda, the True Story of Radical Islam.* (London: Penguin Books, 2007) p. xxv and p. 8.
77. ibid., p. 195.
78. ibid., p. 8.
79. ibid., p. 232.
80. Olivier Roy, *Globalised Islam – The Search for a New Ummah* (London: Hurst & Company, 2002) p. 299; Montasser al-Zayyat, in his biography of Ayman al-Zawahiri, has noted al-Zawahiri's agreement to set up the World Islamic Front in February 1998, pointing out that, while bin Laden was its leader, al-Zawahiri was the most influential role-player. The prominent members of this front brought in by al-Zawahiri from the Egyptian Islamic Jihad are named by him as: Abu Hafs, Sayf Al-Adal, Nasr Fahmi also known as Muhammad Salah, Tariq Anwar, Sayyid Ahmad and Tharwat Salah Shahata. [Bonney, p. 358.]
81. Burke, p. 262.
82. ibid., p. 264.
83. ibid.
84. ibid., p. 265.
85. ibid, p. 267.
86. ibid., p. 268.
87. David Cole, 'Are We Safer?' *New York Review of Books*, Vol. LIII, Number 4, 9 March 2006, p. 15.
88. ibid.
89. Jonathan Raban, 'The Truth About Terrorism', *New York Review of Books*,

Vol. LII, Number 1, 13 January 2005, downloaded from: http://www.nybooks.com/articles/17676.

90. Malise Ruthven, 'The Rise of the Muslim Terrorists', *New York Review of Books,* Vol. LV, Number 9, 29 May 2008, p. 34.

91. ibid.

92. Raban.

93. Michael Scheuer: 'Rumors of Al-Qaeda's Death May be Highly Exaggerated', *Terrorism Focus,* Vol. 5, Issue 21, 4 June 2008; downloaded from: http://www.jamestown.org/programs/gta/archivesgta/2008/?tx_publicationsttnews_ pi2%5Bissue%5D=21.

94. Michael Scheuer: 'Is Global Jihad a Fading Phenomenon', *Terrorism Focus,* Vol. 5, Issue 13, 1 April 2008, downloaded from: http://www.jamestown.org/programs/gta/archivesgta/2008/?tx_publicationsttnews_pi2%5Bissue% 5D=13.

95. For details see Thomas Renard: 'Europol Report Describes Afghanistan-Pakistan Connection to Trends in European Terrorism, *Terrorism Monitor,* vol. 7, Issue 12, 8 May 2009, downloaded from: http://www.jamestown.org/programs/gta/archivesgta/gta2009/?tx_publicationsttnews_pi2%5 Bissue%5D=12.

96. Lawrence Wright: 'The Rebellion Within', *The New Yorker,* 2 June 2008; downloaded from: http://www.newyorker.com/reporting/2008/06/02/080602fa_fact_wrig... .

97. Scheuer

98. George Friedman: 'The Jihadist Strategic Dilemma', *Global Intelligence,* STRATFOR, 8 December 2009; downloaded from: http://www.lebanonwire.com/0912MLN/09120802STR.asp.

99. Michael Scheuer: 'Al-Qaeda Completes its Organisational Mission in Iraq, *Terrorism Focus,* Vol. 5, Issue 3, 23 January 2008; downloaded from: http://www.jamestown.org/programs/gta/archivesgta/2008/?tx_publicationsttnews_pi 2%5Bissue%5D=3.

100. Murad Batal al-Shishani: 'Growth of Salafist Militancy in Palestinian Refugee Camps Poses Security Risks', *Terrorism Monitor,* Vo. 7, Issue 32, dated 30 October 2009; downloaded from: http://www.jamestown.org/programs/gta/archivesgta/gta2009/?tx_publicationsttnews_pi 2%5Bissue%5D=32.

101. Michael Scheuer: 'Yemen's Role in Al-Qaeda's Strategy', *Terrorism Focus,* Vol. 5, Issue 5, 7 February 2008; downloaded from: http://www.jamestown.org/programs/gta/archivesgta/2008/?tx_publicationsttnews_pi2%5 Bissue%5D=5.

102. Abdul Hameed Bakier: 'Al Qaeda Leaders in the Arabian Peninsula Speak Out', *Terrorism Focus,* vol. 6, Issue 3, 28 January 2009; downloaded

from: http://www.jamestown.org/programs/gta/archivesgta/tf2009/
?tx_publicationsttnews_pi2%5Bissue%5D=3.

103. Murad Batal Al-Shishani: 'Ibrahim al Rubaish: New Religious Ideologue of Al-Qaeda in Saudi Arabia Calls for Revival of Assassination Tactic', *Terrorism Monitor*, issue 36, 25 November 2009, downloaded from: http://www.jamestown.org/programs/gta/archivesgta/gta2009/?tx_publicationsttnews_pi2%5Bissue%5D=36.

104. 'Washington Aims Military at New Refuge of Al-Qaeda', *International Herald Tribune*, 29 December 2009, p. 1 and 5.

105. Abdul Hameed Bakier: 'Al-Qaeda Outlines its Strategy Seven Years After 9/11', *Terrorism Focus*, Vol. 5, issue 35, 1 October 2008; downloaded from: http://www.jamestown.org/programs/gta/archivesgta/2008/?tx_publicationsttnews_pi 2%5Bissue%5D=35

106. Syed Saleem Shahzad: 'Osama can run, how long can he hide?' *Asia Times online*, 12 December 2009; downloaded from: http://atimes.com/atimes/South_Asia/KL12Df0.3.html.

107. Wright.

108. ibid.

109. ibid; also, 'Profile: Controversial Jihad Theoretician Dr. Fadl', *Asharq Al-Awsat*, 25 November 2008; downloaded from: http://aawsat.com/english/news.asp?section=3&id=14836.

110. Wright.

111. ibid; also, Abdul Hameed Bakeer; Al-Qaeda's Al-Zawahiri, Repudiates Dr. Fadl's 'Rationalisation of Jihad' *Terrorism Focus*, Vol. 5, Issue 17, 30 April 2008; downloaded from: http://www.jamestown.org/programs/gta/archivesgta/2008/?tx_publicationsttnews_pi2%5Bissue%5D=17.

112. Shafika Mattar: 'Jordan Frees Former Al-Qaeda Mentor', *Associated Press*, 12 March 2008; downloaded from: http://www.boston.com/news/world/middleeast/articles/2008/03/12/jo...;Murad Batal Al-Shishani: 'Jihad Ideologue Abu Muhammad Al-Maqdisi Challenges Jordan's Neo-Zarqawists' *Terrorism Monitor*, Vol. 7, Issue 20, 9 July 2009; downloaded from: http://www.jamestown.org/programs/gta/archivesgta/gta2009/?tx_publicationsttnews_ pi2%5Bissue%5D=20

113. Wright.

114. ibid.

115. ibid.

116. Full Statement downloaded from: http://www.seventhpillar.net/salman_al-awdah

10

Contemporary Islamic Messianism

... the resurgence of [Islamic] apocalypticism should [not] be dismissed as inconsequential. Much of the apocalyptic literature traffics in anti-Semiticism and anti-Westernism and will fuel the already rampant problem of conspiracy theories in the Muslim world. These books are much more widely read than the jihadist literature ... Islamic apocalypticism clearly deserves more attention. As Filiu writes, 'the end of the world is a serious matter, especially for those who are preparing for it.'

Thomas Hegghammer: 'Until the End of Times',
The National, Abu Dhabi, 16 January 2009

Pnina Werbner describes the Islamic millennialist vision as a 'return to the pristine Islam of the time of the Prophet's reign'. This is conceived of as a golden age of unity, harmony, lawfulness, economic prosperity and peace.[1] Sayyid Qutb had described it most eloquently thus:[2]

> That was a remarkable period, sublime summit, an exceptional generation of men, a bright beacon. It was, as we have said, decreed and willed by God, so that this unique image might be materialized in the situations of real life and recourse might later be had to it, in order to repeat it within the limitations of human capacity.

Though mainstream Sunni Islam has generally downplayed 'Mahdism', messianic movements headed by charismatic personalities have been a recurrent reality in Islamic history.[3] Such movements, centred around a self-declared Mahdi, generally sought to effect change in Islamic practice or the existing political order by asserting a new divine mandate for the advent of a new era of rejuvenated faith. On the other hand, the response of the reformist Islamic movements was slightly different. They, too, were led by charismatic personalities who had a similar agenda to that of the

Mahdi, but the emphasis on their part was on the need for 'reform' in *this* life in order to emulate the pristine era of the Prophet. This was primarily to be achieved by rejecting from contemporary Islamic practice all alien infiltrations [seen as innovation (*bid'ah*)] so as to bring Islamic practice as close as possible to the way of the early forefathers of Islam, the *Salaf*.[4]

With the exception of certain unique movements such as those of the Mahdi in Sudan in the late 19th century, and the assertions of Juhayman Al-Utaybi, who seized the Haram Sharief in Makkah, in 1979, the dominant intellectual trend in Islam through the twentieth century was 'reformist', with increasing tendency in favour of a radical discourse, which had little time and space for either Mahdism or speculations about the hereafter.

Still, the thinking of the radical Islamists was messianic in that they remained extremely robust in their aspirations for an Islamic Utopia (albeit in *this* world) and exerted the greatest intellectual effort towards realizing it. Again, like the self-proclaimed Mahdis, these radical ideologues were themselves charismatic figures. Thus, Abbas Amanat has described Hassan Al-Banna as 'a charismatic figure with the zeal of a messianic claimant and with a following as devout and motivated as any millennarian community'.[5] It is true that Al-Banna rejected Mahdism, but, as Amanat has pointed out, he achieved in the eyes of his followers 'the status of a martyrdom messiah reminiscent of Christ's crucifixion'.[6]

Qutb too did not pay much attention to 'signs of the hour' or the nature of resurrection. However, in describing contemporary Muslim society as being in a state of ignorance or barbarism and recommending immigration of true believers from such a society so as to prepare for an inevitable conflict with the forces of disbelief, Qutb too was setting out a 'dormant apocalyptic programme'.[7]

David Cook has pointed out that Abdullah Azzam had had a messianic vision of the Islamic State of Afghanistan which was a truly Muslim state, where the 'emigrants' (presumably the Arab-Afghans) would plan their conflict against corrupt Islamic regimes and prepare the ground for the establishment of a caliphate that would ultimately encompass the entire Muslim world.[8]

Besides being charismatic personalities, the ideology articulated by the radical Islamist writers and adopted by their jihadi followers has many attributes of messianism:

(*i*)   their central belief in the deep division between the faithful Muslim and all others, a division that is unbridgeable and inherently conflictual;

(*ii*) an intense critique of contemporary Muslim leaders and establishment *ulema,* who, in the view of the radical ideologues, have deviated from the path of true Islam and, are, therefore, apostate and require the faithful Muslim to go to war against them;

(*iii*) the radicals see no limit to the violence to be inflicted upon the apostate and unbeliever: since the 'other' is thoroughly demonized, every form and extent of violence has divine sanction, including the killing of women and children, for there are no 'innocents' on the other side; and,

(*iv*) among the weapons of war sanctioned by the radical discourse are 'martyrdom operations', that is, operations in which the protagonist not only places his life in danger but actively seeks death in a violent operation to defend his religion.

Radical Islamists do contemplate the *hereafter,* but only in the context of their own martyrdom. This is illustrated by the note titled 'The Last Night' which contains instructions for a jihadi team embarking on a 'martyrdom operation', where the happiness of the after-life is mentioned:[9]

> Let your breast be filled with gladness, for there is nothing between you and your wedding but mere seconds. Thereby will begin a happy and contented life and immortal blessing with the prophets, the true ones and the righteous martyrs. They are the best of companions. We beseech God for grace. So seek good omens. For the Prophet, may blessings and peace be upon him, used to love divination about every matter.

On similar lines, even as jihad has now become pervasive, jihadi songs celebrating martyrdom and the pleasures of the after-life have become popular; one of these goes as follows:[10]

> *I came to this life*
> *Which is only a short elusive pleasure*
> *A journey through a battle*
> *I became fire and light, a melody and fragrance.*
> *These gardens smell sweet*
> *And their smell is my wound*
> *He is the spirit*

I have been visited by the prophets
And my brothers are martyrs.

Today, in regard to messianism, two clear trends are visible in Islamic discourse: *first,* caution and restraint on the part of Islamist ideologues and contemporary jihadi leaders who focus primarily on realizing an ideal Islamic society in this life but with elements of messianism in their pronouncements; and, *second,* an extraordinary increase in Sunni apocalyptic literature reflecting (and occasionally drawing upon) parallel expressions in Christian millennialist writings. The millennialist vision of the latter writers and the movements led by them are a response to the sense of a cataclysmic failure of Islam and the conviction that the God has abandoned Muslims because of their sinfulness, as exemplified by the Arab defeat in the 1967 war, and the continued violence upon Palestinians, Bosnians, Chechens, Iraqis and Afghans, which taken together are read as a cosmic Islamic crisis.[11] Not surprisingly, such a comprehensive sense of defeat, humiliation and despair can only be effectively confronted with a messianic vision informed by the belief in the ultimate global triumph of Islam. Werbner has set out this deep-seated conviction in the following terms:[12]

> God will not forsake us ... Muslims will remain on this earth; they will not die out but will spread throughout the world. Judaism will die out. Christianity will die out. Hinduism will die out, and one day the name of Islam and only Islam, "God is one and Muhammad is His Prophet", will remain. And when this day occurs – I may or may not be here to see it – it will be a day when the conscience of the Muslims will be fully awakened, and they will be able to differentiate between theirs and others, and will be able to unite.

Contemporary Islamic messianism is an obvious reaction to the sense of Muslim defeat at the hands of the 'West', more specifically the US and its ally, Israel. This hostility to the West and Israel occasionally gets articulated in terms of hostility to the religions of Christianity and Judaism. However, contemporary Muslim millennialist writers also include in their hate-list Arab leaders and the religious establishments supporting them, seeing them as collaborators with the West. Thus, contemporary Muslim millennialist prophecies speak of the inevitable downfall of the US not merely on account of its own sinfulness but primarily on account of its strong engagement with the Zionist cause. In an ironical intellectual twist, a number of contemporary Muslim millennialist writers are increasingly referring to millennialist evangelical Christian writers, at times even giving these writings precedence over traditional Hadith literature![13]

Most of these Islamic apocalyptic writings are founded on an anti-Jewish conspiracy theory which sees in the successes of Israel and commencement of world domination by the Jews, the further humiliation and degradation of the Muslims.[14] It is, therefore, the duty of Muslims to confront and defeat this threat:

> The Zionists control by imposing famine and scientific and technical backwardness upon the Islamic world. The most important thing is that most of the people of the World – Crusader [Christian] world, the Islamic world, and the Buddhist and Hindu worlds – have all become subservient to the evil powers exemplified in institutions and great powers like mountains. And these evil powers, which are like mountains – the Jews sit upon their peaks in the form of the Hidden Government.[15]
>
> It is incumbent upon the Muslims to raise the flag of jihad in the face of the Jews, to exalt the word of God on the earth, and not to leave the reins of their rule and their leadership to those who were satisfied when Zion sheathed its poisoned knife in the breasts of the Muslims, or that their impure feet would pollute the lands of the mosque of Al-Aqsa.[16]

The United States is also demonized in apocalyptic literature for its dominant presence in global and Middle Eastern affairs and its alliance with Israel:[17]

> The principal concern of America became the tending of the interests of the Zionists, and the state of Israel in Palestine became an American state. For this reason the end of the Jews is interconnected with the end of America, and the end of America is interconnected with the end of the Jews.

Apocalyptic writers draw a parallel between the arrogance of the USA and the people of Aad (referred to in the Koran) and their ultimate destruction at the hands of God:[18]

> the similarity between 'Ad the perished and present-day New York is also that both of them were tyrannical, oppressive, haughty, world-class cities imposing their rule by means of unjust force to divide the rest of the peoples and nations of the world. Everything that happened in 'Ad of old has happened in America, just as God said.

David Cook quotes a prominent modern-day millennialist writer, Bashir

Muhammed Abdullah, who drew heavily from modern Christian writers when he wrote of New York thus:[19]

> God's punishment falls on the evil of His creation, and the more evil, the more intense the punishment. Since America is now the chief and first Zionist power, the dragon (of Rev. 12) and the strong arm of the Antichrist (the false prophet,), and the first head of the beast which leads the other six heads, so the punishment will be more intense upon it than upon others. Since in New York especially they are more Jews than in other places, and in it is their wealth, their banks, their political foundations which control the entire world (the U.N., the Security Council, the International Monetary Fund, the World Bank, and the principal media networks), so there is no evil greater than in New York in any other place on the inhabited earth, and for this reason their portion of the punishment will be greater in measure and it will be a total uprooting.

The advent of the Mahdi will result in the salvation of the Muslims:[20]

> The Mahdi will return balance to the globe and honour to the servants of God. He will finish off the monstrous lies of America that the globe has grown old and that there is no further way to restore the atmosphere and clean up the pollution.

The Jews, the followers of the Antichrist, will be annihilated in the final cosmic battle between good and evil:[21]

> The Antichrist is Jewish in aim and intention in that they [Jews] are the greatest corruptors upon the earth, and he is the greatest antichrist of all the ages. His appearance and theirs is one ... The Jews are also antichrists with respect to the aim, the corruption is the means.
>
> The killing of the Antichrist and his Jewish and non-Jewish followers in their totality and their uprooting from the earth will be counted as the uprooting for the great corruption [of the Jews], and the judgment upon the great corruptive arrogance of Banu Isra'il [Israelites] in the third and final stage, and there will be no further Jews upon the face of the earth until the Hour.[22]

Contemporary Mahdist writings have frequently interpreted specific current events in apocalyptic terms, seeing in them signs that would herald the apocalypse. Recalling the messianic tradition that the Muslim world will go through a number of *fitan* (that is, strifes or discords), one Mahdist school has seen two *fitan* in the Iraqi occupation of Kuwait (1990) and the subsequent Gulf War. It anticipates a third *fitna* when

Iran attacks some Gulf sheikhdoms, which will be followed by a US-led assault on Iran.[23]

Is there anything in common between such apocalyptic writings and mainstream Islamist radicalism? On first appearance, the answer would be a firm negative since radical Sunni Islam downplays or totally rejects the notion of the Mahdi. However, as noted earlier, radical Islamist intellectuals have frequently used messianic terminology and imagery, and share with apocalyptic writers their deep concern regarding the Muslim malaise and Muslim salvation through the pursuit of Islam. The Saudi radical cleric, Sheikh Safar Abdul Rehman al-Hawali, is a good representative of such thinking. Though steeped in Saudi Arabia's rigid Wahabbi doctrines, Al-Hawali has authored extensive apocalyptic writings as well. Thus, after the second Intifida, in 2001, in his work, 'Islamic Vision of Prophecy', he interpreted Biblical prophecy texts [Daniel and Revelations] in terms of Islamic connotations; the following list is illustrative:[24]

The New Jerusalem [Rev. 21:2]	Makkah
The son of Man who will come in the Latter days	Mohammed
The beast	Zionism
The little horn [Dan. 8:9] The Abomination of desolation [Dan. 12:11]	Israel
The New Babylon	Modern Western Culture
The New Roman Empire	USA

Al-Hawali also relied on *Daniel* to calculate 'the beginning of the end of the world'; thus, he said:[25]

The final, difficult question remains to be answered: When will the Day of Wrath come? When will Allah destroy the abomination of desolation [Israel]? When will the chains of Jerusalem be broken and its rights returned? The answer has already been implied. When Daniel specified the period between its distress and relief, between the era of anguish and the era of blessing, he put it as forty-five years! We have already seen that he specified the time of the establishment of the abomination of desolation as the year 1967, which is what in fact occurred. Therefore the end—or the beginning of the end—will be 1967 + 45 = 2012 or in lunar year 1387+45 = 1433.

Though Osama bin Laden has himself never given any indication of messianic aspirations, Al-Qaeda has marshalled a powerful messianic appeal in order to attract recruits for its global jihad. First, the USA is referred to as the 'crusader' and as the leader of a Christian–Jewish alliance with a powerful religious agenda;[26] as bin Laden has said:[27]

> One reason behind the symbolic participation of the Western forces ... is to support the Jewish and Zionist plans for expansion of what is called Greater Israel ... We believe that [the US] Administration represents Israel inside America. Take the sensitive ministries such as the Ministry of Exterior and the Ministry of Defence and the CIA, you will find that the Jews have the upper hand in them. They make use of America to further their plans for the world, especially the Islamic world. American presence in the Gulf provides support to the Jews and protects their rear.

Second, the USA has a 'world design' to further divide the Muslim world; thus, in 1998, bin Laden said:[28]

> There is a [US] plan to divide Iraq into three – one in the north for Muslim Kurds, a state in the middle, and a third in the south. The same applies to the land of the two mosques [Saudi Arabia] where there is a plan to divide it into a state for the two mosques, another state for oil in the eastern region, and a state in the middle. This would make the people of the two mosques always busy trying to earn a living, and would leave a few people in the oil region who can be easily controlled.

Later, in 2003, he said:[29]

> .... one of the most important objectives of the new Crusader attack [on Iraq in 2003] is to pave the way and prepare the region, after its fragmentation, for the establishment of what is known as 'the Greater State of Israel,' whose borders will include extensive areas of Iraq, Egypt, through Syria, Lebanon, Jordan, all of Palestine and large parts of the Land of the Two Holy Places.

Against this 'Crusader' agenda, bin Laden (and al-Zawahiri) proposed the establishment of a Muslim state; al-Zawahiri said: '...The restoration of the caliphate and the dismissal of the invaders from the land of Islam ... must remain the basic objective of the Islamic jihad movement, regardless of the sacrifices and the time involved.'[30]

Third, the most effective weapons against the crusader alliance were martyrdom operations; al-Zawahiri said: [31]

> The need to concentrate on the method of martyrdom operations as the most successful way of inflicting damage against the opponent and the least costly to the mujahedin in terms of casualties.
>
> The targets as well as the type and method of weapons used must be chosen to have an impact on the structure of the enemy and deter it enough to stop its brutality, arrogance, and disregard for all taboos and customs. It must restore the struggle to its real size.

The events of 9/11, in bin Laden's view, had divided the world into two mutually exclusive spheres, 'the side of believers and the side of infidels ... Every Muslim has to rush to make his religion victorious.'[32] Thus, as Delong-Bas has noted, the stage is set for a 'cosmic battle between good and evil'.[33] Robert Landes echoes this view and explains bin Laden's apocalyptic view thus:[34]

> In this world view, the West, with its secularism and materialism represents a cosmic enemy that must be destroyed, and Israel, with its control of the holy city of Jerusalem, the insufferable advance column of that assault. As the rest of the world succumbs to Western blandishments and corruption, Islam alone has resisted, at least that element of Islam that has renewed and purified itself in recent times in Islamism.

Certain Mahdist websites have already begun to depict bin Laden in messianic terms. For instance, one site published the text of a play titled: 'It Has Reached Us That Over the Seas There Was A Great God Called America'.[35] This play is set in Kandahar (referred to as the capital of the Islamic Amirate of Afghanistan) in the *hijri* year 1634 (approximately AD 2200), and explains to young Muslim students what 'America' was and how it was destroyed. The Sheikh teaching the students explains that 'America' was a heathen god that the entire world worshipped some centuries earlier, and that God sent Osama bin Laden to save the Muslims from being oppressed by it. Bin Laden destroyed the symbols of the idol's power (the World Trade Centre and the Pentagon), and incurred the wrath of 'America'. The Sheikh and the students then proceed to praise Osama bin Laden as a messianic figure.

In 2003, Al-Qaeda made an attempt to dilute such Mahdi-related enthusiasm by issuing a statement which said:

Many Muslims think an Islamic state will only be established with the appearance of the Mahdi, and so they remain quiescent and implore God to hasten the Mahdi's appearance and so they seize upon any Hadith mentioning him ... and so they also abandon their efforts and just wait for deliverance ... Other Muslims disavow the belief in the Mahdi and attempt to eliminate it.[36]

While there are over 50 Hadith on the Mahdi, the truth is that many are weak or hard to understand ... [and] as for the physical descriptions of the Mahdi, they are all irrelevant. Likewise for the saying that he will have the same name as the Prophet, because tens of thousands of Muslims have that same name ... The truth is, *no one knows yet who will restore the caliphate and restore the ummah to prominence* [Emphasis added.][37]

Furnish examines the various characteristics that are common to millennialist movements and their leaders in different religious denominations, and concludes that, while such characteristics may apply to 'any charismatic Muslim leader', as of now the only serious candidate is Osama bin Laden.[38]

The Appeal of Osama bin Laden

Osama bin Laden is increasingly seen across the Muslim world as an inspiring folk hero. Marc Sageman has noted the romantic appeal jihad now has for Muslim youth, with many viewing bin Laden on par with soccer superstars![39] Bin Laden and al-Zawahiri are idolized as having 'sacrificed everything for their beliefs', that is, being seen as lonely fugitives paying the price for fighting for the Islamic cause. Again, their spartan simplicity in the caves of the Afghan-Pak border contrasts vividly with the opulence of their Western enemy. The image of the cave, of course, has its own special resonance in Islam as the place where Prophet Mohammed had his first revelation and also as the place where he hid when escaping from Makkah to Madinah.

Max Rodenbeck has spoken of the 'mystique' that surrounds bin Laden's persona, pointing out that 'the plot line of his life story fits rather neatly into traditional constructs of the hero'; this consists of:[40]

- a princely birth (his father was a billionaire, who died in a plane crash after claiming to be the only Muslim ever to have prayed at Jerusalem, Medina, and Mecca on the same day);
- physical prowess (he is well over six feet tall);
- courage and cunning (he is still alive);

- sacrifice (of a large personal fortune for the cause of jihad);
- rise to a higher calling (jihad for the salvation of Islam);
- closeness to God (he is pious, and he is still alive);
- respect for ancestors (his puritan version of Islam draws sole inspiration from the semi-mythical first three generations of Muslims);
- experience of exile, and rejection by his own tribe (bin Laden was stripped of Saudi citizenship in 1994, has been disowned by his family, and has spent most of his life abroad, often as a fugitive);
- striking a blow to the eye, or Achilles' heel, of his enemy (September 11).

There are other important factors that have served to exalt bin Laden's standing among Muslims. These emerge from the fact that bin Laden's assertions on behalf of Muslims and his criticism of Western actions, past and present, strike a chord with them, particularly the litany of injustices that Muslims have suffered throughout the twentieth century, especially the Palestinians and, more recently, the Iraqis.[41] Bin Laden has consistently emphasized the centrality of the Palestinian cause while expressing his anger with the 'American-Israeli alliance's' oppression and atrocities against our people'; he set out his feelings most clearly in 2004:[42]

> The events that made a direct impression on me were during and after 1982, when America allowed the Israelis to invade Lebanon ... I still remember those distressing scenes: blood, torn limbs, women and children massacred ... The whole world heard and saw what happened, but did nothing. In those critical moments, many ideas raged inside me, ideas difficult to describe, but they unleashed a powerful urge to reject injustice and a strong determination to punish the aggressors.

Messianic Symmetry of Bush and bin Laden

Observers have noted that the messianic rhetoric of Bush and bin Laden has some remarkable similarities as also some important differences. Bruce Lincoln, comparing President Bush's speech on 7 October 2001, announcing the commencement of military operations against the Taliban and Al-Qaeda in Afghanistan, and bin Laden's response a few hours later, which was carried on Al-Jazeera television, has pointed out that the two speeches share one common attribute: they both present a Manichaean struggle of good versus evil.[43] Thus, President Bush said:

Every nation has a choice to make. In this conflict there is no neutral ground. If any government sponsors the outlaws and killers of innocents, they have become outlaws and murderers themselves. And they will take that lonely path at their own peril ...;

while bin Laden said:

Tell them that *these events have divided the world into two camps*, the camp of the faithful and the camp of infidels. May God shield us and you from them. [Emphasis added.]

The words used by President Bush to describe the 'other' were: outlaws, murderers and killers, as also 'barbaric killers' and 'terrorists'. Bin Laden, on his part, used the word 'infidel', emphasizing the religious character of the offences of the 'other', so that, as Lincoln has noted, the events of 9/11 were 'nothing less than the visitation of divine vengeance on a sinful nation'.

In terms of claims to authority, President Bush invoked his official position as President and Commander-in-Chief, and set out his mission in the war as preserving peace, justice and freedom (the military mission in Afghanistan was called 'Operation Enduring Freedom'). The authority that bin Laden asserted was 'religious and charismatic', highlighting his 'faith' and his status as a 'holy warrior': thus, he spoke of 'the group that refuses to be subdued in its religion' and 'a group of vanguard Muslims, the forefront of Islam', whom 'God has blessed ... to destroy America'.

Given his position as the head of a secular state, President Bush made his presentation in 'ethico-political' and not religious terms, while bin Laden spoke entirely in terms of infidels *vs.* the faithful. However, Lincoln has noted that Bush evoked imagery that had Biblical allusions that would be readily understood by large sections of his audience. He noted two such references: 'the terrorists may burrow deeper into caves and other entrenched hiding places' and the enemies 'will take that lonely path at their own peril'. The former recalls Revelations where the climatic scene of the apocalypse is described thus:

Then the kings of the earth and the great men and the generals and the rich and the strong, and every one, slave and free, hid in the caves and among the rocks of the mountains, calling to the mountains and rocks, 'Fall on us and hide us from the face of him who is seated on the throne, and from the wrath of the Lamb; for the great day of their wrath has come, and who can stand before it?'

The second reference is from Job: 'Such are the paths of all who forget God; the hope of the godless man shall perish.' Lincoln describes these references as 'double coding', and points out that they 'acknowledge a serious cleavage within the American public and address those Americans who could be expected to reject the religious minimalism that otherwise characterizes his [the President's] text'.

Commentators have similarly compared other aspects of the Bush-bin Laden rhetoric and have located some interesting areas of convergence. Thus, soon after the 9/11 attacks, when Bush spoke of launching a 'crusade against the evil-doers', bin Laden felt fully vindicated:[44]

> So Bush has declared in his own words: 'Crusade attack'. The odd thing about this is that he has taken the words right out of our mouth (that this war is a crusade) ... when Bush speaks, people make apologies for him and they say that he didn't mean to say that this war is a crusade, even though he himself said that it was! . ..Bush's image today is of him being in the front of the line, yelling and carrying his big cross. And I swear by the God Almighty, that whoever walks behind Bush or his plan has rejected the teachings of Muhammad, and this ruling is one of the clearest rulings in the Book of God and the Hadith of his Prophet; and ... the proof for this Almighty's word while addressing the true believers: 'O you believe! Take not the Jews and the Christian as allies, they are but allies to one another. And if any amongst you take them as allies, then surely he is one of them'.

In his other speeches, President Bush had invoked religion more freely. Just as bin Laden seems to be supremely confident that Allah is on his side, Bush has expressed equal conviction that God is on his side. In the words of the President:[45]

> Embedded in every soul is the deep desire to live in freedom. I understand freedom is not America's gift to the world; freedom is Almighty God's gift to each men and women in this world ... May God bless the people of this great state. May God bless our troops. And may God bless the United States of America.

Louise Richardson is concerned that, in this regard, the US president is simply mirroring his adversary:[46]

> By using the extreme language of conviction that bin Laden uses, by declaring war, even a crusade, against him in response to his war against the US, Americans are mirroring his actions. They are elevating his stature,

they are permitting him to set terms of their interactions ... Moreover, by placing its troops in Afghanistan and Iraq the US is ensuring that there will be many other actions to be avenged, whether it is the killing of civilians in air strikes, the abuse of prisoners or the desecration of corpses in Afghanistan, or military operations and prisoner abuse in Iraq: those hurt by these actions are likely to swell the ranks of those seeking vengeance.

Conclusion

Contemporary Islamic messianism is inspired by the vision of pristine Islam which flourished during the Prophet's lifetime. Though mainstream Sunni Islam has tended to downplay messianism, its history reveals a robust tradition of the 'Mahdi' movements in response to contemporary crises. In recent times, the most dramatic and successful of these movements have been the Mahdiyya in Sudan in the late nineteenth century and the movement which took over the Haram Sharief in Makkah in 1979.

Though radical Islamic intellectuals have consistently rejected the messianic element in their writings, their aspirations for an Islamic Utopia and their own charismatic personalities have been in the messianic tradition. Again, in their ideological orientation, these writers have manifested many attributes of messianism such as belief in the unbridgeable gap between Muslim believers and others; the acceptance of violence without limits against apostates and unbelievers, and the exaltation of martyrdom.

The later part of the twentieth century has seen the emergence of a number of popular Muslim writers expressing powerful messianic visions based on the ultimate global triumph of Islam. This messianism is a response to the sense of Muslim defeat at the hands of the West and its sense of grievance and victimhood, with hostility to the US and Israel being at the centre of their discourse; the latter are vehemently demonized and their ultimate defeat at the hands of resurgent Islam is confidently predicted.

Though Osama bin Laden has never himself given any indication of messianic aspirations, his persona and pronouncements make it inevitable that he will be increasingly seen in messianic terms in both Islamic and Western popular literature. The mystique of his persona, his spartan lifestyle, his image as a fugitive fighting for Islamic interests, and, above all, his strong assertions on behalf of Muslim causes, all of these have exalted bin Laden's unique status in popular Islamic imagination and given him a special position in contemporary Islamic intellectual and populist discourse.

NOTES

1. Pnina Werbner, 'The Predicament of Diaspora and Millennial Islam: Reflections in the Aftermath of September 11', Social Science Research Council, February 2002; downloaded from: www.sstc.org/sept11/essays/werbner.htm.

2. Quoted in John O. Voll, 'Renewal and Reform in Islamic History: Tajdid and Islah', in John L. Esposito (Ed.), *Voices of Resurgent Islam* (New York: Oxford University Press), 1983) p. 34.

3. See Timothy R. Furnish, *Holiest Wars – Islamic Mahdis, Their Jihads, and Osama bin Laden,* (Westpost, Connecticut: Praeger, 2005) for a new detailed study of the Mahdi movements.

4. See Abbas Amanat, 'The Resurgence of Apocalyptic in Modern Islam', in Bernard J. McGinn et al (Ed.): *The Continuum History of Apocalypticism* (New York: Continuum, 2003).

5. Amanat, p. 596.

6. ibid., p. 597.

7. ibid.

8. David Cook, *Contemporary Muslim Apocalyptic Literature* (Syracuse, New York: Syracuse University Press, 2005) pp. 173–4.

9. Terry McDermott, *Perfect Soldiers – the 9/11 Hijackers: Who They Were, Why They Did It* (New York: Harper Paperback, 2006) p. 250.

10. ibid., p. 83.

11. Werbner; also see Thomas Hegghammer's review of Jean-Pierre Filiu's book, *L'Apocalypse dans l'Islam,* [in French] in *The National,* Abu Dhabi, 16 January 2009, p. 10, which gives a glimpse of the range and content of contemporary Islamic apocalyptic writing.

12. Werbner, p. 10

13. David Cook, 'America, The Second Ad: Prophecies About the Downfall of the United States', Centre for Millennial Studies, Boston University, undated; downloaded from: www.bu.edu/mille/scholarship/papers/adam.htm.

14. ibid., pp. 18–21.

15. ibid., p. 29.

16. ibid., p. 30.

17. ibid., p. 152; Amanat, p. 602.

18. ibid., p. 160.

19. ibid., p. 164.

20. ibid., p. 129.
21. ibid., p 188.
22. ibid., pp. 193–4.
23. Furnish, p. 106.
24. Cook, pp. 48–9.
25. ibid., pp. 89–90.
26. Robert A. Pape, *Dying to Win – Why Suicide Terrorists Do it* (London: Gibson Square Books, 2006) p. 119.
27. ibid., p. 120.
28. ibid., p. 121.
29. ibid.
30. Pape, p. 122.
31. ibid., p. 124.
32. Natana J. Delong-Bas, *Wahhabi Islam – From Revival and Reform to Global Jihad* (New York: Oxford University Press, 2004) p. 278.
33. ibid.
34. Richard Landes, 'Apocalyptic Islam and Bin Laden', Centre for Millennial Studies, Boston University, undated; downloaded from: http://www.bu.edu/mille/people/rlpages/Bin_Laden.html
35. Cook, p. 182.
36. Furnish, p. 153.
37. ibid., p. 154.
38. ibid., p. 156.
39. Quoted in Malise Ruthven, 'The Rise of the Muslim Terrorists', *New York Review of Books,* Vol. LV, No. 9, 29 May 2008, p. 33.
40. Max Rodenbeck, 'The Master's Voice', *New York Review of Books,* Vol. LIII, No. 4, 9 March 2006, p. 8.
41. ibid.
42. ibid.
43. Bruce Lincoln, 'Symmetric Dualisms: Bush and bin Laden on 7 October 2001', Chapter Two of the book, *Holy Terrors: Thinking About Religion After September 11,* University of Chicago, 2003; downloaded from: http://www.isn.ethz.ch/pubs/ph/details.cfm?Ing=en&q51= Symmetric+Dualism&id=46625
44. Meghnad Desai, *Rethinking Islamism: The Ideology of the New Terror* (London: I.B. Tauris, 2007) p. 117.
45. Louise Richardson, *What Terrorists Want – Understanding the Terrorist Threat* (London: John Murray, 2006) p. 239.
46. ibid., pp. 239–40.

11

Children of Abraham at War

The blood of Abraham, God's father of the chosen, still flows in the veins of Arab, Jew, and Christian, and too much of it has been spilled in grasping for the inheritance of the revered patriarch in the Middle East. The spilled blood in the Holy Land still cries out to God – an anguished cry for peace.

Jimmy Carter, *The Blood of Abraham*

The three Semitic traditions share a strong legacy of messianism that has been central to their faith, and a sustained force and abiding influence through the course of their history. While this messianic tradition promised redemption to the believers, it also had the effect of separating believers from the demonized 'other', the 'other' being not just communities within the mainstream religion, but, more frequently, adherents of the other two Semitic faiths. Hence, messianism, while giving comfort and solace to believers, has ensured that the history of inter-faith relations is replete with animosity, conflict and war. This is not surprising since, while the three faiths originated with a common ancestor, Prophet Abraham, and shared broad beliefs and faith, in a number of important areas they parted company, commencing with the central point that the adherents of one faith refused to accept that a later tradition was part of a natural continuum of revelation from the same one true God. Thus, the Jews refused to accept Jesus Christ as the promised messiah, just as both the Jews and the Christians rejected the prophet-hood of Mohammed.

The cleavage between the three faiths evolved from doctrinal differences to a divide that was comprehensive and embraced all aspects of human life–political, economic, social and cultural. Will Durant has noted that the Jews' rejection of Jesus gave rise to 'a thousand suspicions and animosities'.[1] Thus, economic rivalries manifested themselves in all-embracing hatred, so that religious differences and economic competition led to so sharp a divide that 'everything Jewish became distasteful to some Christians and everything Christian to some Jews'.[2] In time, everything about the 'other' came to be seen as obnoxious and unacceptable. Durant has put this most succinctly:[3]

> The Christian reproached the Jew for clannish exclusiveness, and did not excuse it as a reaction to discrimination and occasional physical assault. Jewish features, language, manners, diet, ritual all seemed to the Christian eye offensively bizarre ... Jews were not allowed by their Law to eat food cooked, to drink wine pressed, or to use dishes or utensils that had been touched, by a non-Jew, or to marry any but a Jew; the Christian interpreted these ancient laws – formulated long before Christianity – as meaning that to a Jew everything Christian was unclean; and he retorted that the Israelite himself was not usually distinguished by cleanliness of person or neatness of dress.

Such prejudices led to extraordinarily absurd impressions of the 'other' based primarily on ignorance of the faith and beliefs of the other community. Thus, Jews were accused by Christians of sacrificing Christian children to their God or using the children's blood as medicine or at the Passover. Jews were accused of poisoning the wells of Christians and of defiling the wafers used in the Catholic Mass. Jewish success and prosperity were resented, so that the successful Jew came to be caricatured as the usurious moneylender.[4]

While the Christian Church often made a valiant effort to prevent violence against Jews, the lower clergy were less careful. Again, all too frequently, the Christian Councils issued directives that were derogatory to the Jewish community. The most demeaning of these was the injunction of the Fourth Council of the Lateran which directed, in 1215, that Jews and Saracens of both sexes shall be marked off in the eyes of the public from other people through the character of their dress. This decree was implemented with greater or less rigour across West Europe, and, in several places, was done away with formally only after the French Revolution.[5]

With the Crusades, the demonization of the Jews and violence upon them became institutionalized and continued up to the twentieth century in the shape of pogroms in which entire Jewish communities in different towns were annihilated, compelling communities in West Europe to move eastwards. Durant has conceded that, between such pogroms, there were long periods of peace, but, as he points out:[6]

> ... their [Jews'] traditions carried down the bitter memory of those tragic interludes. The days of peace were made anxious by the ever-present danger of pogroms; and every Jew had to learn by heart the prayer to be recited in the moment of martyrdom.

In traditional Christian demonology, the Jews were seen as endowed with 'uncanny sinister powers' and were identified regularly as the Antichrist.[7] In the medieval period, a recurring aspect of Christian demonology was the suggestion that the Jews worshipped the devil who empowered them with black magic which gave them 'limitless power for evil'.[8] The long tradition of Jewish otherness led to the definition of Jews as alien people; as Cohn puts it:[9]

> In the eyes of most Christians these strange creatures were demons in human form - and some of the demonology that was woven around them in those centuries has proved extraordinarily durable.

With the French Revolution, the role of the divine in messianic belief and expression was replaced by a secular ideal. However, the demonization of the Jewish community even in secular traditions continued, reaching its apogee in the 'final solution' of Nazi Germany. Cohn refers to the drive to exterminate Jews as a 'quasi-religious world view' based on the conviction that the Jews in different parts of the world were part of and constituted a conspiratorial body seeking to dominate all of mankind.[10] Jews could be conveniently made scapegoats by a post-First World War German community that was in a state of acute insecurity, stress and humiliation. Cohn has described this most powerfully: [11]

> The humiliation of defeat and the sufferings that followed it [World War I], the mortification felt over the peace treaties of Versailles and St. Germain, the utter disorientation and widespread financial ruin which accompanied the collapse of the currency – these things produced an entirely new atmosphere. Moreover both Germany and Austria had lost the national minorities on which, formerly, nationalist arrogance and rancour had vented itself; while Germany seemed in addition to have lost any prospect of imperialist expansion. All this gave added appeal to the fantasy of an age-old, mortal struggle between the German and Jewish "races".

German xenophobia drew upon the 2,000-year Christian tradition of demonizing the Jew by projecting him with an inherent will to evil, which could only be effectively responded to with the physical extermination of the entire community. Even this was not enough; Hitler pointed out in an early letter of September 1919 that:[12]

> It is not, he [Hitler] protests, enough to dislike Jews; Germans must realize that Jewry forms a racial entity with very strongly marked racial characteristics, of which the passion for material gain is the most dominant. This is what makes Jewry 'the racial tuberculosis of the peoples'. Mere pogroms are inadequate to cope with such a dangerous foe – 'there must be a rebirth of the moral and spiritual forces of the nation' through 'the ruthless effort of born leaders with a nationalist outlook and an inner sense of responsibility'. A government formed of such men will restrict the legal rights of the Jews, but it will not stop there: its ultimate aim must be 'the removal (*Entfernung*) of the Jews altogether'.

Briefly pausing at this point in the narrative of Jewish-Christian animosity, let us take a look at the ties of the third point of the Semitic triangle – Islam – with its two Abrahamic predecessors.

Muslim Ties with Jews and Christians

The success of Islamic arms in the early decades of the new religion brought substantial Jewish and Christian communities under its rule. Though the two communities were generally treated as 'second class' citizens, they enjoyed a higher status as compared to other subjugated communities since they were seen as 'people of the book'. Generally, under Muslim rule, Jews fared far better than they did under Christian rule. Thus, in the early years of Islam, Jewish communities flourished in Syria, Iraq and Persia in an environment of 'economic prosperity, religious freedom and lively debate'.[13] Jewish scholars generally wrote in Arabic and, being familiar with theological debates within Islam, often utilized similar methods of exposition and argument.

The Jewish communities followed the success of the Muslim arms and spread across Asia, Egypt and North Africa and Europe. During Muslim rule in Spain, the Jews inaugurated, between the tenth and the twelfth centuries, a golden age of Jewish learning and refinement.

Muslim interaction with Christianity has been more complex. The attitude of many Christians in the Arab world was informed by the early biblical references to Ishmael in which he was described as: 'A wild man, his hand against every man's and every man's hand against his; and he shall live at odds with all his kinsmen'.[14] Isidor of Seville, a contemporary of Prophet Mohammed, described the early Muslims thus:[15]

> The Saracens live in the desert. They are also called the Ishmaelites, as the book of Genesis teaches, because they are descended from Ishmael [son of Abraham]. They are also called Hagarenes because they are descended from Hagar [Abraham's slave concubine, mother of Ishmael]. They also, as we have already said, perversely call themselves Saracens because they mendaciously boast of descent from Sarah [Abraham's legitimate wife].

The above negative responses were balanced by other biblical references of a more positive character. Thus, in Genesis it was stated:[16]

> But God said to Abraham: ... I will make a nation of the son of the slave woman [Hagar] also, because he is your offspring [Genesis 21:12-13]

Again, in the same chapter, further assurance was provided: 'I will make him [Ishmael] a great nation'.[17] Later, in Chapter 25 of Genesis, where the descendants of Abraham were detailed, the sons of Ishmael preceded those of Isaac; they were described as twelve in number which conveyed that, like the twelve tribes of Israel, they too were a sacred unit.[18]

Thus, at least some Christians viewed the early successes of Islam as being in line with biblical prediction. An Armenian bishop, writing a few years after Prophet Mohammed's death, said that God would realize in them [Muslims] the promise he had made to Abraham and his successor and it was for this reason that the sons of Ishmael were moving out of the desert towards Jerusalem.[19] On similar lines, a Nestorian monk living in Iraq wrote in the 670s that the sons of Ishmael had been militarily successful since they were following in the footsteps of Abraham.[20]

As the Islamic conquest expanded, this accommodative Christian tone was gradually replaced by concerns that this new community was emerging as a challenge to the Christian people. This led to the view that Muslim successes were a 'judgment of God' upon Romans as punishment for their godlessness and cruelty to Christians. The twelfth-century writer, Michael the Syrian, said:[21]

> The God of vengeance ... raised up from the south the children of Ishmael to deliver us from the hands of the Romans ... It was no light benefit for us to be freed from the cruelty of the Romans, their wickedness, anger and ardent cruelty towards us, and to find ourselves in peace.

As the Muslim armies made inroads into the Byzantium Empire and conquered Jerusalem and other cities holy to the Christians, a certain stability in the relationship between Muslims and Christians emerged, where Christians, while enjoying only second class status, were permitted to worship freely on payment of a special tax (*jizya*).

The principles relating to Muslim-Christian relations were enshrined in the 'Covenant of Omar' which put together comprehensively the agreements between the Muslims and the conquered Christian population. While affirming their second-class status, the Christians and the Jews were seen as 'people of the book' and, in due course, came to be referred to as 'People of the Covenant' or *dhimmis*.[22]

Relations between the Muslims and the Byzantium Empire were marked by substantial cultural and intellectual exchanges. The first mosque in Constantinople was set up during the reign of Pope Leo III (717–41). Byzantium craftsmen sent by the Emperor decorated the Great Mosque in Damascus and the Prophet's Mosque in Madina. There are reports that the Emperor also provided columns for the mosque in Makkah.[23]

In spite of these positive exchanges, harsh criticisms emerged on both sides from which certain stereotypes of the religion and the Prophet emerged which resonate to this day.[24] Mohammed was described as a man of blood, a false prophet, and, while it was acknowledged that Islam shared many beliefs with Christianity in that it venerated the early biblical prophets, Jesus Christ and Virgin Mary, Muslims were despised on doctrinal as well as political grounds:[25]

> They [Muslims] denied the Trinity, the Incarnation and the Resurrection; their holy book was a parody of sacred scripture; they exalted a pseudo-prophet; they made war on the Christians; and they had seized their Holy Places.

These negative views were balanced by other observers who saw in monotheism a common point between Islam and Christianity.[26] Thus, in Byzantium, there were two broad trends in regard to attitude to Islam, one hostile and one accommodative. Overall, as Goddard has noted:[27]

> By medieval standards, the Muslim tretment of Jews and Christians was relatively tolerant and liberal, though it was clearly, by modern standards, still discriminatory to some extent. Comparisons can only fairly be made

with other medieval societies, and on this basis the Muslim world scores extremely well.

During the medieval period, there was much commercial and intellectual interaction between Muslims and Christians but the negative image of the religion and the people endured. The Slovenian scholar, Tomaz Mastnak, has in fact argued that Europe, as a political and civilizational concept, took shape on the basis of anti-Muslim sentiments: he believes that animosity toward the Muslims lies at the core of the historical constitution of Europe and the creation of European identity.[28] While anti-Muslim feelings were widely prevalent from the 8th century as a result of successful Muslim assaults into hitherto Christian territories, the Crusades from the eleventh century onwards contributed to defining Christendom and later Europe on the basis of constructing the Muslim as the enemy. Thus, Pope Urban II, whose speech at the Clermont Council in 1095 initiated the holy war, is reported to have made the following remarks at the Council:[29]

> Oh what a disgrace if a race so despicable, degenerate, and enslaved by demons should thus overcome a people endowed with faith in Almighty God and resplendent in the name of Christ! Oh what reproaches will be charged against you by the Lord Himself if you have not helped those who are counted like yourself of the Christian faith! Let those who are accustomed to wantonly wage private war against the faithful march upon the infidels in a war which should be begun now and be finished in victory. Let those who have long been robbers now be soldiers of Christ. Let those who have once fought against brothers and relatives now rightfully fight against barbarians.

As a result of the Crusades, the Muslim emerged as 'The fundamental enemy of Christianity', even as the Crusades initiated the molding of the Christians into a community and, in time, into a 'self-consciousness collectivity'.[30]

There were some exceptions to this generally negative view of Islam and Muslims. An important contribution on the positive side was that of Abbot Peter the Venerable (c. 1092–1156). While Peter did see Islam as a Christian heresy and part of a satanic scheme to harm the Christian church, he sought to approach Muslims 'not by force but by reason; not in hatred but in love'.[31] While rejecting the Koran and the prophethood of Mohammed, Peter saw several similarities between the two religions and thus attempted to moderate some of the extreme views prevalent in his time that were abusive of Islam and its prophet. While the dominant view of Islam remained negative and indeed venomous, Peter the Venerable provided an alternative moderate view that continued to have some influence in later centuries.

Throughout the medieval period, the principal role played by Muslims was to preserve the earlier knowledge of the Greeks and Romans, build on it in their own empires, and then slowly transmit this knowledge to the Western world. Goddard has noted that at the commencement of the last millennium: 'Europe was backward intellectually, politically weak and divided, and socially and economically primitive compared with the Muslim world'.[32] This situation began to change as Muslims transmitted new knowledge to the Western world. This knowledge included philosophy, science, astronomy, geography, mathematics, physics and politics. Under Islamic influence, universities came to be set up in principal European cities. All these developments taken together prepared the ground for an intellectual renaissance in the West which commenced in Spain and then spread to other parts of West Europe.[33] However, in spite of this positive impact, the inherent hostility between the two religious groups did not abate.

Mastnak has cited numerous sources affirming the enduring animosity for Muslims among Christians in geographical Europe, defining the Muslim—usually represented by the symbolic figure of the 'Turk'— as the evil 'other' of Europe which embodied the 'sense of us-ness'.[34] Over four centuries after the first announcement of the Crusades, the definition of Europe as 'the homeland, fatherland and native soil' of Christians came to be firmly established, alongside demands from European intellectuals and political and religious leaders to 'exterminate the Turks in Europe', 'erase the Turkish name from Europe' or 'chase the Turk out of Europe'. This was to be achieved through a persistent war against the infidel so that the concept of a 'permanent crusade' against the Muslim was kept in place.[35] The views of the great European intellectual and humanist Erasmus (1466–1536) are typical of the thinking of the time; as Mastnak has pointed out:[36]

> ... the Turks were barbarians, argued Erasmus. He called them monstrous beasts, enemies of the Church, a people contaminated with all kinds of crime and ignominies. Muhammad was to him a criminal. Arguably, Erasmus needed these 'barbarians' in order to see himself as European. For it was only in opposition to the Turks, only when facing the 'Turkish peril', that Erasmus considered himself European.

The British intellectual and statesman Thomas More [1478–1535] echoed these views:[37]

> He [More] considered the Turks a 'shameful, superstitious sect,' the 'abominable sect' of Christ's 'professed' 'moral enemies,' representing forces of darkness and Belial.

The Protestant reformer Martin Luther [1483–1546] articulated the same animosity for Islam and Muslims as that of other contemporary Christians. According to him:[38]

> Both Mohammed and the 'Turkish emperor' were possessed by the devil, and their armies were the devil's own. The Turks' faith was scandalous, absurd, and filthy. The Quran was a foul, shameful, and abominable book that distorted Christianity even while it praised Jesus and Mary. It taught a disorderly doctrine of worldly government as well and commanded the Turks to plunder and murder, to devour and destroy, even further, everything around them ... *Mahmet,* the Prophet, was a son of the devil and the devil's apostle. The distinction between him and the pope was that *Mahmet* was the 'rude devil' (*grobe Teuffel*) whereas the pope was the 'subtle devil.' The *Mahmetisten* who professed the lies of the Quran did not deserve to be called human.

The great French intellectual who heralded the Enlightenment in Europe, Voltaire [1694–1778], continued Christian prejudice and hatred of the Muslims into the eighteenth century:[39]

> Voltaire, like many lesser but not necessarily less enlightened contemporaries, desired to annihilate the Turks. He held them, together with the plague, to be the greatest curse on earth. 'It does not suffice to humiliate them,' he said, 'they should be destroyed.' As his personal correspondence shows, he deeply regretted that 'the Christian powers, instead of destroying the common enemy, are busy ruining each other ...'
>
> Voltaire himself confided to the Czarina, his Semiramis of the North: 'Overcome the Turks, and I will die content.' He seems to have felt that his life was not really fulfilled, and that there was more he could have done: 'I wish I had at least been able to help you kill a few Turks.'

Orientalism and Islam

With the commencement of the nineteenth century, European powers began their colonial inroads into the Islamic world. Accompanying these military and political successes was the development of what Edward Said has referred to as the 'Orientalist' discourse which, in time, came to inform all aspects of European/Western approach to Islam and the Muslim people. This discourse consisted of a comprehensive view of the Orient as the 'contrasting image, idea, personality, experience' of the West.[40] This view constructed the Orient in terms that were racist, imperialist and ethnocentric, while focusing on its 'sensuality, its tendency to despotism, its aberrant mentality, its habits of inaccuracy, its backwardness'[41] as the essential, immutable and eternal characteristics of the East, which was viewed as unchanging, uniform and radically peculiar.[42]

In this discourse, Islam and the Muslim people were marked out for special venom, primarily because Islam had historically constituted the 'other' for the West and had been a source of 'lasting trauma' for the Christian world from the eigth century; even over the previous 200 years, it had refused to be entirely subdued by the West. Thus, on the eve of colonial subjugation, the Muslim lands had remained an 'unresolved challenge' on the political, intellectual and, for a time, economic levels.[43] The Orientalist view of Islam drew upon a thousand years of negative imagery which was robustly inflated and strengthened during the colonial period. Thus, in line with earlier Christian tradition, in the Orientalist discourse, given shape alongside colonial conquest, Prophet Mohammed continued to be viewed:[44]

> as the disseminator of a false Revelation, he became as well the epitome of lechery, debauchery, sodomy, and a whole battery of assorted treacheries, all of which derived 'logically' from his doctrinal impostures.

Flowing from this, both in scholarly work and in popular literature, the Muslim continued to be caricatured and demonized. Thus, the great scholar of Islam, William Muir (1820–83) said: 'The sword of Muhammed, and the Koran, are the most stubborn enemies of Civilisation, Liberty, and the Truth which the world has yet known.'[45] The French scholar Chateaubriand (1768–1848), after a visit to Jerusalem and other parts of the Arab world, spoke thus about the encounter between Christianity and Islam during the Crusade:[46]

> The Crusades were not only about the deliverance of the Holy Sepulchre, but more about knowing which would win on the earth, a cult that was civilization's enemy, systematically favourable to ignorance, to despotism, to slavery [that is, Islam], or a cult that had caused to reawaken in modern people the genius of a sage antiquity, and had abolished base servitude [that is, Christianity]?

This Orientalist discourse gained its resonance not just from the innate sense of superiority of Western authors and travelers but also from the fact that, in their writings, they enhanced their authority by citing each others' work. The British clergyman, Thomas Patrick Hughes (1838–1911), in his *Dictionary of Islam* (published in 1885) expressed 'his deep obligations "to Sir William Muir's the *Life of Mohamad*"' as also other British, French and German orientalist activists of his time. He asserted in the preface of his *Dictionary* that his work 'is not intended to be a controversial attack on the religious system of Muhammad, but rather an exposition of its principles and teachings'.[47] However, while discussing the Prophet, he could not restrain himself, and let loose the following verbiage on the founder of Islam:[48]

> ... in the case of Muhammad, his professed inspiration sanctioned and encouraged his own vices. That which ought to have been the fountain of purity was, in fact, the cover of the Prophet's depravity.
>
> The creed of Muhammad ... claims to supersede that of the Lord Jesus. And it is here that we take our stand. We give Muhammad credit as a warrior, as a legislator, as a poet, as a man of uncommon genius raising himself amidst great opposition to the pinnacle of renown; we admit that he is, without doubt, one of the greatest heroes the world has ever seen; but when we consider his claims to *supersede* the mission of the divine Jesus, we strip him of his borrowed plumes, and reduce him to the condition of an imposter!

True to his calling, he contrasted Prophet Mohammed with the sublime character of Jesus Christ:[49]

> - and whilst we wonder at the genius of the hero [Muhammad], we pause at every stage and inquire, 'Is this the Apostle of God, whose mission is to claim universal dominion, to the suppression not merely of idolatry, but of Christianity itself?' Then it is that the divine and holy character of Jesus rises to our view, and the inquiring mind sickens at the thought of the beloved, the pure, the lowly Jesus giving place to that of the ambitious, the sensual, and the *time-serving* hero of Arabia.

The comparison could not but be one-sided:[50]

> We are not insensible to the beauties of the Quran as a literary production (although they have, without doubt, been overrated); but as we admire its conceptions of the Divine nature, its deep and fervent trust in the power of God, its frequent deep moral earnestness, and its sententious wisdom, we would gladly rid ourselves of our recollections of the Prophet, his

licentious harim, his sanguinary battle-fields, his ambitious schemes; whilst as we peruse the Christian Scriptures, we find the grand central charm in the divine character of its Founder. It is the divine character of Jesus which gives fragrance to His words; it is the divine form of Jesus which shines through all He says or does; it is the divine life of Jesus which is the great central point in Gospel history.

An interesting feature of these early Orientalist writings on Muslims and Islam is that several writers failed to distinguish between Jews and Arabs, and referred to them collectively as 'Semites'. Thus, the great scholar, Ernst Renan [1823–92], had this to say about the Semitic race:[51]

> One sees that in all things the Semitic race appears to us to be an incomplete race, by virtue of its simplicity. This race – if I dare use the analogy – is to the Indo-European family what a pencil sketch is to painting; it lacks that variety, that amplitude, that abundance of life which is the condition of perfectibility. Like those individuals who possess so little fecundity that, after a gracious childhood, they attain only the most mediocre virility, the Semitic nations experienced their fullest flowering in their first age and have never been able to achieve true maturity.

Martin Kramer has pointed out that non-Jewish European scholars of the day first brought the Jews and Muslims together 'under this Semitic rubric—benignly, as speakers of cognate languages, Hebrew and Arabic; condescendingly, as peoples limited in their cultural development and mental processes by the languages of their expression; and, ominously, as members of an inferior racial category'. However, he goes on to clarify that, as in the case of Renan quoted above, some of them did distinguish the Jews in Europe from those in the East; he quotes the German philologist Theodor Noldeke (1839–1930) as saying:[52]

> In drawing the character of the Semites, the historian must guard against taking the Jews of Europe as pure representatives of the race. These have maintained many features of their primitive type with remarkable tenacity, but they have become Europeans all the same; and, moreover, many peculiarities by which they are marked are not so much of old Semitic origin as the result of the special history of the Jews, and in particular of continued oppression, and of that long isolation from other peoples, which was partly their own choice and partly imposed on them.

In almost all their writings, British and European Orientalist scholars, who were recognized as authorities on the Eastern peoples and their cultures, spoke glibly about 'Islam', the 'Muslim' and the Arab mind and character, depicting them in essentialized, unchanging terms. Thus, the magisterial Lord Cromer (1841–1917), on the basis of his experience of Arabs in Egypt, had this to say about the Oriental: [53]

> Want of accuracy, which easily degenerates into untruthfulness, is in fact the main characteristic of the Oriental mind ...
>
> The mind of the Oriental ... like his picturesque streets, is eminently wanting in symmetry. His reasoning is of the most slipshod description. Although the ancient Arabs acquired in a somewhat higher degree the science of dialectics, their descendants are singularly deficient in the logical faculty. They are often incapable of drawing the most obvious conclusions from any simple premises of which they may admit the truth...
>
> I content myself with noting the fact that somehow or other the Oriental generally acts, speaks, and thinks in a manner exactly opposite to the European.

Even as recently as 1945, the British authority on Islam and the Arabs, H.A.R. Gibb (1895–1971), noted: [54]

> The Arab mind, whether in relation to the outer world or in relation to the processes of thought, cannot throw off its intense feeling for the separateness and the individuality of the concrete events. This is, I believe, one of the main factors lying behind that 'lack of a sense of law' which Professor Macdonald regarded as the characteristic difference in the Oriental.
>
> It is this, too, which explains – what is so difficult for the Western student to grasp [until it is explained to him by the Orientalist] – the aversion of the Muslims from the thought-processes of rationalism ...

In contrast to 'orientalist' writings by Western (Christian) writers on Islam and the Muslim people, in the nineteenth century there was a powerful tradition in Europe where Jewish scholars made significant contributions to Islamic studies. Sadly, by mid-twentieth century, their pioneering role was slowly erased from public memory. It was brought to public attention for the first time in a systematic manner with the publication in 1999 of *Jewish Discovery of Islam*. Martin Kramer, in his Introduction to the book, pointed out that the approach of Europe's Jewish scholars: [55]

> ... rested upon a heightened empathy and sympathy for Islam, conveyed to the rest of Europe through literature, exploration, and scholarship. And the common rationale, reduced to a sentence, was this: a Europe respectful of Islam and Muslims was more likely to show respect for Judaism and Jews.

Thus, he pointed out, the Jewish scholars highlighted the splendour of Islam in an effort to remind Christian European of the origins of its own civilization and the significant place of Judaism and Islam with it. In this regard, they made:[56]

> A deliberate effort to associate Jews with those periods, places, and elements in Islamic civilization most admired by Europe. The message was straightforward: Jews had helped to bring the civilization of medieval Islam to its apex. Given the chance, they could do the same for the civilization of modern Europe. This interpretation of Islam, emphasizing its achievements and tolerance, had nothing in common with 'Orientalism' as ideology. Its purpose was to facilitate Europe's assimilation of Jews.

Among the great Jewish scholars was Abraham Geiger (1810–74), who, in his study of Islam, showed deep respect for the religion and its prophet and specifically criticized as unjustifiable the harsh judgment traditionally inflicted upon him by European scholars. He contrasted the experience of Jews under Muslims and Christians and pointed out that, while Islam had pursued the study of science and philosophy, the Christian church had nourished repugnance for them.[57]

Another great scholar of Islam was Ignaz Goldziher (1850–1921), who recognized the importance of Islam's oral tradition, the 'Hadith', as a window on early Islam. Scholars have pointed out that Goldziher was supported in his views by his own Jewish identity; as Kramer has said:[58]

> His understanding of Islam was mediated by his intimate familiarity with another religion of law, in constant tension with actual practice, and formulated in a Semitic language: Judaism.

In fact, at one place, Goldziher appeared to elevate Islam above Judaism when he said that Islam had originated as a 'Judaized Meccan cult' but had evolved into 'the only religion which, even in its doctrinal and official formulation, can satisfy philosophical minds. My ideal was to elevate Judaism to a similar rational level'.[59] He worked for a reformed Judaism so that it could attain Islam's degree of rationality without sacrificing its spirituality. Another prominent German Jewish scholar was Franz Rosenthal (1914–2003), who specialized in early and classical Muslim scholarship and historiography.[60]

Kramer has made this general observation about the contribution of European Jewish scholars to Islamic studies:[61]

These (and other) German-Jewish scholars viewed the study of Islam as the perfect point of intersection of classical and Jewish studies. They were drawn to 'golden ages' and those achievements of Islamic civilization that had universal significance, and which demonstrated Islam's tolerance of difference. They worked from the assumption that Islam arose in part upon Jewish foundations, and emphasized that it had provided the civilizational framework for a period of Jewish achievement since paralleled only by the present age. They also were fascinated by the role of this Judeo-Islamic civilization in the preservation and transmission of Greek philosophy and science.

This glorious tradition of Islamic scholarship among Jewish academics was brought to an end by the twin developments of Nazi anti-Semitism (and the Holocaust) and the Zionist project. Even as the Arabs increasingly turned to anti-Semitism in their opposition to Zionism, European Jews too turned their back on Islam and the Muslims, seeing them as having favoured a German victory. In this regard, the intellectual career of Bernard Lewis is instructive. As William Dalrymple has pointed out, Lewis' early enthusiasm for Islam from the late 1950s steadily gave way 'to an increasingly negative, disillusioned and occasionally contemptuous tone', so that, by the 1990s, he was already speaking of an inherent struggle between Islam and Judeo-Christian civilization.[62] At the beginning of this century, Lewis had become deeply entrenched in the neocon movement and was an influential anti-Arab force in the Bush White House. The nineteenth-century sympathetic European Jewish scholarship of Islam and Muslims was over, and the traditional Orientalist approach of animosity and contempt came to be affirmed as the principal (if not the only) Jewish and Christian view of Islam.

Contemporary Jewish-Christian Relations

We left the narrative of Jewish-Christian ties with the idea of the 'final solution' advocated by Hitler whose views were in line with the strong tradition of anti-Jewish racism prevalent in Europe in the nineteenth century. However, after the Second World War, which had witnessed the robust implementation of the Nazi 'final solution' doctrine in the shape of the anti-Jewish holocaust, the emergence of the State of Israel in 1948 effected a fundamental change in the way of Western countries and their scholars regarded the Semitic people. There was now a bifurcation in their view: the Jew migrating from Europe to Palestine was depicted as a hero and an adventurer—pioneer, similar to earlier

Orientalist travellers (such as Sir Richard Burton, Ernst Renan and Edward William Lane).[63] This view culminated in the concept of the 'Judeo-Christian civilization' which is now accepted as the core cultural norm of the West, particularly in the United States. This concept at once nullifies nearly 2,000 years of Christian–Jewish animosity, when the Jew was demonized as the satanic 'Other' and subjected to pogroms and other severe disabilities, restraints and humiliations, and in its place suggests that Judaism and Christianity share common values and beliefs which constitute the foundation of Western civilization.

On the part of the European Jews who originated and gave shape to the Zionist project, there was never any doubt that Israel was strongly affiliated with mainstream Western civilization. Theodor Herzl, the founder of Zionism, had stated in 1895:[64]

> Palestine is our ever-memorable historic home. ... *We should there form a portion of the rampart of Europe against Asia*, an outpost of civilization as opposed to barbarism ... There is a special pain in seeing some of my fellow Western liberals hostile to an ideal and a country I admire. [Emphasis added.]

Several decades later, the Jewish Nobel Laureate (1979, for Physics), Steven Weinberge, echoed the same view:[65]

> Zionism also represents the intrusion – by purchase and settlement rather than conquest, at least until Arab assaults made military action necessary – of a democratic, scientifically sophisticated, secular culture into a part of the world that for centuries has been despotic, technically backward, and obsessed with religion. *For me, it is this essentially Western character of Zionism that gives it an attraction beyond its defensive role.* [Emphasis added.]

In the USA, the term 'Judeo–Christian' emerged in the early part of the twentieth century in response to pervasive anti-Semitism in Europe and the US. It was first used publicly by a prominent American political leader in 1952 when President-elect Eisenhower described the Judeo–Christian concept as being the 'deeply religious faith (on which) our sense of government is founded'.[66] Later, in 1957, former President Truman said before the Zionist Organization of America:[67]

> Here was a country [Israel] founded on the love of human freedom, just as our own country was based on the ideal of freedom. Here, was a country designed to be a haven for the oppressed and persecuted of the earth, just as our own country had been. Here in the land of Moses and the prophets, was a rebirth of a nation dedicated, as of old, to the moral law and to

belief in God ... I believe it has a glorious future before it ... as an embodiment of the great ideals of our civilization.

In recent times, the Jewish–American scholar, Dennis Prager, has been most articulate in promoting the idea of 'Judeo–Christian' values. He sees the contemporary world as witnessing competitions between three rival concepts: European secularism, American Judeo–Christianity and Islam. In support of the Judeo–Christian concept, he has presented the following argument:[68]

> Until the 20th century, European Christianity, as embodied in the church, de-emphasised its Jewish roots, and it usually persecuted Jews (though never ordered, indeed opposed, their physical annihilation – annihilation required a secular ideology, Nazism). No Christian state referred to itself as 'Judeo-Christian.' That identity arose with the Christians of America, who from the outset were at least as deeply immersed in the Old Testament as in the New.
>
> Rather than see themselves as superseding Jews, American Christians identified with them ...
>
> Of course, most Protestant Christians who hold Judeo–Christian values continue to believe that there is no salvation outside of faith in Christ. But precisely because they do hold Judeo-Christian values, they work hand in hand with others whose faith they deem insufficient or incorrect (for example, Jews and Mormons). So while they theologically reject other faiths, *evangelical Christians are the single strongest advocates of Judeo-Christian values.* They are what can be called 'Judeo–Christian.'
>
> But while the Jews provided the text, the Christians brought the text and its values into the world at large and applied them to a society composed of Jews, Christians, atheists, and members of other religions.
>
> *Those Judeo–Christian values have made America the greatest experiment in human progress and liberty and the greatest force for good in history.*
> [Emphasis added.]

The 'Judeo–Christian' concept does have commentators who criticize it on religious and political grounds. Some Jewish critics believe this concept suggests that Christianity is the more evolved form of Judaism, while others have pointed out that it blurs important differences between the two religions. Thus, the Jewish scholar Stephen Feldman is deeply troubled by the hyphenation of the two Semitic traditions:[69]

> Once one recognizes that Christianity has historically engendered anti-Semitism, then this so-called [Judeo–Christian] tradition appears as a

dangerous Christian dogma (at least from a Jewish perspective). For Christians, the concept of a Judeo-Christian tradition comfortably suggests that Judaism progresses into Christianity—that Judaism is somehow completed in Christianity. The concept of a Judeo-Christian tradition flows from the Christian theology of supersession, whereby the Christian covenant (or Testament) with God supersedes the Jewish one. Christianity, according to this myth, reforms and replaces Judaism. The myth therefore implies, first, that Judaism needs reformation and replacement, and second, that modern Judaism remains merely as a 'relic'. Most importantly the myth of the Judeo-Christian tradition insidiously obscures the real and significant differences between Judaism and Christianity.

More seriously, critics believe that the concept is accepted most devoutly by conservative Christians, who ally themselves with conservative Jews, thus excluding the views of liberal Jews who disagree with the various positions of the Christian Right. Thus, Rabbi Gershon Winkler has said:[70]

> Judeo–Christian is purely a Christian myth ... The terms 'Judeo–Christian tradition' and 'Judeo-Christian morality' are wrong and misleading. They are a slap in the face for all the great teachers throughout history, whose responses to today's moral questions would in no way resemble those of the Vatican or the Christian Right, and whose attitude towards sin, physical pleasure, human dignity, and the earth differ vastly from those of Christianity.

Another Jewish scholar, Martin Marty, criticizes the concept on the ground that it is seen by many as 'a code word for those promoting a Christian America'.[71] He is particularly concerned that the concept excludes various liberal sections in the polity such as the secular humanists or the liberal individualists.

While noting the increasing US political support for Israel, promoted assiduously by Israel's leaders working in tandem with various sections of what constitutes the 'Israel lobby' in the US (examined in some detail in Chapter VI), Michelle Mart has provided some interesting insights into the 'cultural foundations' of US–Israel relations.[72] She points out that, by 1962, when President John Kennedy met the then Israeli Foreign Minister, Golda Meir, there was already a pervasive sense among Americans that Israel was 'an ally with unique ties to the US'. In achieving this status, she believes that the popular novel *Exodus* by Leon Uris played a major role in portraying Israel as a nation of pioneers and industrious citizens who were making the desert bloom, in contrast to the squalid life of the backward Arabs. Popular literature was supported by American films that depicted heroic Israelis with 'their pioneering military prowess and Western outlook'. Thus, American popular culture increasingly presented positive images of Jewish characters so that, soon after the war, the status of Jews was transformed from that of outsider to insider.

Alongside this improving image of Jews in general and the deepening of relations between the US and Israel was the increasingly negative discourse relating to the Arab person and the Arab world in general. In the bifurcation of the Orientalist view of the 'Semite' after the Second World War, while the Jew (and Israel) became a hero and, in time, an insider, Orientalist prejudice against the Arab continued in full force, with the Arabs being depicted in popular culture as essentially sadistic, treacherous, low, slave trader, camel driver, moneychanger, colourful scoundrel.[73] Prominent Zionist leaders led the way. Chaim Weizman, in 1918, spoke of Arabs in terms which were very similar to those used by Europeans for the Jews:[74]

> The Arabs, who are superficially clever and quick witted, worship one thing, and one thing only—power and success ... The British authorities ... knowing as they do the treacherous nature of the Arabs ... have to watch carefully and constantly ... The fairer the English regime tries to be, the more arrogant the Arab becomes ... The present state of affairs would necessarily tend toward the creation of an Arab Palestine, if there were an Arab people in Palestine. It will not in fact produce that result because the fellah is at least four centuries behind the times, and the effendi ... is dishonest, uneducated, greedy, and as unpatriotic as he is inefficient.

American scholarship on the Middle East has frequently manifested the same orientalist hostility and contempt for the Arab that had characterized European writing a century earlier. These writings are almost invariably influenced by the view that Israel is the victim of Islamic violence and the consequent need to defend Israel at all costs. Since the end of the Cold War, a number of American writers have come to depict Islam and Muslim people as the 'new empire of evil', with demeaning stereotypes that lump together Islam and terrorism, or Arabs and violence, or the Orient and tyranny. As Edward Said has noted, post-War US scholarship on the Middle East 'accommodated, normalized, domesticated, and popularized' the European tradition of

Orientalist scholarship.[75] In fact, at this time, many of the Near East and Middle East departments in US universities were headed by British and European scholars who had made a name for themselves in the Orientalist tradition and now, in the USA, betrayed the same Orientalist mindset and prejudice. Thus, Gustave von Grunebaum, who headed Middle East Studies at Chicago and UCLA, had this to say in 1964 about his area of expertise:[76]

> It is essential to realize that Muslim civilization is a cultural entity that does not share our primary aspirations. It is not vitally interested in the structured study of other cultures, either as an end in itself or as a means towards clearer understanding of its own character and history...
>
> [Arab or Islamic nationalism] lacks, in spite of its occasional use as a catchword, the concept of the divine right of a nation, it lacks a formative ethic, it also lacks, it would seem, the later nineteenth century belief in mechanistic progress; above all it lacks the intellectual vigor of a primary phenomenon. Both power and the will to power are ends in themselves ...
>
> The resentment of political slights [felt by Islam] engenders impatience and impedes long-range analysis and planning in the intellectual sphere.

Over the years, even as the situation in Palestine has deteriorated, American Middle East academia, particularly the so-called think tanks, has increasingly come to be influenced by pro-Israel views emerging primarily from Right-wing Jewish writers or from the Christian right, so that, in place of academic rigour and objectivity, we find polemical writings and essentialized, one-sided assertions about Islam and Muslims being passed off as scholarship. Noting the prevailing 'highly exaggerated stereotyping and belligerent hostility' pertaining to Muslims and Islam (in 1996), Edward Said said:[77]

> There also seems to have been a strange revival of canonical, though previously discredited, Orientalist ideas about Muslim, generally non-white, people—ideas which have achieved a startling prominence at a time when racial or religious misrepresentations of every other cultural group are no longer circulated with such impunity. *Malicious generalizations about Islam have become the last acceptable form of denigration of foreign culture in the West*; what is said about the Muslim mind, or character, or religion, or culture as a whole cannot now be said in mainstream discussion about Africans, Jews, other Orientals, or Asian. [Emphasis added.]

Thus, the American scholar and former National Security Council member, Peter Rodman, said in 1992:[78]

Yet now the West finds itself challenged from the outside by a militant, atavistic force driven by hatred of *all* Western political thought, harking back to age-old grievances against Christendom ...

Much of the Islamic world is rent by social divisions, frustrated by its material inferiority to the West, bitter at Western cultural influence, and driven by its resentments (what Bernard Lewis calls the 'politics of rage'). Its virulent anti-Westernism does not look like just a tactic.

The events of 9/11 and the consequent Global War on Terror (GWOT) unleashed by the Bush Administration have served to strengthen US-Israel ties, further isolate and demonize Islam and the Muslim people, and harden the cleavage between the Jewish-Christian alliance on one side and Islam on the other. These theatres of contemporary conflict are examined in the next chapter.

NOTES

1. Will Durant, *The Age of Faith* (New York: Simon and Schuster, 1950) p. 385.
2. ibid., p. 386.
3. ibid.
4. ibid.
5. ibid., pp. 387–8.
6. ibid., p. 393.
7. Norman Cohn, *Warrant for Genocide – The Myth of the Jewish World Conspiracy and the Protocols of the Elders of Zion* (London: Serif, 2005) p. 25.
8. Cohn, p. 26.
9. ibid.
10. ibid., p. 197.
11. ibid., pp. 195–6.
12. ibid., p. 197.
13. Durant, p. 367.
14. Richard Fletcher, *The Cross and the Crescent – Christianity and Islam from Muhammad to the Reformation* (New York: Viking, 2003) p. 10.
15. ibid.
16. Hugh Goddard, *A History of Christian-Muslim Relations* Chicago: New Amsterdam Books, 2000) p. 35.
17. ibid.
18. ibid.
19. ibid.

20. ibid., p. 36.
21. ibid., p. 37.
22. ibid., pp. 45–6.
23. ibid., pp. 47–8.
24. ibid., pp. 56–8.
25. Fletcher, p. 18.
26. Goddard, p. 58.
27. ibid., p. 68.
28. Tomaz Mastnak, 'Islam and the Creation of European Identity', Slovene Academy of Sciences and Arts, October 1994, pp. 1-3; downloaded from: http://www.wmin.ac.uk/sshl/pdf/Mastnak%20-%20Islam%20and%20the%20Creation%20of%20European%20Identity.pdf; henceforth Mastnak. Also, Tomaz Mastnak: 'Europe and the Muslims: The Permanent Crusade', in Emran Qureshi and Michael A. Sells (Ed), *The New Crusades – Constructing the Muslim Enemy* (Karachi: Oxford University Press, 2003) p. 205; henceforth respectively Tomaz Mastnak and Qureshi.
29. ibid., p. 8.
30. ibid., p.10.
31. Goddard, p. 95.
32. ibid., p. 97.
33. ibid., pp. 99–101; Michael Hamilton Morgan, *Lost History – The Enduring Legacy of Muslim Scientists, Thinkers and Artists*, National Geographic, Washington DC, paperback 2008, also see two new books on the subject: (a) *Science and Islam – A History*, by Ehsan Masood, Icon, 2009; and (b) *The House of Wisdom – How the Arabs Transformed Western Civilisation*, by Jonathan Lyons, Bloomsbury, 2009, reviewed in 'Culture International', *The Sunday Times*, 1 February 2009, p. 54.
34. Tomaz Mastnak and Qureshi, p. 207.
35. ibid., p. 208.
36. Mastnak, p. 27.
37. ibid., p. 30.
38. Tomaz Mastnak and Qureshi, p. 219.
39. Mastnak, pp. 39–40.
40. Edward W. Said, *Orientalism* (New Delhi: Penguin Books, 2001) p. 2.
41. ibid., pp. 204–5.
42. ibid., p. 98.
43. ibid., pp. 73–4.
44. ibid., p. 62.
45. ibid., p. 151.
46. ibid., p. 172.

47. Thomas Patrick Hughes, *Dictionary of Islam* (New Delhi: first published 1885; in Rupa Paperback, 1988).

48. ibid., p. 398.

49. ibid.

50. ibid., p. 399.

51. Said, *Orientalism*, p. 149; however, Renan carefully distinguished the Jews in Europe from their brethren in Asia; as Martin Kramer has said: 'Renan held that "race" was determined "not by blood, but by language, religion, laws, and customs". A Muslim Turk, in his estimate, was 'today more a true Semite than the Jew who has become French, or to be more exact, European.' Martin Kramer, 'The Jewish Discovery of Islam – Part-I', 'Introduction,' in Martin Kramer (Ed.), *Jewish Discovery of Islam: Studies in Honour of Bernard Lewis*, The Moshe Dayan Center for Middle Eastern and African Studies, Tel Aviv, 1999, p. 15; downloaded from: http://www.genocities.com/martinkramerorg/JewishDiscovery.htm.

52. ibid., pp. 14–15.

53. Said, *Orientalism*, p. 38.

54. ibid., p. 105.

55. Kramer, pp. 3–4.

56. ibid., p. 4.

57. ibid., pp. 12–13.

58. ibid., p. 17.

59. ibid.

60. ibid., p. 22.

61. ibid.

62. William Dalrymple, 'Bernard Lewis and the Neocon View of Islam', *New York Review of Books*, Vol. 51, No.17, 4 November 2004; downloaded from: http://www.nybooks.com/articles/17516

63. Said, *Orientalism*, p. 286.

64. John Trumpbour, 'The Clash of Civilisations, Samuel P. Huntington, Bernard Lewis, and the Re-Making of Post-Cold War World Order', in *Qureshi*, p. 116.

65. ibid.

66. Quoted in Mark Silk, 'Notes on the Judeo-Christian Tradition in America', *American Quarterly*, 36(I), downloaded from: http://en.wikipedia.org/wiki/Judeo-Christian.

67. Michelle Mart, 'The Cultural Foundations of the US/Israel Alliance', *Tikkun Magazine*, Berkeley CA, 11 November 2006.; downloaded from: http://www.tikkun.org/magazine/specials/article.2006-11-11.2313.

68. Dennis Prager, 'Different Theology, Same Morality', *WorldNet daily*, 16

March 2005; downloaded from: http://www.worldnetdaily.com/
index.php?fa=PAGE. printable&pageID=29367
69. Quoted in: http://en.wikipedia.org/wiki/Judeo-Christian
70. ibid.
71. Martin E. Marty, 'A Judeo-Christian Looks at the Judeo-Christian Tradition', *The Christian Century,* 5 October 1986; downloaded from: www.religion-online.org/showarticle.asp?title=188
72. Mart.
73. Said, *Orientalism,* p. 287.
74. ibid., p. 306.
75. ibid., p. 295.
76. ibid., p. 297.
77. Edward W. Said, *Covering Islam – How the Media and the Experts Determine How We See the Rest of the World* (London: Vintage, 1997) p. xi–xii.
78. ibid., p. xvii.

12

The Theatres of Contemporary Conflict

Record!
I am an Arab
I have a name without a title
Patient in a country
Where people are enraged
My roots
Were entrenched before the birth of time
And before the opening of the eras
Before the pines, and the olive trees
And before the grass grew

Record!
I am an Arab
You have stolen the orchards of my ancestors
And the land that I cultivated
Along with my children
And you left nothing for us
Except for these rocks ...
So will the State take them
As it has been said?!

Therefore!
Record on the top of the first page:
I do not hate people
Nor do I encroach
But if I become hungry
The usurper's flesh will be my food
Beware ...
Beware ...

Of my hunger
And my anger!

Mahmoud Darwish, Palestinian National Poet

Religion is the trigger of the fanatic. The bullets are fired by the rising
fundamentalist movements in the USA and Israel and Islam.

Andrew Sinclair: *An Anatomy of Terror*

The Middle East is where various fundamentalists collide, and none
of us can expect to escape the resulting fall out.

Stuart Sim, *Fundamentalist World*

Soon after the 9/11 events, Israeli leaders were seriously concerned about
the possibility of some Americans pointing an accusing finger at Israel
and holding its brutality in suppressing the Palestinian Intifada at least
partly responsible for the carnage in the USA. Israel was quick to pre-
empt this: within a few days of the September 11 attacks, on 18
September 2001, Sharon gave a wide-ranging interview in which he
noted:[1]

> But there have already been some voices raised in America to the extent
> that, if it were not for its relationship with Israel, none of this terror would
> have hit New York or Washington.
>
> We need to understand that the Arab countries now will certainly try
> to use this opportunity to pressure Israel and say that what is bothering
> them is that Israel did not give concessions to the Palestinians. I see that
> possibility. Our clear, unequivocal answer is that this will not be at our
> expense.

Having so clearly noted the problem, Sharon's response was also
categorical: answering a specific question relating to the link between
Islamic rage and the Israeli-Palestinian conflict, Sharon said:

> It is a widespread perception, and there are also Jews, a few, who share
> that perception today. But in my mind, that perception is not widespread.
> Let me make it clear. We know the world very well; we saw [what happened
> in] Europe only 55 years ago. What, are we going to take on the guilt for
> this now? No, not with me. *This is a struggle with extreme Islam, a deep
> struggle of values. What connection does it have to us at all?* And even if you
> would say for a minute that there is a connection with Israel – does that
> mean we are responsible for what happened? For what? [Emphasis added.]

Thus, from the beginning, the Israeli media and its adherents in the
USA forcefully shifted attention away from Palestine and, instead,

focused on extremist Islam and Islamic societies, particularly Saudi Arabia, as being directly culpable for the terrorist attacks in the USA.

Within a few weeks of the September 11 events, US political leaders, academics and journalists began a scathing criticism of Saudi Arabia, obviously on account of the proven involvement of a number of Saudi nationals in the WTC/Pentagon attacks and the identification of the Taliban and Osama bin Laden as the source of this terror. Criticism by prominent senators, such as Joseph Biden, John McCain and Joe Lieberman, led the way, but the content and virulence of much of the later writing in the media was set by two articles: 'King's Ransom–How Vulnerable are the Saudi Royals?' by Seymour Hersh, in *The New Yorker*;[2] and 'Anti-Western and Extremist Views Pervade Saudi Schools', by Neil MacFarquhar, in *New York Times*.[3]

Hersh's piece had the distinction of being based on intelligence briefings, including access to electronic intercepts of conversations between Saudi royals, which gave it a unique authenticity in the fraught atmosphere of the time. At the outset, Hersh categorically stated:

> The intercepts depict a regime increasingly corrupt, alienated from the country's religious rank and file, and so weakened and frightened that it has brokered its future by channeling hundreds of millions of dollars in what amounts to protection money to fundamentalist groups that wish to overthrow it.

Hersh painted a picture of Saudi non-cooperation in the terrorist enquiry; large-scale corruption and self-indulgence on the part of senior royals; and the long-standing reluctance of the US leadership to countenance any public criticism of the Kingdom. Hersh concluded that 'current and former intelligence and military officials' were conveying the picture of 'growing instability of the Saudi regime' and the vulnerability of the Saudi oil facilities to terrorist attack. Hersh also quoted informed sources saying that 'the United States is hostage to the stability of the Saudi system', and that the 'Saudis have been indulged for so many decades. They are so spoiled'.

MacFarquhar, writing from Jeddah, said that an 'extremist, anti-Western world view has gradually pervaded the Saudi education system with its heavy doses of mandatory religious instructions ... It has seeped outside the classroom through mosque sermons, television shows and the Internet, coming to dominate the public discussions on religion'. This assessment was buttressed through an item in 10th grade textbooks in which it was said: 'It is compulsory for Muslims to be loyal to each other and to consider the infidels their enemy', as also interviews with a number of Saudi academics and journalists (some of them named). A prominent editor confirmed that Saudi textbooks promoted 'extremist views of Islam even in the eyes of very devout Muslims'.

MacFarquhar noted that 'the pool of potential recruits [for international terrorist networks] is swelling as tens of thousands of young Saudis emerge with an education that leaves them unqualified for work'. He said that, after every Islamist challenge, the Al-Saud (the Saudi royal family) had ceded more ground on social affairs to the clergy, and had also exported this attitude through substantial funding of Islamic institutions which had preached anti-Western Wahhabi attitudes. The writer concluded that Saudi Arabia 'has revealed itself as the source of the very ideology confronting America in the battle against terrorism'.

The points made by MacFarquhar and Hersh were echoed in numerous editorials and articles in the mainstream US press, including *The New York Times*, *The Washington Post*, *Los Angeles Times*, *The Baltimore Sun* and *The Boston Globe*. These views also came to be expressed in sections of the European press, drawn largely from US writings. Indeed, there was no worse pariah in the international comity of nations than Saudi Arabia. *The Guardian* spoke of the Kingdom as 'the real cancer in the Middle East', and 'a perverted creation of America and its British ally'.[4] The primary grievance of many of these writers was that, with all the 'understanding and even pampering of the Saudis', they were at best reluctant allies and, indeed, in reality, 'false friends'. *Radio Netherlands*, in a commentary titled 'Saudi Arabia: the Weakest Link', thoughtfully concluded: 'With such lukewarm Islamic friends, America hardly needs enemies'.[5]

In all the verbiage poured out in castigating the Kingdom as the fountainhead of terror, no writer made an attempt to address the point made by several Arab and Islamic observers that the injustice meted out to the Palestinians at the hands of Israel was the principal source of Arab and Islamic anger. (*Washington Post* dismissed the then Crown Prince Abdullah's reference to Palestine as 'cheeky'.)[6]

While the Western media onslaughts generally ignored the Palestine issue, they frequently examined the substantial mutuality of interests which had engendered close US ties with Saudi Arabia over several decades. However, this aspect of the bilateral relationship was addressed in a manner as to alienate the average US reader from the compulsions of his government, and to see in the relationship not national interest but sleaze, based on oil and defence contracts and crass economic interest, as influencing 'Washington' (a remote sleaze capital in the eyes of many Middle Americans). This was most apparent in the investigative report of *Newsweek*[7] which spoke of backroom deals involving senior politicians and millions of dollars proffered to corrupt, debauched Arab princes (referred to as 'obscenely rich' in *The Baltimore Sun*).[8]

The other interesting aspect of Western writing was the support that writers derived from previous criticisms, a stratagem which had the advantage of not requiring the case to be proved afresh. The lead role in the criticism against Saudi Arabia was played by *New York Times* (strongly pro-Israel and skeptical of US–Saudi ties), particularly through the writings of influential columnists like Thomas Friedman and William Safire. Friedman forcefully argued the case *for* America and Israel, and condemned the Kingdom for pandering to religious extremism and anti-Westernism. He concluded his piece of 27 November 2001, thus:[9]

> We patronised Islam, and misled ourselves, by repeating the mantra that Islam is a faith with no serious problems accepting the secular West, modernity and pluralism, and the only problem is a few bin Ladens ... Christianity and Judaism struggled with this issue for centuries, but a similar internal struggle within Islam to re-examine its texts and articulate a path for how one can accept pluralism and modernity—and still be a passionate, devout Muslim—has not surfaced in any serious way.

William Safire, Charles Krauthammer in *The Washington Post*, and Daniel Pipes, intellectual-columnist at large, all belonging to the Right-wing in US political discourse, with strong views in support of the US flag, US interests and US Christianity, were particularly vociferous during this period. Krauthammer's views were representative: referring to repeated US statements that the war is not against 'Islam', he wrote:[10]

> ... that great post-Sept. 11 oddity: Deafening silence from the spiritual authorities of Islam, obsessive chatter from Americans, largely Christians, filling that silence with near apologetic professions of good faith and tolerance.
>
> This is not just odd, it is demeaning. Who attacked whom? Who should be doing the soul-searching and the breast-beating? Why are we acting as if we bear guilt for our own victimization? The United States is the most diverse and religiously tolerant society on earth. By far. As regards

Islamic peoples, we have been singularly sympathetic. We waged three successful military campaigns in the 1990s. In every one we rescued a beleaguered Islamic people: Kuwait, Bosnia, Kosovo. And we have just liberated a fourth: Afghanistan.

Points made by these internationally respected columnists were repeatedly quoted in polemical articles written subsequently by less known and less authoritative writers.

An editorial in the *The New York Times* of 14 October 2001, titled 'Reconsidering Saudi Arabia', pointed out that Saudi Arabia not only tolerated terrorism, it had actually 'helped create and sustain bin Laden's terrorist organization'.[11] Nearly a month later, *The Washington Post* published an editorial with exactly the same title ('Reconsidering Saudi Arabia'), which made substantially the same points as the *NYT* leader and, like the *NYT,* strongly urged political reform in the Kingdom.[12] This was a rare instance of two fierce rivals of the East coast publishing nearly the same editorial, with the same title, one month apart!

The sustained and unprecedented assault on the Kingdom's religious affiliation, its political order and its leaders emanating from the United States in such strident tones over several weeks caused both anguish and anger in the country. Saudi bewilderment, uneasiness and rage were heightened by continuous stories of Saudis being arrested and interrogated in the USA, and students being subject to abuse and harassment. Some Saudi commentators responded vigorously to American criticism. Thus, Abdul Aziz Al-Tuweijri, writing in *Al-Watan*, suggested: 'The most important motive behind this [media] attack is to pressurize the Kingdom to relinquish its firm stand on Palestine.'[13] Other motives mentioned by the writer were: to damage the Kingdom's image; to hurt the Kingdom's Islamic charity and relief efforts; and to sabotage the 'excellent relations the Kingdom has with the countries of the world in general and the Western countries in particular'. Besides advocating a more effective media policy to counter the Western assault, the author also ambiguously referred to the need for 'correction of mistakes and shortcomings' of the Kingdom which its enemies were taking advantage of.

Another writer, Dr. Mohammed Shoukany, specifically responded to MacFarquhar's articles on Saudi education and pointed out:[14]

(*i*) the quote from the Saudi textbook used by the writer to make his case was a mistranslation and pulled out of context;

(*ii*) that the author deliberately left out hundreds of other items in Saudi textbooks which advocated moderation and tolerance;

(*iii*) that Saudis in general, products of the same education system maligned in *New York Times,* do not harbour resentment or hatred of the West;

(*iv*) that, indeed, it is Western writing that actually displays hatred and intolerance of Arab and Muslim people; and,

(*v*) that the US media has entirely failed to understand and present the real reasons for Muslim anger, chief among which is 'the blind support of Israeli atrocities in Palestine'.

Many observers in Saudi Arabia were aggrieved about criticism relating to the Kingdom's involvement with mobilizing the mujahideen in Afghanistan as an Islamic jihad and its subsequent affiliation with bin Laden and the Taliban. They believed that in the mujahideen struggle they were allies of the United States in the war against the Soviet Union, that they were serving US ideological and strategic interests, and that the strategy and tactics developed in pursuit of that struggle had the full approval and active participation of the Americans. (For instance, the idea to recruit and induct Arab-Afghans and Muslim radicals from other countries into the Afghan struggle actually originated from the then CIA Chief, William Casey.) Again, with regard to the Taliban, the Saudis pointed out that the Americans themselves were actively engaged with the Taliban: the American government then was promoting US gas pipeline interests across Afghan territory which was founded on a strong pro-Taliban policy, a policy that was given up only in August 1998, after the Al-Qaeda-inspired bombings of US Embassies in Kenya and Tanzania. The Saudis noted that in all the American criticism relating to their funding of Islamic groups, there was no mention of active US participation in it.

Contemporary Conflicts

Today, battles as part of the Global War on Terror (GWOT) are taking place on three fronts: the first, older one is in Palestine, which in its history has witnessed numerous messianic confrontations between adherents of the three Semitic religions. The latest battle originates from 1948 when Israel was set up; it acquired a fresh resonance from 1967 onwards as triumphant Jewish messianism laid exclusive claim to all the territories of the 'Promised Land' and ignited, first, a secular, and later an 'Islamic' resistance that has become central to contemporary Islamic radicalism. Since 9/11, this front has merged with the broader GWOT as a result of Israel's success in defining the Palestinian national struggle as terrorism.

The second more recent battle is taking place in Iraq, where an attempt at neo-imperialist domination has met with fierce resistance that is increasingly imparting to the struggle the character of a messianic religious confrontation. The third battle is centred in Afghanistan but is taking place across the globe, with US-led forces, at home and abroad, battling extremist Islam in its varied manifestations, but broadly represented by the Al-Qaeda as a movement and as a concept. These three battles are analyzed in the following paragraphs.

Palestine

The Palestinian-Israeli confrontation is a key factor in fomenting violence and terror in West Asia, though it has suited Israel and its supporters to focus on others, such as: authoritarian politics in West Asia; the corruption and venality of Arab leaders; extremist state religion; education that breeds hate; and, in general, a hatred of modernity, all of which together constitute 'the cultural malaise' of the Arab/Muslim world.

The Arab/American writer, Shibley Telhami, in his book, *The Stakes: America in the Middle East*, rejects this approach and asserts: 'No other issue resonates with the public in the Arab world, and many other parts of the Muslim world, more deeply than Palestine.'[15] Even on occasions when Arab governments, in their anxiety to appease the USA, have attempted to downplay the issue of Palestine, they have been reminded of the 'depth of public anger' by their populations. For the Arabs, the Palestinian issue, according to Telhami, 'is an issue of *identity*'. He says:[16]

> Its role in the collective Arab consciousness over the past 50 years has been akin, though not identical, to the role that the state of Israel has come to play in the contemporary Jewish identity ... [Following from this] *the contemporary political consciousness of the region has been largely defined in relation to Israel and Palestine.* (Emphasis added.)

However, as noted earlier, within a few days of the 9/11 events, the Israeli media and its supporters in the USA forcefully shifted attention away from Palestine and, instead, focused on extremist Islam and Islamic societies, particularly Saudi Arabia, as being directly culpable for the terrorist attacks in the USA. At the same time, the Israeli forces stepped up their attacks on the Palestinians. In a report written in March 2004, the US diplomat and academic, Edward Sheehan, gave a graphic account of the depredations wreaked by the Israelis in different parts of the Occupied Territories. Since mid-December 2003:[17]

> (Israel) has intensified its incursions, seeking suspected terrorists, militants of Hamas, and munitions makers. Using bulldozers, tanks, helicopters, and F-16 aircraft, the Israelis have destroyed or badly damaged two mosques, three churches, and hundreds of other buildings and homes.

Sheehan reported that serious violence had been perpetrated upon the civilian population when thousands of young and old people were interrogated and hundreds of young men indefinitely detained. Economic life was almost totally destroyed. He pointed out that the breakdown of civil order and social services witnessed by him in Nablus had been repeated in other Palestinian areas such as Jenin, Hebron, the Gaza Strip and other areas. In response to these Israeli depredations, popular support for Hamas rose even as the power of the Palestinian Authority disintegrated. Suicide bombings, most of them encouraged by Hamas, killed or wounded dozens of Israelis. There were pitched battles between Israelis and the Palestinians in the Gaza Strip in which dozens of Arabs have been killed. On 20 March 2004, Israel carried out the targeted assassination of the Hamas spiritual leader, Sheikh Ahmed Yassin, followed by the killing of his successor, Dr. Abdul Aziz Rantissi.

According to the United Nations Relief and Works Agency for Palestinian refugees, UNWRA, Israel had, in May 2004, destroyed 191 homes in Gaza, making 2,197 Palestinians homeless.[18] Amnesty International reported in May 2004, that since the start of the Intifada, three years earlier, Israel destroyed 3,000 Palestinian houses in Gaza, throwing over 18,000 Palestinians on the street. It damaged a further 15,000 houses, in addition to the destruction of hundreds of factories, workshops, greenhouses, wells, pumps, irrigation canals and orchards. It uprooted 226,000 trees and destroyed some 10 per cent of Gaza's agricultural land. Amnesty International denounced as 'war crimes' these grave breaches of international law and of the Fourth Geneva Convention. Three years of wanton destruction drove 60 per cent of Gaza inhabitants below the poverty line and threw some 50 per cent out of work.[19]

For Sharon, whose propaganda machine equated the Palestine Authority Chairman, Yasser Arafat, with Osama bin Laden, September 11 provided an incentive to use force without restraint – since the West would now give carte blanche to any policies aimed at fighting terrorism, regardless of the methods or means. Palestinian Islamist radicals, following Al-Qaeda's example, showed no more restraint than did Israel, and embarked on a fresh cycle of suicide bombings.

Within the Arab and Islamic world, there is no escaping the fact that the Arab–Israeli conflict is the biggest source of anger and humiliation. Given the near-total US support to Israel, the anger toward Israel is increasingly becoming anger toward the United States as well.[20] Telhami has set out a detailed and substantial critique of US policies which, in his view, have encouraged the wellsprings of extremism and violence in the Arab and Muslim world. He points out that, in responding to violence in West Asia, the Bush Administration only focused on the Palestinian attacks without setting any moral limits to those responses. Thus, in regard to the Israeli counter-attacks, it made no demand that these actions not be sweeping and that such disproportionate force should not be used so indiscriminately.

A prominent Palestinian writer, Mustafa Barghouti, has pointed out that, in Israel, 'any humiliation or abuse is permissible if it goes under the spurious banner of security'; the writer says:[21]

> Over 7,000 Palestinian prisoners currently remain in Israeli prisons, many of them held without charge or trial. Most will have suffered some degree of torture before their release. It is shocking to recognize that *around 650,000 Palestinians have spent time in Israeli custody since 1967*, most of them adult males. This means that almost every second Palestinian adult male has been imprisoned. (Emphasis added.)

Many objective observers have noted with concern the similarity in Palestinian and US/Israeli violence. *Human Rights Watch* [HRW], in its response to Israeli criticism to its report on Israeli violence in Palestine, said:[22]

> Any objective assessment would show that, horrendous as the terrorist attacks on Israel have been, *the Israeli government has chosen to mount a defence not within the ample leeway provided by international human rights and humanitarian law but in violation of that law*. Assassinating suspects when they could be arrested, punishing families for the acts of one of their members, employing abusive interrogation techniques, imposing punitive

restrictions on the Palestinian population that go well beyond security requirements, building a security barrier not on the Green Line but with deep incursions into the West Bank to protect settlements that themselves violate the Geneva Conventions–all of these flout fundamental legal norms that Israel itself has subscribed to, along with most of the rest of the world.

By fueling hatred for Israel among Palestinians, this disregard for human rights has arguably made Israel less safe. And it does enormous damage to Israel's global reputation, transforming the country in the eyes of many from a sympathetic victim of terrorism to another (particularly powerful) human rights abuser.[Emphasis added.]

HRW pointed out that, by ignoring criticism of its actions, Israel discourages understanding of a major cause of increasing Palestinian animosity toward Israel and growing global disquiet about Israeli government practices. The issue, HRW said, is not Israel's right to defend itself from the scourge of suicide bombing but the method of defence. In many parts of the world, public horror at the bombing and sympathy for the Israeli victims too often gives way to outrage at Israeli indifference to the same body of international human rights and humanitarian law that prohibits deliberate attacks on civilians.

The bloodshed from 2002 to date has had a broader impact on the regional psyche. On the Israeli side, the escalation of suicide bombing, including a horrific bombing in Netanya on Passover in May 2005 that left scores of people dead and wounded, created deep scars. Among the Palestinians, the ruthlessness of Israeli actions in the West Bank and Gaza, including severe violations of human rights, increased the urge for revenge. In the Arab world, the live televised images of helpless Palestinians facing Israeli tanks, while the world watched, left a mark on the collective consciousness of a new generation that rivals the scars of the 1948 war. Telhami points out that there is an increasing perception in Muslim countries that the United States is specifically targeting and weakening Muslims, matched by the heightened fears of many Americans about Muslim aims toward America and the West.[23] Increasingly, public attitudes in the Arab world and much of the Muslim world have included not only strong resentment of American foreign policy but also a sense of deep despair and humiliation that people connect in their minds to that policy. Telhami concludes:[24]

Not all, or even most, people who are desperate or feel a sense of deep humiliation are inclined to be recruited by groups engaged in terror. But when one looks at a society as a whole and finds that majorities are enraged, it is usually an indication that people on the margins of that society are being radicalised into sometimes brutal action.

Amidst all this carnage, resurgent Jewish messianism has continued to expand and consolidate its presence in the territories occupied in 1967 so that, between the fall of the Likud Government in 1993 and the end of the Barak government in 2000, the number of settlers at the West Bank doubled, with conservative estimates of the construction cost of the settlements, excluding military expenditure, exceeding $20 billion.[25]

The areas actually inhabited by Jewish settlements are about three per cent of the West Bank; however, the municipal borders of these settlements and their infrastructure support take up about 50 per cent of the West Bank. The building of the fence affirms to the beleaguered Palestinians that Israel has no intention of leaving its settlements, and it proposes to limit the Palestinian population to about half the West Bank, which would be about 10 per cent of pre-1948 Palestine.[26]

The influential Israeli historian, Benny Morris, has radically transformed our understanding of the context of the historic Israeli occupation of Palestine by pointing out that, in 1948, the secular Zionist leadership concluded that the Jewish state proposed to be set up by the United Nations required the removal of 700,000 Palestinians. Accordingly, between April and May 1948, Jewish forces of the Haganah were instructed to uproot the villagers, expel them, and destroy the villages. According to Morris, this action resulted in 'far more Israeli acts of massacre than I had previously thought', including 'many cases of rape [that] ended in murder' and executions of Palestinians who were lined up against a wall and shot in operation Hiram.[27]

This expulsion was not the result of war but a deliberate and planned operation to 'cleanse' (word used in the original documents) those parts of Palestine that had been assigned to the Jews as part of their state. Morris has justified this decision, saying: 'Ben-Gurion was right. Without the uprooting of the Palestinians, a Jewish state would not have arisen here.' Morris has gone on to explain these early Israeli actions thus: 'There are circumstances in history that justify ethnic cleansing ... The need to establish this [Jewish] state in this place overcame the injustice that was done to the Palestinians by uprooting them.' Morris has even suggested that the need to accommodate the fence and Sharon's plans for 'Bantustans' could require a second transfer of the Palestinian population.[28] In response, Henry Siegman has asked why Palestinian actions, including suicide bombings in support of *their* 'national cause' should not be seen as equally noble or compelling as to justify violence against the Israeli population; Siegman has concluded:[29]

> There is not much that distinguishes how Jews behaved in 1948 in their struggle to achieve statehood from Palestinian behaviour today. At the very least, this sobering truth should lead to a shedding of the moral smugness of too many Israelis and to a re-examination of their demonization of the alestinian national cause.

Iraq

Seven years after the US invasion of Iraq, a near consensual position has emerged that the invasion was a disaster and did not serve US interests. Jonathan Freedland has said that:[30]

> the 2003 invasion of Iraq was a calamity, ... the presidency of George W. Bush has reduced America's standing in the world and made the United States less, not more, secure, leaving its enemies emboldened and its friends alienated.

Dennis Ross, who has held senior positions in earlier US Administrations, had this to say about Iraq:[31]

> It is hard to exaggerate the Bush administration's fundamental miscalculations on Iraq, including but not limited to unrealistic policy objectives; fundamental intelligence failures; catastrophically poor understanding of what would characterize the post-Saddam period, and completely unrealistic planning as a result; denial of the existence of an insurgency for several months; and the absence of a consistent explanation to the American people or the international community about the reasons for the war.
>
> Small wonder that after nearly four years of warfare, Iraq has been a disaster, costing thousands of lives, requiring the expenditure of hundreds of billions of dollars, stretching our forces and reserve system to the breaking point, and becoming a magnet for terrorists and hostility towards the United States throughout the Muslim world.

The prominent Amrican statesman and foreign affairs commentator, Zbigniew Brzezinski, has said:[32]

> The Iraq War in all its aspects has turned into a calamity—in the way it was internally decided, externally promoted, and has been conducted - and it has already stamped the Bush presidency as a historical failure.

One of the extraordinary aspects of the deliberate official mis-information relating to Iraq that has been fed to the US population is that Saddam Hussein had a 'personal role' in the 9/11 attacks: a poll in August 2003 found that 69 per cent of Americans were convinced about this. Surprisingly, a later poll of July 2006 indicted that 64 per cent of all Americans still believed that Saddam Hussein had had strong links with Al-Qaeda, an increase of two per cent from two years earlier. Again, 50 per cent Americans, in July 2006, still believed that Saddam Hussein had developed weapons of mass destruction (WMD), an increase over 38 per cent two years earlier.[33] Max Rodenbeck has pointed out that this false information, assiduously encouraged by US administration officials, was possibly responsible for the aggressive behaviour of American soldiers in Iraq, encouraging in turn fierce Iraqi resistance to the US forces. What the Iraq war has succeeded in doing is to create 'the world's principal breeding and training ground for anti-American terrorists'.[34]

Besides the physical damage that has been inflicted upon the Iraqi people and their country, and the encouragement it has given to sectarian and extremist forces there, the greatest harm that the Iraq war has done is the opportunity it has provided to the US forces to give vent to their visceral hatred for Arabs and Muslims. Human Rights Watch, in their report published on 25 September 2005, have given graphic details of the abuses that US armed forces personnel have inflicted upon the Iraqi population, whose actions were not subject to the Geneva Conventions since the US Administration has placed the war outside the purview of international and even domestic law; hence, prisoners arrested in Iraq (as in Afghanistan) are referred to as 'person(s) under control' (PUC) not prisoners of war. The report made the following main points:[35]

(*i*) US armed forces routinely used physical and mental torture as a means of intelligence gathering and, astonishingly, for stress relief.

(*ii*) The torture and other mistreatment of Iraqis in detention was systematic and known at various levels of command.

(*iii*) The mistreatment of prisoners by US military is even more widespread than has been acknowledged to date.

(*iv*) The torture of detainees was so widespread and accepted that it became a means of "stress relief" for soldiers who would routinely subject detainees to beatings and forced physical exertion.

(*v*) The torture and other cruel and inhuman treatment described in the Human Rights Watch report included:

severe beatings (in one incident, a soldier reportedly broke a detainee's leg with a baseball bat), blows and kicks to the face, chest, abdomen, and extremities, and repeated kicks to various parts of the detainees' bodies; the application of chemical substances to exposed skin and eyes; forced stress positions, such as holding heavy water jugs with arms outstretched, sometimes to the point of unconsciousness; sleep deprivation; subjecting detainees to extremes of hot and cold; the stacking of detainees into human pyramids; and the withholding of food (beyond crackers) and water.

David Forsythe has pointed out that these abuses were part of state policy from the very outset:[36]

From the beginning of the US war on terrorism, President Bush and his closest advisors (and their lawyers), Vice President Cheney, Secretary of Defense Rumsfeld, and Legal Counsel Gonzales, opted for abusive interrogation over humane interrogation. They were backstopped by lawyers primarily from the Justice Department. State Department officials and those from the National Security Council (NSC), including even NSC Advisor Condoleeza Rice, were apparently shunted aside early in deliberations. So were many uniformed lawyers in the Department of Defense. All of the lawyers centrally involved were civilian political appointees. These lawyers may have engaged in the unethical practice of advising their clients about how to violate the law.

In spring 2003, the US forces invading Iraq found themselves with large numbers of detainees. In addition, they were faced with a persistent and violent insurgency against their occupation of the country. The poor management of prisoner affairs was only one part of a broader bungled occupation. In that situation, Major General Geoffrey Miller was transferred from Guantanamo to Iraq in August 2003 to improve intelligence gathering, which set the stage for considerable abuse of the detainees. In May 2004, the world was presented with shocking evidence that the new dispensation of abuse had reached Iraq, with the publication of photographs from Iraq's Abu Ghraib prison showing naked prisoners chained like dogs, forced to simulate sex with each other, and hooded prisoners with electric wires linked to their fingers. Forsythe has described these abuses thus:[37]

Some prisoners were sexually and religiously taunted and humiliated. They were restrained in painful positions. They were subjected to extremes of heat and cold. They were subjected to loud music or other noises, as well as to flashing lights. They were kept in isolation for long periods. They were force-fed liquids, then made to urinate on themselves. They were also made to defecate on themselves. They were intimidated by military police dogs. The interrogation process was such that both FBI agents and CIA agents sought to distance themselves from it, lest they be held legally responsible. The CIA might have been doing something similar, by way of similar interrogation in other places, but the agency did not want to be tagged for the abuses at Gitmo. In addition, some prisoners were physically beaten and otherwise abused by US Military Police in actions that did not seem to be approved by Military Intelligence or higher authorities.

Afghanistan/Pakistan

US bombings in Afghanistan after 9/11 led to at least 3,000-8,000 Afghan dead or injured. The bombings also caused major dislocations as people fled their homes for safety; food aid was halted and revenge killings became the norm. It is estimated that up to 20,000 Afghans may have died indirectly due to hunger, displacement and drought. Hundreds of casualties also occurred due to wrong targeting of villages.[38]

However, the Taliban and Al-Qaeda fighters escaped; they just went across the border into Pakistan—a move that was facilitated by Pakistani security officials, who saw them as the 'future of Afghanistan'—to be protected till the opportune moment arrived to send them back to their home country. As Ahmed Rashid has pointed out, over the next five years not a single Taliban commander was handed over to the Americans. The Americans, on their part, were, at this stage, only interested in pursuing the Al-Qaeda and were not bothered about the Taliban.[39] Mullah Omar, in an interview in May 2002, made his own views clear:[40]

> The battle in Afghanistan has (just) started, its fire has been kindled and it will engulf the White House, the seat of injustice and tyranny.

The American future in Afghanistan, he said, would be 'fire, hell and total defeat'.

Within a few months of the 9/11 events, senior Al-Qaeda and Taliban leaders were given sanctuary in different parts of Pakistan; as William Dalrymple has pointed out:[41]

> only months after September 11, ... the ISI was giving refuge to the entire Taliban leadership after it fled from Afghanistan. Mullah Omar was kept in an ISI safe house in the town of Quetta, just south of the tribal areas in Baluchistan, near the Afghan border, while his militia was lodged in

Pashtunabad, a sprawling Quetta suburb. Gulbuddin Hikmetyar, the leader of the radical Mujahideen militia Hizb-e-Islami, was lured back from exile in Iran and allowed to operate freely outside Peshawar, while Jalaluddin Haqqani, one of the most violent Taliban commanders, was given sanctuary by the ISI in North Waziristan, a part of FATA

From late 2002, the Taliban began to move weapons, ammunition and food supplies to Afghanistan from their sanctuaries in Pakistan. They raised funds from a variety of sources in Pakistani commercial and official circles and from sympathizers in the Gulf. Hundreds of fighters of Arab and Central Asian origin, hiding in the Federally-Administered Tribal Areas (FATA) on the Afghan-Pak border also joined them.[42]

Taliban-led military campaigns in Afghanistan began from the spring of 2003, with back-up support provided by the leaders of the Pakistani provinces of FATA and the North-West Frontier Province (NWFP). According to Rashid, the Taliban did not have a detailed agenda beyond wanting to 'drive out the foreigners', but still were able to make considerable headway in the country. This was due to the failure of the US and Afghan authorities to successfully implement programmes to reconstruct the country. The failure was particularly serious in the south of Afghanistan due to poor security and inadequate funds for development.[43]

The expansion of Taliban strength in Afghanistan led to deep concerns in the USA and among NATO countries about Pakistan's role in their success. In June 2007, a joint US, NATO and Afghan report indicated that the Taliban were made up of four elements: hardcore leaders linked to Al-Qaeda; militants from Pakistan; disaffected tribesmen, and unemployed youth. The report spoke of Pakistan's role thus:[44]

> ISI operatives reportedly pay a significant number of Taliban living/ operating in both Pakistan and Afghanistan to fight ... A large number of those fighting are doing so under duress as a result of pressure from ISI. The insurgency cannot survive without its sanctuary in Pakistan, which provides freedom of movement, safe havens, logistic and training facilities, a base for recruitment, communications for command and control, and a secure environment for collaboration with foreign extremist groups. The sanctuary of Pakistan provides a seemingly endless supply of potential new recruits for the insurgency.

One significant development in the Afghan scenario was the connection that was established between the Iraqi and Afghan militants from 2003 onwards. As Rashid has noted, by 2005, there was 'a steady traffic of extremists between Afghanistan-Pakistan and Iraq'. Taliban fighters were trained in military techniques and subversion in Iraq as also through Arab trainers who came to Afghanistan. More seriously, suicide bombers from Europe and North Africa on their way to Iraq, were diverted to Afghanistan, where they could reach Al-Qaeda training camps in a few weeks.[45]

The Taliban insurgency was fuelled by funds provided by opium cultivation, which soon became 'the largest production of drugs the world had ever seen'. In 2004, 4,200 tonnes of opium were harvested; farmland under poppy cultivation increased by over 64 per cent, being grown in all of Afghanistan's thirty-four provinces. According to Rashid, the opium economy is worth $2.8 billion, 60 per cent of the country's legal economy. Again, over 80 per cent of the Afghan opium is now being refined within the country.[46]

NATO-led military operations against the Taliban escalated in 2006, with 2,100 air strikes against them in June-December (as against 88 in Iraq). The Taliban responded by stepping up suicide bombings, which, in 2006, numbered 141 attacks, causing about 1,200 casualties. In 2007, the number of attacks was nearly the same (137), but the number of casualties was over 1,700. Taliban strength was also buttressed by fresh foreign fighters from Central Asia, Western China, Turkey and Arab countries. These fighters provided training to the Taliban cadres, while the Arabs among them also brought in Muslim militants from Europe, mainly UK, France, Germany and Scandinavia.[47]

Though a number of prominent Taliban leaders were killed or captured by 2007, the lethality of suicide bombings, the availability of fresh recruits, and improvements in military and subversion capabilities, besides the full support of sections of the Pakistani security forces, all of these factors have ensured that, eight years after 9/11, the Taliban had once again become a powerful force in Afghanistan, while the USA, NATO and the Karzai Government seemed incapable of providing the country with the peace and development it desperately needed.[48] Rashid described the scenario in 2008 most graphically:[49]

> Today, seven years after 9/11, Mullah Omar and the original Afghan Taliban Shura still live in Balochistan province. Afghan and Pakistani Taliban leaders live on farther north, in FATA, as do the militias of Jalaluddin Haqqani and Gulbuddin Hikmetyar. Al[-]Qaeda has a safe haven in FATA, and

along with them reside a plethora of Asian and Arab terrorist groups who are now expanding their reach into Europe and the United States.

The United States and NATO have failed to understand that the Taliban belong to neither Afghanistan nor Pakistan, but are a lumpen population, the product of refugee camps, militarized madrassas, and the lack of opportunities in the borderland of Pakistan and Afghanistan. They have neither been true citizens of either country nor experienced traditional Pashtun tribal society. The longer the war goes on, the more deeply rooted and widespread the Taliban and their transnational milieu will become.

Within a year, Ahmed Rashid's dire predictions came to pass. By early 2009, Taliban controlled 70 per cent of Afghanistan as against just 50 per cent in November 2007.[50] In March 2009, the newly elected US President, Barack Obama, announced that the US would shift its attention from operations in Iraq to Afghanistan and Pakistan, referred to by him as 'Af-Pak', suggesting that problems relating to the two countries would be viewed as an integrated issue.[51] This was quickly given up: the new American thinking was that, in terms of its strategy in Afghanistan, the US should distinguish between Al-Qaeda and Taliban. Later, further fine-tuning was done when a number of senior US officials began to suggest that not only should US strategy distinguish between Al-Qaeda and Taliban in Afghanistan but it should also view the extremist problem in Pakistan quite separately. The thinking in support of these ideas was that Al-Qaeda 'is a threat not only to the U.S. homeland and American interests abroad, but it has a murderous agenda'.[52] Hence, Al-Qaeda's leadership, infrastructure and military capability should be destroyed. On the other hand, the Taliban in Afghanistan were primarily an indigenous group that wanted to bring the maximum possible Afghanistan territory under their control to set up their own government. Further, Al-Qaeda, being made up of foreign elements, could be evicted from Afghanistan; this was not possible in the case of the Taliban who were operating in their own homeland. In any case, several Afghan warlords and sections of the local population were supporting the Taliban primarily on account of local grievances rather than due to belief in global jihad.

This view has been rejected by a number of prominent strategic thinkers who believe that Taliban and Al-Qaeda are closely linked with each other and draw their strength from each other, and that the Taliban would continue to give sanctuary to Al-Qaeda fighters even as they expanded their control over different parts of the country. Henry Kissinger intervened in this debate by asserting that Al-Qaeda and Taliban could not be separated, nor did he believe that the Taliban would implement the 'civic actions' desired by the US in territories occupied by them.[53] He felt that a soft line towards the Taliban was 'a disguised way of retreating from Afghanistan all together'.

The total number of Taliban insurgents in Afghanistan today is estimated at 17,000, as compared to 10,000 at the end of 2007.[54] There is some dispute about the extent of Al-Qaeda presence in Afghanistan at present. While some senior US officials and commentators maintain that Al-Qaeda and Taliban enjoy a symbiotic relationship and they cannot be distinguished on the ground, others suggest that, while in the last days of the fighting in Afghanistan before 9/11 there were about 1,500–2,500 Arab and Central Asian frontline fighters, today Al-Qaeda in Afghanistan would number only around 100 foreign fighters, or, at most between 200 and 250. The bulk of foreign fighters in Afghanistan are Pashtun tribals from Pakistan who, while educated in madrassas in Pakistan, do not have any affiliation with Al-Qaeda.[55]

While there could be differences about the exact number of Al-Qaeda militants in Afghanistan and the extent of their proximity to the Taliban, there is little doubt that Al-Qaeda has a strong military presence in Pakistan (in NWFP and FATA), while in Afghanistan a Pakistani of Kashmiri origin, Mohammed Ilyas Kashmiri, heads the Al-Qaeda-affiliated fighting unit Lashkar Al-Zil, or 'Shadow Army'.[56] This unit has a cross-border presence, being active in NWFP and Eastern and Southern Afghanistan. It is believed that the 'Shadow Army' is made up of three or four brigades and has a military command structure. In this unit at least the line between the Taliban and Al-Qaeda is blurred, with Taliban and Al-Qaeda elements working so closely together that, in the view of one observer, 'the alliance is essentially indistinguishable at this point except at a very abstract level'.[57]

Some observers believe that, in the last months of 2009, a schism had possibly emerged between Al-Qaeda and Taliban. Based on analyses of Internet messages on jihadi websites, commentators concluded that the Taliban were possibly offering a separate political settlement to the Americans in that, in exchange for withdrawal of all foreign forces from the country, the Taliban would restrain the Al-Qaeda within its territory and have normal relations with its neighbours. This emerged from

Taliban leader Mullah Omar's statement on the occasion of Eid-ul-Fitr, on 19 September 2009, when he made the following main points:[58]

- he promised social reforms,
- he expressed his determination to discipline Taliban members and to get rid of rogue elements,
- he expressed his commitment to international norms, promising to establish friendly bilateral relations with other countries and to respect the sovereignty of neighbouring countries, and,
- he asserted that Islam rejected extremism.

Since many of these points were not in keeping with Al-Qaeda's commitment to global jihad, the statement led observers to suggest that the relationship between Al-Qaeda and Taliban is now quite different from what it had been up to 2001: the Taliban were now seen as a nationalist organization seeking to govern Afghanistan under sharia but not interested in attacking the USA.[59]

The Al-Qaeda–Taliban 'schism' is being extensively discussed on jihadi websites, with some participants seeing in it signs of moderation and appeasement of the Americans and the West on the part of the Taliban. One commentator has pointed out that the agenda of the two organizations is quite different, in that the Taliban wish to obtain control over all of Afghanistan and win support of other Islamic countries, including 'infidel-ruled' Islamic states; thus, it is moving away from Al-Qaeda's global war on Islamic and non-Islamic countries.[60] Another contributor said angrily:[61]

> We must not look for excuses for what the Mullah [Omar] said. The Mullah and the Taliban leaders must know that we are angry and denounce his stated shift in policy. We demand that the Mullah apologise or renounce the statement. We expect Shaykh Osama to denounce the statement as well.

Other contributors are more optimistic: they believe the two organizations are close to each other, but have different roles:[62]

> Al[-]Qaeda works globally, whereas the Taliban offer an incubator for the group and a refuge for Muslims in general. Taliban Afghanistan is a safe haven and a launch pad that will lead to an eventual bright future for Muslims. Afghanis' love for Islam and Arabs is genuine, as is evident from their sacrifices for Arabs on the battlefields of Afghanistan.

Along with Afghanistan, there has been a significant expansion in the power and influence of the Al-Qaeda and Taliban in Pakistan itself. After 9/11, a large number of Al-Qaeda and Taliban militants had been given sanctuary in the Federally Administered Tribal Areas (FATA) of Pakistan which border Afghanistan and are home to 4.5 million Pashtun tribals. Soon, the radicalized Pashtun leaders set up their own private militias which supported the Taliban operations in Afghanistan while spreading their own influence in FATA. As attacks on US/NATO forces increased, the US pressurized General Musharraf to remove the militias from FATA. The Pakistani army was unsuccessful, and bought peace by entering into agreements with the militia to give them a free hand in the FATA areas dominated by them. In 2007, the various Pashtun militia set up a unified group, the Tehrik-e-Taliban-e-Pakistan (TTP), or the 'Movement of the Pakistani Taliban', under the militant leader, Baitullah Mehsud, who was later responsible for several suicide bombings and, possibly, the assassination of former Prime Minister Benazir Bhutto in December 2007. The TTP is affiliated to Al-Qaeda.[63]

Another unsuccessful military operation by the Pakistan army in Swat in February 2009, led to a 'peace agreement' with the TTP in terms of which the militias would be disarmed while the TTP, in turn, would be free to enforce strict sharia laws in the territory. This agreement followed heavy fighting involving 12,000 Pakistani soldiers and 3,000 Taliban militia, and resulted in several hundred civilian casualties and displacement of 1.5 million people from Swat. TTP rule in Swat meant summary executions, floggings, destruction of homes and girls' schools and severe restrictions on women.[64]

In violation of the peace agreement, instead of surrendering their arms, the TTP began to expand their influence outside Swat. Their armed strength increased to eight thousand fighters, including hundreds of Al-Qaeda militants, other Pashtun fighters, and trained extremists from Punjab and Karachi. The TTP spread to the districts of Dir, Shangla and Buner, the last being just 100 km from the national capital, Islamabad.

On 24 April 2009, once again under American pressure, the Pakistan army launched a new offensive against the TTP in the three newly acquired districts. Within a few weeks, Pakistani leaders were declaring total success in removing the TTP elements from the Swat Valley, stating that, within a week of the operation, at least 700 Taliban militants had been killed.[65] However, some observers were skeptical about the extent of the Pakistani army's success, pointing out that some parts of Swat still remain under Taliban control and that many Taliban elements had actually taken refuge in other parts of FATA.[66]

After Swat, the Pakistani forces turned their attention towards Waziristan where the TTP head, Baitullah Mehsud, was killed by an American Drone in early August 2009, after which, from October onwards, the TTP elements responded with a series of terrorist attacks in different parts of Pakistan in which more than 250 persons were killed and several hundred others injured.[67] At the end of the year, military operations in South Waziristan were ongoing with more than a quarter of a million local civilians displaced from their homes. Certain Pakistani leaders also declared success in these operations, but observers suggest that the Taliban elements could either take refuge across the border in Southern Afghanistan or even go southwards towards Balochistan and the border city of Quetta.[68]

Pakistan's prominent political commentator, Imtiaz Gul, has approvingly quoted an observer as saying that the threat faced by Pakistan from extremist elements operating in its tribal areas is a 'direct existential threat to the state and constitution of Pakistan'.[69] He then quotes the remarks of Pakistani Army Chief, General Ashfaq Pervez Kayani, who told Pakistani military cadets that 'Pakistan's current fight is against extremism and terrorism. It is not a fight based on religion, ethnicity, sub-nationalism or provincialism'.

Thus, at the end of 2009, the TTP and their Afghan brethren controlled the Khyber Pass (the land route through which the bulk of US supplies pass to Afghanistan), most of Afghanistan, and most of FATA and NWFP in Pakistan.[70] The Taliban were poised to penetrate Punjab province: they were already closely associated with extremist groups in Punjab that had been built up by the ISI in the 1990s to carry out jihadi operations in Jammu and Kashmir and other parts of India. These groups are providing the suicide bombers who are wreaking havoc in the different cities of Pakistan.[71]

The reason for the Pakistan army's pusillanimous approach to Al-Qaeda, the Taliban (both Afghan and home grown) and other extremist elements is quite obvious: as far as Afghanistan is concerned, the ISI is awaiting the imminent departure of American and other Western forces, after which it will install a Taliban government in Kabul, as it had succeeded in doing in the mid-1990s. The other extremist elements operating within the country, i.e., the TTP and the Punjabi extremists, it would like to use to continue jihadi violence against India.[72]

Global War on Terror (GWOT)

As in the case of the Iraq war, there is now a consensus that the GWOT launched by the Bush Administration was also a mistake. Jonathan Freedland has argued that the assaults of 9/11 should have been treated as an outrageous crime; by declaring a war on Al-Qaeda and extremist Islam, the US actually gave Al-Qaeda the exalted position it wanted. Moreover, as Freedland points out, the original error has been compounded by serious mistakes made by the US administration after the GWOT had been declared, such as the abuses at Guantanamo an Abu Ghraib, which have radicalized young Muslims in different parts of the world.[73]

Echoing these views, Jonathan Raban has noted that, soon after September 11, the US President, George Bush, had described the attacks as a 'criminal atrocity' and had said that the perpetrators would be 'brought to justice'. However, within a few days, he was already describing 9/11 as 'a new brand of war'.[74] Vice President Cheney said that this war would be fought 'in the shadows: this is a mean, nasty, dangerous, dirty busines. We have to operate in that arena'.[75] Earlier, in 1989, William Lind with four other military officers had spoken of this kind of war as a 'fourth generation war', which they had described as follows:[76]

> In broad terms, fourth generation warfare seems likely to be widely dispersed and largely undefined;the distinction between war and peace will be blurred to the vanishing point. It will be nonlinear, possibly to the point of having no definable battlefields or frots. The distinction between 'civilian' and 'military' may disappear ... Success will depend heavily on effectiveness in joint operations as lines between responsibility and mission become very blurred.

Raban has described such a conflict as a world of 'chronic blur', where 'peace wears the face of war, and war dis-simulates as peace'.[77]

Believing that the atrocity committed against it on 11 September 2001, was so grave that, in its response, there could not be any constraints placed on the exercise of its power, the US, as Louise Richardson has noted, pursued policies 'that alienated its allies, turned neutrals against it, swelled the ranks of its adversaries and destroyed its chances of achieving its long-term objective, that is, the containment of the resort to terrorism'.[78] US General Antonio Taguba, in his relatively moderate (and limited) report on the Iraq abuses, spoke of them as 'sadistic, blatant, and wanton, criminal abuses'.[9] Amnesty International, in its 2004 report, said that the Bush Administration had 'openly eroded human rights' to win the war on terror, and had sparked a backlash that had made the world a more dangerous place. In her introduction to the Report, the Amnesty Secretary General said:[80]

> The Baghdad tragedy was a clear reminder (though by no means the only one) of the global threat posed by those who are ready to use any means to further their political objectives. We condemn their acts unequivocally. They are guilty of abuse of human rights and violation of international humanitarian law, sometimes amounting to crimes against humanity and war crimes.
>
> There is no path to sustainable security except through respect for human rights. *The global security agenda promulgated by the US Administration is bankrupt of vision and bereft of principle.* Sacrificing human rights in the name of security at home, turning a blind eye to abuses abroad, and using pre-emptive military force where and when it chooses have neither increased security nor ensured liberty.
>
> Double speak brings disrepute to human rights but sadly, it is a common phenomenon. *The USA and its allies purported to fight the war in Iraq to protect human rights – but openly eroded human rights to win the "war on terror".* (Emphasis added.)

Jane Mayer is convinced that the GWOT has now become a battle for the soul of the United States. She points out that, after 9/11, the US administration has pursued a 'policy of deliberate cruelty' that would have been unthinkable earlier. This has been done, she believes, on the basis of 'dubious legal opinion that has enabled the administration to circumvent American laws and traditions'.[81] She echoes the widespread view that the war in Iraq, the Israeli-Palestinian conflict and the deteriorating security situation in Afghanistan and Pakistan have all 'contributed to the radicalization of the Muslim world'. In this regard, she quotes a senior US official who, after an extensive tour of West Asia, said that 'no subject was described by Muslims he spoke with as more deeply disturbing than America's abuse of the detainees'. He believed that US abuses had served to alienate the next generation of Arab youth; he said:[82]

I came away from my many visits to the Middle East convinced there is a widespread belief that if *America* abuses prisoners then there can be no true freedom for anyone ... It seemed to me that our greatest sin in the eyes of Muslims was not invading the Middle East, or even our support of Israel: our greatest sin was robbing Muslims of hope. (Emphasis in original)

Commenting on the pattern of abuse on the part of the US administration, Jane Mayer has noted the following facts:[83]

(*i*) Seven years after the 9/11 events, not a single terror suspect held outside the US criminal court system has been tried.

(*ii*) Of the 759 detainees acknowledged to have been held at Guantanamo, 270 still remain there, with very few of them having been charged.

(*iii*) Since much of the information from detainees has been obtained by means of torture, the administration has not been able to pursue cases against such high profile detainees as: Mohammed [A]l Qahtani, suspected of having been the 20th hijacker; Mohamedou Ould Slahi, who was believed to be a senior Al[-]Qaeda leader assisting the Hamburg Cell to plan the 9/11 attacks; and Abu Zubaydah, a prominent Al[-]Qaeda member, whose torture was captured on videotape.

(*iv*) Till early 2008, no senior administration official had been prosecuted or removed from office for abuse of prisoners: according to Human Rights Watch, more than 600 US military and civilian personnel were involved in abusing about 460 detainees at Abu Ghraib.

Given the mountain of evidence marshalled by different observers, there is little doubt that the GWOT has seen the most extreme forms of 'state terrorism', compelling Richard Falk to point out:[84]

'Terrorism' as a word and concept became associated in US and Israeli discourse with anti-state forms of violence that were so criminal that any method of enforcement and retaliation was viewed as acceptable, and not subject to criticism ... With the help of influential media, the state over time has waged and largely won the battle of definition by exempting its own violence against civilians from being treated and perceived as 'terrorism'. Instead such violence was generally discussed as 'use of force', 'retaliation', 'self-defence' and 'security measures'.

The neocon understanding of the events of 9/11 was clear and straightforward: this was a war launched by radical Islam with 'the sole desire to destroy the US out of remorseless theologically inspired hatred for its values';[85] Thus, Richard Pipes said:[86]

The attacks on New York and the Pentagon were unprovoked and had no specific objective. Rather, they were part of a general assault of Islamic extremists bent on destroying non-Islamic civilizations. As such, America's war with Al[-] Qaeda is non-negotiable.

Norman Podhoretz rejected the suggestion that the wrath of radical Islam had any connection with unconditional US support for Israel; he stated confidently: 'Hatred of Israel is a surrogate for anti-Americanism, rather than the reverse ... If the Jewish state had never come into existence, the United States would still have stood as an embodiment of everything that most of these Arabs considered evil'.[87]

The neocon effort was to deny that the grievances mentioned by Al-Qaeda in its various statements deserved a serious look even though some of the points made by bin Laden and al-Zawahiri were quite specific, such as: the removal of the US bases from Saudi Arabia; end to US aggression against the Iraqi people, and allegations that the US was making efforts to fragment the Arab states of the region in order to guarantee Israel's survival and the continuation of the crusade for the occupation of the Arabian Peninsula.

Michael Scheuer rejects the neocon view and sees the following as constituting the wellsprings of Al-Qaeda animosity:[88]

> *The United States is hated across the Islamic world because of specific US government policies and actions.* That hatred is concrete not abstract, material not intellectual, and it will grow for the foreseeable future ... America is hated and attacked because Muslims believe they know precisely what the United States is doing in the Islamic world. They know partly because of bin Laden's words, partly because of satellite television, but mostly because of the tangible reality of US policy. We are at war with an Al[-]Qaeda-led, worldwide Islamist insurgency because of and to defend those policies, and not, as President Bush has mistakenly said, 'to defend freedom and all that is good and just in the world.' [Emphasis added.]

After seven years of the GWOT, the overall scenario from the US perspective was described by Ahmed Rashid thus:[89]

> As the Bush era nears its end in 2008, American power lies shattered, the US Army is overstretched and broken, the American people are disillusioned and rudderless, U.S. credibility lies in ruins, and the world is a far more dangerous place. The Iraq war has bankrupted the United States, consuming upto $11 billion a month. Ultimately the strategies of the Bush administration have created a far bigger crisis in South and Central

Asia than existed before 9/11. There are now full-blown Taliban insurgencies in Afghanistan and Pakistan, and the next locus could be Uzbekistan. The safety of Pakistan's nuclear weapons is uppermost in the minds of Western governments. There are more failing states in the Muslim world, while Al[-] Qaeda has expanded around the world.

Conclusion

Today, there are three principal theatres of conflict between 'Islam' and the West: Palestine, Iraq and Afghanistan, with the latter having worldwide ramifications as part of the 'global war on terror'. Each of these battles has seen large-scale destruction of nations, cultures and societies built over centuries that are today reduced to stone-age conditions of anarchy and deprivation, not far from the Hobbesian 'Kingdom of darkness'. In each of them, Muslims are targets of Western wrath, paying the price for the effrontery of their radical co-religionists in assaulting the world's sole superpower.

Day by day, as war becomes more intense, the saga of mutual abuse and terror worsens, which not only devastates the target community, but also debilitates the West's own national principles and ideals so that the West is unable to project to itself as an exemplar to a world seeking models for self- improvement.

Specific episodes of violence over the last ten years, so dramatic and horrific at the time they were perpetrated, now fade in memory and constitute today merely a grim background to the leitmotif of violence that has systematically undermined the peace process and brought about the deepest possible estrangement between the West and Muslims, an estrangement that is now based on visceral assertions of religious and ethno-nationalist identities, with hardly any prospect of co-existence.

NOTES

1. 'Terror-Principal Danger to Middle East Security: Sharon', reproduced in *Middle East Mirror*, 18 September 2001.
2. Seymour M. Hersh: 'King's Ransom: How Vulnerable Are the Saudi Royals?' *The New Yorker*, 22 October 2001.
3. Neil MacFarquhar: 'Anti-Western and Extremist Views Pervade Saudi Schools', *New York Times*, 19 October 2001.
4. David Leigh and Richard Norton-Taylor: 'House of Saud Looks Close to Collapse', *The Guardian*, 21 November 2001.

5. Bertus Hendriks, 'Saudi Arabia: the Weakest Link', *Radio Netherlands*, 2 November 2001.
6. Jim Hoagland, 'On a Precipice With the Saudis', *Washington Post*, 11 November 2001.
7. 'The Saudi Game', *Newsweek*, 13 November 2001.
8. 'Mideast "Friends" Could Do More', *Baltimore Sun*, 25 November 2001.
9. Thomas L. Friedman, 'The Real War', *New York Times*, 27 November 2001.
10. Charles Krauthammer: 'The Silent Imams,' *Washington Post*, 24 November 2001.
11. 'Reconsidering Saudi Arabia', *New York Times*, 14 October 2001.
12. 'Reconsidering Saudi Arabia', *Washington Post*, 11 November 2001.
13. Abdul Aziz Al-Tuwejri, 'Furious Media Attack on Saudi Arabia – Its motives and goals', *Al-Watan*, Abha, Saudi Arabia, 11 November 2001.
14. Dr. Mohammad Shoukany, 'More Passion, Less Reason', *Saudi Gazette*, Jeddah, 29 October 2001.
15. Shibley Telhami, *The Stakes – America in the Middle East* (Cambridge, MA: Westview Press, 2004) p. 96.
16. ibid., p. 101.
17. Edward R.F. Sheehan, 'The Disintegration of Palestine', *New York Review of Books*, 29 April 2004, p. 21.
18. Patrick Seale, 'Sharon At It Again – This Time He Targets Gaza', *Gulf News*, Dubai, 21 May 2004.
19. 'Israel and the Occupied Territories: Under the Rubble: House Demolition and Destruction of Land and Property', Amnesty International, Index No. MDE 15/033/2004, dated 18 May 2008; downloaded from: http://www.amnesty.org/en/library/info/MDE15/033/2004.
20. Telhami, p. 178.
21. Mustafa Barghouti, 'Israel's Use of Torture Must Be Exposed', *Gulf News*, Dubai, 26 May 2004.
22. 'The Truth Hurts', *Jerusalem Post*, April 12, 2004; downloaded from: http://hrw.org/english/docs/2004/04/12/isrlpa8422_txt.htm
23. Telhami, p. 177.
24. ibid.
25. Amos Elon, 'War Without End', *New York Review of Books*, Vol. L I, No. 12, 15 July 2004, p. 28.
26. Henry Siegman, 'Israel: The Threat from Within', *New York Review of Books*, Vol. L I, No. 3, 26 February 2004, p. 15.
27. Siegman, p. 17.
28. ibid.

29. ibid.
30. Jonathan Freedland, 'Bush's Amazing Achivement', *New York Review of Books*, Vol. L IV, No. 10, 14 June 2007, p. 16.
31. ibid.
32. ibid.
33. Max Rodenbeck, 'How Terrible Is It?', *New York Review of Books*, Vol. LIII, No. 19, 30 November 2006, p. 33.
34. ibid.
35. 'Torture in Iraq – A Report by Human Rights Watch', *New York Review of Books*, Vol. L II, No. 17, 3 November 2007, pp. 67–72.
36. David P. Forsythe, 'United States Policy Toward Enemy Detainees in the "War on Terrorism"', *Human Rights Quarterly*, Vol. 28, 2006, pp. 470–1.
37. ibid.
38. Ahmed Rashid, *Descent Into Chaos – How the War against Islamic Extremism is being lost in Pakistan, Afghanistan and Central Asia* (London: Allen Lane/Penguin Books, 2008) pp. 97-8;.
39. ibid., pp. 240–1.
40. ibid., pp. 241–2.
41. William Dalrymple, 'Pakistan in Peril', *The New York Review of Books*, Vol. LVI, Number 2, 12–25 February 2009, p. 41.
42. Rashid, p. 244.
43. ibid., p. 251.
44. ibid., p. 368.
45. ibid., p. 282.
46. ibid., pp. 317–25.
47. ibid., p. 365.
48. ibid., pp. 365–7.
49. ibid., p. 401.
50. Dalrymple, p. 39.
51. In his remarks on 27 March 2009, President Obama announced 'a comprehensive, new strategy for Afghanistan and Pakistan'. Noting that the situation is 'increasingly perilous', the President set out America's concerns thus:

> Al[-]Qaeda and its allies – the terrorists who planned and supported the 9/11 attacks – are in Pakistan and Afghanistan. Multiple intelligence estimates have warned that [A]l[-] Qaeda is actively planning attacks on the United States homeland from its safe haven in Pakistan. And if the Afghan government falls to the Taliban – or allows [A]l[-] Qaeda to go unchallenged – that country will again be a base for terrorists who want to kill as many of our people as they possibly can.

The future of Afghanistan is inextricably linked to the future of its neighbour, Pakistan. In the nearly eight years since 9/11, [A]l[-]Qaeda and its extremist allies have moved across the border to the remote areas of the Pakistani frontier. This almost certainly includes [A] l [-] Qaeda's leadership: Osama bin Laden and Ayman al-Zawahiri. They have used this mountainous terrain as a safe haven to hide, to train terrorists, to communicate with followers, to plot attacks, and to send fighters to support the insurgency in Afghanistan. For the American people, this border region has become the most dangerous place in the world.

But this is not simply an American problem - far from it. It is, instead, an international security challenge of the highest order.

The President added: 'We must recognize the fundamental connection between the future of Afghanistan and Pakistan—which is why I'hve appointed Ambassador Richard Holbrooke, who is here, to serve as Special Representative for both countries, and to work closely with General Petraeus to integrate our civilian and military efforts.'

52. Peter Baker and Eric Schmitt, 'War Strategy Debate Focuses on Al Qaeda', *International Herald Tribune*, 9 October 2009, p. 8; Gareth Porter: 'Hawks Still Link Taliban to Al-Qaeda', *Asia Times online*, 15 Oct 2009; downloaded from: http://www.atimes.com/atimes/South_Asia/KJI5Df01.html.

53. Henry A. Kissinger, 'Afghanistan's Cruel Options', *International Herald Tribune*, 5 October 2009, p. 12.

54. Porter.

55. ibid.

56. Bill Roggio, 'The Long War Journal: Al Qaeda's paramilitary 'Shadow Army,' *The Long War Journal*, 9 February 2009; downloaded from: http://longwarjournal.org/archieves/2009/02/al_qaedas_paramilita.phb

57. ibid; American commentators have made a valiant effort to explain the confusing situation in the 'Af-Pak' region pertaining to the two Talibans and Al[-]Qaeda, and the role of the Pakistan armed forces in this imbroglio. Thus, in an article in the *International Herald Tribune*, Scott Shane explained that, from the point of view of American interests, 'the Afghan Taliban is the primary enemy, mounting attacks daily against the 68,000 U.S. troops in the country'.

He added that the US's principal concern is that, once the Afghan Taliban take over the country, they will invite Al[-]Qaeda back into Afghanistan.

Shane then explained that the Pakistan Taliban have little in common with the Afghan Taliban since the former's principal interest is to expand their influence in Pakistan's tribal areas and ultimately gain control over

Islamabad. In this campaign they are at war with the Pakistani armed forces. On the other hand, the Pakistani armed forces have a long, mutually beneficial relationship with the Afghan Taliban: they hope that once the Americans withdraw from Afghanistan, the Taliban with the help of the Pakistan army, will fill the power vacuum in the country. [Scott Shane: 'Two Talibans Equal a Lot of Confusion', *International Herald Tribune*, 23 October 2009, p. 4.]

58. Abdul Hameed Bakier, 'Jihadis Debate Growing Rift Between Al-Qaeda and the Taliban', *Terrorism Monitor*, Vol. 7, Issue 38, 15 December 2009; downloaded from: http://www.jamestown.org/programs/gta/single/?tx_ttnews%5Btt_new.

59. Bakier; also see Porter; Gareth Porter: 'The Taliban-Al-Qaeda Schism', *Counterpunch*, 7 December 2009, downloaded from: http://www.counterpunch.org/porter12072009.html; and Gareth Porter: 'US Silent on Taliban's Al-Qaeda Offer', *Asia Times online*, 17 December 2009, downloaded from: http://www.atimes.com/atimes/South_Asia/KL17Df02.htm.

Graham Usher has also pointed out that this idea has been consistently promoted by the Pakistani army: since the late 1990s, Pakistan has been stressing the importance of US/NATO engagement with the Taliban on the basis that foreign forces will be withdrawn from Afghanistan in exchange for the Taliban sharing power with other Afghan groups and preventing elements like the Al-Qaeda from carrying out extremist activity from Afghan soil. Usher says:

The logic of negotiations [with the Taliban] assumed that the fundamental relationship between the Afghan Taliban and [A]l[-]Qaeda is tactical or material, rather than ideological, and that the Taliban is at heart a Pushtum movement before it is an Islamist one. In return for a share of power the Taliban leaders can be turned against their jihadi allies, argues Asif Ahmed Ali, a former Pakistani foreign minister. "We have to talk to the Taliban. There will be no peace in Pakistan and Afghanistan without it. The Taliban is the only force that can expel [A]l-Qaeda."

[Graham Usher: 'Obama, Pakistan and the Afghan Wars to Come', *Middle East Report*, 2 January 2010; downloaded from: http://www.lebanonwire.com/1001MLN/10010205MER.asp; henceforth Usher.]

60. Bakier.

61. ibid.

62. ibid.

63. Ahmed Rashid: 'Pakistan on the Brink' *The New York Review of Books*,

Vol. LVI, No. 10, 11 June-1 July 2009, pp. 12-14; henceforth Ahmed Rashid.

64. Ibid; for political and strategic implications of the Swat 'agreement', see Sadia Sulaiman, Syed Adnan Ali Shah Bukhari: "The Swat Conflict": An Arc of Instability spreading from Afghanistan to Central Asia and Xinjiang', *Terrorism Monitor*, Vol. 7, Issue 13, 18 May 2009; downloaded from: http://www.jamestown.org/programs/gta/single/ ?tx_ttnews%5Btt_new.

65. Manan Ahmed, 'Start a War', *The National Review*, Abu Dhabi, 6 November 2009, p. 3.

66. ibid.

67. ibid.

68. ibid.

69. Imtiaz Gul, 'Drain Pakistan's Tribal Swamps', *Sunday Times of India*, Mumbai, 6 September 2009, p. 14.

70. Dalrymple, p. 39.

71. Ahmed Rashid, p. 14.

72. ibid; Dalrymple, p. 41; Graham Usher has also set out the thinking of the Pakistani army thus:

As far as the Pakistani military is concerned, it faces two adversaries in Afghanistan – neither of which is the Taliban or even Al[-]Qaeda. One foe is the regime of President Hamid Karzai, particularly its nascent military and intelligence directorates. Those forces, for the most part, are commanded by Tajik warlords formerly belonging to the Northern Alliance ...

The second adversary is India, with which Pakistan is embroiled in a long-running conflict. The Indian footprint in Afghanistan, in the words of one Kabul-based Ambassador, is "strategic and vast," and Pakistan is duly alarmed. New Delhi was the regional backer of the Northern Alliance and is now Karzai's strongest ally in South Asia. It is one of Afghanistan's largest foreign donors and has helped train the armed forces. Along with Iran, India has built a road network in Western Afghanistan that allows Kabul access to the Persian Gulf without using Pakistani ports – facilities Islamabad deems vital to its economic future.

With most of its army still stationed on the eastern border with India – and an unfinished war in Kashmir – Islamabad's nightmare is that India and pro-Indian Afghan forces will fill the void left by departing US and NATO forces on its Western flank. [Usher.]

73. Freedland, p. 16.

74. Jonathan Raban, 'The Truth About Terrorism', *New York Review of Books*, Vol. LII, No.1, 13 January 2005, p. 22.

75. ibid.
76. ibid.
77. ibid.
78. Quoted in: Max Rodenbeck, p. 38.
79. 'Gen. Miller Said to Have Urged Use of Dogs at Iraqi Prison', *Washington Post*, published in *Arab News*, Jeddah, 27 May 2004.
80. Irene Khan, 'Why Human Rights Matter,' *Amnesty International, 2004 Annual Report*, downloaded from www.web.amnesty.org
81. Jane Mayer, 'The Battle for a Country's Soul', *New York Review of Books*, Vol. LV, No. 13, 14 August 2008, p. 41.
82. ibid., p. 42.
83. ibid., pp. 42–3. From 7 October 2001 onwards, a total of 715 detainees were brought to Guantanamo. Over the years, several detainees were released without charge, so that by November 2009 only 215 remained in detention.

     Only three detainees were convicted under the system of 'military commissions' set up under the Bush administration. The present US government is likely to try 60-80 of them and release the rest, though the legal and judicial framework within which the proposed prosecutions will take place has not been finalized so far.

     In January 2009, soon after his inauguration, President Obama signed an executive order directing that the Guantanamo Bay Detention Camp be closed within a year. However, taking into account administrative problems, he later clarified that the closure might be delayed to late 2010. [Information downloaded from: http://www.usatoday.com/printedition/news/20080602/oppose02.art.htm; http://www.npr.org/templates/story/story.php?storyID=9940966; and, http://www.indybay.org/newsitems/2009/03/23/18580989.php]
84. Richard Falk, *The Great Terror War* (Gloucestershire, U.K.: Arris Books, 2003) pp. xviii-xix.
85. Raban, p. 22.
86. ibid.
87. ibid., p. 23.
88. ibid., p. 24.
89. Rashid, p. lvii.

13

The Badge of All Our Tribe

SHYLOCK

...

For sufferance is the badge of all our tribe.
You call me misbeliever, cut-throat dog,
And spit upon my Jewish gabardine,
And all for use of that which is mine own.

...

You, that did void your rheum upon my beard
And foot me as you spurn a stranger cur
Over your threshold: moneys is your suit

ANTONIO

I am as like to call thee so again,
To spit on thee again, to spurn thee too.
If thou wilt lend this money, lend it not
As to thy friends; for when did friendship take
A breed for barren metal of his friend?
But lend it rather to thine enemy,
Who, if he break, thou mayst with better face
Exact the penalty.

William Shakespeare, *The Merchant of Venice*

People are very frightened of losing what they used to have, what they have now. We have not dealt with the trauma of 9/11. We have not found any closure. There is a vindictiveness that has transmitted itself into religion and into foreign policy and they have become partners. We're in shock and we're feeling threatened, not just about terrorism, but gay marriage, abortion. The issues are boiled down to black and white and there's no discussion about them. There's a real cultural revolution. We are seeing a significant struggle and it is not going to go away any time soon.

— Stephen Bales, *God's Own Country*

In contemporary times, religion, particularly its messianic impulse, is seeing a revival; as Mark Lilla has noted:[1]

> Today we have progressed to the point where we are again fighting the battles of the sixteenth century–over revelation and reason, dogmatic purity and toleration, inspiration and consent, divine duty and common decency. We are disturbed and confused. *We find it incomprehensible that theological ideas still inflame the minds of men, stirring up messianic passions that leave societies in ruin.* We assumed that this was no longer possible, that human beings had learned to separate religious questions from political ones, that fanaticism was dead. We were wrong. [Emphasis added.]

Lilla recalls that great Western thinkers, such as Hobbes, had in their time been 'disturbed by the messianic passions then debasing European life' and had sought alternatives to the traditional political theology; but he also notes the 'fragility' of such alternative traditions.[2] In spite of the efforts of Hobbes and the 'Great Separation' advocated by him, messianism survived resolutely, both in its religious and secular incarnations. Today, we are experiencing the full implications of an alliance, in the USA, between these two elemental forces, however opportunistic it might be, in the shape of the neocons and the Christian Right. This alliance is influential because it responds to the essential need for man to hope: he draws strength from his faith (religious messianism) and intellect (secular messianism), which not only imbues him with optimism, but also with conviction about the justice of his expectations and the inevitability of their realization. Sadly, since man is part of a larger multitude, his own aspirations often put him in competition with the expectations of others. Hence, he draws upon the other powerful impulse that informs his being: the demonization of the 'other' as evil, even satanic; but, since the divine entity is on *his* side, the total defeat and annihilation of the 'other' is to be confidently expected. Messianic expectation, both religious and secular, brings together like-minded adherents who bond in a powerful camaraderie which excludes not just the demonized 'other', but other possible hostile conspirators on one's own side, who lurk in the shadows and whose destruction for the success of the messianic expectation is as necessary as that of the 'other'.

Today, the days of the secular version of the messianic impulse seem to be drawing to a close, to be replaced by 'old-time religion ... at the heart of global conflict'.[3] Iraq, as Gray has pointed out, was initially a conflict of secular ideologies (neocons *vs.* Baathism), but later became a 'many-sided war of religion'. Gray blames the West's belief in faith-based violence as necessary for human salvation for the ignominious end of the 'great separation'; he says:[4]

> *The age of utopians ended in Fallujah, a city razed by rival fundamentalists.* The secular era is not in the future, as liberal humanists believe. It is in the past, which we have yet to understand. [Emphasis added.]

In the following paragraphs, we analyze the various strands that constitute the contemporary clash of messianic militarisms.

The Right-wing Christian-Jewish Alliance

During the Bush Administration, the neocon movement in the United States was the most influential secular messianic movement. Jacob Heilbrunn's book on the neocons was simply titled *They Knew They Were Right: The Rise of the Neocons*. The title of Grant Havers' review of this book was even more instructive: 'The Neocons: The Chosen People Without God'.[5] In true messianic tradition, the neocons also saw 'humanity advancing from darkness to light by way of the fires of war and revolution', embracing the 'pursuit of Utopia' with faith in revolution and force.[6] The most significant development in the evolution of the neocons' strategy was the alliance they set up with the Christian Right-wing in the USA, putting in place a truly 'Utopian Right' messianic movement.[7]

This alliance functioned in a number of different political contexts that, coming together, imbued it with unique authority and power in the pursuit of its messianic agenda. The first was the context of the US's historic belief–system that makes its citizens deeply religious, while conscious of their nation being 'exceptional' and having a God-given 'special destiny in the world'. As Gray has noted, what is unique about the USA is 'the persistent vitality of [its] messianic belief and the extent to which it continues to shape the public culture'.[8] The second context was the personal religiosity of President Bush and his willingness to assert it in the public domain to an extent greater than any of his predecessors. With his presidency, 'religion began to move into the centre of American politics'.[9]

The third context were the events of 9/11: this assault upon the United States' mainland, after nearly 200 years, not only traumatized the nation and made it vulnerable, but it also made it aware of dark hostile forces that envied its success, despised its values and challenged its prowess. These fears and anxieties touched the deep-seated religiosity of the American people who, in this period of national crisis, delved into their messianic belief system and, led by their president, came up with an understanding of their enemy and weaponry to be used to vanquish him. Thus, the events of September 11 became, for Americans, a messianic 'time of tribulation'.[10]

Jewish lobbies supporting Israel's interests in the USA had been working closely with the Christian Right movement since 1967.[11] Through the 1990s, the neocons, too, saw the merits of this rather opportunistic alliance; now, in the wake of 9/11, this alliance was consolidated into a solid strategic partnership, headed by a president, who, with the unstinted support of the Christian Right, believed in end-times and saw in 9/11 an apocalyptic event that defined their God-given mission to battle the forces of evil.[12]

In this environment of messianic excitement, the neocons, albeit secular messianics but in alliance with true religious messianism, commenced the implementation of their agenda in West Asia: regime change in Iraq and the ushering in of democracy in all of West Asia. The agenda was truly messianic: it involved the demonization of the enemy (Saddam Hussein), and use of violence to effect regime change in the confident belief that, from this (necessary) violence, salvation in the form of a democratic order for the Iraqi people would emerge; regime change, as John Gray has said, would be an instrument of progress.[13] This is illustrated by Deputy Defence Secretary Wolfwitz's messianic enthusiasm for the Iraq war which James Mann has described tus:[14]

> In the midst of the invasion, Americans working in the war zone came up with the nickname Wolfowitz of Arabia for the deputy secretary of defence; the phrase captures the degree of intensity, passion and even, it sometimes seemed, romantic fervour with which he pursued the goals of overthrowing Saddam Hussein and bringing democracy to the Middle East.

The Global War on Terror (GWOT) was similarly defined and pursued in messianic terms; as Gray has said:[15]

> The 'war on terror' is a symptom of a mentality that anticipates n unprecedented change in human affairs – the end of history, the passing

of the sovereign state, universal acceptance of democracy and the defeat of evil. *This is the central myth of apocalyptic religion framed in political terms, and the common factor underlying the failed utopian projects of the past decade.* [Emphasis added.]

The GWOT was to be a 'universal crusade' which would yield progress and support good causes; it would lead, in Paul Berman's words:[16]

to a politics of human rights and especially women's rights, across the Muslim world; a politics against racism and anti-Semitism, no matter how inconvenient that might seem to the Egyptian media and the House of Saud; a politics against the manias of the ultra-right in Israel, too, no matter how much that might enrage the Likud and its supporters; a politics of secular education, of pluralism, and law across the Muslim world; a politics against obscurantism and superstition; a politics to outcompete the Islamists and Baathis on their left; a politics to fight against poverty and oppression; a politics of authentic solidarity for the Muslim world, instead of the demagogy of cosmic hatred. A politics, in a word, of liberalism, a 'new birth of freedom' – the kind of thing that could be glimpsed, in its early stages, in the liberation of Kabul.

As in the case of all enterprises pursuing Utopia, this enterprise too has failed, with extraordinary death and destruction visited upon peoples, societies and nations in West Asia, whose only role in these upheavals is that of innocent victims of the 'cleansing' onslaught of messianic fervour.

Messianic zeal has not just wreaked havoc in West Asia; one of the most serious implications of the GWOT has been the abridgement of civil liberties within the USA itself and the coarsening of national values in pursuit of an elusive 'security'. A concentration camp was set up at Guantanamo[17] and a tradition of wanton torture and abuse was established in Iraq. Both these enterprises, during the Bush era, were beyond the scrutiny of international and domestic law. It is noteworthy that all these measures were in line with precedents set by the Japanese in World War II, the Khmer Rouge in Cambodia, Stalin's Soviet Union and the Chinese during the Korean War.[18]

In the messianic paradigm that informs the GWOT, demonization of the adversary has been an important feature of contemporary conflict. A few days after the 9/11 attacks, President Bush told reporters that 'this crusade, this war on terrorism, is going to take a while'. The word 'crusade' could have been a slip of the tongue had it not been repeated in a set speech to the troops in Alaska some months later. At that time, the President said of the Canadians: 'They stand with us in this incredibly important crusade to defend freedom.'[19] Louise Richardson notes:[20]

> While Westerners may see the crusades as a romantic military episode in ancient history, in the Middle East today the crusades are well remembered. The charter of Hamas, for example, deals at length with the fate of the crusaders who held Jerusalem for 200 years before being expelled by the Muslim warrior Saladin. Hamas regards the Israeli occupation of Jerusalem today along the same lines. By their own account the crusaders slaughtered 70,000 Muslims when they conquered Jerusalem in 1099, and while they probably exaggerated the number, the memory runs very deep. *By using the term "crusade" President Bush appeared to many in the Middle East to demonstrate that the US war on terrorism was actually a war of Christianity against Islam, just as bin Laden has sought to cast it.* [Emphasis added.]

The GWOT launched by the US after 9/11, had, from the Arab perspective, the character of a broad and sustained assault on Arab and Muslim people. As they saw it, in response to the attacks on the World Trade Centre and the Pentagon, the US killed several thousand Afghans and Iraqis, and imprisoned several hundred of them in conditions of physical and mental abuse. Besides this, the USA targeted and humiliated Muslims in general through ethnic/religious profiling, abridgement of civil rights, denial of judicial hearings and appeal, and, in general, presented the picture of an intrusive regime that indulged in illegal surveillance, arrest, detention and demeaning incarceration.

A review of this contemporary reciprocal demonization leads one to conclude that ideology-driven, messianic, Right-wing state-powers, in their confrontation with the 'other' that opposes their hegemony or occupation, themselves assume the identity, characteristics and instrumentalities of their enemy. Indeed, in the process, such state-powers make Right-wing extremist/terrorist groups in their country irrelevant, as the governments themselves assume the mantle, identity and zeal of non-official perpetrators of violence.

Unfortunately, with every passing day, in US/Israeli (=Western?) eyes, the identity of the Muslim 'other' is acquiring a sharper focus. President Bush, in his interviews with Bob Woodward for *Plan of Attack*, justified the Iraq war even in the absence of any recovery or evidence of WMD; he said:[21]

> ... there is no doubt in my mind we should have done this [that is, gone to war on Iraq]. Not only for our sake, but for the Iraqi citizens.

Again, in respect of the conduct of the Iraq war itself, Bush was self-congratulatory, saying that the carefully targeted war:[22]

> will enable other leaders, if they feel like they have to go to war, to spare innocent citizens and their lives ... To me the big news is America has changed how you fight and win war.

Both these self-serving remarks of the President, in the Arab view, had the ring of cruel irony for the Iraqi people. As many Arabs see it, the US occupation of Iraq has been imbued with a racist/fascist attitude that demeaned the conquered people and deprived them of their identity and dignity. This was most obvious in the systematic abuse and humiliation meted out to inmates at Guantanamo and Iraq. It is particularly noteworthy that, in some instances, the religious and ethnic identity of the prisoners was deliberately undermined, with prisoners being made to abuse Islam and forced to consume alcohol and pork. An American soldier explained this mindset thus:[23]

> You just sort of try to block out the fact that they are human beings and see them as enemies. You call them *hajis*, you know? You do all the things that make it easier to deal with killing them and mistreating them.

American liberal commentators have also noted with deep concern the serious abridgement of civil liberties in the United States itself, put in place legislatively by the Bush Administration after the events of September 11. Thus, Anthony Lewis pointed out:[24]

> We are in another bad time for civil liberties now. Under the mantle of his War on Terror, President Bush has imprisoned American citizens without trial, detained thousands of aliens in this country, and persuaded Congress to let government intrude more deeply into our private lives. In a significant respect, the danger to liberty is more serious than in past episodes.

Taking into account the fact the GWOT was open-ended in terms of time, Lewis was concerned that 'repressive measures may go on indefinitely, unless they are stopped by the courts or by political second thoughts'.[25]

Soon after the events of September 11, the Bush Administration had rushed through the Congress, the *USA Patriot Act 2001*, which had provided the broadest possible definition of terrorism. The Act, according to an observer:[26]

> greatly expanded the power of Government to conduct secret searches of private homes, permitted the attorney general to detain aliens as security

threats whenever he wanted, stipulated new rules enabling government to demand records of any person's book purchases or borrowings from bookstores and libraries, and increased the government's surveillance authority in many other ways. A recent report by an internal Justice Department inspector alleged 'dozens of violations of civil rights in the enforcement of the Act.'

Observers also noted the general passivity of the American population in the face of these assaults on their civil liberties. Michael Ignatieff explained this thus: [27]

> The historical record suggests, disturbingly, that *majorities care less about deprivations of liberty that harm minorities than they do about their own security.* [Emphasis added.]

Ronald Dworkin believed that these draconian measures would primarily affect the USA's Muslim population:[28]

> But with hardly any exceptions, no American who is not a Muslim and has no Muslim connections actually runs any risk of being labeled an enemy combatant and locked up in a military jail.

The demonizing of the Muslims in Jewish–Christian Right-wing discourse has included an effort to link Islam with fascism and the Palestinians with the Nazis. The distinguished Canadian journalist Eric Margolis has noted that the term 'Islamofascism' has become the new hot buzz word among America's Right-wing and Christian fundamentalists; he points out:[29]

> The term 'Islamofascist' is utterly without meaning, but packed with emotional explosives. It is a propaganda creation worthy of Dr. Goebbels, and the latest expression of the big lie technique being used by neocons in Washington's propaganda war against its enemies in the Muslim World.

He goes on to say that 'Islamophobia' or the 'hatred of Muslims has become a key ideological hallmark of rightwing parties' in the US and in different parts of Europe. Thus, references to 'Islamofascism' have been frequently made by American Right-wing Christian leaders. Gary Bauer, described as a conservative Christian power broker, conveyed the following idea:[30]

> The war against Islamofascism is in many respects a "values issue". That may seem like an odd statement at first glance, but, as I have often said, *losing Western Civilisation to this vicious enemy (Islam) would be immoral.* [Emphasis added.]

These views were echoed by another prominent Christian Right-wing leader, Rick Scarborough, who said: 'If radical Islam succeeds in its ultimate goals, Christianity ceases to exist. It's the ultimate life issue.'[31] During the 2008 Presidential campaign, the then Presidential candidate, Mike Huckabee, described Islamofascism, as 'the greatest threat this country (USA) has ever faced'.[32]

In Right-wing American and Israeli writings, Arab resistance to Israel has often been depicted in terms of its similarity to the Nazi violence against Jews, and, in this way, links the Palestinians and Arabs to the Holocaust. Thus, a prominent American intellectual referred to Palestinians and many of the Arab leaders in the 1930s and 1940s as 'Hitler's little helpers in the Middle-East'.[33] Another writer spoke of 'Arab intransigence' growing 'more violent and being politically sympathetic to Nazism', while still another, Daniel Bell, spoke of the Palestinians as having 'sustained themselves by the emotions of race hatred against Israelis'. Other Jewish writers have traced Muslim animosity towards Israel to the millennial political hatred between Islam and Christendom.[34] Thus, the Israeli political leader Benjamin Netanyahu said: 'The soldiers of militant Islam and pan-Arabism do not hate the West because of Israel; they hate Israel because of the West.'[35]

The Islamophobia of the Jewish and Christian Right has its mirror image in burgeoning anti-Semitism in sections of the Muslim community. That modern-day militant Islam has a strong element of anti-Semitism is confirmed by the various writings of Al-Qaeda leaders such as Osama bin Laden and al-Zawahiri. Bin Laden has frequently spoken of the alliance between Jews and Crusaders, and has pointed out that American leaders 'have fallen victims to Jews' Zionist blackmail'.[36] Again, in a number of popular Arab writings, the discredited *Protocols of the Elders of Zion* is still treated as an authentic document that refers to the Jewish plan for world domination.

Anti-Semitism among Arabs manifested itself only from the early part of the twentieth century, primarily in response to Western support for the Zionist project. In this, the Arab side merely mirrored the near-racist animosity of the extremist Zionists. Thus, as noted in Chapter III, Vladmir Jabotinski, founder of the Union of Zionist Revisionists, saw Zionism as a colonial enterprise that had necessarily to be based on military force. Thus, he said:[37]

Zionism is a colonizing adventure and it therefore stands or falls by the question of armed force. It is important to build, it is important to speak Hebrew, but, unfortunately, it is even more important to be able to shoot– or else I am through with playing at colonization.

He went on to say that only an 'iron wall of Jewish bayonets' could force the Palestinian Arabs to accept the inevitable–'the transformation of Palestine into Eretz Israel'.[38] Even David Ben Gurion had recognized in the 1930s that Zionist support for the 'partition plan' was a purely short-term tactical move; he had said:[39]

I favour partition of the country because when we become a strong power after the establishment of the state, we will abolish partition and spread throughout Palestine.

Thus, armed violence against the resident Palestinian population was inherent in the Zionist project and made violent resistance by the dispossessed Palestinians and their Arab supporters inevitable. However, in spite of this well-known historical background, Western Right-wing writers continue to make vicious attacks on Muslims on account of their perceived anti-Semitism. Thus, the Right-wing British writer, Andrew Sullivan, said the following in a newspaper article:[40]

Fanatical anti-Semitism, as bad as or even worse than Hitler's, is now a cultural norm across much of the Arab Middle East and beyond. It's the acrid glue that unites Saddam, Arafat, al Qaeda, Hezbollah, Iran and the Saudis. They all hate the Jews and want to see them destroyed.

Other writers have echoed this view. Christopher Hitchens has spoken of 'fascism with an Islamic face', while Clive James pointed out that 'a typical Muslim terrorist believes that Hitler had the right idea, that *The Protocols of the Elders of Zion* is a true story, and that the obliteration of the state of Israel is a religious requirement'.[41]

Peter Partner, after a detailed study of the Christian West's 'holy wars' against Islam over the last fourteen centuries, refers to present-day conflicts among the adherents of the Semitic traditions as 'modern revivals of the language of holy war'[42] and categorically points out:[43]

the dynamic that moves people to commit acts of war and terrorism is not some sort of cultural imperative that arises from the texts themselves. *For both modern Islamism and modern Zionism, the moving power behind their sacred vocabulary is entirely of their own times.* [Emphasis added.]

After analyzing the history of anti-Semitism in militant Islam, he has pointed out that its origins lie *not* in Islam the religion, or even in early Islamic history; it is in fact 'distinctly Western'.[44] But, there is an interesting irony in this: Western anti-Semitism had been based on the canard that the Jewish community was seeking world domination. Today, the votaries of Islamophobia strongly argue that Islam, on its part, is seeking world domination and that anti-Semitism is the natural offspring of this impulse. However, the factual position is that the urge for world domination of radical Islamists is an exact mirror image of the same Western fantasy and, indeed, the anti-Islamic demonology developed in the West is based on demonizing the 'other' who is seen as a rival in the same competition.

Given the central role of 'Islam' in the discourse of present-day messianic militarisms, it would be useful to place radical Islam in a broader contemporary political context.

Contextualizing Radical Islam

If today we pore over the writings of radical Islamists of the mid-twentieth century, it is only because their visions and strategies, until recently obscure and marginal and largely confined to their own countries, were able to acquire practical shape and character during the mujahideen struggle in Afghanistan. What the political progenitors of the global jihad in Afghanistan,— the USA, Saudi Arabia and Pakistan, failed to anticipate was that, if 'Islam' could be mobilized in a global jihad against godless communism, it could also direct its wrath and weaponry on the older villain and hate-figure –Western imperialism, particularly when people in the Muslim lands were voicing considerable anger against the injustices in Palestine and the pusillanimity (and, indeed, *collaboration* with imperialism) of their own rulers. This anger in Muslim lands was not expressed in terms of 'Islam' the religion: though its protagonists made frequent references to the faith and its history, in the twentieth century, they manifested strong affinities with contemporary Christian as also Western secular developments so that radical Islam, in many ways, mirrors its avowed enemies.

Radical Islamic thinkers of the twentieth century were not fanatical mullahs burning with age-old anti-Christian or anti-Western animosity emanating from the time of the Crusades. They were actually deeply familiar with Western writings, and many of their ideas reflect those of contemporary Western thinkers. Thus, Sayyid Qutb drew his idea of the 'revolutionary vanguard' (echoed later by Abdullah Azzam and bin Laden) from Lenin. The idea of using revolutionary violence to achieve a new world, of course, originated with the Jacobins, and then was repeated in Western secular tradition right up to modern times. Finally, Qutb's messianism, that is, belief in the imminence of a new ideal world, originates in the Islamic tradition of the Mahdi, which is itself drawn from the Christian and the earlier Jewish tradition of the messiah.[45]

The votaries of an inherent Islam—West conflict often fail to note that there are, in fact, many similarities between mainstream Islam and Christianity: based on their common Semitic origins, both share monotheism and believe that history moves immutably towards progress. Again, they are both proselytizing faiths and, ideally, would like to convert all of mankind.[46] Historically, there has been no firewall between them: Islam preserved the culture of the Greeks and Romans, while developing its own rich culture through interaction with other developed civilizations, and then passed on this valuable amalgam to the West to lay the basis for the Renaissance. Up until recent times, Islam and the West, as we have seen, have interacted with each other in a spirit of benign accommodation and in pursuit of mutual interests.

It is interesting to note that even the fundamentalist movements of Christianity and Islam share several characteristics. Both seek to define religion in its 'pure' sense, that is, divorced from its cultural, social or anthropological moorings.[47] Thus, they tend to reject the familial or cultural heritage in which religious beliefs and practices took shape. Again, they view established religion as lukewarm (or even pagan), and assert what they think of as its authentic 'born-again' character. Both emphasize faith-based rather than intellect-based religion, believing that faith-based religion gives religion greater popular appeal. They stress social homogeneity, believe in admonition rather than benign administration and emphasize the importance of distinguishing between the sexes and between believers and unbelievers. Not surprisingly, their appeal is greatest amongst populations that are in acute distress because they that have been uprooted or fear that their cultural identity is in danger (due to their being in the diaspora or, generally, due to globalization). Flowing from this, it is not surprising that adherents of both traditions strongly espouse messianic beliefs.

Moving beyond the religious discourse, it is important to note that contemporary radical 'Islam', represented by Al-Qaeda and other kindred

Islamist groups, is more akin to Western secular Left-wing and Right-wing movements than to traditional religious entities. Thus, there are several similarities between Al-Qaeda and the radical Left movement in Europe of the 1960s in that:[48] both draw their strength from a pool of alienated youth; both use similar symbols of non-conformity and revolt such as beards and guns; both believe in sanctified texts; both hark back to inspirational figures and have been headed by charismatic leaders; both have similar targets in political and cultural terms, that is, imperialism, globalization, modernization; both have a global mission; both movements have become de-territorialized in that their members belong to different countries and were brought together through a sense of shared alienation, which Marc Sageman has referred to as 'in-group love';[49] both use violence in pursuit of their mission; both seek to tear the curtain of hypocrisy and expose the 'real face' of their enemies. The Left seeks to expose the violence, selfishness and materialism of the capitalist West, while radical Islam is seeking to reveal the real character and nefarious agenda of Western, crusader imperialism. Finally, both have a messianic belief of their inevitable destiny, that is, the triumph of socialism then, the triumph of Islam now. Interestingly, both movements, as Gilles Kepel has noted, have been seen by their enemies as a danger to the Western way of life![50]

Again, the demand of radical Islamic protagonists for an 'Islamic State', also referred to as a 'caliphate' modeled on the polity of Prophet Mohammed in Madinah, though couched in theological terms that go back to pristine Islam, incorporates several modern concepts. In the first place, the details of such a vision have never been adequately spelt out: 'no-one has ever seriously gone in search of that Caliph', Roy points out.[51] The UK-based Hizbul Tahrir has suggested that the Caliphate is vested in the party itself, thus harking back to the Marxist tradition of party as political actor.[52]

The establishment of an Islamic state had pre-occupied Maududi, Al-Banna and Sayyid Qutb in the last century. Maududi had clearly stated that 'the real objective of Islam is to establish the kingdom of God on earth.'[53] In April 1939, he said this would be achieved through jihad: '... the objective of the Islamic jihad is to eliminate the rule of an un-Islamic system, and establish in its place an Islamic system of State rule'.[54] While such an attempt would initially be confined to the countries where the 'members of the Party of Islam' lived, their ultimate aim was 'none other than a world revolution'.[55] In his *Islamic Law and the Constitution*, finalized in 1953–5, he set out some of the contours of his 'Islamic State'. He described the state as a 'theo-democracy' ruled by the whole community of Muslims led to power by the Islamist party: the seizure of political power by the party was not just 'positively desirable', it was 'obligatory'.[56] This Islamic state would be 'universal and all-embracing', possibly even resembling a fascist or communist state, but without the dictatorship.[57] According to commentators, Maududi's Islam was a 'political religion' and even an ideology that supported 'state might' and would be an 'opponent of human freedom and equality'.[58]

In defining his Islamic state, Hasan Al-Banna was nostalgic about the caliphate, but advocated it only as a long-term goal, and satisfied himself with an entity based on Koranic injunctions promoting good and prohibiting evil.[59] His polity was more open and accommodative than that of Maududi, since it would be based on consultation (*shura*). He even accepted the notion of a secular government if chosen by the people, though, in regard to jihad, he was a militant and a staunch anti-colonialist.[60]

Sayyid Qutb saw the end of jihad as the establishment of a religio-political unit (under the sovereignty of God) achieved by the Islamic vanguard that separated itself from the jahili (ignorant) society.[61] Both Al-Banna and Qutb in defining their concept of the Islamic state went far beyond traditional thinking. Al-Banna's state accommodated parliamentary democracy and elections. On the same lines, Sayyid Qutb too rejected the contributions of the traditional ulema and in his writings pursued a 'freedom of interpretation' that caused misgivings not only among traditional scholars but even among senior members of the Muslim Brotherhood.[62]

The most important political achievement of these three intellectuals of early resurgent Islam was the 'recasting of Islam as a comprehensive ideology to address the conditions of modern Muslims'.[63] This 'recasting' was actually based on a new interpretation of the Islamic faith to suit contemporary circumstances. Thus, the Islamist demand for an Islamic Caliphate is rooted neither in religious dogma nor in Islamic tradition. It, in fact, emerges from a *modern* protest against an illegitimate state authority (seen as servile before Western hegemonic interests) and in support of 'nationalist legitimacy';[64] it thus treats Islam not as a traditional faith but as a modern political ideology.

The Badge of All Our Tribe

Amidst the venom and strife that animates the children of Abraham today, Karabell has soberly noted: 'There is known history and forgotten history, history that supports our sense of present and history that suggests other pathways'.[65] While the Western view is largely influenced by memories of conquests by Muslim arms, the Islamic view is overwhelmingly influenced by memories of imperialism and of recent defeat centred around the emergence of Israel. Karabell points out:[66]

> If the Holocaust stands as a never-ending rebuke to relations between Christians and Jews, then the intractable conflict between the Palestinians and the Israelis has come to colour not just discussions about Judaism in the Muslim world but discussions about Islam and the West in general.
>
> The creation of Israel is a historical Rubicon. On one side is a dynamic past of coexistence and cooperation along with episodes of antagonism and cruelty. On the other is an increasingly simplistic picture of hostile relations between the parties. *In short, the creation of Israel led to disturbing revisions of the past in light of the present. Muslims, Christians, and Jews are all guilty of revisionism.* [Emphasis added.]

The central issue that divides the children of Abraham today and instills in them animosities based on messianic belief is that of Palestine. No other issue defines identities so robustly and or sharpens present differences so acutely on the basis of recalled ancient claims and grievances. At one level, the Palestine issue is simple, that is, it is a land dispute over which two contending parties have laid claims on different bases; at the same time, it is a complex issue, since it is imbued with religious history, tribal memory, grievances emerging from a sense of dispossession and victimhood, and a sustained and deeply ingrained demonization of the 'other', so that the conflict assumes the character of a messianic confrontation.

The Israeli position emerges from the Holocaust: as pointed out by Avraham Burg in his recent book, *The Holocaust is Over: We Must Rise from its Ashes*, Israel has, from the very beginning, inculcated in its citizenry a conviction that they are the eternal victims of the Holocaust.[67] Today, the memory of the Holocaust defines the identity of the Israeli and appears to justify the extraordinary violence with which Israel's state authorities deal with the Palestinian people. Burg, with other earlier liberal Israeli writers, has seen the emergence in Israel of a 'toxic anti-Arab racism' that is not only part of the Israeli mainstream but even reflects the anti-Semitism of Weimar Germany which prepared the way for Hitler's 'final solution'.[68]

As of now, the Palestinian scenario seems rather bleak and incapable of yielding a resolution that would bring peace to the peoples involved. This is because the centrepiece of Israeli policy is the systematic eviction of Palestinians; as Alan Philps has pointed out:[69]

> Before 1948, the Palestinians owned – either outright or through customary title – 93 per cent of the land in Mandatory Palestine. After the *Nakba* (1948), this declined to 25 per cent, and now stands at a mere four per cent.

The dispossession of lands and properties owned by Palestinians has been part of a systematic policy to induce Palestinians to leave the occupied territories, a project that Jonathan Cook has described as 'ethnic cleansing not by butchers in uniform but technocrats in suits'.[70]

The results of these forced evictions have not been particularly impressive from the Israeli perspective: while the expansion of settlements on the West Bank has been an article of Zionist faith, Israel's distinguished academic, Zeev Sternhell, has pointed out that of the 250,000 Israelis living in the West Bank settlements, four-fifths are there for practical non-ideological reasons, such as having access to better housing and quality of life.[71] According to him, only 50,000 settlers are ideology-oriented and just a small handful of these, between one to two thousand, would resort to violence in support of continued occupation.

However, the defence of the interests of these few xenophobic zealots has led to considerable hostility toward the Palestinians, yielding a near-universal culture of abuse by Israeli state authorities. An Israeli group calling itself 'Breaking the Silence', founded in 2004, has taken it upon itself to publicize the behaviour of Israeli soldiers in Palestinian territories, highlighting the routine abuse of Palestinian civilians.[72] The co-founder of the group, Yehuda Shaul, has provided numerous instances of prolonged curfews, long detentions of Palestinians, random gunshot firings and destruction of Palestinian property so that, over time, in Shaul's words, 'The Palestinians stopped being a people and simply become objects'.

The violence in Gaza in January 2009 was in line with the systematic use of disproportionate force by Israel against Palestinian and other Arab targets. Early commentaries on the assault indicated that the Gaza assault had been planned for over six months, and the Israeli armed forces were only waiting for an appropriate opportunity to unleash their firepower upon the hapless population.[73] While the Israeli media campaign highlighted the fact that Israel had evacuated all its settlements and citizens from Gaza in 2005, what it failed to mention was that, for several months before the attacks, Gaza was under sustained economic blockade and that, over the previous six months before the attacks, there had been no rocket attacks from Hamas.

In fact, Hamas was voted to power in January 2006 primarily on account of the Gaza population's frustration with the inability of the Fatah government of Mahmoud Abbas to get the blockade lifted so that the people could lead a normal life. The rocket attacks were almost entirely due to the economic blockade. Again, before the aerial assault from end-December 2008, the Israeli forces had been engaged in systematically provoking the Hamas authorities by sending in patrols to destroy tunnels and inflicting casualties on Hamas fighters resisting them. Again, before Hamas revoked the ceasefire in mid-December, Israel cut deliveries of food supplies, medicine, fuel, cash and spare parts, so that, on the eve of the assault, the Gaza administration was in a state of near breakdown.[74]

The aim of the Israeli assault upon Gaza was clearly stated by its leaders as the destruction of Hamas as a military and political force and the ending of Hamas's rule in Gaza. Towards this end, besides large-scale destruction of civilians and property, the Israeli assaults also targeted symbols of local importance, such as the Islamic University, the Interior Ministry, the Gaza seaport, the Justice Ministry, civil defence buildings, etc. These actions, according to most observers, have actually strengthened the Hamas, made the Palestinians more angry and bitter, and have ensured the emergence of the next generation of radicals and suicide bombers.[75]

Questions have been raised as to why the Hamas has pursued its rocket attacks upon Israel, given that they hardly inflict any serious damage on the enemy even as they provoke harsh retaliation. The British journalist, Peter Beaumont, on the basis of firsthand discussions with Palestinians in Gaza, has explained that these attacks revolve around the idea of resistance; according to those interviewed by him, the attacks serve: [76]

> as a form of psychological release; as a focus for social cohesion and national identity, generating 'martyrs' to celebrate; and, finally, as a constant

reminder to the 'Other' – the enemy – that the Palestinians had not been defeated.

This mindset is clearly reflected on the Israeli side as well. Soon after the end of the Gaza military operations by Israel, news reports appeared about the role played by the Israeli Army's Rabbinate in this assault. The reports referred specifically to Chief Rabbi Avichai Ronsky (holding the rank of Brigadier), who encouraged the soldiers to inflict the maximum possible violence upon the Palestinians in Gaza. The soldiers were given a booklet which extensively quoted Shlomo Aviner, an extreme Right-wing rabbi, who has compared Palestinians to Philistines, the biblical enemies of the Jews.[77] Aviner was quoted as saying: 'When you show mercy to a cruel enemy, you are being cruel to pure and honest soldiers … This is a war on murderers.' He also cited a biblical ban on 'surrendering a single millimeter' of Greater Israel.[78]

In an editorial, the Israeli liberal newspaper, *Haartez*, described Ronsky as 'an instrument of divine punishment' and as 'the spiritual mentor of the most violent and extremist settlers'.[79] It said that under him, the soldiers were 'being exposed to chauvinist and racist incitement, which is illegal'. Later, *Israel Opinion* published the views of two reserve soldiers who saw action in Gaza. They expressed concern about the major role played by religious groups, who were involved with the soldiers at different stages of the operation. The two soldiers concluded their report with the following comment:[80]

> There is a problem with the growing tendency to provide religious elements with a monopoly on values and fighting spirit, and particularly with *the legitimacy granted to organizations with a missionary and messianic character to operate amongst the soldiers.* Most of the commanders in our division are religious, yet up until the last war there was complete separation between their private world and their military position.
>
> If we fail to clearly draw the line right now, *in a few years we shall find ourselves shifting from wars of choice or no choice to holy wars.* [Emphasis added.]

Jonathan Cook, in a detailed report in the Abu Dhabi-based *The National*, has quoted a number of Israelis as saying:[81]

> Extremist rabbis and their followers, bent on waging holy war against the Palestinians, are taking over the Israeli army by stealth.
>
> Their influence in shaping the army's goals and methods is starting to be felt, as more and more graduates from officer courses are also drawn from Israel's religious extremist population.

Even while the Israeli attacks upon Gaza were going on between December 2008 and January 2009, large sections of the international community had been appalled at the ruthlessness of the assault and the extent of the carnage. However, the publication of a report of the UN Fact-Finding Mission on Gaza, headed by Justice Richard Goldstone, on 15 September 2009, revived memories of the Gaza violence, and focused fresh attention globally on the Palestine predicament in the occupied territories.[82] While the Goldstone report did criticize Hamas for war crimes by firing rockets indiscriminately into Israel, as a result of which four people were killed and hundreds injured, the report severely castigated the Israeli military operation. Some of the findings of the report were as follows:

> The Mission found that, in the lead up to the Israeli military assault on Gaza, Israel imposed a blockade amounting to *collective punishment* and carried out a *systematic policy of progressive isolation and deprivation* of the Gaza Strip. During the military operation, houses, factories, wells, schools, hospitals, police stations and other *public buildings were destroyed*, with families, including the elderly and children, left living amid the rubble of their former dwellings long after the attacks ended, as no reconstruction has been possible due to the continuing blockade.
>
> *Significant trauma*, both immediate and long-term, has been suffered by the population of Gaza. More than 1400 people were killed. The Gaza military operations were directed by Israel at the people of Gaza as a whole, in furtherance of an overall policy aimed at punishing the Gaza population, and in a deliberate policy of *disproportionate force* aimed at the civilian population.
>
> The destruction of food supply installations, water sanitation systems, concrete factories and residential houses was the result of *a deliberate and systematic policy to make the daily process of living, and dignified living, more difficult for the civilian population.*
>
> Israeli forces also *humiliated, dehumanized and carried out an assault on the dignity of the people in Gaza*, through the use of human shields, unlawful detentions, unacceptable conditions of detention, the vandalizing of houses, the treatment of people when their houses were entered, graffiti on the walls, obscenities and racist slogans.
>
> The Israeli operations were carefully planned in all their phases as a *deliberately disproportionate attack designed to punish, humiliate and terrorize a civilian population*, radically diminish its local economic capacity both to work and to provide for itself, and to force upon it an ever increasing sense of dependency and vulnerability. Responsibility lies

in the first place with those who designed, planned, ordered and oversaw the operations.

> There is strong evidence that Israeli forces committed grave breaches of the Fourth Geneva Convention in Gaza, including: willful killing, torture or inhuman treatment, willfully causing great suffering or serious injury to body or health, and extensive destruction of property. As grave breaches, these acts give rise to individual criminal responsibility. [Emphasis added.]

The report also looked at certain larger issues pertaining to the Israeli occupation of Palestinian territories and its treatment of Palestinians in general. It spoke of the violence of Israeli settlers against Palestinians; the use of excessive force against Palestinian demonstrators; large-scale detentions of Palestinians in Israeli prisons, and humiliation of Palestinians at various Israeli checkpoints.

The report evoked outrage from the Israeli government and a number of prominent Israeli commentators, with considerable personal abuse being heaped on Justice Goldstone, in spite of his being Jewish and a judge of international standing.[83] At the same time, a number of prominent Jews also defended the report. Thus, Richard Falk felt that Israel's reaction to the report had been 'panicked', primarily because it had been authored by an eminent international personality who could not credibly be accused of an anti-Israel bias.[84] Falk noted that since the Gaza war, 'the solidity of Jewish support for Israel has been fraying at the edges. This will likely now fray even further'.

A number of prominent Jewish writers criticized Israel not just for the abuses perpetrated in Gaza but also for its policies against Palestinians in general. Thus, David Shulman pointed out:[85]

> No one who regularly visits the Palestinian territories controlled by Israel has to speculate about whether or not Israel is engaged in the routine abuse of human rights. Such abuse is the very stuff of the occupation – a daily reality exacerbated above all by the endless hunger for more land and the ever-expanding settlement project. That reality has been amply documented by Israeli human rights organizations.

Shulman sorrowfully concluded:

> the occupation–and above all the settlement project–have profoundly eroded the moral fiber of Israel, corroded central institutions of the society, and undermined our integrity as a political community.

Demonization of Islam and Muslims

The issue of Palestine has led to a widespread demonization of Islam and Muslims in much of the Western world. Israel has succeeded in portraying itself as the victim of Islamic violence, with its votaries, primarily from the Jewish Right-wing, positing in defence of Israel a theory of 'continued violence and cultural inferiority' to depict the Palestinian opposition to Israeli occupation.[86] The success of the Israeli information effort is confirmed by the fact that a large majority of Americans have come to see Muslims as 'gun-toting, bearded, fanatic terrorists hell bent on destroying the great enemy, the US'.[87] There is little attention paid to the legitimate concerns and grievances of the Palestinians, the entire focus being on the inherent defects and shortcomings of the religion and its people, and how they could be 'reformed'. In fact, in Western discourse:[88]

> The search for a new foreign devil has come to rest, as it did beginning in the eighth century for European Christianity, on Islam, a religion whose physical proximity and unstilled challenge to the West (a vague term used by Lewis and Huntington that denotes 'our' civilization as opposed to 'theirs') seem as diabolical and violent now as it did then.

This was the mindset that shaped the GWOT and defined it, in popular perception, as a global war on Muslims. The deaths through aerial bombardment and ground action in Afghanistan and Iraq, accompanied by the abuses of Guantanamo and Abu Ghraib, affirmed to most Muslims that the US had now joined Israel in a modern-day crusade against Islam and Muslims. As the GWOT progressed, the US side was buttressed ideologically by a vast array of officials and academics drawn from the American Right-wing, at the head of whom were the neocons and their media and academic affiliates. Bernard Lewis headed this cavalcade, providing it with 'intellectual muscle',[89] while giving free play to his deep-seated prejudices.

In his numerous writings, Lewis repeated much that he had written earlier. His main points were helpfully put together in two books, *What Went Wrong* and *The Crisis of Islam*, published respectively in 2002 and 2003. At the same time, his fresh writings and pronouncements were at best eccentric: he stoutly supported armed action against Saddam's Iraq,[90] and, after the war, advocated (with former CIA chief, R. James Woolsey) a Hashemite solution for Iraq that would place a scion of the old royal family on Baghdad's throne.[91] Later, in an article published on 8 August

2006, he predicted that, on 22 August, Iran could unleash nuclear weapons on the US or Israel, since 22 August marked the day when Prophet Mohammed had taken flight to Jerusalem and then had ascended to heaven.[92] In March 2007, Lewis, in an hour-long speech, extolled the Crusades as an 'understandable response to Muslim onslaught of the preceding centuries', and regretted that the West was 'losing its conviction in facing off against Islamic expression and migration', unlike the zeal it had shown earlier.[93] These and other shoddy 'intellectual' inputs led Edward Said to note bitterly:[94]

> It is surely one of the intellectual catastrophes of history that an imperialist war confected by a small group of unelected US officials was waged against a devastated Third World dictatorship on thoroughly ideological grounds having to do with world dominance, security control and scarce resources, but *disguised for its true intent, hastened, and reasoned for by Orientalists who betrayed their calling as scholars.* [Emphasis added.]

The resilience of such perceptions was recently affirmed in the article 'Going Muslim' by the Indian-origin American academic and journalist, Tunku Varadarajan, which was written just after the Fort Hood killings by Major Nidal Malik Hasan, an American army officer of Arab (Palestinian) origin.[95] Varadarajan described 'going Muslim' as a moment unique to a Muslim when he:

> ... discards his apparent integration into American society and elects to vindicate his religion in an act of messianic violence against his fellow Americans.

This moment of 'going Muslim' is not an act of psychological 'snapping' (under some dire external pressure), but is merely 'a calculated discarding of the camouflage of integration – in an act of revelatory catharsis'.

Having set out his understanding of the general Muslim psyche in America, Varadarajan then makes some rather loose remarks about Islam, the faith: Muslims, according to him, 'may be more extreme because their religion is founded on bellicose conquest, contempt for infidels and an obligation for piety that is more extreme than in other schemes'. Muslims, he concludes, are 'the most difficult "incomers" in the ongoing integration challenge' in America.

Varadarajan affirms the essentialist view of the 'Muslim' propagated by US Right-wing academics and commentators, and now expanding to become part of pervasive popular perception. In this view, a Muslim in America is not permitted the privilege of a *personal* crime or misdemeanour: every act of his, trivial or horrendous, epitomizes the *entire* Muslim community; he is the ideal, the supreme 'other', with a shallow two-dimensional personality, whose essential, indeed, only character is his 'Muslim' identity that is inherently violent and fanatical. It is also a persona he is barely able to camouflage: his American personality is a veneer so thin that his *real* persona is not exposed through 'snapping' under external pressure, as is the case of all other Americans who periodically snap and perpetrate mass murder upon their countrymen. In fact, the Muslim does not need to 'snap', since his civil personality is superficial, and only lightly camouflages the inherent, all-consuming violence that defines his essential being. Such a person, and, by extension, the entire Muslim community, therefore, does not deserve even the 'mindset' of political correctness, much less understanding of its concerns and interests, since the community can never be trusted. No Muslim in any case will ever be able to integrate into the wonderful cultural mosaic that every other individual and community has come together to build in the United States.

The events of 9/11, the Afghanistan and Iraq wars, the violence in Palestine and the GWOT, all of these have now consolidated the discourse relating to Islam and Muslims, placing it firmly in the Orientalist tradition, though updated to take account of late twentieth and early twenty-first century events. Thus, the pervasive view in the West is of an essentialized stereotype of the faith and its followers centred around violence, fanaticism and terrorism. This discourse projects the monolithic character of Islam, asserts that violence and terror are integral to Islamic doctrine due to the all-encompassing character of the faith and culture, avers that the faith is inherently anti-modern, anti-secular and anti-democratic, and, above all, is imbued with a deep animosity for the West, particularly the USA.[96] The twenty-first century contribution to the discourse goes further: it sees in 'Islam' a serious threat to the security of the West, and its democracy, civilization and way of life. It goes on to assert that this threat is 'new' in comparison with other threats the West has faced, such as from Nazism and communism, since it is based on fanatical *religious* belief, with which no reasonable negotiation or accommodation is possible.[97]

A number of more objective academics, both Western and Arab, have intervened in the debate and challenged the Right-wing discourse by presenting alternative assessments both of the history of Islam's ties with the West and of the present scenario relating to Muslim politics in different parts of the world. Thus, Karabell points out that the narrative of inherent and sustained Islam-West conflict 'distorts the past, constricts our present, and endangers our future'.[98] It not only ignores the substantial historic give-and-take between the Christian and Muslim peoples over the last 1,000 years, it also fails to note the very real and substantial cooperation between the West and a number of Muslim countries as recently as the twentieth century, as evidenced by the 60-year-old strategic partnership between the US and Saudi Arabia; the close cooperation between the USA, Saudi Arabia and Pakistan in the jihad in Afghanistan, and the generally accommodative approach of most Gulf and North African states in regard to issues of crucial significance to US interests.

Thus, the contemporary quarrel of Muslims with the West is neither inherent, nor historical nor even ideological. It emerges from contemporary concerns relating to certain specific issues, such as Palestine, and, more recently, Iraq and Afghanistan, as also the support given by the West to authoritarian regimes in Muslim countries which is believed to have retarded the political evolution of the countries of West Asia.[99] On a philosophical plane, it also reflects a desire to assert a native authenticity, though this does not necessarily imply a rejection of the West, for there is still considerable scope for understanding and accommodation. Generally, such views had little influence during the Bush presidency, which responded to what it saw as a messianic Islamic challenge with messianic zeal of its own. As a result, issues that agitate the Muslim world and have a certain validity went largely unrecognized and unaddressed, even as sanction was secured to inflict the maximum pain and suffering on those seen as extremists, be they individuals at Guantanamo, or collective groups in Palestine, Iraq and Afghanistan. Such violence, in turn, also had a corrosive effect on the avowed national values of the US and Israel, leading to an abridgement of human rights at home and intensifying attitudes of racism, intolerance and bigotry. Not surprisingly, this only intensified counter-violence through rocket attacks, wayside incendiary devices and, above all, suicide bombings.

To combat this xenophobic we *vs.* they mindset, Gray advocates a return to what he calls 'realism', that is, a rejection of utopian thinking and, in its place, an acceptance that governments will have to pursue their goals in an environment that combines competition and conflict.[100] Realism restrains the excesses of messianic and other faith-based impulses, and encourages policies of accommodation, based on the conviction that the movement of history (contrary to religious and secular messianism) is *not* one of uni-linear progress but of alternatives of order and chaos.[101] Though Gray sees the advantages of such an approach in an untidy and disorderly world, at the end of his monumental work he is pessimistic and concludes that, in tandem with the competition for natural resources, 'the violence of faith looks set to shape the coming century'.[102]

Such pessimism is well-placed, since the children of Abraham are today defining their identities and pursuing their messianic destinies with the utmost ferocity, each believing that God is with him. Ian Buruma has explained how such competitions over identity and destiny usually turn out:[103]

> ... 'identity' is what gets the blood boiling, what makes people do unspeakable things to their neighbours. It is the fuel used by agitators to set whole countries on fire. *When the world is reduced to a battle between 'us and them,'* ... *only mass murder will do, for 'we' can only survive if 'they' are slaughtered.* Before we kill them, 'they' must be stripped of our common humanity, by humiliating them, degrading them, and giving them numbers instead of names.
>
> [In] the extraordinary bloodlust of identify warriors, Sadism must play a part. Once their basest instincts are given the official nod, some people feel a sense of pleasure, even liberation. The degradation of one's victims, stripped of their identity, is a way to soothe one's conscience. This results in a ghastly paradox: *the more brutal the method of slaughter, the easier it is on the killers, for the victims are no longer regarded as fully human.* [Emphasis added.]

The echoes of 9/11, Palestine, Iraq and Afghanistan reverberate in these lines.

NOTES

1. Mark Lilla, *The Stillborn God – Religion, Politics, and the Modern West* (New York: Alfred A. Knopf, 2007) p. 3
2. Lilla, p. 9, 6.
3. John Gray, *Black Mass – Apocalyptic Religion and the Death of Utopia* (London: Penguin Books, 2008) p. 200.

4. ibid., p. 261.
5. Grant Havers: 'The Neocons: The Chosen People Without God', *Book Review*, 15 March 2008; downloaded from: http:// davidaslindsay.blogspot.com/2008/03/neocons-chosen-people-without-god.html
6. Gray, pp. 44–6.
7. ibid., p. 46.
8. ibid., pp 159–60.
9. ibid., p. 161.
10. Lilla, p. 51.
11. For a detailed account of this relationship see: Victoria Clark, *Allies for Amageddon–The Rise of Christian Zionism* (London: Yale University Press, 2007).
12. Gray, p. 161.
13. ibid., p. 231.
14. ibid., p. 219.
15. ibid., p. 259.
16. ibid., p. 230.
17. ibid., p. 40.
18. ibid, p. 231; from the last days of the Bush presidency there has been a steady flow of literature pertaining to the pervasive use of torture against the prisoners at Guantanamo and other detention centres and the official US sanction provided for these actions. Reviewing a few books on the subject, Anthony Lewis, wrote in August 2008:

> ...a steady accumulation of disclosures, capped in June by a Senate committee report and hearing, has made it clear that abusive treatment of prisoners was a deliberate policy that came from the top – the Pentagon, the Justice Department, and the White House. [Anthony Lewis: 'Official American Sadism', *The New York Review of Books*, Vol. LV, No. 14, 25 September 2008, p. 45.]

> Other reviews of books on the subject may be seen at: David Bromwich: 'The Co-President at Work', *The New York Review of Books*, Volume LV, Number 18, 20 November 2008, pp. 29–33; and, David Cole: 'What to Do About the Torturers?' *The New York Review of Books*, Volume LVI, Number 1, 15 January-11 February 2009, pp. 20–4.

> *The New York Review of Books'* issue of 9 April 2009, published a long article by Mark Danner based on the report of Red Cross officials who had looked into the torture of some prisoners at Guantanamo. The Red Cross report had concluded:

> > The allegations of ill-treatment of the detainees indicate that, in many cases, the ill-treatment to which they were subjected while held in the

CIA program, either singly or in combination, constituted torture. In addition, many other elements of the ill-treatment, either singly or in combination, constituted cruel, inhuman or degrading treatment. [Mark Danner: 'US Torture: Voices from the Black Sites', *The New York Review of Books*, Vol. 56, No. 6, dated 9 April 2009; downloaded from: http://www.nybooks.com/articles/22530]

19. Louise Richardson, *What Terrorists Want-Understanding the Terrorist Threat* (London: John Murray, 2006) p. 237.
20. ibid.
21. Brian Urquhart: 'A Cautionary Tale', *New York Review of Books*, Vol. LI, No.10, 10 June 2004, p. 10.
22. ibid.
23. Quoted in: Bob Herbert: 'How to Kill an Iraqi,' *The Asian Age*, New Delhi, 22 May 2004.
24. Anthony Lewis: 'Bush and the Lesser Evil', *New York Review of Books*, Vol. LI, No. 9, 27 May 2004, p. 9.
25. ibid.
26. Ronald Dworkin: 'Terror and the Attack on Civil Liberties', *New York Review of Books*, Vol. L, No.17, 6 November 2003, p. 37.
27. Lewis, p. 10.
28. Dworkin, p. 38; Even before the 9/11 events, a number of scholars had drawn attention to the negative images of Arabs and Muslims depicted in the American media. Thus, in 1984, Jack Shaheen had noted that Arab images on television and in Hollywood had perpetuated four myths about Arabs:

"...they are all fabulously wealthy; they are barbaric and uncultured; they are sex maniacs with a penchant for white slavery; and they revel in acts of terrorism." [Lawrence Pintak, *America, Islam, and the War of Ideas – Reflections in a Bloodshot Lens* (Cairo: The American University in Cairo Press, 2006) p. 31.]

Edward Said's book, *Covering Islam,* re-published in 1997, confirmed that this tradition of negative stereotyping had continued. It seems to have become even more intense after 9/11, as recent studies have shown. Thus, Suad Joseph, an anthropologist at the University of California, Davis, has noted how the US mainstream press [*New York Times* and *Wall Street Journal*] has associated Arabs and Muslim Americans with terrorism and the demonized globalized Islam; she has identified seven principal characteristics of such writings:

(i) they represent Arabs and Muslims in ways that differentiate them from other Americans and project them as a collective essentialized identity;

(ii) Arabs/Muslims are shown as intimately tied to their countries of origin rather than to the USA;

(iii) they are represented as being highly religious, perhaps more religious than most other Americans;

(iv) they are depicted as devoted to Islam and other Muslims before they were devoted to the USA or other Americans;

(v) they have links with international Muslims and Islamic movements;

(vi) their religious devoutness is very close to religious fanaticism; and,

(vii) such fanaticism is again very closely linked with global Islamic fanaticism.

['Racial Profiling of Arab, Muslim Americans in US Media', *Pak Tribune*, 18 April 2006; downloaded from: http://www.paktribune.com/news/index.shtml?140992.]

29. Eric Margolis: 'The Big Lie About "Islamic Fascism",' 29 August 2006; downloaded from: www.lewrockwell.com/margolis/margolis46.html.

30. 'US Evangelicals Raise Specter of "Islamofascism" to Rouse Voters', *Associated Press*, 11 November 2007; downloaded from: http://www.haaretz.com/hasen/spages/922592.html

31. ibid.

32. ibid.

33. John Trumpbour: 'The Clash of Civilisations: Samuel P. Huntington, Bernard Lewis, and the Remaking of Post Cold War World Order', in Emran Qureshi and Michael A. Sells (Ed), *The New Crusades – Constructing the Muslim Enemy* (Karachi: Oxford University Press, 2005) p. 117.

34. ibid.

35. Trumpbour, p. 99.

36. See the Section, 'The Zionist Lobby', in Raymond Ibrahim (Ed), *The Al Qaeda Reader* (New York: Doubleday, 2007) pp. 274–8; Suha Taji-Farouki traces the origins of the contemporary Muslim construct of the essentialised Jewish/Zionist 'other' to the Zionist project which resulted in the emergence of a 'New Tradition' of anti-Jewishness in Arab/Muslim discourse; the 'essential' Jewish characteristics included in this discourse are: 'ingratitude, selfishness, disbelief in the truth, hatred for good for others, love for life and cowardice'. Sayyid Qutb, on the other hand, in line with modern Islamist thinking, saw the origins of the Jewish-Muslim divide in early Islamic history, particularly in the interaction of Prophet Mohammed with the Jews in Madinah and Khayber, and visualized an ongoing 'cosmic struggle' between the Jews and Islam in these words:

the Jews have confronted Islam with enmity from the moment the Islamic state was established in Medina ... the Muslim community

396 Children of Abraham at War

continues to suffer the same Jewish machinations and double-dealing which discomfited the early Muslims ... This is a war which has not been extinguished: for close on fourteen centuries its blaze has raged in all the corners of the earth and continues to this moment. [Suha Taji-Farouki and Basheer M. Nafi (Ed), *Islamic Thought in the Twentieth Century* (London: I.B. Tauris, 2008) p. 329.]

Such thinking is now pervasive in Muslim anti-Semitic writings, which have proliferated after the 1967 war, borrowing heavily from European anti-Jewish writings as also the *Protocols of the Elders of Zion.*

37. Quoted in Richard Webster: 'Israel, Palestine, and the Tiger of Terrorism', *New Statesman*, 29 November 2002; p. 10; downloaded from: http://www.richardwebster.net/israelpalestine.html.
38. ibid.
39. ibid.
40. ibid., p. 2.
41. ibid., p. 3.
42. Peter Partner, *God of Battles–Holy Wars of Christianity and Islam* (Princeton, NJ: Princeton University Press, 1997) p. xvii.
43. ibid.
44. ibid., p. 8.
45. Gray, pp.97–8.
46. ibid., p. 99.
47. ibid.
48. Max Rodenbeck: 'The Truth About Jihad', *New York Review of Books*, vol. LII, No. 13, 11 August 2005, downloaded from: http://www.nybooks.com/articles/18177.
49. ibid.
50. ibid.
51. Olivier Roy, *Secularism Confronts Islam* (New York: Columbia University Press, 2007) p. 58; compare Francis Fukuyama:
    The Islamic revival was rather the nostalgic re-assertion of an older, purer set of values, said to have existed in the distant past, that were neither the discredited 'traditional values" of the recent past, nor the Western values that had been so poorly transplanted to the Middle East. In this respect, Islamic fundamentalism bears a more than superficial resemblance to European fascism.' [Francis Fukuyama, *The End of History and the Last Man* (New York: Free Press, 1992, reprinted 2006) p. 236].
52. Olivier Roy, p. 58.
53. Richard Bonney, *Jihad - From Qu'ran to bin Laden* (Basingstoke, UK: Palgrave/Macmillan, 2004) p. 205.
54. ibid., p. 200.

55. ibid.
56. ibid., p. 207.
57. Alan Philps: 'Grab Every Hilltop', *The National*, Abu Dhabi, 5 September 2008, p. 9.
58. ibid.
59. ibid., p. 212; see also David Commins: 'Hasan al-Banna (1906-1949)', in Ali Rahnema (Ed), *Pioneers of Islamic Revival* (London: Zed Books, reprinted 2005) pp. 133–8
60. Bonney, p. 213.
61. ibid., p. 222.
62. Charles Tripp, 'Sayyid Qutb–The Political Vision', in Rahnema, p. 176.
63. Bonney, p. 223.
64. Olivier Roy, p. 62.
65. Zachary Karabell, *People of the Book – The Forgotten History of Islam and the West* (London: John Murray, 2007) p. 3.
66. ibid., pp. 260–1.
67. Tony Karon: 'A Late Divorce', *The National*, Abu Dhabi, 16 January 2009, p. 12.
68. ibid.
69. ibid.
70. Ibid.
71. Tim Butcher: 'Jewish Terrorism Threatens Israel', *The Telegraph*, London, 4 October 2008; downloaded from: http://www.lebanonwire.com/0810MLN/08100407TGR.asp
72. Cherrie Heywood: 'Israel: Breaking the Silence', *Inter Press Service*, 3 October 2008; downloaded from: http://www.lebanonwire.com/0810MLN/08100302IPS.asp
73. 'Israel's Gaza Offensive planned six months ago', *Times of India*, Mumbai, 5 January 2009, p. 8.
74. ibid; Peter Beaumont: "Gaza: A Supreme Emergency", *The Hindu*, Chennai, 13 January 2009.
75. Uri Avnery: 'Israel's New Election War', *Khaleej Times*, Dubai, 6 January 2009, p. 13.
76. Beaumont.
77. Jonathan Cook: 'Religious Groups are 'Penetrating' Israeli Army', *The National*, Abu Dhabi, 4 February 2009, p. 14.
78. ibid.
79. 'A Rabbinate Gone Wild, Editorial, *Haaretz*, 27 January 2009; downloaded from: http://www.haaretz.com/hasen/spages/1059124.html
80. Shamir Yeger and Gal Einar: 'In the name of God', *Israel Opinion*, 2 February 2009; downloaded from: http://www.ynetnews.com/articles/

2 February 2009; downloaded from: http://www.ynetnews.com/articles/ 0,7340, L-3665302, 00.html.

81. Cook; In March 2009, the international media carried new reports, based on statements of Israeli soldiers involved in the fighting in Gaza, which described 'wanton vandalism to Palestinian homes, humiliation of civilians and loose rules of engagement that resulted in unnecessary civilian deaths.' ['New details of Israeli war conduct emerge', *Associated Press*, 21 March 2009; downloaded from: http://www.lebanonwire.com/ 0903MLN/09032109RR.asp] In these reports, the soldiers described the 'messages' given to them by the army's Rabbinate thus: 'We are the Jewish people, we came to this land by a miracle. God brought us back to this land, and now we need to fight to expel the gentiles who are interfering with our conquest of this holy land.'

Earlier, some sections of the Israeli press had carried reports that, in the Gaza offensive, Israeli commanders, anxious to avoid endangering the lives of soldiers even at the price of seriously harming the civilian population, caused extensive damage and the deaths of many Palestinian civilians. According to IDF statistics, almost two-thirds of Palestinians killed were civilians. [Reuven Pedatzur: 'The war that wasn't', *Haaretz*, 25 January 2009; downloaded from: http://www.lebanonwire.com/ 0901MLN/09012503HZ.asp]

Also see: Ethan Bronner: 'A Religious War in Israeli Army', *New York Times*, 22 March 2009; downloaded from: http://www.lebanonwire.com/ 0903MLN/09032205NYT.asp; and, Peter Beaumont, 'Gaza War Crime Claims Gather Pace as More Troops Speak Out', *The Observer*, 22 March 2009, downloaded from: http://www.lebanonwire.com/0903MLN/ 09032207GDN.asp

82. Quotes from "Unofficial Summary—For Media Use Only", 15 September 2009; downloaded from: http://goldstone-report.org/the-report/the-contents/98-media-summary...; full report available at: http://www2.ohchr.org/english/bodies/hrcouncil/specialsession/9/ FactFindingMission.htm

83. Israeli Finance Minister Yuval Steinitz accused the international community of anti-Semitism for endorsing the report; he said:

It is an anti-Semitic attempt to rule that what is permissible for the US in Afghanistan, Russia in Chechnya and Turkey in northern Iraq is forbidden for the State of Israel that is defending itself in the Gaza Strip. We won't lend a hand to the accusations; Jews will not be led once again like lambs to the slaughter. The land of the Jews has a right and a duty to protect its citizens no less than the US, Russia or Turkey. [*Jerusalem Post*, 18 October 2009, downloaded from:http:www.jpost.com/servlet/

Satellite?pagename=JPost/JPArticle/Sh..]

Jerusalem Post in an editorial said:

The exploitation of Judge Goldstone's Jewish background by our enemies intensifies our obligation to confront the enemy within – renegade Jews – including Israelis who stand at the vanguard of global efforts to demonise and delegitimise the Jewish state. Such odious Jews can be traced back to apostates during the Middle Ages who fabricated blood libels and vile distortions of Jewish religious practice for Christian anti-Semities to incite hatred which culminated in massacres. It was in response to these renegades that the *herem* (excommunication) was introduced... [Downloaded from: http:asiapacific.mediamonitors.net/content/view/full/689.]

The Zionist Organisation of America issued a press release, dated 16 September 2009, titled 'ZOA Condemns Goldstone's Despicable Anti-Israel U.N. Report, Based On Unsubstantiated Testimony & Perversion Of Legal Norms'. The press release stated that the ZOA is:

... appalled that Justice Goldstone was willing to ruin his legal reputation by participating in this dishonestly-conceived and fraudulent investigation. Most serious, perhaps, is the fact that Richard Goldstone was willing to bend and pervert legal norms – such as the definition of occupation and of combatants – in order to pin non-existent legal responsibility on Israel for acts were both justified and indeed necessary in self-defence ...

This is a Report that should be condemned and ignored by all people of goodwill. The leaders of Hamas and Iran must be clearly delighted in this Report. For shame on Goldstone and the UN. Every anti-Semitic racist bigot in the world is smiling.

[Downloaded from: http://www.zoa.org/sitedocuments/pressrelease_view.asp?pressrelease]

A number of Israeli commentators have also defended Justice Goldstone and his report: thus, Larry Derfaer said:

The context of the war – the full context – was that we had blockaded Gaza by air, sea and to a great extent by land, we were racking up a kill ratio of nearly 50 to 1 – then we invaded the country, destroyed thousands upon thousands of homes and public buildings and bumped up the ratio to more than 100-to-1.

We've tried to smear them all [critics], to silence them, to drown out the messages that keep repeating itself from one source to another. Now we have the message, the same message again, from one of the world's most respected, accomplished men of justice.

Amira Hass, prominent Israeli journalist, said:

Like the Serbs of yore, we Israelis continue thinking it's the world that is wrong, and only we who are right.

Israel struck a civilian population that remains under its control, it didn't fulfill its obligation to distinguish between civilians and militants and used military force disproportionate with the tangible threat to its own civilians.

Gideon Levy, a journalist with *Haaretz*, wrote:

For almost a year Israel has been trying to argue that the blood spilled in Gaza was merely water. One report followed the other, with horrifyingly identical results: siege, white phosphorous, harm of innocent civilians, infrastructure destroyed – war crimes in each and every report. Now after the publication of the most important and damning report of all, compiled by the commission led by Judge Richard Goldstone, Israel's attempts to discredit them look ludicrous, and the empty bluster of its spokespersons sound pathetic ... This time though, the messenger is propaganda-proof ... On the eve of the Jewish New Year, Israel, deservedly, is becoming an outcast and detested country. We must not forget it for a minute.

Zeev Sternhell, emeritus Professor at Hebrew University, said:

The Goldstone report was inevitable. Even if it is not balanced, even if it does not take Hamas into account properly – it has sounded a harsh warning signal by expressing the international public's attitude towards Israel after Gaza. The bottom line is that Operation Cast Lead has contributed another brick to the wall of delegitimization that is gradually closing in on the Jewish state. Even if no Israeli is brought to court in The Hague in the near future, the moral stain will not be erased and the repercussions are yet to be seen.

[All quotes from: http://asiapacific.mediamonitors.net/content/view/full/689]

84. Richard Falk: "Why the Goldstone Report Matters", *Sabbah Report*, 22 September 2009; downloaded from: http://sabbah.biz/mt/archives/2009/09/22/richard-falk-why-the-goldstone...

85. David Shulman: "Israel Without Illusions", *The New York Review of Books*, Volume LVI, 17 December 2009 – January 13, 2010, p. 32.

86. Edward W. Said, *Covering Islam*, Vintage, London, 1997, p. xxiv; henceforth, *Covering Islam*.

87. ibid.

88. ibid., p. xxxiv.

89. Renel Marc Gerecht: 'The Last Orientalist', *The Weekly Standard*, Vol. 011, Issue 36, 5 June 2006; downloaded from: http://

12267&R=1130E...

90. Bernard Lewis: "The Region after Saddam", 3 October 2002; downloaded from: http://www.aei/docLib20030317_Lewispub.pdf

91. Bernard Lewis and R. James Woolsey: 'King and Country', 29 October 2003; downloaded from: http://www.mideastweb.org/log/archives/00000094.htm

92. Bernard Lewis: 'August 22–Does Iran have something in store?' 8 August 2006; downloaded from: http://www.opinionjournal.com/extra/?id=110008768

93. 'Bernard Lewis Applauds the Crusades', 8 March 2007; downloaded from: http://blogs.wsj.com/washwire/2007/03/08/bernard-lewis-applauds-the-crusades/

94. Edward Said: '*Orientalism* 25 years Later: Worldly Humanism v. the Empire Builders', 5 August 2003; downloaded from: http://www.counterpunch.org/said08052003.html.

95. Tunku Varadarajan: "Going Muslim", *Forbes*, 8 November 2009; downloaded from: http://www.forbes.com/2009/11/08/fort-hood-nidal-malik-hasan-muslims-opinions-colum...

   Major Nidal Malik Hasan, a psychiatrist in the US army, killed 12 soldiers and a civilian in a shooting spree at Fort Hood, Texas, on 5 November 2009. Later reports revealed he had possibly come under the influence of a radical Muslim cleric from Yemen, Anwar al-Awlaki, who, on his website, applauded Major Hasan's deed and advised that he be emulated by other Muslims in the US army. These reports also said that Major Hasan had acted on his own, and his actions were the result of a number of factors, including his opposition to the wars in Iraq and Afghanistan and his increasing religious fervour.

   [David Johnston and Scott Shane: "US Knew of Suspect's Tie to Radical Cleric", *The New York Times*, November 10, 2009; downloaded from: http://www.nytimes.com/2009/11/10/us/10inquire.html?pagewanted=pr]

96. See Richard Jackson: 'Religion, Politics and Terrorism: A Critical Analysis of Narratives of "Islamic Terrorism,"' University of Manchester, Centre for International Politics, Working Paper Series, No. 21, October 2006, downloaded from: http://www.socialsciences.manchester.ac.uk/disciplines/politics/researchgroups/cip/publications/documents/Jackson_000.pdf, for an excellent analysis of the subject.

97. ibid., pp. 10-12.

98. Karabell, p. 5.

99. Gray, p. 100.

100. ibid., pp. 271–82.

100. ibid., pp. 271–82.
101. ibid., pp. 263–5.
102. ibid., p. 297.
103. Ian Buruma: 'The Blood Lust of Identity', *New York Review of Books*, Vol. 49, No. 3, 11 April 2002; downloaded from: http://www.nybooks.com/articles/article-preview?article_ id=15241

14

The Way Forward

Too many tears have flowed. Too much blood has been shed. All of us have a responsibility to work for the day when the mothers of Israelis and Palestinians can see their children grow up without fear; when the Holy Land of three great faiths is the place of peace that God intended it to be; when Jerusalem is a secure and lasting home for Jews and Christians and Muslims, and a place for all of the children of Abraham to mingle peacefully together as in the story of Isra, when Moses, Jesus, and Mohammed (peace be upon them) joined in prayer.

—*President Barack Obama's Address to the Muslim community,* Cairo, 4 June 2009.

Ten years after the proclamation of global jihad by Osama bin Laden and eight years after the commencement of the GWOT by President Bush, it is a matter of considerable irony, as Gilles Kepel has noted, that 'the war between George W. Bush and Osama bin Laden defeated both of its protagonists', so that neither US-led 'reform' nor Al-Qaeda-led jihad have succeeded in West Asia.[1] This sets the stage for the emergence of a new strategic vision that would wean West Asia and the world away from messianism-driven confrontations into a new scenario of mutual accommodation and respect.

Some positive glimpses are already apparent in Israel itself. Over the last few years, there has been a robust questioning of some of the myths that had surrounded the emergence of the Israeli state, particularly through the writings of commentators such as Ilan Pappe, Zeev Sternhell, Akiva Eldar, Avraham Burg, and recently Shlomo Sand. These writers have not yet captured the mainstream, but, with their academic rigour, they have already begun to make a mark and compel Israeli popular opinion to recognize the ugly face of occupation, particularly the pervasive anti-Arab racism. In this regard, Shlomo Sand has made a very significant contribution with his new book, *The Invention of the Jewish People*.[2]

Sand examined in considerable detail the various ways in which Jewish scholars from the nineteenth century onwards attempted to define Jewish identity, an enterprise that later became central to the Zionist project and its claims on Palestine. This effort required the acceptance of continuity in Jewish religious and ethnic identity from biblical times to the present, and assertions about the uniqueness and separateness of the Jews from other communities and 'nations'. From this emerged the immutable claim on the 'Holy Land'. As Sand has pointed out, Zionism's early fathers flourished in Germanic culture and, hence, imbued their nascent movement with 'the ethnoreligious and ethnobiological ideologies' that were flourishing in Germany, Russia, Poland and Austria-Hungary in the second half of the nineteenth century.[3]

The principal challenge before the early Zionist project was 'to forge a single *ethnos* from a great variety of [Jewish] cultural-linguistic groups, each with a distinctive-origin', which were then flourishing in different parts of Europe as also in Asia and Africa. As Sand puts it: [4]

> To achieve their aim, the Zionists needed to erase existing ethnographic textures, forget specific histories, and take a flying leap backward to an ancient, mythological and religious past.

He concludes:[5]

> Zionism from its inception was an ethnocentric nationalist movement that firmly enclosed the historical people of its own invention, and barred any voluntary civil entry into the nation its platform began to design.

Having set out the 'invention' of the unique exclusiveness of Jewish identity that emerged from the Zionist project, Sand then looks at the character of the state of Israel. He points out:[6]

> The Jewish nationalism that dominates Israeli society is not an open, inclusive identity that invites others to become part of it, or to coexist with it on a basis of equality and in symbiosis. On the contrary, it explicitly and culturally segregates the majority from the minority, and repeatedly asserts that the state belongs only to the majority; moreover . . . it promises eternal proprietary rights to an even greater human mass that does not choose to live in it. In this way, it excludes the minority from active and harmonious participation in the sovereignty and practices of democracy, and prevents that minority from identifying with it politically.

Obviously, the assertion (and acceptance) of Israel's *democratic* character is important to the Israeli leadership if only to assert the superiority of the Israeli political order over the other Arab regimes in West Asia and to obtain international (but primarily American) support for its expanding settlements project. However, the state's avowed Jewish character, the privileging of the Jewish majority (as also *all* the Jews in the diaspora), and the lack of equal rights for its 20 per cent Arab citizens, all of these have ensured that Israel's democratic credentials do not enjoy universal acceptance. Sand has described the Israeli state thus:[7]

> ... Israel must still be described as an "ethnocracy." Better still, call it a Jewish ethnocracy with liberal features – that is, a state whose main purpose is to serve not a civil-egalitarian *demos* but a biological-religious *ethnos* that is wholly fictitious historically, but dynamic, exclusive and discriminatory in its political manifestation. Such a state, for all its liberalism and pluralism, is committed to isolating its chosen *ethnos* through ideological, pedagogical and legislative means, not only from those of its own citizens, who are not classified as Jews, not only from the Israeli-born children of foreign workers, but from the rest of humanity.

Sand is part of the group of Israeli post-Zionist writers who are taking a fresh unblinkered look at their nation's and people's past. They are already making a mark, though the field continues to be dominated by mainstream thinkers who robustly affirm the Zionist tradition. But, the efforts of Sand and others like him are worthy of commendation, for, as he has himself put it: ' I don't think books can change the world, but when the world begins to change, it searches for different books'.[8]

An important indication of the impact of this new thinking on the Israeli political leadership was apparent in the remarks made by Prime Minister Olmert when, in September 2008, he spoke of the need for Israel to define its territories and prepare itself to live side by side with a Palestinian state.[9] Though Olmert's remarks were made *after* he had formally stepped down as Prime Minister and was heading a 'caretaker' administration, the fact remains that such sentiments had rarely been expressed in public earlier by so senior a political leader. Of course, a few months later, the same Olmert led the Israeli assault upon Gaza and, hence, at this point it is difficult to determine whether his remarks were sincere or merely tactical. In any case, the Netanyahu Government, with its present uncompromising position on the settlements issue, appears to have frozen the peace process. Obviously, the Palestinian cause has also not been helped by the persisting dispute between Hamas and Fatah, and Hamas' own rigid posture in regard to dealing with Israel.

Some winds of change are also apparent in the US. The monopolistic control over the Israel-Palestine discourse exercised by pro-Israel Rightwing Jewish and Christian writers was dented with the publication of *The Israel Lobby and US Foreign Policy* by John J. Mearsheimer and Stephen M. Walt in 2007. Just two years earlier, due to the opposition of the Israel lobby, the very subject of their critical research, these authors had failed to get an 80-page article on the same subject published by the prestigious journal, *Atlantic Monthly.* Later, there had been a storm of protest when a much shorter version had appeared in London. Now, the publication of a 484-page tome, its wide circulation and its availability in a paperback version, suggest the beginning of some balance in academic writing relating to West Asia. Again, former President Jimmy Carter's book, *Palestine–Peace Not Apartheid,* published in 2006 amidst considerable criticism, was the first effort by a senior American political leader to provide some balance to discussion relating to Palestine in American public circles.

Coinciding with these path-breaking developments in regard to writings on West Asia, we have the emergence of a new Jewish organization in the US that, for the first time, has challenged the pervasive control on discussion relating to West Asia exercised by the Israel lobby headed by the American Israel Public Affairs Committee (AIPAC). This organization, called 'J Street', was founded in April 2008, and is located in Washington DC. According to its website:[10]

> J Street was founded to change the dynamics of American politics and policy on Israel and the Middle East. We believe the security and future of Israel as the democratic home of the Jewish people depend on rapidly achieving a two-state solution and regional comprehensive peace. Our mission is to promote meaningful American leadership to achieve peace and security in the Middle East and to broaden the debate on these issues nationally and in the Jewish community
>
> J Street represents Americans, primarily but not exclusively Jewish, who support Israel and its desire for security as the Jewish homeland, as well as the right of the Palestinians to a sovereign state of their own - two states living side-by-side in peace and security. We believe ending the Israeli-Palestinian conflict is in the best interests of Israel, the Untied States, the Palestinians, and the region as a whole.

J Street supports diplomatic solutions over military ones, ncluding inIran; mltilateral ver unilateral approaches to conflict resolution; and dialogue over confrontation with a wide range of countries and actors when conflicts do arise.

J Street hosted a conference in ashington DC in October 2009 under the title 'Driving Change, Securing Peace', wich attracted an unprecedented 1,500 participants, including a large number of US Congressmen albeit overwhelmingly from the Democratic Party.[11]

J Street has fundamentally changed the discourse relating to Israel in the US. Mearsheimer and Walt had earlier described AIPAC as:[12]

a de facto agent for a foreign government, [with a] stranglehold on Congress, with the result that U.S. policy towards Israel is not debated there, even though that policy has important consequences for the entire world.

In contrast to the hardline approach of AIPAC, J Street advocates the creation of a viable Palestinian State as part of a negotiated two-state solution, based on the 1967 borders with agreed reciprocal land swap, and is alo in favour of Jrusalem as th shared capital of the two states. After the commencement of the Israeli assault upon Gaza on 27 December 2008, J Street issued a press release stating that 'there is no military solution to what is fundamentally a political conflict', and calling for 'immediate, strong diplomatic intervention' to negotiate a resumption of the ceasefire.[13] The next day, J Street's Campaign Director, Issac Luria, stated:[14]

While there is nothing 'right' in raining rockets on Israeli families or dispatching suicide bombers, there is nothing 'right' in punishing a million and a half already-suffering Gazans for the actions of the extremists among them.

According to Edward Witten, the main reason for J Street's popularity is *timing* in that J Street represents the views held by a new generation of American Jews whose thinking is at odds with the views of those in the mainstream community represented so far by AIPAC.[15] J Street conducted a poll of Jewish opinion in July 2008 and found that a significant majority of American Jews (60 per cent) opposed further Israeli settlements; they also overwhelmingly supported the position that the US should be actively engaged in the peace process even if there were public disagreements with Israel.[16] The other aspect of timing pertains to President Obama's own commitment to pursuing a peace settlement in the West Asia. J Street has thus provided a voice to the Jewish majority to change, in the words of its executive director Jeremy Ben-Ami, 'the unconstructive way this issue plays out in American policies and policy'.[17]

Not surprisingly, J Street has been subjected to considerable criticism from the Right-wing both in Israel and in the US. Jeremy Ben-Ami understands the wellsprings of such criticism, particularly when it emerges during moments of crisis for Israel, when the discourse is dominated by 'the emotional side of the communal history, and ... the fear of not wanting in some way to be responsible for the next great tragedy that will befall the Jewish people'.[18]

These important developments in Israel and the US have been matched by the 'Arab Peace Plan' which originated as a Saudi proposal in 2002, and was approved by the Arab League at Beirut that year. It foundered soon thereafter amidst violence in Palestine and Iraq. However, it was re-adopted by the Arab League in Riyadh in 2007.[19] It offers Israel full diplomatic, political and economic ties with the Arab countries in return for Israel relinquishing the territories occupied in 1967 and setting up a Palestinian state. The plan includes provision for discussion and fine-tuning in terms of the details of the withdrawal and the issue of refugees. For some time Israel ignored the proposal, but, recently, some words of cautious welcome have emerged from Israeli leaders. In the context of the Gaza assault, Arab leaders have pointed out that the plan is still on the table though they have warned Israel that, in face of its continued obduracy and violence, the peace plan might not be available forever.

A number of brave peace initiatives have been made over the last few years by well-meaning Israeli and Arab politicians and scholars, with most of them being summarily rejected or ignored by political leaders, so that their details are now available only to meticulous scholars. One such recent effort was that of the Washington DC-based United States Institute of Peace, which prepared a special report, in October 2008, titled 'Abrahamic Alternatives to War – Jewish, Christian, and Muslim Perspectives on Just Peacemaking'.[20]

This initiative brought together a number of prominent Christian, Jewish and Muslim scholars who went back to their respective scriptures to identify those which promoted violence and sanctioned war, and those that could be utilized to promote peace. The study revealed that many of the texts relied upon to sanction conflict had either been pulled out of their historic context or had been misinterpreted. The scholars also discovered:

> ... a wealth of material in their sacred texts comprising a coherent ethic and method for Just Peacemaking that can not only strengthen the means to address conflict nonviolently but that can address some of the root causes that lead to violent conflict.

Thus, in the Jewish tradition, human rights and poverty relief were recurrent themes. In Islam, the Koran rejected violence as a means to settle disputes, encouraged forgiveness, advocated equality and upheld pluralism and diversity as core values. In the Christian tradition, the central principle was that of pacifism in the face of violence and war, non-violent conflict resolution and the prominent position given to social, political and economic justice. The scholars issued a joint statement which rejected holy war or crusades and upheld 'just peace making' as the best option to resolve human conflict. The report has received some favourable press coverage, but it has still to resonate in the public domain.

As far as West Asia is concerned, the past, particularly the remote past, continues to have a powerful influence on the present and gives every indication of determining the future. In Roger Cohen's chilling words:[21]

> France and Germany freed themselves after 1945 from war's cycle. So, even more remarkably, did Poland and Germany. China and Japan scarcely love each other but do business. *Only in the Middle East do the dead rule.* As Yehuda Amichai, the Israeli poet, once observed, *the dead vote in Jerusalem. Their demand for blood is, it seems, inexhaustible. Their graves will not be quieted.* Since 1948 and Israel's creation, retribution has reigned between the Jewish and Palestinian national movements. [Emphasis added.]

Not surprisingly, amidst this despair, from time to time people in the region have seized upon certain developments as promising a way out of the dark tunnel, such as: the agreement of Camp David-I, the Madrid-Oslo Peace Process, the discussions at Camp David-II, the Annapolis Conference, and various non-official peace plans and proposals, such as the Geneva Initiative, that have been put forward by thinkers, diplomats and political leaders. A similar defining moment emerged with the inauguration of President Obama, an event that clearly marked an important change in the evolution of US politics and foreign policy. His campaign was based on the promise of change and this permeated every paragraph of his inaugural address.[22] This document has already been analyzed threadbare by commentators in different parts of the world who have read specific meanings and messages in certain general assertions.

The address promised positive change in the approach of the new presidency to West Asia and to the issues that have brought such violence and grief to the region. Thus, in regard to the domestic scenario, Obama carefully de-hyphenated the link between the Jew and the Christian (as exemplified by the term Judeo-Christian); he spoke instead of the US as a 'nation of Christians and Muslims, Jews and Hindus and non-believers'. By giving precedence to Muslims over Jews, and mentioning them just after Christians, Obama clearly took the first step toward addressing the persistent demonization of Muslims in Western discourse over the last several years, but particularly after the initiation of the GWOT after 9/11. Obama also rejected the abridgement of human rights and other national principles which had been cynically compromised during the earlier administration, when he asserted: 'As for our common defence, we reject as false the choice between our safety and our ideals'.

Again, with regard to the Israel–Palestine (or the Muslim–Jew) issue, Obama clearly referred to age-old animosities propelling conflict and hatred in West Asia, when he said:

> We cannot help but believe that *the old hatreds shall someday pass; that the lines of tribe shall soon dissolve*; that as the world grows smaller, our common humanity shall reveal itself; and that America must play its role in ushering in a new era of peace. [Emphasis added.]

Finally, responding to the sense in the Muslim world that it was being targeted with a broad-brush demonization, Obama carefully separated the Muslim world from extremists within its fold. He addressed the Muslim world by saying: 'We seek a new way forward, based on mutual interest and mutual respect.' At the same time, his message to Al-Qaeda and other Islamic extremists was also unambiguous: 'We will not apologize for our way of life, nor will we waver in its defence. And for those who seek to advance their aims by inducing terror and slaughtering innocents, we say to you now that our spirit is stronger and cannot be broken–you cannot outlast us, and we will defeat you.'

Following the inaugural address, President Obama went further when he addressed the global Muslim community in Cairo on 4 June 2009.[23] He frankly noted at the outset that serious problems had emerged between the USA and the Muslim world:

> We meet at a time of tension between the United States and Muslims around the world – tension rooted in historical forces that go beyond any current policy debate. The relationship between Islam and the West includes centuries of co-existence and cooperation, but also conflict and religious wars. More recently, tension has been fed by colonialism that denied rights and opportunities to many Muslims, and a Cold War in which Muslim-majority countries were too often treated as proxies without regard to their own aspirations. Moreover, the sweeping change brought by modernity and globalization led many Muslims to view the West as hostile to the traditions of Islam.

Following this candid admission, President Obama referred to a number of serious issues which needed to be addressed frankly: 'We must say openly the things we hold in our hearts and that too often are said only behind closed doors'.

His most important remarks pertained to 'the significance of the relationship between Israelis, Palestinians and the Arab world'. After referring to America's strong bonds with Israel, which were 'unbreakable' and based on 'cultural and historical ties', and recalling the persecution of the Jewish people in Europe, President Obama had this to say about the Palestinians:

> On the other hand, it is also undeniable that the Palestinian people – Muslims and Christians – have suffered in pursuit of a homeland for more than sixty years. They have endured the pain of dislocation. Many wait in refugee camps in the West Bank, Gaza, and neighbouring lands for a life of peace and security that they have never been able to lead. They endure the daily humiliations – large and small – that come with occupation. So let there be no doubt: the situation for the Palestinian people is intolerable. America will not turn out backs on the legitimate Palestinian aspiration for dignity, opportunity and a state of their own.
>
> For decades, there has been a stalemate: two peoples with legitimate aspirations, each with a painful history that makes compromise elusive. It is easy to point fingers – for Palestinians to point to the displacement brought by Israel's founding and for Israelis to point to the constant hostility and attacks throughout its history from within its borders as well as beyond. But if we see this conflict only from one side or the other, then we will be

blind to the truth. The only resolution is for the aspirations of both sides to be met through two states, where Israelis and Palestinians each live in peace and security.

He then committed himself to pursuing a peace process 'with all the patience that the task requires'. In terms of basic principles, he set out the following:

> To play a role in fulfilling Palestinian aspirations, and to unify the Palestinian people, Hamas must put an end to violence, recognize past agreements, and recognize Israel's right to exist.
>
> At the same time, Israelis must acknowledge that just as Israel's right to exist cannot be denied, neither can Palestine's. The United States does not accept the legitimacy of continued Israeli settlements. This construction violates previous agreements and undermines efforts to achieve peace. It is time for these settlements to stop.

President Obama's speech to the Muslim world in Cairo constituted an unprecedented and robust intervention to stem the tide of deteriorating relations between a global religious community, the 'Muslim World', and the 'West', particularly the United States. It is in effect an attempt to undo the damage caused most recently by the Bush Presidency, founded as it was on the neocon ideology and informed by unstinted support for Israel and the abuses of the occupation in Iraq. The recurring theme of the address was for a 'new beginning' in the Muslim-West relationship, not as a 'prisoner of the past' but through pursuing new ties on the basis of justice, mutual respect, tolerance and dignity while doing away with stereotypes on both sides.

On the eve of President Obama's speech, both bin Laden and Ayman al-Zawahiri expressed severe criticisms of the US President and US policies in general. Thus, bin Laden said:[24]

> He [Obama] has followed the steps of his predecessor in antagonizing Muslims ... and laying the foundation for long wars ...Obama and his administration have sowed new seeds of hatred against America. Let the American people prepare to harvest the crops of what the leaders of the White House plant in the next years and decades.

Ayman al-Zawahiri said:[25]

> His [Obama's] bloody messages were received and are still being received by Muslims, and they will not be concealed by public relations campaigns or by farcical visits or elegant words.

The Iranian leader, Ayatollah Ali Khamenei, declared on the day of President Obama's address: 'The nations of this part of the world … deeply hate America. Even if they [American leaders] give sweet and beautiful [speeches] to the Muslim nation, that will not create change. Action is needed.'[26]

These voices represent the most extreme and the most demanding forces in the Muslim world against traditional US policies in West Asia. Al-Qaeda has drawn its appeal, inter alia, from US failures in Palestine and its wars in Iraq and Afghaistan, while Iran has based and nurtured its grievances on the American rejection of the Islamic revolution and Iran's place in regional and world affairs. These forces constitute the greatest challenge for the Obama presidency for he would have to show concrete achievement fairly quickly in regard to the Palestine issue and the two wars, and in his dialogue with Iran. He would have to do this while ensuring that the Right-wing government in Israel and its xenophobic supporters, both in Israel and the USA, do not scuttle his efforts in this turbulent and tortured land. The difficulties he has already had since his address in regard to these issues only confirm how rocky the path ahead is going to be.

The stage is now set for the rejection of messianic dreams and demonizations which have led to such wanton hatred and destruction among the children of Abraham, and the emergence of a new era of dialogue, understanding and respect between the three brothers. They have been estranged from each other for far too long, so that they have forgotten the essential truth of their faiths, which the tenth century Arab scholar, Abu Mansur al-Maturdi (c. 873–944), had described in these simple words:[27]

> Religion is to believe in the unity of God. The religion of all the Prophets is one and the same religion. All th Prophets invite human beings to belief in the unity of God, the knowledge of God's unity, and to the worship only of the One God...

NOTES

1. Gilles Kepel, *Beyond Terror and Martyrdom–The Future of the Middle East* (Cambridge MA and London: The Belknap Press of HarvardUniversity Press, 2008) p. 257.
2. Shlomo Sand, *The Invention of the Jewish People* (London & New York: Verso, 2009).

3. ibid., p. 252.
4. ibid., p. 255.
5. ibid., p. 256.
6. ibid., p. 305.
7. ibid., p. 307.
8. ibid., p. xi.
9. Ehud Olmert, 'The Time Has Come to Say These Things', *The New York Review of Books*, Vol. 55, No. 19, 4 December 2008; downloaded from: http://www.nybooks.com/articles/22112
10. Downloaded from: http://www.jstreet.org/about/about-us
11. Edward Witten, 'The New J-Lobby for Peace', *The New York Review of Books*, Vol. LVI, No. 19, 3-16 December 2009, p. 69.
12. James Traub, 'The New Israel Lobby', *The New York Times Magazine*, 13 September 2009; downloaded from: http://www.nytimes.com/2009/09/13/magazine/13JStreet-t.html?_r=1&
13. ibid.
14. ibid.
15. Witten, p. 69.
16. Traub.
17. Witten, p. 69.
18. Traub.
19. Ian Black, 'Time to Resurrect the Arab Peace Plan', *The Guardian*, 18 October 2008; downloaded from: http://www.guardian.co.uk/world/2008/oct/18/middle-east
20. Susan Thistlethwaite and Glen Stassen, 'Abrahamic Alternatives to War – Jewish, Christian, and Muslim Perspectives on Just Peacemaking', *Special Report 214*, United States Institute of Peace, Washington DC, October 2008; downloaded from: http://www.usip.org/pubs/specialreports/sr214.pdf
21. Roger Cohen, 'Eyeless in Gaza', *The New York Review of Books*, Vol. 56, No. 2, 12 February 2009; downloaded from: http://www.nybooks.com/articles/22270
22. 'President Barack Obama's Inaugural Address,' 21 January 2009; downloaded from: http://www.whitehouse.gov/blog/inaugural-address/
23. 'A New Beginning', President Obama's speech to the Muslim community, Cairo, 4 June 2009; downloaded from: http://www.obama-mamas.com/blog/?p=255.
24. 'Bin Laden Pours Scorn on Obama Charm Offensive', *AFP Report*, 3 June 2009; downloaded from: http://www.france24.com/en/20090603-osama-bin-laden-slams-obama
25. 'Al Qaeda Number Two Hits Out At Obama's "Bloody Messages",' *AFP*

Report, 2 June 2009; downloaded from: http://www.france24.com/en/2009-0602-al-qaeda-number-two-hits-out.

26. 'Barack Obama Begins Key Egypt Speech', *BBC News*, 4 June 2009; downloaded from: http://news.bbc.co.uk/go/pr/fr/-/2/hi/middle_east/8082333.stm

27. Hugh Goddard, *A History of Christian – Muslim Relations* (Chicago: New Amsterdam Books, 2000) p. 63.

Glossary

Ad	A possibly mythical tribe or people of ancient Arabia, said to have been giants and to have left monuments.
Ahl al-Kitab	'People of the Book', usually Jews and Christians.
ailiyya	(Arabic: **familialism**) a reference to an individual's affiliation to his 'extended family', which, in the view of some social anthropologists, determines the identity and notions of pride and honour in traditional Arab society, particularly in the Arabian peninsula.
Al-Akhira	(**Arabic**) The 'Hereafter'.
aliya	(**Hebrew:** ascension, immigration.) Originally it described the ascent of the Temple Mount by Jewish pilgrims to Jerusalem, and thus meant 'pilgrimage'. The Zionists used it to describe migration to the land of Israel.
Amir	(**Arabic:** one who commands) it means either a military commander or a prince.
Ansar	(**Arabic:** The Helpers) the name given to Prophet Mohammed's followers in Madinah.
Antichrist	From certain prophecies in the New Testament, early Christians evolved a belief in a figure that would rise to power at the end of time, heralding the 'Last Days'. He was the opposite of a Messiah, because he was the enemy of Christ and of all Christians. An ordinary human being, he would be a person of absolute evil. Antichrist would deceive many people and attract a large following, while persecuting the faithful. He would be crowned in Jerusalem. Eventually, God would send down the Archangel Michael to fight him and

Christians would join the last terrible battle. The 'Second Coming' of Christ would then occur and an era of peace and glory would begin.

Apocalypse (**Greek:** revelation.) All three Semitic regions have developed an apocalyptic tradition relating to the events that will occur at the end of time, when God's power and justice will be finally revealed and, after a long war against the forces of evil, there will be final victory for the true religion.

asabiyya (**Arabic:** tribalism), the sense of solidarity or group affiliation emerging from *ailiyya*, or familialism.

Bid'ah (bida) (**Arabic**) Reprehensible innovation in Islam; heresy.

Bil-saif Jihad with the sword.

Caliph (Arabic: Khalifa) (**Arabic:** successor, deputy.) The caliph was the successor and deputy of the Prophet Mohammed and was recognized as the supreme authority of the Muslims by the Sunni until the Mongol invasions in the late thirteenth century. According to the Sharia, the caliph exercised full authority in both spiritual and political matters. After the rise of the sultans and amirs throughout the Muslim world, the caliph became a figurehead.

Canon Literally, a rule or decree, it refers to the list of officially accepted books in the Hebrew and Christian Bible.

Chansons de Geste (**French: 'the Songs of Deeds'**) Refers to those songs which began to be composed at the time of the First Crusade, celebrating the glorious achievements and heroism of the age of Charlemagne and exalting the military prowess of the Franks. The most famous of these was *The Song of Roland*.

Christ (**Greek:** *christos*): A Greek translation of the Hebrew *meshiah* ('anointed one'); a title applied by the early Christians to Jesus of Nazareth.

Dar al-Harb (**Arabic:** Land of War) In Islamic holy law, this describes the non-Muslim world outside the frontiers of Islam. In Islamic legal theory, there must be a perpetual state of war until the whole world submits to the supremacy of Islam, the true religion. The state of war may be suspended by truces, but cannot be ended by a permanent peace. In practice, Muslims abandoned this notion in the eighth century, accepted that Islam had reached its territorial limits and had normal trading and political connections with non-Muslim countries.

Dar al-Islam   (**Arabic:** Land of Islam): Any territory or country governed by the tenets of Islam.

Dar al-kufr   (**Arabic:** Land of unbelief): the term used by Prophet Mohammed to describe the society of Mecca between his flight (Hijra) in 622 AD and his triumphant return in 630. The more commonly used term to describe non-Islamic societies is '*Dar al- Harb*'.

Dawa (daawat)   (**Arabic:** The Call): i.e. invitation to unbelievers to Islam.

Dawlat al haqq   (**Arabic:** Land of truth), i.e., the territory governed by Islamic law and norms.

Deobandi   *A* person who follows the views, values and approach of the Islamic religious institution Darul Uloom Deoband, set up in Deoband, India, in 1866. Deobandis are Sunni Muslims and follow the Hanafi School. Unlike other Salafi movements, Deobandis also accept Sufism, particularly the Chishti, Naqshbandi, Qadiri and Suhrawardi orders. The Deobandi movement in India was hostile to British rule, while also opposing the movement for Pakistan. However, on the eve of India's independence, some Deobandis migrated to Pakistan where they established a political movement called *Jamiat-ul-Ulema-e-Islam* (JUI). During the 1980s, JUI established a number of madrasas along the Afghanistan-Pakistan border, which were attended by Afghan refugee children in their hundreds. In the 1990s, these students were organized by the JUI, with the active support of the Pakistani government and its armed forces, into the Taliban. While the term 'Deobandi' is loosely applied by certain scholars to the radical Islamic movement in Pakistan and Afghanistan, the latter is quite different from the Deobandi movement in India which remains moderate and apolitical.

Dhimmi   (**Arabic** *Dhimma*): This was a pact between the Muslim state and all non-Muslims living under Muslim rule in terms of which non-Muslims were afforded full religious liberty and given military and civil protection, on condition that they respected the supremacy of Islam. The term therefore means 'protected minorities'.

Dhu'l-fiqar
(also, Zulfiqar)   (**Arabic:** Wearing the armour of the Prophet and wielding his sword.), the name of the sword presented by Prophet Mohammed to his cousin and son-in-law, Ali ibn Abi Talib, which he used to fight non-believers.

Diaspora   This refers to the 'dispersal' of the Jewish people throughout the world and to those Jews who live outside the Land of Israel.

Eretz Israel   The Land of Israel: The usual name of the region which was promised by God to the descendants of Abraham through his son Isaac and to the Israelites, descendants of Jacob, Abraham's grandson. The biblical definitions of *Eretz Israel* encompass different regions; the actual area defined by these Bible passages is also subject to differences of opinion. Prior to the foundation of the State of Israel, the term *Eretz Yisrael* was used by Jews to refer to the area then generally known among non-Jews as the Holy Land or as Palestine.

Eschatology   Derived from the Greek, *eskaton*: 'the end', it is the study of the 'last days' and the 'end times'.

Exegesis   (**Greek:** To 'lead or guide out'); the art of interpreting and explaining the biblical text.

faqih   (**Arabic**) A Muslim jurisprudent who is deemed capable and sufficiently knowledgeable to give a *fatwa*.

fard' Ayn   (**Arabic**) A legal obligation incumbent on individual Muslims.

fard kifaya   (**Arabic**) A legal obligation incumbent on the community of Muslims as a whole.

fatwa   (**Arabic**) An opinion or a ruling given by an appropriate Islamic authority *[faqih]*, who interprets a point of holy law in a way that will be binding on those Muslims who accept him as their guide.

fedayeen	(**Arabic**, singular *fidai*) Literally 'one who sacrifices himself', a fighter who is prepared to risk his life for the sake of a belief or cause. It came into use in modern times while referring to the various Palestinian militants belonging to different organizations who attacked Israel and Israel-related interests, but were not motivated by religion. Now, however, it primarily refers to Muslim militants, particularly 'suicide bombers'.
fiqh	(**Arabic**) Islamic jurisprudence; the study and application of the body of sacred Muslim law.
Gentile	A non-Jew; derived from the Latin *gentes*, a translation of the Hebrew *goyim*, the 'foreign nations'.
ghazis	Muslim warriors.
ghayba	(**Arabic**: Occultation): In Shia tradition, it refers to the disappearance of the twelfth and last Imam Mohammad bin Hasan al-Askari in 873 AD. (See *'Hidden Imam'.*)
Gospel	Literally 'good news' (from the Anglo-Saxon *god spel*): the 'proclamation' (Greek, *evangelion*) of the early Church; the term is also applied to the various biographies of Jesus.
Gush Emunim	(**Hebrew: the 'Bloc of the Faithful'**) A religio–political group formed in Israel in 1974 to Judaise the occupied territories by setting up settlements there, and by encouraging Jews in the Diaspora to emigrate to Israel and join them in Gaza or the West Bank.
Hadith	(**Arabic**) A tradition handed down orally through a reliable train of sources relating to a saying or deed of Prophet Mohammed for the guidance of Muslims, which were gathered together during the ninth century. The whole corpus of the *Hadith* is one of the major sources of Islamic law.
hajis	(**Arabic**) those who perform the annual pilgrimage to Makkah.
Halakha	(**Hebrew**): Literally, the 'path' or 'way of walking', it is the part of the Talmud concerned with legal matters.
halakhic	Rulings made by priests on the basis of religious texts.
Hamas	(**Arabic acronym for 'Movement of the Islamic Resistance'**)

Islamic movement founded in 1988 in Palestine during the first *intifada*; its military wing, Izz al-Din al-Qassam, has been engaged in a guerrilla and violent campaign against Israel from 1988.

haram   (**Arabic**): Sacred; forbidden – hence 'sanctuary', especially the sanctuary surrounding the Kabah where all violence was prohibited; also, any holy Islamic site open only to Muslims.

Al-Haram
al-Sharif   (**Arabic: 'Noble Sanctuary'**) It refers to Islam's third holiest site in Jerusalem, encompassing the Al-Aqsa Mosque and the Dome of the Rock, which were built between 685 and 709 AD. According to Jewish tradition, these structures are located atop the site of the First Temple (destroyed in 586 BC) and the Second Temple (destroyed in AD 70), so that the site is also referred to as Temple Mount.

haredim   ('Fearful', meaning 'God-fearing' in Hebrew): name of those Jewish believers who refuse modern innovations. (*Haredi* is the singular form.)

Hermeneutics   (**Greek**): The art of interpretation, especially of scripture.

hesb   (**Arabic: accountability**) the principle of holding government officials accountable.

hezb   Literally "Party" or organization (also spelt as *'hizb'* in English*)*.

Hezbollah   (**Arabic for 'Party of God'**): Shiite radical movement in Lebanon founded in 1982, it is both a political party and a paramilitary organization.

Hidden Imam   In 'Twelver Shiism', the Hidden Imam is an Islamic Messiah figure. The Shiites took as their leader (imam) the direct descendants of Ali, the cousin and son-in-law of Prophet Mohammed. There were twelve of these imams. Eventually, the Twelfth Imam went into hiding in AD 874. After that the Shiites claim that there can be no more legitimate authority in the absence of this Hidden Imam, who, they say, is in a state of 'occultation'. They believe that one day the Twelfth Imam will return and inaugurate a golden age.

Hijra   (**Arabic: migration**) The migration of Prophet Mohammed from Makkah to Medina in 622. The beginning of the year in which this emigration took place is the starting point of the Muslim era. The term has been used by later Muslims to describe a migration from the community in order to live a more truly Islamic life.

Holy Spirit Term used by rabbis in the Talmudic age to denote God's presence on earth. In Christianity, this divine presence, along with Father and Logo, constitutes the revelation of God as Trinity.

Ijmah: (**Arabic**) The 'consensus' of the Muslim community that gives legitimacy to a legal decision; the third source of Shariah law after the Koran and the Hadith.

ijtihad (**Arabic**): The 'independent reasoning' used by a jurist to apply the *Shariah* to contemporary circumstances. One who was expert enough to develop Islamic tradition by means of individual reasoning was called a *mujtahid* (one who exercises *ijitihad*). During the fourteenth century Sunni Muslims declared that the 'gates of *ijtihad*' were closed, and that scholars must rely on the legal decisions of past authorities instead of upon their own reasoned insights. In Iran, however, another Muslim tradition does allow *mujtahids* of sufficient standing to exercise individual reasoning and to make a contribution to the Islamic tradition.

Ilm (**Arabic**) knowledge of what is right and how Muslims should behave.

Imam (**Arabic**: leader) Generally, the word is used to describe any leader of the Muslim community or a Muslim who leads the prayers in the mosque. In the Shia tradition, the word is applied to Prophet Mohammed's descendants through his daughter Fatima and his son-in-law, Ali.

Intifada (**Arabic** for 'shaking off') Palestinian uprising against the Israeli occupation, the first in 1987 and the second in 2000.

Irgun The underground military and extremist wing of the Revisionist Zionists, which operated in Palestine and in Israel from 1931 to 1949, led by Menachem Begin, who became Prime Minister of Israel in 1977. It blew up King David Hotel in 1946 and was heavily involved in terrorist attacks against the Palestinian population. During the 1948 war, it

	became part of the Israel Defence Force (IDF) and committed the Dir Yassin massacre; dissolved later that year.
Islam	(**Arabic**) the name of the religion of Muslims. It means submission to God, and a 'Muslim' is 'one who submits'.
islah	(**Arabic**: to repair) generally translated as 'reform' and, in this sense, is used in the name of several parties in the Muslim world.
Isra	A night journey, specially that of Prophet Mohammed to Jerusalem.
istibdad	(**Arabic**) Despotism, autocracy, arbitrariness, tyranny.
Jahiliyyah	(**Arabic**) Traditionally translated as 'Age of Ignorance', and used to apply to the pre-Islamic period in Arabia. Today, radical Muslims often apply it to any society, even a nominally Muslim society, which has, in their view, turned its back upon God and refused to submit to God's sovereignty.
jahili	(**Arabic**: ignorant) those who do not follow the tenets of Islam.
Jama'a (*jamaat*)	(*Arabic:* 'group'): the collectivity of Muslims.
Jihad	(**Arabic: striving, effort**) Greater *jihad* speaks of internal struggle for righteousness; lesser *jihad* is the defence of the Muslim community. Usually used to mean 'holy war' against unbelievers or against Christians, who oppressed and persecuted Muslims in their Crusades.
jizya	(*Arabic*): a tax levied upon non-Muslims in a Muslim state, in return for freedom to them to practice their faith and obtain state protection from external aggression as also exemption from military service and payment of *Zakat* (obligatory alms).
Kafir	(**Arabic: Plural: *kuffar*) Traditionally translated as 'unbeliever'. More accurately, it refers to somebody who ungratefully and aggressively rejects Allah and refuses to acknowledge his dependence on the Creator.
Kach	Far-right Israeli party, led by the late Rabbi Meir Kahane, barred from running in elections.
Kabbalah	(**Hebrew**) The system of Jewish mysticism.

klipa	In Jewish mysticism, it symbolizes the forces of evil in the universe.
Koran	(**Arabic: recitation**) The name given to the holy book of Islam, which Muslims believe was dictated to Mohammed by God himself. Mohammed, who could not write, was told to recite the words after the divine voice. These utterances were written down by those of his disciples who were literate, and were collected by his disciples by the middle of the seventh century. As the revelations came to Mohammed, he passed them on to the Muslims who had to learn them by heart and place each new revelation in the place that the Prophet prescribed.
Labour Zionism	This is the group of Zionists led by David Ben-Gurion, who became the first Prime Minister of Israel in 1948. These were secular socialists who originally believed that they would create a model, equal society in Palestine. They ruled Israel till 1977, when the Right-wing Likud came to power under Begin.
Lehi	(**Hebrew; an acronym for *Lohana Herut Israel*: 'Fighters for the Freedom of Israel'**) This was a militant Zionist organization that fought the British and the Arabs in Palestine before the establishment of the state of Israel. It was founded by Abraham Stern in 1939, a former Irgun leader, killed by the British in 1942. Responsible for assassination of UN mediator Count Bernadotte. One of its leaders, Yitzhak Shamir, was intermittently Prime Minister between 1983 and 1992.
Likud	(**Hebrew for 'cohesion'**): Parliamentary bloc representing the Right-wing parties in Israel formed in September 1973. First won election in 1977 and has been intermittently in power since then.
Mahdi	(**Arabic**) Literally 'one who is rightly-guided [by God]', the term came to have messianic overtones and referred to the awaited saviour who would restore justice and return the community to the proper path.
Madrassa	(**Arabic**) A seminary or college of Islamic learning, which is often, though not always, attached to a mosque.
Maseeh Al-Dajjal	(**Arabic**) Antichrist

Al-maslaha al amma	(**Arabic**) Matters of public welfare
Messiah	(**Hebrew** *meshiah*, 'anointed one'): Originally the term applied to anybody who was given a special task by God – notably the king, who was anointed at his coronation and became a 'son of God'. But, the term was also used for prophets and priests, and also for Cyrus, king of Persia, who permitted the Jews to return to Judah and rebuild their temple after their long exile in Babylon. Later, some Jews in the first century AD expected a *meshiah* to redeem Israel, assist Yahweh during the last days, and establish his reign on earth. The Christians believed that Jesus was this messiah.
Mufti	(**Arabic**) An expert in Islamic law. Unlike the Qadi, his status is usually personal and voluntary rather than an official appointment; it is a title bestowed on a Muslim who is renowned for his scholarship and personal reputation.
Muhajireen	(**Arabic**) (Singular. *Muhajir)* 'Migrants', people leaving a place for the sake of Islam. Originally it referred to the migration of Prophet Mohammed and his companions from Mecca to Medina.
Mujahid	(**Arabic, plural:** *mujahideen)*: A freedom fighter who takes part in a *jihad* or struggle for the liberation of his people from tyranny and persecution.
Mujtahid	(**Arabic**) An Islamic scholar qualified to exercise *ijtihad* or independent judgment in all matters pertaining to Islamic practice. This means he can issue authoritative opinions on the basis of his knowledge of Islamic law and this can also be a political judgment.
National Religious Party	Often referred to by its acronym 'NRP', it represents the radical Jews in Israel who are not Haredim.
Al-Naqba	(**Arabic**: 'catastrophe') Term used by the Palestinians and the Arab world for the 1948 war and the creation of Israel.
Palestine Authority	Title of the body running legislative and executive affairs in the 'Occupied Territories' according to the 1993 Oslo Accord; became largely ineffective after the second Intifada in 2000.

Pogrom	(**Russian:** destruction) An organized massacre which is directed towards the annihilation of any one body or class of people, particularly Jewish communities.
Prophet	(**Latin:** to speak on behalf of) In all three Semitic traditions, the Prophet is a person who speaks on behalf of God: he is an intermediary between God and man, who will correct, guide and lead a community to a closer approximation of God's will.
Al-Qaeda	(**Arabic:** 'The base'.) Name of the radical Islamic organization headed by Osama bin Laden and Ayman al-Zawahiri, responsible for the 9/11 strikes on US soil. Al-Qaeda members often refer to their organization as the 'base of jihad' (*Qaedat al-Jihad*).
Qaim	(**Arabic:** The Standing One, the one who will rise), refers, in Shia tradition, to the appearance of the Mahdi on the Day of Judgement. [See *'Hidden Imam.*]
qaraba	(**Arabic**) Closeness that is engendered by *ailiyya* and *asabiyya* which enjoins familial solidarity and requirement of obligatory mutual support and responsibility in traditional Arab societies, particularly in the Arabian peninsula.
Al-Qiyaamah	(**Arabic**) Resurrection, Hereafter.
qiyas	(**Arabic:** precedent) In Sunni jurisprudence, it is the process of analogical reasoning to derive a new injunction from precedents set out in the Koran or Hadith. This is the fourth source of Sharia law after the Koran, *Hadith* and *ijmah*.
Qadi	(**Arabic**) A judge who officially administers the Sharia.
Rabbi	(**Hebrew:** master) A Jewish religious teacher.
Redemption	For the Jews, it refers to the coming of the Messiah and the dawning of a new era of peace and harmony, when God's chosen people will live in their land according to the Torah and the whole world will acknowledge the truth of Judaism and be redeemed through this recognition. Christians call the death and resurrection of Christ their redemption because they believe that by this means he saved the world.
Revisionist Zionism	This was an ideology propounded by Vladimir Jabotinsky, which broke away from Labour Zionism. Revisionists

tended toward an extreme nationalism and were affected by the racial chauvinism widespread Europe at the end of the nineteenth century.

Sahib al-sayf   (**Arabic**) Lord of the sword.

Salafism   It is a Sunni Islamic movement that takes the pious ancestors, the *(Salaf)* of early Islam, as exemplary models. Salafism seeks to revive the practice of Islam that more closely resembles the religion and society during the time of Mohammed. Salafis in general are opposed to both Sufi and Shi'a doctrines, which they regard as having many aspects of *shirk, bidah* and impermissible intercession of religious figures. In recent years they have been associated with the 'jihad' of Al-Qaeda and other radical Islamic movements, collectively referred to by some scholars as 'Jihadi-salafism'.

Salvation   This word describes those events in which God's elect are rescued from an impending and apparently inevitable destruction by a sudden reversal of fortune that seems miraculous and can only be explained by positing divine intervention. This experience has befallen Jews, Christians and Muslims throughout the story of the holy wars.

Saracen   (**Greek *Sarakenoi* and Latin *Saracenus*:** 'The people that dwells in tents'.) This was the word used by Greeks and Romans and by Greek and Latin Christians to describe the people of the Arabian Peninsula, who lived in tents.

Sharia   (**Arabic**) The word literally means the road or way to a watering hole, which must always be followed; it refers to Islamic holy law which was compiled and codified by the great Muslim jurists of the eighth and ninth centuries, who applied the principles of the Koran and the *hadith* to the smallest details of everyday life.

Shas   (**Hebrew abbreviation of 'Guardian of the Torah'**) Founded in 1984 by ultra-orthodox Mizrachi Jews (i.e., Jews from the Arab countries), who broke away from *Agudat Israel*, the major ultra-orthodox party; calls for the creation of a theocracy in Israel and for equal rights for Mizrachi Jews. Has done well in all elections since 1988.

Sheikh   (**Arabic : old man, elder**) The word used in a number of contexts: a Sheikh can be a religious leader, a chief of a tribe or a man who has won respect and renown in the community; in several Gulf countries, it is also the title of royal family members.

shekhina (**Hebrew**) Divine presence.

Shia/Shiite (**Arabic**, *Shiah al-Ali*: the partisans of Ali.) Originally this was a political movement of a minority of Muslims in the community, who believed that the Prophet Mohammed had wanted Ali ibn Abi Talib, his cousin and son-in-law, to succeed him instead of Abu Bakr, the first Caliph. Over the years, Shiites developed different beliefs and religious practices from the Sunni Muslims, but there is no difference in the essentials of the faith in the two traditions.

Shoah (**Hebrew**) The Nazi Holocaust

shirk (**Arabic**: idolatry), associating other beings with God, putting other deities or purely human values on the same level as Allah; the cardinal Muslim sin.

shura (**Arabic**) Consultation.

Sitra ahra (**Hebrew**) The other side, the devil's camp.

Sultan (**Arabic: originally government.**) The Sultan wielded military and political authority over a group of Muslims, but theoretically he was subservient to the Caliph.

Sunna, Sunni (**Arabic**, *Sunna*: the way) The *Sunna* is the way of the Prophet Mohammad and includes everything he said, did, caused, ordered or allowed to happen. Much of *Sharia* law is based on the sunna, since it is believed that upholding Mohammed's practices and habits is the perfect form of Islam. A Sunni is a Muslim who follows this way. The word is commonly used to distinguish the majority of Muslims from the Shiite minority.

taasul (**Arabic**) Fanaticism

tajdid (**Arabic**) Renewal

Takfir (**Arabic**, from the root *kafir*, non-believer) An assertion that the action or pronouncement of an apparent Muslim indicates his abandonment of his faith, thus exposing him to extreme punishment, including execution.

Talmud	(Hebrew, 'teaching, study') The body of Jewish civil, ceremonial and traditional law which developed from the Torah and from the oral and written commentary upon it by the great rabbis.
tawhid	(Arabic) Unity and authority of God and religion.
Torah	(Hebrew: the Law) The Hebrew name (the Arabic form is *tawrat*) for the Pentateuch – the first five books for the Old Testament attributed to Moses. The whole of the Torah comprises the 613 commandments that bind observant Jews and regulate the conduct of everyday life.
Ulama/Ulema	(Arabic, singular: *alim*) The learned men who devote their lives to the study of the holy law of Islam, extending to the entire world of Islamic belief and practice. As guardians and interpreters of the *sharia,* the *ulema* have traditionally held a prominent place in Muslim society. The consensus of the *umma* – which in reality translates into the consensus of the *ulema* - is second only to the Koran and *sunna* in authority and is generally seen as binding on the entire *umma.* Their backing is therefore often sought by the governments of Muslim countries as they confer religious legitimacy.
Umma	Arabic: The global community of Islam.
Wahhabism	Muslim Sunni reform movement that emerged in the Arabian Peninsula in the mid-eighteenth century under Mohammed Ibn Abdul Wahhab (1703–92). His followers reject the name 'Wahhabi' and call themselves the *Muwahidin,* i.e., 'those who believe in God's unity'. The ancestors of the present royal family of Saudi Arabia accepted the reformist doctrines of Ibn Abdul Wahhab (c. 1740), and, armed with this religious support, they embarked upon bringing different parts of the Arabian Peninsula under their rule. After some setbacks, this effort culminated with the emergence of the 'Kingdom of Saudi Arabia' in 1932. All aspects of public life in the Kingdom are regulated on the tenets proclaimed by Ibn Wahhab.
Yahweh	This is the name that God gives to himself in the Jewish Scriptures. In English versions of the Bible, Christians often translate Yahweh as 'Jehovah'.

Yishuv (Hebrew: settlement) the Jewish community in Palestine, before the creation of the state of Israel in 1948. This Community was made up of the "Old Yishuv", who lived in Palestine up to 1918 (numbering about 25,000), and the "New Yishuv" who migrated to Palestine from 1922 onwards, and, by 1948, numbered about 700,000.

Zion Zion was the name of the ancient citadel which King David conquered in about 1000 BC. It is often used as a synonym for Jerusalem. The Zionists, who wanted to return the Jewish people to the land of their fathers, looked back to the old religious dream of a Jewish return to Zion.

Zoroastrianism The official religion of the Persians before they converted to Islam. It was a dualistic religion in which a good spirit fights an evil spirit in a constant battle. The Jews in exile in Babylon (586–38 BC) were influenced by its beliefs and practices, though there is academic dispute in regard to details. Generally, Jewish ideas of heaven, hell, the afterlife and the coming of the Messiah have been traced by scholars to Zoroastrianism.

Bibliography

Messianism / Extremism / Terrorism

Burleigh, Michael. *Blood & Rage – A Cultural History of Terrorism*. London: Harper Press, 2008.

Burleigh, Michael. *Sacred Causes – Religion and Politics from the European Dictators to Al Qaeda*. London: Harper Press, 2006.

Falk, Richard. *The Great Terror War*. Gloucestershire, U.K.: Arris Books, 2003.

Fenn, Richard K. *Dreams of Glory – The Sources of Apocalyptic Terror*. Hampshire, England: Ashgate Publishing, 2006.

Gray, John. *Black Mass – Apocalyptic Religion and the Death of Utopia*. London: Penguin Books, 2008.

Harris, Sam. *The End of Faith, Religion, Terror, and The Future of Reason*. London: The Free Press, 2005.

Hobsbawm, Eric. *Globalisation, Democracy and Terrorism*, London: Little Brown, 2007.

Juergensmeyer, Mark. *Global Rebellion, Religious Challenges to the Secular State, from Christian Militias to Al Qaeda*. Berkeley, California: University of California Press, 2008.

Juergensmeyer, Mark. *Terror in the Mind of God – The Global Rise of Religious Violence*. New Delhi: Oxford University Press, 2000.

Junaid, Shahwar. *Terrorism and Global Power Systems*, New York: Oxford University Press, 2005.

Lacqueur, Walter. *The New Terrorism – Fanaticism and the Arms of Mass Destruction*. New York: Oxford University Press, 1999.

Lilla, Mark. *The Stillborn God – Religion, Politics, and the Modern West*. New York: Alfred A. Knopf, 2007.

Pallmeyer, Jack Nelson. *Is Religion Killing Us? Violence in the Bible and the Quran*. Harrisburg, PA : Trinity Press International, 2003.

Pape, Robert A. *Dying to Win – Why Suicide Terrorists Do It*. London: Gibson Square, 2006.

Richardson, Louise. *What Terrorists Want – Understanding the Terrorist Threat.* London: John Murray, 2006.

Stern. Jessica. *Terror in the Name of God – Why Religious Militants Kill.* New York: HarperCollins, 2003.

Messianism in the Semitic Traditions

Al-Ashqar, Umar S. *The Day of Resurrection – In the Light of the Qur'an and Sunnah.* Riyadh, Saudi Arabia: International Islamic Publishing House, 2005.

Amanat, Abbas and Magnus Bernhardsson, Eds.. *Imagining the End: Visions of Apocalypse from the Ancient Middle East to Modern America.* London: I.B. Tauris Publishers, 2002.

Armstrong, Karen. *The Bible – The Biography.* London: Atlantic Books, 2007.

Armstrong, Karen. *The Battle for God-Fundamentalism in Judaism, Christianity and Islam.* London: Harper Collins Publishers, 2001.

Armstrong, Karen. *A History of God.* London: Vintage Books, 1993.

Cook, David. *Contemporary Muslim Apocalyptic Literature.* Syracuse, New York: Syracuse University Press, 2005.

Cohn, Norman. *Europe's Inner Demons – The Demonisation of Christians in Medieval Christendom.* London: Pimlico, 2005.

Cohn, Norman. *Warrant for Genocide – The Myth of the Jewish World Conspiracy and the Protocols of the Elders of Zion.* London: Serif, 2005.

Cohn, Norman. *Cosmos, Chaos & The World to Come.* London: Yale University Press, 1995.

Cohn, Norman. *The Pursuit of the Millennium – Revolutionary Millenarians and Mystical Anarchists of the Middle Ages.* London: Pimlico, 2004.

Hoffmann, R. Joseph. *The Just War and Jihad – Violence in Judaism, Christianity, & Islam.* New York: Prometheus Books, 2006.

McGinn, Bernard J., John J. Collins and Stephen J. Stein, eds. *The Continuum History of Apocalypticism.* New York: Continuum, 2003.

Mendel, Arthur P. *Vision and Violence.* Ann Arbor, Michigan: The University of Michigan Press, 2002.

Rinehart, James F. *Apocalyptic Faith And Political Violence – Prophets of Terror.* Hampshire, England: Palgrave MacMillam, 2006.

Siddiqui, Moid. *The Return of Christ – The End is Close: The Jewish, Christian and Islamic Perspective.* New Delhi: Adam Publishers, 2007.

Williamson, G. A. *Josephus – The Jewish War,* London: Penguin Books. 1959.

Historical Ties Between the Semitic Communities

Akbar, M. J. *The Shade of Swords – Jihad and Conflict Between Islam & Christianity.* New Delhi: The Lotus Collection, 2002.

Armstrong, Karen. *Islam – A Short History.* London: Phoenix Press, 2000.

Armstrong, Karen. *Holy War – The Crusades and their Impact on Today's World.* London: Macmillan, 1988.

Berkey, Jonathan P. *The Formation of Islam – Religion and Society in the Near East, 600-1800.* New York: Cambridge University Press, 2003.

Bulliet, Richard W. *The Case for Islamo-Christian Civilization.* New York: Columbia University Press, 2004.

Durant, Will. *Our Oriental Heritage.* New York: Simon & Schuster, Reprinted 1980.

Durant, Will. *The Age of Faith.* New York: Simon & Schuster, 1950.

Durant, Will. *Caesar and Christ.* New York: Simon & Schuster, 1944.

Goddard, Hugh. *A History of Christian – Muslim Relations.* Chicago: New Amsterdam Books, 2000.

Hourani, Albert. *A History of the Arab Peoples.* Cambridge, MA: The Belknap Press of Harvard University Press, 1991.

Karabell, Zachary. *People of the Book – The Forgotten History of Islam and the West.* London: John Murray, 2007.

Kennedy, Hugh. *The Great Arab Conquests – How the Spread of Islam Changed the World We Live In.* London: Phoenix, 2008.

Lewis, David Levering. *God's Crucible – Islam and the Making of Europe, 570-1215.* New York: W.W. Norton, 2008.

Morgan, Michael Hamilton. *Lost History – The Enduring Legacy of Muslim Scientists, Thinkers, and Artists.* Washington, DC: National Geographic Society, 2008.

Partner, Peter. *God of Battles – Holy Wars of Christianity and Islam.* Princeton, New Jersey: Princeton University Press,1997.

Said, Edward W. *Orientalism.* New York: Random House, 1979.

Walker, Christopher J. *Islam and the West – A Dissonant Harmony of Civilisations.* Gloucestershire, United Kingdom: Sutton Publishing Ltd., 2005.

Zein, M. Faruk. *Christianity, Islam and Orientalism.* London: Saqi Books, 2003.

Israel / Palestine

Armstrong, Karen. *Jerusalem – One City, Three Faiths.* New York: Alfred A. Knopf, 1996.

Carter, Jimmy. *Palestine-Peace Not Apartheid.* New York: Simon & Schuster, 2006.

Cook, Jonathan. *Israel and the Clash of Civilisations – Iraq, Iran and the Plan to Remake the Middle East.* London: Pluto Press, 2008.

Cook, Jonathan. *Blood and Religion – The Unmasking of the Jewish and Democratic State.* London: Pluto Press, 2006.

Dieckhoff, Alain. *The Invention of a Nation- Zionist Thought and the Making of Modern Israel*. Cape Town: David Philip, 2003.

Freedman, Lawrence. A *Choice of Enemies - America Confronts the Middle East*. New York: Published by Public Affairs, 2008.

Hamilton, Jill. *God, Guns and Israel – Britain, The First World War and the Jews in the Holy City*. Gloucestershire, U.K.: Sutton Publishing, 2004.

Horowitz, Elliott. *Reckless Rites*. Princeton: Princeton University Press, 2006.

Keay, John. *Sowing the Wind – The Seeds of Conflict in the Middle East*. London: John Murray Ltd., 2003.

La Guardia, Anton. *Holy Land, Unholy War – Israelis and Palestinians*. London: Penguin Books, 2001.

Landau, David. *Piety & Power – The World of Jewish Fundamentalism*. New York: Farrar, Straus and Giroux, 1993.

Lehmann, David & Batia Siebzehner. *Remaking Israeli Judaism – The Challenge of Shas*. London: C. Hurst & Co., 2006.

Magi, Giovanna. *Jerusalem*. Florence, Italy: Bonechi & Steimatzky, 1999.

Masalha, Nur. *Imperial Israel and the Palestinians – The Politics of Expansion*. London: Pluto Press, 2000.

Mearsheimer, John J. and Stephen W. Walt. *The Israel Lobby and US Foreign Policy*. London: Allen Lane/Penguin Books, 2007.

Morris, Benny. *Righteous Victims – A History of the Zionist – Arab Conflict 1881-2001*. New York: Vintage Books, 2001.

Oren, Michael B. *Power, Faith and Fantasy – America in the Middle East, 1776 to the Present*. New York: W.W. Norton & Company, 2007.

Pappe, Ilan. A *History of Modern Palestine* – Second Edition. New York: Cambridge University Press, 2004.

Pappe, Ilan. *The Ethnic Cleansing of Palestine*. Oxford, England: Oneworld Publications, 2006.

Pappe, Ilan. *The Making of the Arab-Israeli Conflict 1947 – 1951*. London: I. B. Tauris & Co. Ltd, 1992.

Sand, Shlomo. *The Invention of the Jewish People*. London: Verso, 2009

Shahak, Israel and Norton Mezvinsky. *Jewish Fundamentalism in Israel*. New Edition, London: Pluto Press, 2004.

Shindler, Colin. *The Land Beyond Promise – Israel, Likud and the Zionist Dream*. London: I. B. Tauris, 2005.

Sternhell. Zeev. *The Founding Myths of Israel – Nationalism, Socialism, and the Making of the Jewish State*. Princeton, New Jersey: Princeton University Press, 1999.

Telhami, Shibley. *The Stakes – America in the Middle East – The Consequences of Power and the Choice for Peace*. Cambridge, MA: Westview Press, 2004.

Zertal, Idith and Akiva Eldar. *Lords of the Land – The War Over Israel's Settlements in the Occupied Territories, 1967-2007.* New York: Nation Books, 2007.

United States : Religion and Politics

Bates, Stephen. *God's Own Country – Tales from the Bible Belt.* London: Hodder & Stoughton, 2007.

Campbell, David E. *A Matter of Faith – Religion in the 2004 Presidential Election.* Washington DC: Brookings Institution Press, 2007.

Carpenter, Joel A. *Revive us Again – The Reawakening of American Fundamentalism.* New York, USA: Oxford University Press, 1997.

Clark, Victoria. *Allies for Armageddon – The Rise of Christian Zionism.* London: Yale University Press, 2007.

Friedman, Murray. *The New Conservative Revolution – Jewish Intellectuals and the Shaping of Public Policy.* New York: Cambridge University Press, 2005.

Fukuyama, Francis. *After the Neocons - America at the Crossroads.* London: Profile Books Ltd., 2006.

Jenkins, Philip. *Mystics and Messiahs – Cults and New Religions in American History.* New York: Oxford University Press, 2000.

Micklethwait, John and Adrian Woodridge. *The Right Nation – Why America Is Different.* London: Penguin Books, 2005.

Phillips, Kevin. *American Theocracy - The Peril and Politics of Radical Religion, Oil and Borrowed Money in the 21ˢᵗ Century.* New York: Penguin Books, 2007.

Sniegoski, Stephen J. *The Transparent Cabal – The Neoconservative Agenda, War in the Middle East, and the National Interest of Israel.* Norfolk, Virginia: Enigma Editors, 2008.

Stelzer, Irwin, ed., *The Neocon Reader,* New York: Grove Press, 2004.

Stelzer, Irwin. *A Matter of Faith – Religion in the 2004 Presidential Election.* Washington: Brookings Institution Press, 2007.

Victor, Barbara. *The Last Crusade – Religion and the Politics of Misdirection* London: Constable & Robinson Ltd., 2005.

Wallis, Jim. *God's Politics – Why the Right Gets it Wrong and the Left Doesn't Get it (A New Vision for Faith and Politics in America).* New York: Harper Collins Publisher, 2005.

Weisberg, Jacob. *The Bush Tragedy – The Unmaking of a President.* London: Bloomsbury, 2008.

Zunes Stephen. *U.S Foreign Policy and the Roots of Terrorism.* London: Zed Books, 2002.

Resurgent Islam and Jihad

Ahmed, Akbar. *Journey into Islam – The Crisis of Globalization.* Washington, DC: Brooking Institution Press, 2007.

Armstrong, Karen. *Muhammad – Prophet For Our Time*. London: Harper Collins Publishers, 2006.

Atwan, Abdel Bari. *The Secret History of al-Qaeda*. London: Saqi Books, 2006.

Berkey, Jonathan P. *The Formation of Islam, Religion and Society in the Near East, 600-1800*. New York: Cambridge University Press, 2003.

Bonney, Richard. *Jihad – From Quran to Bin Laden*. New York: Palgrave/ Macmillan, 2004.

Burke, Jason. *Al Qaeda – The True Story of Radical Islam*. London: Penguin Books, Third Edition, 2007.

Burke, Jason. *The Road to Kandahar – Travels through conflict in the Islamic World*. London: Penguin Books, 2007.

Choueiri, Yousef M. *Islamic Fundamentalism*. London: Pinter Publishers, 1990.

Delong-Bas, Natana J. *Wahhabi Islam – From Revival and Reform to Global Jihad*. London: Oxford University Press, 2004.

Desai, Meghnad. *Rethinking Islamism: The Ideology of the New Terror*. London: I.B. Tauris, 2007.

Devji, Faisal. *Landscapes of the Jihad – Militancy, Morality, Modernity*. London: C. Hurst & Co., 2005.

Enayat, Hamid. *Modern Islamic Political Thought*. London : I.B. Tauris & Co., 2005.

Ernst, Carl W. *Following Muhammad – Rethinking Islam in the Contemporary World*. Chapel Hill, NC, USA: The University of North Carolina Press, 2003.

Esposito, John L., ed., *Voices of Resurgent Islam*. New York: Oxford University Press, 1983.

Esposito, John L. and Azzam Tamimi. *Islam and Secularism in the Middle East*. London: Hurst & Company, 2000.

Esposito, John L. and John O. Voll, eds., *Islam and Democracy*. New York: Oxford University Press, 1996.

Fandy, Mamoun. *Saudi Arabia and the Politics of Dissent*. New York: St. Martin's Press, 1999.

Furnish, Timothy R. *Holiest Wars-Islamic Mahdis, Their Jihads, and Osama bin Laden*. Westport, CT: Praeger, 2005.

Glasse, Cyril. *The Concise Encyclopedia of Islam*. London: Stacey International, 1989.

Gray, John. *Al Qaeda and What it Means to be Modern*. London: Faber and Faber, 2003.

Halliday, Fred. *Two Hours that Shook the World – September 11, 2001: Causes & Consequences*. London: Saqi Books, 2002.

Halliday, Fred. *Nation and Religion in the Middle East*. London: Saqi Books, 2000.

Hefner, Robert W. *Remaking Muslim Politics - Pluralism, Contestation, Democratization*. Princeton, New Jersey: Princeton University Press, 2005.

Ibrahim, Raymond, ed., *The Al Qaeda Reader*. New York: Doubleday, 2007.

Islamic Movements-Impact on Political Stability in the Arab World. Abu Dhabi: The Emirates Centre for Strategic Studies and Research, 2003.

Jansen, Johannes J. G. *The Dual Nature of Islamic Fundamentalism*. London: Hurst & Co., 1997.

Kedourie, Elie. *Islam in the Modern World*. New York: Holt, Rinehart and Winston, 1980.

Kepel, Gilles. *Beyond Terror and Martyrdom: The Future of the Middle East*. Cambridge MA and London, UK: The Belknap Press of Harvard University Press, 2008.

Kepel, Gilles and Jean-Pierre Milelli. *Al Qaeda in its Own Words*. London: The Belknap Press of Harvard University Press, 2008.

Kepel, Gilles. *The Roots of Radical Islam*. London: Saqi Books, 2005.

Kepel, Gilles. *Jihad-The Trail of Political Islam*. London: I.B. Tauris, 2004.

Kepel, Gilles. *The War for Muslim Minds – Islam and the West*. USA: The Belknap Press of Harvard University Press, 2004.

Lewis, Bernard. *The Crisis of Islam: Holy War and Unholy Terror*. London: Weidenfeld & Nicolson, 2003.

Lewis, Bernard. *What Went Wrong? The Clash Between Islam and Modernity in the Middle East*. London: Weidenfeld & Nicolson, 2002

Mamdani, Mahmood. *Good Muslim, Bad Muslim – America, The Cold War, and the Roots of Terror*. Lahore, Pakistan: Vanguard Books, 2005.

Mohammed, Arkoun. *Islam: To Reform or to Subvert?* London: Saqi Books, 2006.

Ottaway, Marina and Julia Choucair-Vizoso. *Beyond The Façade – Political Reform in the Arab World*. Washington: United Book Press, 2008.

Qureshi, Emran and Michael A. Sells. *The New Crusades - Constructing the Muslim Enemy*. New York: Oxford University Press, 2005.

Randall, Jonathan. *Osama – The Making of a Terrorist*. London: I.B. Tauris, 2006.

Rehnema, Ali, ed., *Pioneers of Islamic Revival*. New Updated Edition, Kuala Lumpur: SIRD, 2005.

Roy, Olivier. *The Politics of Chaos in the Middle East*. New York: Columbia University Press, 2008.

Roy, Olivier. *Secularism Confronts Islam*. New York: Columbia University Press, 2007.

Roy, Olivier. *Globalised Islam – The Search for a New Ummah*. London: Hurst & Company, 2006.

Ruthven, Malise. *Islam in the World*. London: Penguin Books, 1984.

Sageman, Marc. *Leaderless Jihad - Terror Networks in the Twenty-First Century.* Philadelphia, Pennsylvania: University of Pennsylvania Press, 2008.

Said, Edward W. *Covering Islam – How the Media and the Experts Determine How We See The Rest Of The World.* London: Vintage, 1997.

Salame, Ghassan. *Democracy without Democrats? – The Renewal of Politics in the Muslim World.* London: I. B. Tauris & Co. Ltd., 2001.

Schulze, Reinhard. *A Modern History of the Islamic World.* London : I.B. Tauris, 2002.

Sivan, Emmanuel & Menachem Friedman. *Religious Radicalism & Politics in the Middle East.* New York: State University of New York Press, 1990.

Taji-Farouki, Suha and Basheer M. Nafi. *Islamic Thought in the Twentieth Century.* London: I.B. Tauris, 2004.

Takeyh, Ray & Nikolas K. Gvosdev. *The Receding Shadow of the Prophet – The Rise and Fall of Radical Political Islam.* London: Praeger Publishers, 2004.

Trofimov, Yaroslav. *The Siege of Mecca – The Forgotten Uprising.* New York: The Doubleday Broadway Publishing Group, 2007.

Vertigans, Stephen. *Militant Islam – A Sociology of Characteristics, Causes, and Consequences.* London & New York: Routledge, 2009.

Westerlund, David. *Questioning the Secular State – The Worldwide Resurgence of Religion in Politics.* London: C.Hurst & Co., 1996.

Wright, Robin. *Dreams and Shadows – The Future of the Middle East.* New York: The Penguin Press, 2008.

Wright, Lawrence. *The Looming Tower – Al Qaeda and the Road to 9/11.* New York: Alfred A. Knopf, 2006.

Wright, Robin. *Sacred Rage - The Wrath of Militant Islam.* London: Andre Deutsch Limited, 1986.

Contemporary Politics

(A) Iraq

Glantz, Aaron. *How America Lost Iraq.* New York: Penguin Group, 2005.

Gourevitch, Philip and Errol Morris. *Standard Operating Procedure – A War Story.* New York: Penguin Press, 2008.

Hiro, Dilip. *Secrets and Lies – The True Story of the Iraq War.* New York: Nation Books, 2004.

Packer, George. *The Assassins Gate – America in Iraq.* New York: Farrar, Straus and Giroux, 2005.

Scheuer, Michael. *Marching toward Hell – America and Islam After Iraq.* New York: Free Press, 2008.

Woodward, Bob. *The War Within – The Secret White House History 2006-2008.* New York: Simon & Schuster, 2008.

Woodward, Bob. *State of Denial – Bush At War, Part III.* New York: Simon & Schuster, 2006.
Woodward, Bob. *Plan of Attack.* Great Britain: Simon & Schuster, 2004.
Woodward, Bob. *Bush At War.* New York: Simon & Schuster, 2002.

(B) Afghanistan

Coll, Steve. *Ghost Wars – The Secret History of the CIA, Afghanistan, and bin Laden, from the Soviet Invasion to September 10, 2001.* New York: Penguin Press, 2004.
Rashid, Ahmed. *Descent Into Chaos – How the War against Islamic Extremism is being lost in Pakistan, Afghanistan and Central Asia.* London: Allen Lane/ Penguin Books, 2008.
Rashid, Ahmed. *Taliban – The Story of the Afghan Warlords.* London: Pan Books, 2001.

(C) General

Buruma, Ian and Avishai Margalit. *Occidentalism – The West in the Eyes of Its Enemies.* New York: The Penguin Press, 2004.
Fukuyama, Francis. *The End of History and the Last Man.* New York: Free Press, 1992.
Huntington, Samuel. *The Clash of Civilizations and the Remaking of World Order.* London: Simon & Schuster, 1997.
Pitank, Lawrence. *America, Islam, And The War of Ideas – Reflections in a Bloodshot Lens.* Cairo, Egypt: The American University, 2006.
Taylor, Charles. *A Secular Age.* Cambridge, Massachusetts: The Belknap Press of Harvard University Press, 2007.

Index of Subjects

messianic vision and ideology
220, 225, 295-97, 300-02,
307
messianic stature of Osama bin
Laden 302-04
impact of Western secular
leftwing and rightwing
traditions on radical Islam
378-81, 396
influence of Christianity on
297-98
Religious Violence 1, 55
alliance of fundamentalism with
messianism 2-4
early instances of 56-8, 70-71
characteristics of 'sacred terror' 57
messianism and violence 58-60
assassination of Sadat and Rabin
59-60
radical religious movements 62-4
jihad (see under 'Jihad')
Republican Party 148, 152, 167, 179
Rome (also Empire, Emperor) 27-30,
32-5, 39, 49, 56
Russia 144, 248, 404

Salaf/Salafism (see under 'jihad')
Satan or Antichrist 37, 59, 64, 137,
139, 144, 220
Saudi Arabia 14, 47, 177, 181, 229,
236, 239, 241-42, 244-5, 247,
249, 257, 268, 280-81, 336-37,
340, 360, 378
and Pakistan 248
response to 9/11 339
education system 336
funds 240
royal family 47, 235, 240
September 11 (*also* 9/11) 66, 150-52,
173, 177, 180, 186, 191, 255,
258, 260, 262, 264, 268, 270,

272-73, 277-78, 280, 286, 302,
305-06, 330, 335, 341, 347, 349,
353, 357-59, 361, 368, 371-72,
390
Shia Islam 4, 45, 50
Shi'ite traditions 44
Shia 274, 284
hagiographic literature of the 45
Shia messianic tradition 44
Sinai 85
Six-Day War 83
Somalia 226, 245, 268, 279
South Lebanese Army 124
Southern Baptist Convention (SBC)
136
Soviet Union 7-8, 162, 176, 230, 241,
243, 340
State Terrorism 118,
differences over definition 118-22
implications for the Israel-
Palestine conflict 123-25
State Department definition
122-23, 133-34
Suicide attacks (also: suicide bombings, martyrdom operations)
64-9, 111, 125, 261, 268, 276,
342-43, 356, 384
increase in incidents of 64-5
effectiveness of 65-6
profile of perpetrators 66-8
"martyrdom operations" 296,
302, 307
Sunni (see 'Islam')
Syria 85, 105, 179, 181, 273, 278,
313

Tajiks 274
takfir 283
Tehrik-e-Taliban Pakistan (TTP)
355-56

Index of Names